Anti-Americanism

Anti-Americanism

History, Causes, and Themes

Volume 1: Causes and Sources

Edited by
Brendon O'Connor

Greenwood World Publishing
Oxford / Westport, Connecticut
2007

First published by Greenwood World Publishing 2007

1 2 3 4 5 6 7 8 9 10

Greenwood World Publishing
Wilkinson House
Jordan Hill
Oxford OX2 8EJ
An imprint of Greenwood Publishing Group, Inc
www.greenwood.com

British Library Cataloguing-in-Publication Data: a catalogue record for this book is available from the British Library

Library of Congress Cataloging-in-Publication Data

Anti-Americanism: history, causes, themes/edited by Brendon O'Connor.
     p. cm.
  Includes bibliographical references and index.
  ISBN 1-84645-004-7 (set: alk. paper) – ISBN 1-84645-024-1 (vol 1: alk. paper) – ISBN 1-84645-025-X (vol 2: alk. paper) – ISBN 1-84645-026-8 (vol 3: alk. paper) – ISBN 1-84645-027-6 (vol 4: alk. paper) 1.   Anti-Americanism – History.   2.   United States – Foreign public opinion.   3.   United States – Relations – Foreign countries.
I.   O'Connor, Brendon, 1969–

  E183.7.A66 2007
  303.48'273009045 – dc22

                                                    2006039656

ISBN 978-1-84645-004-4 (set)
     978-1-84645-024-2 (vol. 1)
     978-1-84645-025-9 (vol. 2)
     978-1-84645-026-6 (vol. 3)
     978-1-84645-027-3 (vol. 4)

Designed by Fraser Muggeridge studio
Typeset by TexTech
Printed and bound by Bath Press

Contents

Series Preface vii
Brendon O'Connor

Introduction: Causes and Sources of Anti-Americanism xiii
Brendon O'Connor

Chapter 1: What is Anti-Americanism? 1
Brendon O'Connor

Chapter 2: The Anti-Americanism Mindset 23
Andrei S. Markovits

Chapter 3: Americanisation and Anti-Americanism 41
Andrei S. Markovits

Chapter 4: Guns, Capital Punishment and Anti-Americanism 59
Robert Singh

Chapter 5: George W. Bush, Religion and European Anti-Americanism 85
D. Jason Berggren and Nicol C. Rae

Chapter 6: Anti-Americanism and the American Personality 115
Richard Boyd and Brandon Turner

Chapter 7: The Environment and Anti-Americanism 139
Navraj Singh Ghaleigh

Chapter 8: American Democracy and Anti-Americanism Since 2000 163
Graeme Orr

Chapter 9: Bush, the Iraq War and Anti-Americanism 187
Pierangelo Isernia and Sergio Fabbrini

Chapter 10: The Washington Consensus and Anti-Americanism 217
Iwan Morgan

Chapter 11: American Popular Culture and Anti-Americanism 239
Cheryl Hudson

Chapter 12: Modernity, Resentment and Anti-Americanism 263
Michael Werz and Barbara Fried

About the Series Editor and Contributors 287

Notes 293

Index 333

Series Preface

Brendon O'Connor

The United States of America is the primetime show of our age. Despite prognostications of America's demise, as of 2007, the American century appears set to continue. American presidential elections, speeches and bloopers, American foreign policy, and American movies, music, food, television, computer games and celebrities are more broadly known than the politics, culture and people of any other single country. As a result, 'America' is a common reference point, a *lingua franca*, a threat, a friend and a source of anxiety for the peoples of the world. Indeed, if some newspaper reports are to be believed, even Osama bin Laden spends some of his spare time fantasizing about American pop singers – in his case Whitney Houston.[1] More seriously, if you were to put a group of teenagers from around the world in a room, American culture would be their common reference point. For a group of international academics, it is more than likely that they would find common ground in condemning George W. Bush.

Given this breadth of influence, it is hardly surprising that anti-Americanism, pro-Americanism and widespread ambivalence towards the United States exists in all societies. More noteworthy is that until September 11, 2001, so little of substance had been written on anti-Americanism. Academics largely ignored the subject, possibly seeing it as unimportant and akin to writing about sexism against men, or discrimination against white people. When I informed a colleague that I was editing a four-volume series on anti-Americanism, I was asked why I was not spending my time on a more worthy subject, such as poverty. Two responses to this question drive this project. Firstly, not all important scholarship is advocacy; understanding the origins, sources and causes of anti-Americanism in as objective a manner as possible is a valuable contribution to knowledge. Secondly, many of the essays in this series put forward political arguments, with various chapters debating anti-Americanism from different and, at times, opposing positions. As editor, I have encouraged this pluralism and see it as crucial in reflecting the contested nature of the concept of anti-Americanism. If my own chapters have a prescriptive aim, it is to call for debates on America to proceed armed with information and evidence rather than cant and prejudice (which seems all too common). As the most powerful state in the world, America will rightly be the focus of much attention and often criticism. However, there is a difference between criticism, which is healthy and necessary, and anti-Americanism, which is prejudicial and often counter-productive. A central characteristic of this prejudice is that it reduces American society and policies to a series of tropes and caricatures and ignores the fact that this is one of the most diverse countries on earth. To return to the television metaphor, anti-Americanism is often based on an unwillingness to see America as a 'variety show' with appealing, unappealing and indeed mundane features. In the realm of foreign affairs, anti-Americanism is often the result of a disinterest in differentiating between various US actions and policies, fixating instead on the worst aspects of America's role in international relations.

The four volumes in this series attempt to build a composite picture of anti-Americanism that reveals both the breadth of this topic and some of its central themes. Volume one starts with the crucial task of defining anti-Americanism and exploring the anti-American mindset. Volume one, and the series in general, emphasize an historical approach, showing how negative tropes and narratives about America and Americans that developed in the nineteenth century have been recycled in more recent debates. There are clear continuities in attitudes toward American culture, gun use, commerce and religion. However, not all sources of anti-Americanism have strong historical legacies. In volume one, American environmental policies and US intervention in Iraq are examined with respect to the new resentments and distrust they have created toward America.

Volume two examines the crucial events and ideas throughout history that have shaped the development of anti-Americanism. The contrast between America as the uncouth orphan child of Europe and as an exceptional and promised land is discussed in many of the chapters. Meanwhile, within America, this legacy of exceptionalism and the consecration of Americanism as something almost akin to a national ideology[2] have created at times an intolerance of dissent, which has led to anti-war or black nationalist activists being labeled un-American or anti-American. Volume two also explores how the Cold War created a world often divided into two competing camps. This deadly loyalty test made anti-Americanism both an ideological badge of honor for some communists and a lethal label placed on the enemies of America, particularly in the Third World.

Volume three explores anti-Americanism in a comparative perspective. It begins by contrasting anti-Americanism with Anglophobia and anti-globalization, pointing to similarities and overlap between these two terms. This raises a question that runs throughout the series: namely, are the powerful always blamed for the ills of the world? In the historical volume two, it is argued that anti-Americanism predates America being a significant global power and that anti-Americanism is certainly not divorced from American actions. Power alone does not account for marked rises in anti-Americanism. America has not become suddenly more powerful since the end of the Clinton Administration, but anti-Americanism has certainly risen significantly since Bill Clinton left the Oval Office. In other words, actions are also crucial to understanding anti-Americanism. Volume three provides an excellent opportunity to examine how American interactions with certain countries and regions have created tensions and outright hatred, and illustrates most strikingly how one's definition of anti-Americanism has a significant impact on one's findings. The authors who view anti-Americanism principally as a response to what America supposedly is, rather than a reaction to what America does around the world, see anti-Americanism in a narrower more pejorative way. Those who see anti-Americanism as growing out of a struggle for greater independence and better treatment by America tend to be more sympathetic in their descriptions of anti-Americanism and treat it as a much broader concept. However, all contributors are united in the understanding that anti-Americanism is not, in most places and at most times, the dominant response to America, but rather it is ambivalence that typifies the response of most peoples and nations to the United States.

Finally, in volume four, twenty-first century anti-Americanism is explored through issues such as the war in Iraq, recent US economic and human rights policies and other actions that have been key sources of recent anti-Americanism. The volume's three concluding chapters ask the big questions: (1) does anti-Americanism really inhibit American foreign policy-making; (2) what is being done by the US government to combat anti-Americanism; and (3) what could be done to enhance America's image abroad? Of all the volumes, volume four contains the least consensus of opinion, reflecting the polarized nature of recent debates over the Bush Doctrine and responses to Islamic terrorism. However, despite the obvious differences of opinion within the volume, the authors all express their views in a detailed and thoughtful manner. This is entirely in line with the aim of this series: to raise the level of sophistication of discussion about anti-Americanism, while recognizing the essentially contested nature of debates about America. This series is unlikely to be the last word on anti-Americanism, but hopefully it offers its most comprehensive overview to date.

This series owes its roots to a lifetime interest in American politics, and the first thanks must go out to those who have stimulated this interest and helped me make a career of it. Thanks to those who listened to the ideas in this book at various seminars and workshops, including my own presentations at Griffith University, Ohio State University, Florida International University, Georgetown University, the University of London and the University of East Anglia, as well as conference presentations at the European Consortium for Political Research workshop in Nicosia and the International Political Science Association conference in Fukuoka. And those who facilitated these talks: Alexander Stephan in Columbus, Richard Crockatt in Norwich, Iwan Morgan and Robert Singh in London, and Nicol Rae in Miami.

At Griffith University, I must thank my colleague and friend Martin Griffiths for drawing me into this multivolume series on anti-Americanism and for continuing to collaborate with me on this topic; you have made the project a lot more fun, bringing your own unique edge to the series. Thanks also to my research centre director Pat Weller for your generous assistance to this project.

Thanks also to my colleagues and friends in Washington, DC, who made my Fulbright Fellowship at Georgetown University such a pleasure in 2006. A special thanks to Alan Tidwell, Helen Riordan and Tain and Grace Tompkins for making me feel most welcome.

To the contributors, thank you for your excellent work and respect for deadlines; you have made editing these volumes a lot less fraught than most people suggested it would be. It has been a pleasure to work with both old friends and new ones. The work of some of the chapters is path-breaking in the relatively underdeveloped sub-field of anti-American studies, and deserves a wide readership. Thanks to Andrei S. Markovits for your multiple contributions to this series. It has been a pleasure to get to know you first via lively e-mail exchanges and then in person; you have been a great inspiration for this project.

Thanks to my editor Simon Mason for commissioning this series and for his continual encouragement, and to Vikas Kanchan and Premlal

Premkumar for their copyediting. Thanks are also due to Paul Norton and Srdjan Vucetic for their assistance on proof reading.

Most of all, thanks to my family for their support and encouragement. My parents Carole and Barry have helped this happen in many ways large and small. My son Finnegan has provided many moments of relief from worrying about W. and WMDs and all the other largely weighty issues discussed in these books. However, my heaviest debt of gratitude goes out to my wife Katherine whose support and involvement in this project helped make it a reality. I look forward to reciprocating the support with your novels in the future.

Introduction: Causes and Sources of Anti-Americanism

Brendon O'Connor

What are the principal causes and sources of anti-Americanism? Some obvious candidates would be American manners, gun-slinging cowboys, Wall Street, 'over here, oversexed, overpaid' GIs, Dresden, Hiroshima, gum-chewing, the Korean War, Coca-Cola, the Central Intelligence Agency (CIA) in Guatemala, Iran and Chile, Hollywood, the Vietnam War, Ronald Reagan, cruise missiles, religiosity, support for Israel, rap music, McDonald's, Guantánamo Bay, sport-utility vehicles, unilateralism, the 2003 Iraq War, and George W. Bush. As these answers suggest, anti-Americanism is not just a response to what America does around the world but also what it symbolises. Just as McDonald's represents more than just a hamburger company, these names and events are catch-cries for what is wrong with America and its role in the world. Every bellicose American president is a gun-slinging cowboy in the cartoon pages of the world press. Wall Street, well before Oliver Stone's movie, was synonymous with greed and corporate ruthlessness. American SUVs are not only blamed for global warming, they are seen as a sign of American arrogance.[1] Or as Amnesty International states: 'Guantánamo Bay has become a symbol of injustice and abuse in the US administration's "war on terror"'.[2]

As contradictory as this list is, all the items on it have engendered animosity and at times hatred towards the United States. However, which of these animosities can fairly be called anti-Americanism and which are better seen as criticism is too often left unanswered, or if addressed, is done so in an overly partisan manner. To confront this crucial question, 'What is anti-Americanism?', I attempt in the first chapter of this volume to set a standard for what constitutes anti-Americanism. I outline different conceptual understandings of anti-Americanism, look at the merits and demerits of various definitions, and conclude that anti-Americanism is best understood as a prejudice that has, at times, ideological overtones. I situate this conceptual debate in the contemporary context where, by any measure, it is hard to dispute that since the election of George W. Bush, anti-Americanism has risen dramatically around the world. The chapter relies upon opinion polling data, particularly the invaluable Pew surveys, to document the recent rise in anti-Americanism, but argues these polls should be the starting point and not the endpoint for understanding the concept of anti-Americanism.

Two events in the early twenty-first century have made anti-Americanism one of the central issues of our age: the terrorist attacks of September 11, 2001, and the Iraq War. 9/11 was the quintessential anti-American act in modern history, fulfilling all sensible definitions of anti-Americanism. However, despite its absolute malice, it was followed by enormous debate about the rights and wrongs of American foreign policy and American society; some of this debate and commentary suggested that America had brought these attacks upon itself. Whether such views were anti-American quickly became the subject of even more heated debate. This series contributes to this debate by suggesting criteria for judging what is sensibly called anti-Americanism and what is better viewed as legitimate criticism. The second critical event in debates about anti-Americanism was the US decision to go to war against Iraq in 2003, an action that has clearly led to much negativity worldwide, not only towards the Bush administration, but also towards America more generally. This decision, and the post-invasion quagmire in Iraq, has given a particular edge to debates about America in recent years. As misguided as US policy in Iraq has often been, in my view, these failings have opened the door for a great deal of anti-American prejudice, often not aimed at American foreign policy in particular but at Americans and American society in general. The contributions of Andrei Markovits to this volume are crucial in documenting this contempt within Europe.

Markovits focuses on responses to what America supposedly *is* as opposed to reactions to what America *does*. His research points to a common want or need to see America as inferior within Europe. For example, he suggests that the American movie *Bowling for Columbine*, released in 2002, was enormously popular in Europe not because of any interest Europeans had in joining American gun-control campaigns but because the movie allowed them to look down their noses at Americans. Markovits substantiates his views with his survey of 1,500 articles selected from a range of European newspapers covering the decade between 1992 and 2002. Deliberately avoiding the political pages, he analyses largely cultural issues to expose the underbelly of anti-Americanism – the negative responses to what America apparently *is*.

What he finds are regularly gratuitous and snide remarks about America and Americans in articles that range from the world of accounting through to sports. Markovits further shows the historical continuity of these anti-American tropes, drawing particularly on examples from German history. Lastly, in his essay 'Americanisation and anti-Americanism', Markovits asks what political end might anti-Americanism serve in Europe? He suggests the possible formation of a European super-state, although he notes that this seems more the wishful thinking of certain academics than a popularly supported goal.

Robert Singh's chapter addresses the supposed divide between Europe and America by examining two issues at the forefront of European claims of difference: gun control and the death penalty. Singh suggests that the attitudes of the public in Europe and America on the death penalty have often been fairly similar in surveys. The difference has been due to the governing class in Europe deeming the death penalty illegitimate, whereas in the more plebiscitary democracy of the United States, the people's will has ruled, leading to the death penalty becoming law in certain states. On guns, Singh points out the tendency to exaggerate US gun culture and to ignore the fact that 98 percent to 99 percent of all American gun owners use their weapons responsibly. While not making light of these seriously contentious public policies, Singh questions whether these policy differences represent a fundamental transatlantic values divide. He thinks not, seeing them more realistically as a disagreement between a family of rather similar nations. It is tempting to see such fracas as part of what Freud called the 'narcissism of minor differences'.

Nicol Rae and Jason Berggren examine what one recent prominent book on America suggests is the most crucial cultural divide between America and Europe: the contrasting levels of religiosity.[3] In their comprehensive chapter on religion and anti-Americanism, Rae and Berggren document the regional nature of American religious exceptionalism. Certain regions of America, particularly the South, do have patterns of religious adherence and a style of religiosity that is quite different from most of Europe, but religiosity in Northeastern America is not that different from Europe as a whole. One of the most fascinating questions asked by the 2005 Pew Global Attitudes survey was whether people thought America was 'too religious or not religious enough'. Sizeable majorities in France and the Netherlands thought America was too religious, whereas slim majorities in Canada, Spain and Russia thought America was not religious enough. Moreover, sizeable majorities in

Poland, Indonesia, Jordan and Pakistan thought America was not religious enough.[4] This simple question serves up a complicated set of responses and makes it hard to say that the world, or Europe, sees America as overly religious.

The same Pew survey asked respondents what they thought of the American character or Americans as individuals. Americans are broadly seen as inventive and hardworking, but also as greedy and violent.[5] Various British Broadcasting Corporation (BBC) surveys on what the world thinks of America and Americans have strongly highlighted the widespread perception that Americans are less cultured than Europeans, Asians or Australians. These views reflect historical understandings of the American personality, as outlined in Richard Boyd's and Brandon Turner's chapter, which examines the views of three prominent nineteenth-century critics of America – Alexis de Tocqueville, Frances Trollope and Karl Marx – to demonstrate that contemporary currents of anti-Americanism have strong historical precedents in the nineteenth century. The Germans saw Americans as too commercial and spiritually lacking, the French emphasised the lack of cultural or culinary taste in America, and the British complained about the lack of respect for social norms or hierarchy and the deleterious effect this had on manners. As with the Pew survey results, whether these observations tell us more about Germany, France and Britain than America is an open question.

More contemporary concerns about American policy – its flawed democracy, its role in global warming, and the impact of the 'Washington Consensus' – are also dealt with in this volume. The chapters by Graeme Orr and Navraj Singh Ghaleigh argue that the common put downs of American democracy and environmental policy only tell part of the story, and then often in a distorted manner. Orr's chapter examines seven sins of American democracy, in each case revealing a more complicated picture than the one generally painted. Ghaleigh suggests that while opposition to George W. Bush's stance on global warming might be considered a respectable and even legitimate prejudice, blanket condemnation of America as ecologically repressive ignores the long history of US government action on environmental issues both within the United States and in international forums. Ghaleigh cites the initial US response to the growing hole in the ozone layer, and America's key role in the banning of chlorofluorocarbons. He then contrasts this with the current administration's response to the Kyoto Protocol where economic concerns have trumped ecological concerns and solid scientific evidence of climate change. As one scholar put it, if the prediction about global warming turns out to be as bad as some scientists argue, it could lead to centuries of anti-Americanism.

Iwan Morgan's chapter deals with the global policies of the International Monetary Fund (IMF) and the World Bank, the so-called Washington Consensus (a term often used in a pejorative manner). Morgan suggests that in general terms, Asian and European opposition to the Washington Consensus tends to be ideological, whereas in Latin America, it has generally been more prejudicial. He argues, however, that unless American foreign policy is able to deal more effectively with the current 'Bolivarian Revolution', there is a risk of anti-Americanism in Latin America also becoming ideological.

The volume ends by turning to anxieties about American popular culture in particular and modernity in general. Cheryl Hudson's chapter on American popular culture examines the variety and success of American movies and television shows and suggests that the popularity of American products is due more to their quality and universal themes than to the imperial dominance of the American cultural industry. Hudson explores how the adjective 'American' has come to be shorthand for inferior; thus the very terms 'American television' or 'American movies' are often used to imply a lack of class, or to refer to products that are good for neither your mind nor your body. My own view is that the anxieties created by fast food give us a key insight into contemporary anti-Americanism. Fast food is undoubtedly wonderfully convenient and its most famous brand of McDonald's is an expert marketer. Nonetheless, many of the people who eat the convenient fried goods on offer at McDonald's must face, outside its walls, a plethora of campaigns promoting healthy living and encouraging the fight against obesity. The tension between these two lifestyles is bound to create anxieties and fears. Some within and outside America will blame particular fast food restaurants; however, non-Americans have the tantalising and, some might say irresistible, possibility of simply making a scapegoat of the country most associated with this type of food – the so-called 'fast food nation' as one author put it. Anxieties and reactions to American fast food chains, television and films are often inchoate, but so is much anti-Americanism. It represents a generalised fear that something is wrong, and America seems the easiest nation at whose feet we can place the blame.

The standardisation and homogenisation of products and services common in the fast food industry has spread to many sectors. Once again, this hyper-modernist trend is more pronounced in America than elsewhere. The globalisation of US companies and ideas has contributed to anti-Americanism near and far. A small personal example is illustrative. In the 1980s, while studying in New Zealand, I worked at a government-owned betting agency (the TAB) that took bets on horseracing via phone accounts. Towards the end of my time at the TAB, corporatisation began to take hold, with new management ideas sweeping through the organisation. One of the ideas was to make it compulsory for staff to answer all phone calls with a standard greeting and to end all calls (no matter how rude the gambler had been) with a compulsory 'good luck'. Friends of mine who were working in other service sectors experienced a similar revolution. Some of us had worked for McDonald's and noted the obvious similarities. The sophisticated response is to see these developments as part of the 'fine tuning' of capitalist profitability and new management ideas that were certainly not solely driven by America; however, America has been the originator of many of these ideas and the base for many of the global companies using this business model. On a personal level, many around me saw these shifts not as part of broader global economic change, but rather as an invasion of their culture by American ideas. Such concerns about America forcing standardisation and homogenisation on people are not new. They form a crucial part of French critiques of America as far back as the early twentieth century and were a key element of what was first named anti-Americanism.[6] Although many of these concerns could be better called anti-technocratic and at times anti-modernist and anti-capitalist, they have for a century been a part of an ideological anti-Americanism that has been bubbling away, often at a subconscious level. Michael Werz and Barbara Fried deal with these complex issues adroitly in their chapter on modernity and anti-Americanism.

In summary, how does this multitude of causes and manifestations of anti-Americanism mesh together? When underlying cultural anxieties combine with political disagreement, anti-American opinion noticeably increases. These rapid increases (as shown in Figure 1.1 and charted in Pierangelo Isernia's and Sergio Fabbrini's chapter) are possible because there is always a subconscious layer of fear and resentment about America that can easily percolate into anti-Americanism, given the right ingredients. Conversely, in the twentieth century, such upward trends subsided rapidly due to an accumulation of cultural and political goodwill towards America, particularly in the West. Prior to the current Bush administration,

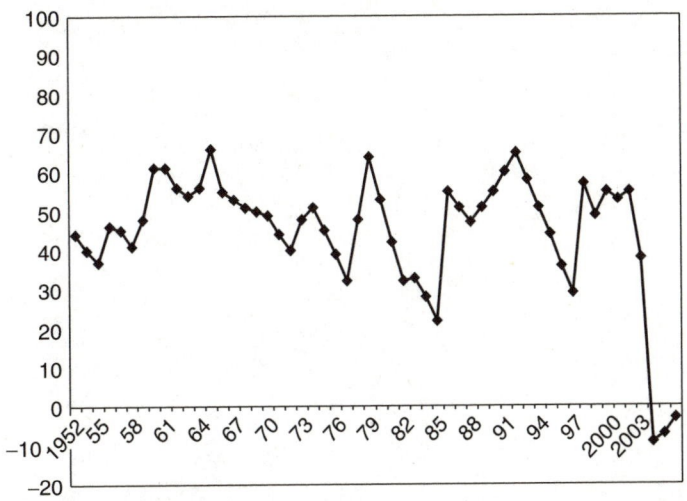

Figure 1.1
Opinions of the United States in Four European Countries, 1952–2003
(in Percentage net "Favourable" Opinion).
Source: Various, including Eurobarometer, Pew, USIA.[7]

it seemed likely that this undulating pattern of anti-Americanism would continue during the twenty-first century; however, the current strength of disfavour brought about by the unpopularity of both America's leader and its foreign policy may make it much more difficult for the United States to regain a more favourable reputation abroad. As I mentioned earlier, proceeding armed with information and evidence rather than cant and prejudice would be judicious in such unsteady times. My hope is that the work of the authors in this volume will pave the way for such an undertaking.

Chapter 1
What is Anti-Americanism?

Brendon O'Connor

'I am large, I contain multitudes' wrote Walt Whitman in *Song of myself*, but these words can also be read as a hymn to his nation. America,[1] seen from this Whitmanesque viewpoint, is a vast and contradictory land. This emphasis on American variety and paradox would seem a very obvious starting point from which to understand America, but it is an outlook that is increasingly disregarded. Instead, America's vastness is often reduced to a series of stereotypes and caricatures, while its essence is exclusively described through negative examples drawn from history or the contemporary world. From this narrow and biased focus emerges the spectre of anti-Americanism.

What is said to be America, or representative of America, has long been subject to selectivity and caricature. On this theme, Oscar Wilde opined that: 'English people are far more interested in American barbarism than they are in American civilisation.'[2] Similarly, a man whose quotes are often confused with Wilde's, George Bernard Shaw, ventured that 'one must distinguish between civilised America and barbarian America'.[3] This polarisation suggests that there are at least two Americas, but it misses the bigger point that America is good, bad and all that is in between.[4] The ordinariness of much American life is lost as America is constantly fantasised, sensationalised and caricatured. James Russell Lowell recognised this when he wrote in 1869, 'for some reason or other, the European has rarely been able to see America except in caricature'.[5] Undoubtedly, America has produced more global icons[6] than any other contemporary nation and its proclaimed exceptionalism, and differences, are constantly referred to by Americans and non-Americans alike. However, this tendency to see this mythologised or Hollywood screen version of America as the reality leads to an exaggeration of all things American. In one of the first, and still one of the most considered books on anti-Americanism, Henry Pelling summed up the above strands of thought with the following conclusion:

Hope and disillusion will long continue to colour the European view of America, as they did when [Samuel] Gompers crossed the

Atlantic in 1909 to discover that people in Western Europe looked
at his country as if in one of two distorting mirrors, either convex or
concave. ... To understand the Americans as they really are requires
not only an appreciation of the peculiarities of the American
environment, but also a recognition that, in its better features
and its worse, human nature everywhere and at all times is,
as Thucydides said, very much the same.[7]

The dismissal of American pluralism has allowed a renewed anti-
Americanism to take hold. The core markers of this anti-Americanism
are a distorted or narrowcast focus, a reflexive dislike, an undifferentiated view of American behaviour and policies and a tendency
to conflate the nation's people with their government and its policies.
One of the most egregious examples of this anti-Americanism was the
statement often aired after September 11, 2001, that 'they had it
coming'.[8] This is the type of comment that Todd Gitlin seems to have
had in mind when he wrote: 'When hatred of foreign policies ignites into
hatred of an entire people and their civilisation, then thinking is dead and
demonology lives.'[9] I write none of this seeking to defend the current US
president or his controversial foreign policies in Iraq; in fact quite the
opposite. At a time when intelligent critiques of American foreign and
domestic politics are needed more than ever to provide wise foreign
counsel to the United States,[10] the rise of anti-American prejudice is
unfortunate and likely to be counterproductive. My position is simply
that criticism of any nation needs to be based on detailed evidence rather
than sweeping generalisations and prejudices. Given the unprecedented
power and influence of the United States, close scrutiny is a necessity but
a narrowcast or *a priori* view of America's motives and behaviour will
inevitably lead to distortions and foreclose sensible conversations and
debates.[11]

As these opening remarks would suggest, I see anti-Americanism
pejoratively and as something quite distinct from criticism; thus, for
me, separating these two outlooks is crucial. Although the call to differ-
entiate criticism from anti-Americanism is regularly uttered, few
scholars provide a sound analytical basis for effectively achieving this.
Anti-Americanism for me is a term in desperate need of a more precise
definition rather than something that we shrug our shoulders about in a
post-modernist manner declaring that it is 'all about interpretation'. In
asking and trying to answer the question, 'What is anti-Americanism?',

I seek to rectify this failing by providing an analytical basis for conceptualising anti-Americanism.

Before developing my argument any further, one last preliminary point needs to be made. When writing on anti-Americanism, one is forced to put one's generalist pretensions on the line: after all, we are entering into a debate about global opinions on 297 million Americans and their culture, politics and history. Further, given the vastness of the topic, one needs to be sceptical about coming to conclusions too hastily. In the pages that follow I will firstly examine what I see as the two big issues in any current conversation on anti-Americanism: September 11, 2001, and the Iraq War (and its aftermath). From these much commented-on events, I will move on to discuss how anti-Americanism has been measured in public opinion surveys and defined in popular commentary, arguing that most analysis is inadequate and generally far too vague. Finally, I will present my own typology of anti-Americanism.

The Two Elephants in the Room

Any current discussion of contemporary anti-Americanism occurs in the shadows of September 11, 2001, and America's invasion of Iraq. Analysing these events, however, is not easy. Events such as wars and terrorist attacks take the subtleties out of politics, with the ensuing debates often reduced to 'which side are you on' clichés, which often disable critical and nuanced thinking. The terrorist attacks of September 11, 2001, and the ensuing response of the American media and the Bush administration began an unprecedented global conversation about the virtues and vices of the United States. These violent attacks were widely condemned by most governments and peoples around the world; however, it was also apparent that many people, including a number of prominent commentators, saw the United States less as a victim and more as reaping the consequences of years of unscrupulous behaviour in the Middle East and elsewhere.[12] Some less versed or interested in the details of foreign affairs simply seemed pleased to see America brought down a peg or two. These negative responses reflected a widespread distrust and resentment towards the United States that, while not entirely new, surprised many Americans, particularly during a time of national shock and mourning. Summing up this mood, one writer went as far as suggesting that the events following September 11, 2001, 'have increased

the visceral loathing not of terrorism or of Islamic fundamentalism but
of President George Bush'.[13] Although this overstates the situation somewhat, a 2004 Pew survey showed that Osama bin Laden is seen much more
favourably in a number of Muslim countries than George W. Bush.[14] Other
reputable surveys provide evidence that the United States is widely viewed
as a greater threat to world peace than China, Russia or Iran.[15]

If 9/11 revealed to Americans a strong ambivalence in world opinion
towards their nation, the decision to go to war in Iraq tipped global
opinion clearly against the United States. A range of national surveys
and the influential global Pew surveys provided clear evidence that the
decision to go to war against Iraq was widely unpopular and has turned
people against the United States more generally. As the Table 1.1 shows,
polls taken during the lead-up to the Iraq War and since confirm that the
United States is currently more unpopular globally than at any other point
in the history of such polls. Other surveys show that comparatively, the
United States is less popular than France, Germany, Japan or China.[16]
While attitudes towards America have generally become more favourable
since 2003, the United States is still viewed unfavourably in the majority
of countries surveyed by the Pew Research Center.

Table 1.1
Global Attitudes Towards the United States (Percent Unfavourable).

	2002	2003	2004	2005	2006
Britain	16	40	34	38	33
France	34	67	62	57	60
Germany	35	71	59	54	60
Spain	–	74	–	50	73
Poland	11	–	–	23	–
Russia	33	68	44	40	47
Turkey	55	84	63	67	76
Pakistan	69	81	61	60	56
Jordan	75	99	93	80	85

Source: Pew Research Center for the People and the Press, June 23, 2006.

Other polls yield similarly negative results. For example a recent survey
showed that 'Saudis expressing confidence in America shrank from
60 percent in 2000 to just 4 percent in 2004.'[17]

Measuring a Politically Contested Term

While it is widely agreed that the terrorist attacks on the World Trade Center and the Pentagon were unambiguous instances of violent anti-Americanism, whether much of the broader antipathy towards America is fairly labelled anti-Americanism is frequently contested, not least because what one person will call anti-Americanism will be defended by another as reasonable criticism. In fact it is a rare person who openly acknowledges their anti-Americanism.[18] And like most political debates, the tendency to caricature one's opponents is commonplace.[19] Scholars have an important role in negotiating the way through such politicised discourses.

From the outset, it is crucial that we acknowledge that anti-Americanism is a highly politicised term, with some seeing it everywhere while others almost deny its existence. Commentators on FOX News and the like are inclined to use the term to imply that critics of the United States are sympathetic with Al Qaeda and other similar terrorist organisations in the current global 'war on terror'. (This response repeats a familiar pattern; some Cold War warriors never tired of labelling criticisms of US foreign policy anti-Americanism, implying sympathy with the Soviet Union). Recognising this usage of the term, Kenneth Minogue writes, 'anti-Americanism thus often functions in argument as an incapacitating device, just like such charges as "sexism" and "racism"'; it is, he argues, 'an attacking move in any discussion of international affairs'. However, he also correctly acknowledges that the claim is 'conventionally blocked by a denial whose point is to restore credibility to whatever point the critic of America is making'.[20]

One side of this debate overuses and abuses the term as a blanket term to describe any criticism of the United States.[21] Conversely, those on the other side of the fence deny their opinions are anti-American at all, despite the fact that similar comments made about almost any other peoples or nation would be quickly called racism or prejudice. This polarised debate, although disappointing, is not particularly surprising; however, what is curious is that scholars have done little to help clarify and elevate discussions on anti-Americanism. The existing literature on this important topic of international debate is more limited and more impressionistic than might be imagined.

Perhaps some of the difficulty we have in ascertaining whether the undoubted rise in negative feelings towards the United States equates to something as strong as anti-Americanism is because rather blunt instruments are being used to measure it. The Pew Global Attitudes Project survey is the most influential ongoing survey in the world on attitudes to America. In it, respondents are asked their attitude towards America by choosing from the following statement: 'Please tell me if you have a very favourable, somewhat favourable, somewhat unfavourable or very unfavourable opinion of the United States.' Respondents are asked to judge an entire nation in the same manner as they would an individual political leader or party. The assumption is that we can judge the United States as a monolithic entity. There is no doubting the influence of the Pew surveys. Their analysis has had a profound impact on commentary on anti-Americanism. However, while they certainly provide solid data of America's unpopularity in nearly all the countries where they are conducted, to be really useful to the ongoing study of anti-Americanism, these surveys need to be prefaced by a more precise definition of the term; at present, the poll data is too often presumed to explain what is clearly a more complicated question.

Anti-Americanism in Popular and Scholarly Debate

In the months and years following September 11, 2001, there has been a steady outpouring of newspaper and magazine articles discussing anti-Americanism. A number of best-selling books also appeared, such as *Why do people hate America?*[22] Although these early contributions identified key points of conflict, often little time was spent defining anti-Americanism. Similarly a number of the superstars of European and American academia have ventured opinions on the recent rise of anti-Americanism, including Timothy Garton Ash, Simon Schama, and Tony Judt. These historians of the present, as Ash has occasioned to call himself, have neatly summarised the growing anti-American mood of today with historically informed articles in the *New Yorker*, *The Guardian* and that 'other American'[23] journal of ideas, *The New York Review of Books*. However, as readable as these articles are, they similarly spend little time on defining anti-Americanism.

The best scholarship offers a number of ways of dividing the anti-American pie. This includes Andrei Markovits' four-squared division of anti-Americanism into left/right and cultural/political.[24] Moisés Naím identifies 'five "pure" types: politico-economic, historical, religious, cultural, and psychological',[25] while Rubinstein and Smith separate anti-Americanism into the following categories: issue oriented, ideological, instrumental and revolutionary.[26] Robert Singh distils the various sources of anti-Americanism down to three principal strands: the first is leftist critiques of America's unjust and self-centred use of its wealth and power; the second source is rival nationalisms and the universal pretensions of American nationalism; and the third encompasses cultural concerns about the Americanisation of cultural products, norms and public policies.[27] Katzenstein and Keohane outdo all comers by suggesting there are six prominent types of anti-Americanism: liberal, social, sovereign-nationalist, radical, elitist and legacy.[28] The other noteworthy division is between what Moisés Naím calls 'lite' and 'murderous' anti-Americanism.[29]

These divisions are all useful tools to understand the different sources and motivations behind anti-American actions and ideas. However, my interest is in starting one step further back and asking what anti-Americanism is. This concrete definition of the term would seem necessary before we can classify it into the various strands. Such definitions have been elusive as the term is generally acknowledged by most authors to be slippery. As Tony Judt and Denis Lacrone suggest in their recent book *With us or against us*: 'Anti-Americanism is above all about perceptions'.[30] Given the troublesome nature of the term, which can include so many different varieties, a number of authors are drawn to the Justice Potter Stewart line of 'I know it when I see it ...'[31] However, with anti-Americanism being such a politicised term, this definition opens one up to the claim that you see or do not see anti-Americanism when it is convenient to your argument. While individuals will always argue about how their thoughts are classified, this should not deter scholars from attempting to create categories and more robust definitions. It also seems important to give the term a precise and rigorous definition in order to rescue it from political abuse and misuse. The existing academic literature provides endless divisions between different so-called sources of anti-Americanism but there is too little scholarship on what anti-Americanism conceptually is and thus how anti-Americanism can be effectively differentiated from criticism.

What is Anti-Americanism? Five Conceptions

I have extracted five understandings of how the term is used across both popular and scholarly debates. Simply stated, these competing conceptions can be characterised as identifying anti-Americanism to be: firstly, as one side of a dichotomised worldview; secondly, as a tendency; thirdly, as a pathology; fourthly, as a prejudice; and fifthly, as an ideology.

Anti-Americanism as one side of a dichotomy. As one half of a dichotomy, anti-Americanism is understood in a binary or oppositional fashion where people, groups or nations are seen as either pro- or anti-American. Thus anti-Americanism is simply the views and actions of those deemed not to be pro-American. This is the most straightforward, but also the most straitjacketed, interpretation of the term.

Anti-Americanism as a tendency. A little less crude but still straightforward, this term sees anti-Americanism as a tendency that slides across a pro- and anti-American scale, depending on the issues, the time or the place. Opinion pollsters generally adopt this understanding with their questionnaires that aim to measure negative and positive perceptions of America. Ultimately this interpretation of anti-Americanism is too situational to provide a durable definition of anti-Americanism.

Anti-Americanism as a pathology. This understanding sees anti-Americanism as akin to an allergic reaction to all things American. It is probably the most precise and literal way of defining anti-Americanism, but if adopted, the outcome would be such a limited application of the term that almost no one's actions or thoughts apart from bin Laden's and those of other extremists could correctly be labelled anti-Americanism. This definition thus takes the term too far from its common usage and has limited utility.

Anti-Americanism as a prejudice. This definition is often suggested by conservative commentators. Scholars too would do well to take this approach more seriously rather than being blindsided by their view of prejudice as something only experienced by dispossessed and disadvantaged peoples. Much anti-Americanism has the traditional markers of prejudice as it *prejudges*, it is often clearly *one-sided* and offers an *undifferentiated* view of America and Americans.

Anti-Americanism as an ideology. This is a far more complex and speculative way of defining anti-Americanism, complicated not least by the fact that the term 'ideology' itself is multifaceted and frequently contested. At its crudest, we have the anti-American ideologies of Castro and the post-1979 Iranian leaders. Whether contemporary anti-Americanism in general can sensibly be called ideological I am less certain.

Having briefly outlined these five conceptions of anti-Americanism, I will now provide a much more detailed overview of each of these understandings.

Anti-Americanism as One Side of Dichotomised Worldview

At its simplest, one is either pro- or anti-American. This dichotomy reduces politics down to crude polarisations. At its worst, this is the 'with us or against us' view of the Bush administration and the 'which side are you on' demand of left-wing ideologues. It also represents the worldview of tabloid journalism where, for the sake of speed and simplicity, politics is constantly polarised. A recent interview I gave to an Australian newspaper journalist is a case in point, albeit on a personal level. Given I was writing on the topic, the journalist asked if I was anti-American. I answered in the negative, explaining that the terms 'pro-American' and 'anti-American' were too simplistic to describe my views on America. I added that my outlook towards the United States was one of ambivalence. However, when the article appeared in the newspaper, it stated that I described myself 'as pro-American …'[32] In the mind of that journalist and others of the same ilk, there are only two options. This understanding may suffice for bar room conversation or within certain parts of the media but is far too broad to specifically define anti-Americanism. It overstates the degree of anti-Americanism and falsely labels any critic of America an anti-American.

Anti-Americanism as a Tendency

Public opinion surveyors personify this understanding of the term with their ongoing questionnaires, which chart the rise and fall of anti-Americanism from year to year. In the social sciences, this is the view taken by behaviouralists and their measuring of preferences. In standard behaviouralist analysis, anti-Americanism and pro-Americanism are placed at the two opposite ends of a continuum. In the hands of these surveyors, one's attitudes to America can be plotted at some point along this continuum and accumulated with the opinions of others to allow for pronouncements to be made on trends in global anti-Americanism.

The Pew survey results certainly paint a clear picture that the election of George W. Bush, and even more significantly, the Iraq War of 2003 have increased negative global attitudes towards the United States as a country. This is starkly illustrated by simply picking two of the countries surveyed over time. By 2003, 71 percent of Germans and 99 percent of Jordanians expressed an unfavourable attitude to the United States. One year earlier, German negativity stood at only 35 percent and the Jordanians were also significantly less negative towards the United States at 75 percent. One is given an even greater sense of how far America's reputation has fallen with the fact that all surveyed nations – except for the United States, Canada and Poland – view China more favourably than the United States. France and Germany are also seen more favourably by all nations apart from respondents in the United States; and Japan was favoured over the United States by all except the Chinese and Americans. This seems a major public diplomacy indictment for the United States.

On the other hand, if you are looking for a more positive reading for America in the data, you could point to evidence that European respondents clearly think it will be a 'bad thing' if 'China were to become as powerful militarily as the United States'. And quite revealingly, when asked, 'If an innocent people were being killed by the army, the police or another tribe, in another country, who would you trust most to do something to stop the killings?', the United States tops the list as the country most regularly named (from the six options of France, Germany, China, Great Britain, Japan, Russia and the United States).[33] Furthermore, as a people, Americans were seen favourably by the majority of people in Canada, Great Britain, France, Germany, the Netherlands, Russia, Poland, India, Nigeria and Japan in the most recent fifteen-nation Pew survey.[34]

Whatever angle you take on these data, it is clear that it provides us with shifting tendencies in world opinion. On the continuum, the most important shift is the change in how respondents generally view

America – before the Iraq War, their view was 'somewhat favourable', but during and since the Iraq War, it has shifted to 'somewhat unfavourable'. Although it seems alarming that recent, post–World War II allies of the United States such as France, Germany, Spain and the Netherlands all have a more unfavourable than favourable attitude towards the United States, the negative attitude of the vast majority of respondents was only 'somewhat unfavourable' as opposed to 'very unfavourable'. The reporting of the survey data seems to miss this very crucial point. Furthermore, looking at the data, it seems that much of what the Pew survey calls anti-Americanism could just as easily be renamed 'anti-Bushism'. When the Pew survey asks: 'Why do you have an unfavourable view of the US? Is it mostly because of President George W. Bush or is it a more general problem with America?', strong majorities of respondents in Canada and in all the Western European countries surveyed state 'mostly Bush'.[35] It seems quite a conceptual leap to label visceral dislike of an individual president the same as dislike for an entire nation of people.

The Pew report writers use the term 'anti-Americanism' liberally, undoubtedly making their influential survey more marketable, but they offer no definition of the term. Rather, they boldly open their most recent report with the statement: 'Anti-Americanism in Europe, the Middle East and Asia, which surged as a result of the US war in Iraq, shows modest signs of abating. But the United States remains broadly disliked in most countries surveyed, and opinion of the American people is not as positive as it once was.'[36] But is it anti-Americanism? If taken to mean a negative attitude towards the United States as a country, then the answer is a resounding yes. But this would suggest the 'anti' in anti-Americanism means 'somewhat unfavourable' rather than a narrower and more intense dislike. This approach empties the term of much of its intended pejorative meaning, reducing the dialogue to degrees of tendency for or against America rather than looking at whether the attitude is anti-American even to begin with. I favour building a definition of anti-Americanism that retains pejorative overtones, rather than simply describing whether someone is more or less negative towards the United States on a given day. Although the data from the Pew surveys have highlighted some important trends, they have only scratched the surface; to dig deeper, we need a more analytical understanding of the term 'anti-Americanism' before asking further questions that determine more accurately the levels of anti-Americanism around the world.

Anti-Americanism as a Pathology

In *The Rise and Fall of Anti-Americanism* (1990), an edited collection
of French scholarship, the authors argue for the adoption of a narrow
approach to the term by taking the word 'anti-Americanism' quite
literally and suggesting it implies a dislike of all things American.
Theodore Zeldin examines what he calls '[t]he pathology of anti-
Americanism' in an essay that examines the phenomenon from a clinical
point of view.[37] Marie-France Toinet writes in the same volume: 'As for
the term "anti-Americanism", we feel that its use is only fully justified
if it implies systematic opposition – a sort of allergic reaction – to
America as a whole. It is clear that if defined in this very narrow way,
anti-Americanism either does not exist or is extremely rare. Nonetheless,
accusations of anti-Americanism are bandied about with ease.'[38]

Seen as a pathology, anti-Americanism is an aversion to all things
American. This would place one at the extreme end of the tendency
continuum described previously. The word 'pathology' suggests that anti-
Americanism is the preserve of the irrational fanatic.[39] At first take, this
definition holds much appeal. It is neat, precise and narrowly defined.
Sensibly, the advocates of this definition warn against picking out
particular quotes as a way of labelling an individual an anti-American.
Most famous commentators on the United States have written things
that can be construed to reveal their anti-Americanism. For example
Tocqueville famously wrote, 'I know of no country, where, by and large,
there exists less independence of mind or true freedom of discussion than
in America.' Of course, such quotes need to be seen in the context of the
person's general views about America. In the case of Tocqueville, it
would have to be balanced against the many positive things he said about
the United States. Toinet certainly takes this into account, arguing that in
sum, it would seem Tocqueville's attitudes towards America, like that of
most people's, is ambivalence rather than anti-Americanism.[40] Similarly,
Robert Singh has written, 'the sole unifying and main animating feature
of anti-Americanism is ambivalence: admiration co-existing with disapproval and disappointment'.[41] This emphasis on ambivalence and the
recognition that very few individuals or groups are disapproving of all
things American is an eminently sensible understanding of most people's
attitude towards the United States. However, this understanding is too
narrow in its conception of anti-Americanism. Under this pathological
definition of anti-Americanism, only a small number of people, such as

bin Laden and some of his supporters, could be labelled true anti-Americans. Most people's dislikes would be considered something less than real anti-Americanism. The term thus would be reserved for only the most fanatical haters of America, with everyone else labelled a critic. This is a position advocated by some who believe they are falsely labelled anti-American, such as the Indian writer and activist Arundhati Roy.[42] If one wants to put the term 'anti-Americanism' out of circulation as a term, this definition is appealing. However, it is too far from the commonplace usage of the term; in my opinion, academic definitions should generally seek to build on and work with the everyday usage of words rather than re-invent them anew. The word 'anti-Americanism' is already too set in the collective vocabulary to be easily pared back to this sparse definition. Also there is enough anecdotal evidence from Americans of experiences of 'anti-Americanism' to warrant the term needing a wider definition than the one of pathology allows.

Anti-Americanism as a Prejudice

My preference for defining anti-Americanism more precisely is to largely view it as a prejudice. In most instances, prejudice is seen as wrong and thus something to combat. The current strength of this normative position in the West has been very effective in reducing racism and other forms of discrimination. The markers of prejudice include: undifferentiated attacks, assumption of inferiority or an *a priori* belief that only bad intentions drive one's ideas and actions. Prejudice encompasses negative stereotyping, but goes beyond this to include more direct forms of hatred and vitriol. Prejudiced opinion easily leads to exaggerations and conspiratorial ideas. These generally recognised signs of prejudice are all too familiar in discussions about America, and it seems high time to honestly acknowledge them as prejudice. Moreover, at least ideally, calling anti-Americanism a prejudice would force the accuser to not abuse a term that has significant cultural and political resonance in the fight against racism and discrimination.

Although it is true that many people's views on America bear the common signs of prejudice as listed above, most would deny this. They would argue that anti-Americanism is in fact not a prejudice because you can only be prejudiced towards 'oppressed' or 'disadvantaged' groups.[43] Some people, however, choose to openly acknowledge that their views

are prejudicial, arguing that anti-Americanism is a legitimate or necessary prejudice. Nick Cohen in an article entitled 'Why it is right to be
anti-American' brazenly adopts this position. He makes the following
admission: 'Anti-Americanism is a prejudice, and it remains crass
to identify a people with their government. But with no alternative to
the present regime in Washington in sight, a depressingly convincing
justification for anti-Americanism remains: that there is little about
modern America to be for.'[44]

Todd Gitlin's apposite criticism that anti-Americanism is often 'an
emotion masquerading as an analysis'[45] seems fair to direct at Cohen and
his defence of anti-American prejudice. The Bush administration is a long
way from my favoured politics, but to sweepingly dismiss all that modern
America produces is to reveal a remarkably narrow focus. It is a common
viewpoint on the left, from where Nick Cohen hails, that there have been
no decent American politicians for a considerable time and that America
has been a lost cause since the 1960s.[46] These arguments are remarkably
selective. From a progressive point of view and for those who bother to
examine the details, good and bad decisions and policies come out of the
United States every year at the federal, state and city levels (a lack of
concern for details or counter evidence is one of the common traits of
anti-American prejudice). Further, the America's environmental,
women's rights and gay rights movements still provide inspiration for
many around the world. If we move to the cultural realm, there is clearly
very much in modern America to be 'for' from a progressive position. To
let one's disgust at the Bush administration overshadow appreciation for
the good aspects of America is to be blinded by prejudice.

Viewing anti-Americanism as a prejudice as opposed to a pathology
has a number of advantages. It does not let us allow the exceptions to
disprove the rule (an argument commonly accepted in discussions on
racism). Just because a person has an Aboriginal friend does not mean
that person is not racist towards Aboriginal people. Those accused
of anti-Americanism often bring up the objection that they cannot
be labelled in this way as they like Toni Morrison or John Coltrane
or Jonathan Richman; or they have American friends; or that they were
born in America; and, in E.P. Thompson's case, he claimed he could not
be accused of being anti-American because he was 'ethnically half-
American'[47] himself. These objections are beside the point; those who
are prejudiced towards America may be all of these things and more.
However, it is the nature of the comment or action that needs to be

analysed, not a person's music collection or birth certificate. Of course comments and actions need to be set in context. However, to ask whether these actions or attitudes are prejudiced, or not, is a relatively straight-forward question that helps us get to the heart of people's views about America in a way that is widely understood and allows for necessary debate on this issue.

Once the question of prejudice has been raised, the critical issue to judge is the breadth and degree of perniciousness in the prejudice held by the individual or group. Recognising this, a number of authors distinguish between anti-Americanism 'lite' and 'murderous' anti-Americanism.[48] I would not see this distinction as a dichotomy but rather as a continuum, with some forms of non-violent anti-Americanism being more pernicious than others. Whether this prejudice is best seen as part of a wider and more comprehensive anti-American ideology will now be explored.

Anti-Americanism as an Ideology

James Caeser has written that: 'Only one opinion or ideology in the world today has a truly global reach. It is anti-Americanism.'[49] To take this definition seriously, one first needs to ask what ideology is. Of course there is no simple answer. My understanding of the conceptual nature of the term 'ideology' owes much to the brilliant scholarship of Michael Freeden.[50] Although the term was coined by Antoine Destutt de Tracy to connote the study of ideas, the more negative understanding of ideology set forth by Marx and Engels in *The German Ideology* has profoundly shaped subsequent discussions. Marx and Engels presented ideology as a distortion and manipulation of reality that masks the truth;[51] the importance of this interpretation is apparent in the common perception that ideology is cant or propaganda that distorts or misrepresents reality. This usage is invoked when people dismiss an argument as being 'just ideology' as opposed to what they believe the 'evidence shows' or is 'in the best interests of society' (in debates about privatisation or education, for instance). This pejorative understanding of the term 'ideology' is the one used by Philippe Roger in *The American Enemy* and by Jean-François Revel in his far less sophisticated *Anti-Americanism*. For both authors, French anti-Americanism is presented as an ideological attack on a distorted and imagined America; an attack that significantly misrepresents reality. This leads both authors to conclude that anti-Americanism tells us more about French fears and anxieties than it does about American society or politics.

The understanding of ideology as falsehood is never likely to disappear entirely from a sensible description of what ideology is, but it is only part of the story. The Marxian distinction between bourgeois capitalist ideology and communist truth alerts us to one of the obvious weaknesses of this conception. Clearly, communism too is an ideology, as history attests. Recognising this, many modern scholars of ideology have been drawn to talk of competing ideologies, with less emphasis placed on the division between ideology and truth. During the twentieth century, scholars were drawn to increasingly seeing all major schools of thought as ideologies, with the experience of the so-called 'age of ideologies' – the 1920s and 1930s – particularly shaping this outlook. It was during this period that anti-Americanism emerged as a recognised concept;[52] this historical timing goes some way to explaining why anti-Americanism emerged as an 'ism' rather than as a 'phobia'.

Coming back to the notion of competing ideologies: this is often presented too simply as major conflicts between fairly fixed ideologies with names like socialism, liberalism and fascism. This is the *Politics* 101 approach to ideologies and is a perception that misses much of the subtlety and dynamism regarding how ideologies develop. I am disinclined to see ideologies as monolithic, fixed positions; the insights gained from anthropologic studies of 'ideology as a cultural system' and behaviouralist studies of belief systems have added important nuances to the study of ideologies. At the same time, there are limits to the number of belief systems we can contemplate; we need to herd ideas into widely recognised labels and concepts to have any chance of engaging in dialogue and politics in general. Ideologies are after all mass belief systems, not private philosophies.

Minogue has suggested that, 'No one, if we get right down to it, is anti-American in quite the same way.'[53] For these different anti-American thoughts and outpourings to be called an ideology, there needs to be a certain commonality, or what Freeden calls an ideological 'core', that these ideas coalesce around. While not entirely rigid, this core gives them what Freeden describes as 'flexible coherence'.[54] Freeden also argues that to qualify as an ideology, a belief system needs to have discernable views on important political questions and political concepts such as freedom, democracy and equality (anti-Americanism would seem to generally fall short of this standard).[55] Anti-Americanism does provide a public policy position but it is rather limited, simply arguing against American culture, ideas and policies. Where you can see anti-Americanism clearly as an ideology is in the hands of ideologues such as Fidel Castro. As a number of authors have remarked, anti-Americanism has overtaken communism as Castro's dominant guiding ideology.[56]

At first, I was tempted to argue that anti-Americanism is simply too incoherent to make it sensible to talk about it as an ideology beyond specific instances, but this possibly misses the commonalities within much anti-American opinion. If one focuses particularly on what America symbolises rather than its actions, it becomes imaginable to talk of an anti-American ideology. James Caeser's assertion that on 'every continent, large contingents of intellectuals, backed by significant numbers in the political class, organise their political thinking on the basis of anti-Americanism'[57] certainly suggests that anti-Americanism is a mass belief system. This claim certainly requires further research and analysis, the likes of which have been begun most fruitfully by Andrei Markovits, with his detailed empirical work on anti-Americanism in Germany.[58] An anti-American mindset, if we can call it that, is certainly nowhere near as coherent as ideologies such as liberalism or even conservatism; but it does have similarities with nationalism, which has been called a 'thin-centred ideology'.[59]

To see anti-Americanism as ideology inevitably draws one into debates about what America symbolises and thus to the question of what is Americanism? Richard Hofstatder's observation that, 'it has been our fate as a nation not to have ideologies but to be one',[60] would seem a perfect starting point from which to understand firstly Americanism and then in turn anti-Americanism as an ideology. However, Hofstatder's quote is a siren call that quickly grounds much analysis because an exact understanding of Americanism is far from simple. Beyond vague notions such as 'American exceptionalism', there is little agreement on what this ideology is; and exceptionalism itself is certainly not universally accepted as a valid way to describe America.[61] Theodore Roosevelt in 1909 popularised the word 'Americanism', declaring that 'Americanism signifies the virtues of courage, honour, justice, truth, sincerity and strength – the virtues that made America'.[62] In his seminal book *American Exceptionalism*, Seymour Martin Lipset embraces Americanism as an ideology, suggesting that its core values are 'liberty, egalitarianism, individualism, populism, and laissez-faire'.[63] There are a number of problems with these definitions. Firstly, the values associated with Americanism are simply too general to really define a distinct American creed; all of these so-called core values could be equally said to define Australianism if we were to invent such a term. Once these values are articulated beyond motherhood phrases such as truth, courage and liberty, they become contested – the most obvious example is the constant competition between the liberal and conservative interpretations of the American tradition. American liberals and conservatives alike see their version as the more authentic understanding of Americanism. Scholars such as Lipset paste over these conflicts by adopting Louis Hartz's line that America has a dominant liberal tradition; I would argue this position pays far too little attention to the importance of an indigenous form of American conservatism and its impact on the United States.[64]

For me, talk of Americanism in the current environment is often confused with what would be more accurately called an intensification of American nationalism. This nationalism of course borrows from long standing myths and traditions, but I am less certain these should be called Americanism. Richard Crockatt eloquently puts the case for the position I am wary of, thus:

> What is not in doubt is the allegiance of a majority of Americans to certain profoundly unifying symbols, attitudes, and values that can collectively be called *Americanism*. There is no more eloquent expression of this sentiment, which is sufficiently potent and historically grounded to qualify as an ideology, than the unity displayed by the American people's reaction to September 11. Equally clear is the curious mixture of attraction and repulsion that this ideology arouses in peoples around the world.[65]

One of the reasons I am sceptical of notions of Americanism is that they often lead to a polarisation between the 'real America' (what is seen as typically American) and the 'other America' (or what is also called alternative America). For example George W. Bush is often called a typical American as opposed to John Kerry, or Al Gore, who are somehow seen as less typically American. Such pontificating about what is typically American is often heard when people talk about their dislike of 'American movies' or 'American food'. Americanism simply becomes a hackneyed set of stereotypes, where personal tastes dictate over serious analysis. Such conversations reveal how malleable the term 'Americanism' is. For example, how would one sensibly talk about widely popular alternative heroes like Bob Dylan or Woody Allen? Do they represent Americanism or something else? To me, once you have an appreciation of the conflicting ideologies and cultures within America, summing up the essence of America with a pat definition or examples of Americanism seems impossible. This all makes me a sceptic of analysis that argues the best way of understanding anti-Americanism is through a thorough understanding of Americanism.

In this chapter, I have argued for a critique based on details and evidence, rather than broad prejudices and stereotypes; for analysis, not knee-jerk rejection. I have offered five different understandings of what anti-Americanism is; all of these interpretations provide us with various insights. Seeing anti-Americanism as one side of a dichotomy neatly encapsulates how many polemicists see the world. The view of anti-Americanism as a tendency is likely to continue to predominate in discussions on anti-Americanism, despite its analytical limitations. The rich data available from the Pew and other quality surveys provide an almost irresistible basis for discussing year-to-year variations in 'anti-Americanism'. From my perspective, these surveys provide solid evidence that antipathy towards the United States has risen in recent times, but these trends do not in themselves provide us with a means of distinguishing genuine anti-American sentiment from disappointment with particular US policies such as American involvement in Iraq. Furthermore, anti-Americanism for me is something more specific than seeing the United States 'somewhat unfavourably', the response that much of the Pew analysis is built upon.

I am inclined to see anti-Americanism principally as a prejudice. This allows for a relatively straightforward debate over what should be called anti-Americanism and what should more fairly be regarded as criticism. This approach, however, has failed to be widely adopted in commentary on anti-Americanism because unlike most other prejudices, anti-Americanism is more regularly associated with intellectuals who apparently know better than to be prejudiced. So to overcome anti-American prejudice, we first need to overcome the prejudice against seeing anti-Americanism as a form of prejudice. Of course this may be difficult but I think it is far more achievable than trying to find an entirely new definition for anti-Americanism itself – such as the term 'Americanophobia' suggested by Lacorne.[66]

Seeing anti-Americanism as a pathology is at times tempting, given the simplicity of this literal interpretation; however on closer examination, this conception means that almost no one ends up being anti-American. Lastly, my discussion of anti-Americanism as an ideology sees it as a conception that covers all four of the previous understandings. However, as we presently know them, the various strands of anti-Americanism lack even a 'flexible core', making it too early to admit the term as a member of the family of ideologies. More empirical research is required that examines the commonalities of various anti-American views. This analysis would also need to ask whether anti-Americanism is more than just an amalgam of other recognised ideologies.

Last Words

Certainly not everyone will be persuaded by this academic analysis of anti-Americanism. Some see these as desperate times that require general outrage towards America, not more nuanced analysis. A recent personal experience highlighted this for me. At the end of one of my lectures on American foreign policy, by chance an American peace activist arrived to give a talk on the Iraq War. I told the activist I was writing a book about anti-Americanism and asked her if she had experienced anti-Americanism in her travels. She said she certainly had and that she welcomed it. 'The more anti-Americanism the better' was her line. Her argument was that America needed to be totally isolated by the rest of the world; only then might it change its ways for the better. It is a position I have heard promoted in a number of forums over the last year.

Apart from being an unrealistic wish, promoting isolationism seems a very naïve view of history. Over the last hundred years, nations isolated from the rest of the world have often wrought disastrous results. Isolation certainly did not help post–World War I Germany or Japan, or post–1945 China, or more recently, North Korea, become more progressive nations. For me, apart from being the only realistic approach to the United States, engagement is also desirable on the major challenges of time: from poverty to AIDS, from the Israeli/Palestinian conflict to Darfur. Thomas Jefferson long ago wrote that, 'every man has two countries – his own and France'. Today every person has two countries, their own and America. This incorporation of America into our lives, dreams and nightmares is suggestive of why isolating the United States is not really a realistic option. Of course there are many reasons to be critical of the United States, and certainly the Bush administration could have been a much fairer, wiser and better global leader than it has, but anti-Americanism is not a solution. Rather, by inflaming issues, it is an obstacle to real debate and becomes part of the problem. Too many critics of the 'them versus us' politics presented by President Bush do the same only in reverse. For me, such polarisations and claims of loyalty to a particular 'side' represent the death of the independent mind.

My work here is really only a starting point for further analysis on this topic that until recently has been largely neglected by scholars. For those less convinced that this is a subject worthy of further study and analysis, I offer these reasons. Firstly, prejudice, be it against Indonesians or Americans, should be challenged and confronted. In its most extreme form, this prejudice led to the terrorist attacks of September 11, 2001. In its more commonplace expression, it leads to reflexive discrimination against Americans and American ideas and products. Secondly, for the policies of the Bush administration (and his successors) to be effectively questioned, a more differentiated understanding of America is crucial. Thirdly, the consecration of an anti-American ideology that automatically rejects American policy and even culture is reactionary and the enemy of intelligent thought and discernment. In closing, American politics and Americanisation is rightly the concern of people around the world; the challenge is how to engage with America without letting anti-American prejudices overwhelm critique in all its various forms. Whether one cares about this distinction is set to be one of the most challenging questions of our age.

Chapter 2

The Anti-Americanism Mindset

Andrei S. Markovits

Introduction and Definition

One need not be a diligent student of survey research to know that
antipathy towards America and Americans has become a worldwide
phenomenon.[1] As the Italian political scientist Pierangelo Isernia
demonstrates in his excellent paper, 'The Nature of the Beast. Anti-
Americanism in Western Europe', anti-Americanism has become a *lingua
franca* of political elites in France, Britain, Germany and Italy, who are
currently using this resentment for political purposes of mobilisation
like never before in the 50-year period following World War II.[2] By
concentrating on public opinion surveys of the past four decades, Isernia
delineates very convincingly the presence of anti-Americanism in the
publics of these four countries. Yet, he does not view this phenomenon as
deep and decisive. In contrast, I most certainly do. My research, which
includes public opinion polls but also other data, reveals that anti-
Americanism is a deep-seated prejudicial structure in contemporary
West European discourse, with a massive historical lineage. Newspaper
headlines, editorials, and television talk shows, as well as casual
conversations at parties and dinner tables reveal a widely held hostility
towards the United States that remains seemingly unprecedented.

The study at hand will concentrate on Europe alone, though in a
comparative context. By any measure, American–European relations
have reached a nadir over the past few years, with no aspect of public life
immune to this tension fraught with recrimination, antipathy and even
open hostility. When even the world of accounting, hitherto hardly
a hotbed of cultural wars and transatlantic disagreements, witnesses
overt hostilities from Europeans towards their American colleagues,
it would seem the situation has indeed reached a very low point. Claude
Bebear, the chairman of AXA, the French insurer, recently compared
accounting rulemakers to Iranian religious leaders: 'Most of them are
from the United States', he said, 'but there is a super-super-ayatollah who
is not even American but is from Scotland and has a fascination with

market value'.[3] Regardless of the issue involved, about which I claim zero expertise, the tone says it all. The German proverb *Der Ton macht die Musik* (the tone makes the music) comes to mind. Indeed, this proverb's wisdom will inform much of this study, since the saying clearly denotes the important fact that form matters at least as much as substance, or better still, that form is in fact substance. Accordingly, this study is as much about the 'how' as it is about the 'what'. In particular, it will demonstrate that a steady – and growing – resentment of the United States (indeed, of most things American) has permeated European discourse and opinion since the fall of the Soviet Union in 1991 and thus the end of the bipolar world of the Cold War that dominated Europe since 1945. However, it will also argue that the manifest nature of this antipathy hails from a very long and fertile history and that it is only marginally related to dislike of George W. Bush and his administration's policies. The latter have merely served as convenient caricatures for a much deeper structural disconnect between Europe as an emerging political entity and a new global player on the one hand and the United States, its only genuine rival, on the other. As this chapter will argue, anti-Americanism in Europe has long preceded George Bush and will persist long after his departure, even though the current US president and his policies have catapulted contemporary anti-Americanism in Western Europe into 'overdrive'. My study does not explain this overdrive. Instead, it concentrates on the structures that permitted this overdrive and fostered its presence. To continue with this metaphor, my study thus looks at the road, the car, the driver, in short all the necessities that rendered this overdrive possible. A couple of caveats are in order at this juncture: This study is *not* about American–European relations. Were it that, it would also have to take European pro-Americanism into account, which it does not. Just as any study of Jewish–Gentile relations would have to include the important phenomenon of philo-Semitism in order to be complete, while an analysis only of anti-Semitism on its own is perfectly legitimate, so, too, is the study of anti-Americanism *sui generis*. Moreover, just because millions consume key ingredients of American culture on a daily basis does not *eo ipso* mean that one cannot simultaneously harbour resentments and antipathies towards America and many things American. Perhaps one does so all the more. We know quite well that regular and massive consumption of artefacts of black culture in the United States has never led to racists lowering their prejudices and resentments of African-Americans.

Anti-Americanism is a particularly murky concept, because it invariably merges antipathy towards what America *does* with what America *is* – or rather is projected to be in the eyes of its beholders.[4] The difference between 'does' and 'is' corresponds well with Jon Elster's fine distinction between 'anger' and 'hatred'. Elster writes: 'In anger, my hostility is directed towards another's action and can be extinguished by getting even – an action that re-establishes the equilibrium. In hatred, my hostility is directed towards another person or a category of individuals [Americans in the case of this chapter] who are seen as intrinsically and irremediably bad. For the world to be made whole, they have to disappear.'[5] Thus, it has characteristics like any other prejudice in that its holder 'prejudges' the object and its activities apart from what actually transpires in reality. And just as in the case of any prejudice, anti-Americanism too says much more about those who hold it than the object of its ire and contempt. But where it differs so markedly from 'classical' prejudices such as anti-Semitism (about which there will be more in this study), homophobia, misogyny and racism is the fact that unlike in these latter cases – where Jews, gays and lesbians, women and ethnic minorities rarely, if ever, have any actual power in and over the majority of populations in most countries – the real existing United States most certainly does have power. Because of this unique paradox, the separation between what America *is* – i.e., its way of life, its symbols, products, people – and what America *does* – its foreign policy writ large – will forever be jumbled and impossible to disentangle. I would argue that it is precisely because of this fact that – unlike these other prejudices which, as a fine testimony to progress and tolerance over the past forty years, have by and large become publicly illegitimate in most advanced industrial democracies – anti-Americanism remains not only acceptable in many public circles, it has even become commendable, indeed a badge of honour, and perhaps one of the most distinct icons of being a progressive these days. After all, by being anti-American, one adheres to a prejudice that *ipso facto* also opposes a truly powerful force in the world. Thus, in the case of anti-Americanism, one's prejudice partially assumes an antinomian purpose, thereby attaining a legitimacy in progressive circles that other prejudices – thankfully – do not anymore, at least in the accepted public discourse of advanced industrial democracies. Anti-Americanism, as with any other prejudice, is an acquired set of beliefs, an attitude, an ideology, not an ascribed trait. Thus, it is completely independent of the national origins of its particular holder.

Indeed, many Americans can be, and are, anti-American, just as Jews can be, and are, anti-Semitic; blacks can, and do, hold racist views, and women misogynist ones.[6] The reason I am mentioning this is because often the very existence of anti-Americanism is denied by dint of Americans also adhering to such positions. It is not a matter of the holder's citizenship or birthplace that ought to be the appropriate criterion but rather one's set of acquired beliefs about a particular collective. But here, too, context means everything. Delighting in Michael Moore's *Bowling for Columbine* in an artsy movie theatre in Ann Arbor, Madison, Cambridge or Berkeley is a completely different experience and has a vastly different meaning from having this film become the movie of choice about the United States among German youth, including right-wing and left-wing radicals in towns of the former East Germany, who use it as a bonding experience between and among them. *Bowling for Columbine* and *Fahrenheit 9/11* have become far and away the most successful documentary films in German history, and Michael Moore's books grace Europe's bestseller lists, even before they are translated into the local languages.[7] Thousands thronged to his lectures on his European tour in December 2003 when he was received like a rock star by an adoring public. Conservative CSU voters delighted in his films and books, just as did radical leftists. This had never happened to any other documentary filmmaker, American or European. It behoves us to seek an explanation for the reasons of Michael Moore's immense popularity in contemporary Europe across generations and political allegiances. Clearly, the texture of the admiration bestowed upon him by these adoring Europeans hails from a source that goes much deeper than disagreements over policy or even the dislike of a particular president and members of his cabinet. Indeed, as I have argued elsewhere in detail, Michael Moore continues to serve as a shill for Europeans to utter their resentment of America and Americans with panache and without any fear of being labelled prejudicial or hateful since – after all – an American himself, namely Michael Moore, says precisely what millions of Europeans feel.[8] It is not Michael Moore the filmmaker who matters but Michael Moore the public speaker who denounces Americans as stupid, vapid and ignorant in front of thousands of appreciative Europeans who reward him with thunderous applause and adoration. Their actions have nothing to do with the merit of his films, which indeed are interesting and worth seeing, and everything to do with Michael Moore being an American who – by dint of his being that – can utter any and all derogatory statements about Americans without ever risking being labelled 'anti-American'. Racist lyrics by rappers do not become less racist by virtue of their being articulated by African-American artists, but their very quality changes completely if the same lyrics are uttered by whites. Few people have a more deprecating sense of humour than Jews. Yet it makes a whale of a difference whether the jokester is Jewish or not. The content defines but the context lends meaning.

As much as possible, this study is about the *is*, not the *does*. I will argue that in Europe, anti-Americanism has been much more about the essence of America – or put more precisely, the interpretation of how Europeans constructed this essence for their own purposes – than its actual activities. This is clearly not the case with other manifestations of contemporary anti-Americanism. Thus, for example, as my colleague Meredith Woo-Cummings argues in a perceptive paper on changing public opinion in the Republic of Korea, Korean antipathies towards the United States have none of the depth, characteristics and tradition that their European counterparts have, and remain clearly much more anchored in dislike of America's actual activities – its doing – rather than its character, its essence – its being.[9] Unlike elsewhere in the world, at least until very recently, America represented a particularly loaded concept and complex entity to Europeans precisely because it was a European creation which, however, more than any other former European extension, consciously defected from its European origins. Anti-Americanism in Europe has always been much more about America's being, as opposed to the rest of the world's antipathy which has been much more anchored in America's doing.

To be sure, just as to the Europeans this imagined America served all kinds of purposes, not least of which was to delineate a clear 'other' to themselves, the exact obverse pertained as well to Americans, who throughout their history created all kinds of imagined Europes that fulfilled an 'othering' function. This America as Europe's 'other' and vice versa has best been characterised as a 'compulsive *folie à deux* for over three centuries with a remarkably stable set of choreographies, but with a rather uneven, historically specific set of performances'.[10] However, I perceive an important difference in the respective agencies of this *folie à deux* on the two continents. In the United States, the carriers of prejudice and antipathy towards Europe have predominated – if at all – in the lower social strata while American elites – particularly cultural ones – have consistently extolled Europe, and continue to do so. This love for and emulation of European tastes, mores, fashions and habits remained a staple of American elite culture even during the country's most nativist and isolationist periods. It is safe to say that virtually all of America's highbrow culture continues to be European. One need only look at the humanities departments of any leading American university to observe this continuing cultural hegemony, which, even in the persistent attempt of negating its Eurocentrism, resorts to ideas and methods that are completely European. (Of course it goes without saying that those among America's cultural elites who decry European culture's hegemony in America's history are equally critical of established American culture and mainstream America. If anything, they see the latter merely as a cheapened version of the former.) The word 'European' invariably evokes positive tropes among Americans (elite and mass alike) such as 'quality', 'class', 'taste', and 'elegance', be it in food, comfort, cars (as in the recent ad for the Ford Focus which – of course – sports a 'European-inspired transmission') tradition, romance, eroticism (as in European massage, European decor, European looks and the list can go on). Virtually every context of advertising in which the word 'European' is used in America is highly favourable. Any resentment of Europe by American mass opinion is of a completely different order of magnitude than anti-Americanism's presence in Europe. The risible 'freedom fries' had zero traction in any segment of American society. First of all, the parallel words to 'anti-Americanism' namely 'anti-Europism' or 'anti-Europeanism' are virtually nonexistent. (Indeed, my computer's spell checker knows neither, as opposed to 'anti-Americanism', with which it seems totally familiar.) Second, Americans in their history have been known to be anti-French, anti-German, anti-Russian, anti-British, and anti-Communist, but never anti-European. To be sure, one important aspect of acculturation to America was to oppose things from 'the old country', to try to distance oneself from the 'old world' in an attempt to create a new one. (This, too, changed in the course of the twentieth century, since by its end, the ideology of a multicultural America demanded pride in one's origins as opposed to the ideology of the melting pot of the pre-1960s era, which exacted distancing from one's previous culture.) In that sense, one could speak of a distancing from Europe.

The *folie à deux* viewed from the European side could scarcely be more different. In Europe, the word 'American' conjures up outright negative and pejorative – at best ambivalent – notions. Here too, though there have been differences according to social class and status;

'ordinary' Europeans have never exhibited the aversion towards America
that their elites have. Indeed, as demonstrated by regular public opinion
surveys since the early 1960s, a solid majority of Europeans have
expressed positive views of America, with only about 30 percent holding
negative ones. Tellingly, the higher the social scale of the respondents is,
the greater the negative attitude towards America becomes. As such, anti-
Americanism is arguably one of the very few prejudices in contemporary
Europe that correlates positively with education and social status: the
higher the education, the greater the prejudice. Until the mid-1960s, this
was also the case with anti-Semitism in Austria and Germany where,
since the nineteenth century, the most virulent anti-Semites were to be
found at universities and among their graduates, such as doctors, lawyers
and engineers. In the course of the past four decades, conventional anti-
Semitism in these two countries has assumed the pattern of other kinds
of collective prejudices and hatreds: the lesser the respondent's education
and the lower her or his social standing, the greater the probability of her
or his having prejudices and collective dislikes. This has never been the
case with anti-Americanism and – as will be discussed later – might yet
again have received a new twist in terms of anti-Semitism as well.
Thus, a sort of inverted mirror image has characterised this European –
American *folie à deux*, with very different weights in their respective
agencies: European masses have by and large liked and respected
America while European elites have certainly not, whereas American
elites have liked and respected Europe and American masses less so.

Perhaps what differentiates the current level and quality of European
anti-Americanism from all its predecessors is the fact that, for the very first
time, a solid majority of European publics also bear negative attitudes
towards the United States, thus establishing – maybe for the first time – a
complete congruity with their elites on this topic. There can be no doubt
that the Bush administration's actions, tone and demeanour have greatly
contributed to this congruity – this voluntary *Gleichschaltung* (a general
state of consensus) – between European publics and elites in terms of their
massively felt and politically mobilised anti-Americanism.

Lest there be any misunderstandings and conceptual uncertainties as
to what exactly I mean by anti-Americanism, here is the definition offered
by Paul Hollander in his superb and definitive book on the subject:

Anti-Americanism is *a predisposition to hostility* toward the United
States and American society, a relentless critical impulse toward

American social, economic, and political institutions, traditions, and values; it entails an aversion to American culture in particular and its influence abroad, often also contempt for the American national character (or what is presumed to be such a character) and dislike of American people, manners, behavior, dress, and so on; rejection of American foreign policy and a firm belief in the malignity of American influence and presence anywhere in the world.[11]

It is a generalised and comprehensive normative dislike that often lacks distinct reasons or concrete causes.

Anti-Americanism is an 'ism', thus bespeaking its established institutionalisation and common usage as a modern ideology. Whereas the word itself might not have been explicitly used until the beginning of the twentieth century, the sentiments that it denotes had been commonly understood and employed in Europe since the late eighteenth century, if not before.[12] Anti-Americanism exists: it is visible, palpable, audible and readable. Lest we get bogged down in fruitless definitional squabbles, Justice Potter Stewart's famous dictum about pornography (obscenity) applies here as well: 'I shall not today attempt further to define the kinds of material I understand to embrace in that shorthand description; and perhaps I could never succeed in intelligibly doing so. But I know it when I see it.'[13]

A Brief Historical Overview

In my research of the topic, I reached back into history in order to ascertain whether the current anti-Americanism sweeping Europe is indeed unique. While some of its manifestations might indeed be (as will be discussed later), it is also quite clear that there never was a 'golden age' in which European elites genuinely liked America. To be precise, there never existed an era in which European intellectuals and literati – European elites – viewed the United States without a huge residue of *ressentiment,* perhaps a more apt characterisation of how Europeans feel about America than the aforementioned hatred.[14] As odd as this may seem, this goes back all the way to 1492 and the so-called 'discovery' of the so-called 'New World' – what was to become America and the Americas – by Christopher Columbus. As Ira Strauss argues in a perceptive paper, a simpler, pre-ideological fear of and *ressentiment* towards America emerged among Europe's elites – both the aristocracy and the clergy – who understood all too well that the changes in the world that Columbus's journeys wrought could potentially undermine their established positions and ordered views.[15] Well before America had any power, and well before it was an independent country, tropes emerged that were to become mainstays of European anti-Americanism and continue to be so to this day: venality, vulgarity, mediocrity, inauthenticity but also a clear sense of danger in its undefinable but clearly evident attraction. Thus, the argument that it has been America's disproportionate power when compared to Europe's alleged powerlessness that lies at the heart of European *ressentiment* towards the United States and things American simply does not hold up. For clearly, even when the United States had virtually no power, certainly when compared to the big European players such as Britain and France, Europeans bore hostility towards this new entity. From the very beginning until today, European elites have continued to view America as this threatening *parvenu*. By the eighteenth century, Europeans begin to depict America as 'degenerate', which is particularly odd since the country had barely been born. The French anthropologist Georges Louis Leclerq, better known as Count de Buffon, argued that, in comparison with Africa, Asia and even South America, North America's native population was particularly retarded and 'degenerate' and that this physiological and psychological inferiority somehow transferred onto the new European immigrants who, too, regressed once they reached America. According to de Buffon, this inevitable process of degeneration initiated via contact with America also affected the domestic animals that the Europeans brought with them.[16] Just like their human masters, they regressed once contact was made with this New World. Count de Buffon's 'degeneration thesis' gained immense popularity among Europe's elites throughout the eighteenth and nineteenth centuries and was also seconded by other European interpreters of America such as the Dutch naturalist Cornelius de Pauw, who decried the existence of America as 'the worst misfortune' that could have happened to all humanity, upsetting even the New World's dogs who – according to de Pauw – never barked.[17] This view of America as 'degenerate' has remained a major staple of European elite opinion to this day.[18] As I have argued repeatedly, concurring with others, European antipathy towards America can easily be traced to July 5, 1776, the beginning of the republic. Thus Herbert J. Spiro said: 'Anti-Americanism has been endemic among the ruling classes in continental Europe since 1776 at the latest.'[19] No lesser observer of the United States than the French aristocrat Alexis de Tocqueville completely understood – and in part reflected – this European *ressentiment* towards America, which already by the early nineteenth century bespoke a clear fear of a loss of control on the part of the Europeans, which rested partly in America's potential as a powerful country but also in its undeniable – almost irresistible – attraction, especially to Europe's masses, surely not the aristocracy's friends. When Tocqueville predicted the rise of Russia and America as the two superpowers of the twentieth century, mainly by virtue of their continental expanse, he clearly understood that one would be much more attractive and successful than the other: the United States, according to Tocqueville, would become a hegemon under the banner of freedom, whereas Russia would do so by means of repression. Tocqueville's claim that the latter would fail whereas the former would flourish not only uncannily foresaw the events of the last decades of the twentieth century, but also underlined the European elites' continued fear of and disdain for America.[20] From the get go, there was something eerily attractive about the place well beyond the new life that it offered to millions of Europe's masses. It was similar, yet different; weak, yet powerful; repellent, yet attractive. In notable contrast to any other country, from the very beginning, the enemy for European elites was not 'America the Conqueror – not the Imperial Republic – but America the Beguiling'.[21] Nowhere has this consistently powerful sentiment been better expressed than in the lyrics of Johnny Hallyday, that self-styled French Elvis Presley, when he sings in his song 'Quelque chose de Tennessee': 'Cette force, qui nous pousse vers l'infini; Y a peu d'amour avec tell'ment d'envie' (that force which pushes us towards infinity; there is so little love but so much desire/envy).

In the following few paragraphs, I will give examples only from Germany, not because Germany represents a special case in Europe's *ressentiment* towards the United States, but because I happen to know German thinkers and literature better than any other in Europe. To attest to the Europe-wide nature of this phenomenon, one could easily give parallel examples from Russia, France, Britain or Italy. From the late eighteenth century until today, a strong negative assessment of things American outdistanced any positive views of the United States on the part of German intellectuals and elites. The dichotomy of Germany's 'Kultur' versus America's 'Zivilisation' arose to contrast the latter's materialism, vulgarity and shallowness with the former's idealism, nobility and depth. Beginning with Hegel, virtually all German observers condemned the political immaturity of the United States, mainly by virtue of its not having a European-style state. As long as the United States failed to establish a European-style polity and state structure – and the prognosis looked bad given the size of the country as well as its civil turbulence (which was an outgrowth of its multiethnic and immigrant population) – the United States, Hegel concluded, would remain forever peripheral to world history. Accordingly, Heine wrote of America that it was a 'colossal jail of freedom' where 'the mob, the most disgusting tyrant of all' carries out 'its crude authority'. He continued: 'You dear German farmers! Go to America! There, neither princes nor nobles exist; there, all people are equal; there, all are the same boors!'[22] Jacob Burkhardt equated the allegedly a-historical and anti-historical nature of American society with barbarism. He discussed the 'a-historical Bildungsmensch [educated class]' who exist in America's blandness, monotony, mediocrity and uniformity, and thus whose only escape lay in an inevitable – and pathetic – imitation of Europe's mores and values.[23] Nikolaus Lenau, a major America enthusiast before his trip to the United States, was so disappointed in all things American after his arrival that he returned to Germany in a completely dejected state, informing his countrymen that there were 'serious and deep reasons that there were no nightingales and no singing birds at all' in this awful country of 'worn out people' and 'scorched forests'.[24] To the Romantics, America's 'Bodenlosigkeit' (rootlessness) was an unforgivable sin. Simon Schama has argued that the flimsy frame construction of American houses was *prima facie* evidence for Germans of America's rootlessness. This association of America with rootlessness became, of course, a major staple of German views of America, well beyond the radical right's and the Nazis' blood and soil ideology. Thus, for example, in many a current discussion pertaining to the alleged advantages of the 'Rhenish' as opposed to the American model of economic and social management, one often hears that in contrast to the ills of America's 'flexible' labour markets, which exact a high degree of geographic mobility by workers, Germans are much more tied to home and hearth.

Whether the aforementioned German intellectuals had actually visited the United States, as had Lenau, or whether they made their judgements from afar (as did Heine, Burkhardt and Nietzsche) mattered little in terms of their disseminating anti-Americanism among Germany's intellectuals and political and cultural elites, as well as its growing *Bildungsbürgertum* (educated middle-class). Friedrich Nietzsche hated America as the epitome of the modern, which he foresaw as the inevitable conqueror of Europe as well. Long before the advance of Hollywood movies, and rock and rap music, the spread of American culture was likened to a form of disease. Its progress in Europe seemed ineluctable. 'The faith of the American is becoming the faith of the European as well', Nietzsche warned.[25] And Nietzsche's student Arthur Moeller Van den Bruck, 'best known for having popularised the phrase "The Third Reich", proposed the concept of *Amerikanertum* (Americanness) which was to be "not geographically but spiritually" understood'.[26] Sigmund Freud viewed the United States as embodying the most pronounced manifestation of everything that he found despicable in modern civilisation. It was a place that was solely governed by the almighty dollar, that had 'no time for libido', that was simply an 'anti-Paradise'. 'What is the use of Americans, if they bring no money?' he asked Ernest Jones. He confided to Jones that, 'Yes, America is gigantic, but a gigantic mistake.' At least Freud had the good sense to admit that the United States was the embodiment of an enemy he simply could not do without, especially after his *Civilisation and Its Discontents* became a bestseller in America, making Freud a wealthy man.[27] Peter Gay points out in his superb study of Freud how, to Freud, America represented something inferior, primitive, materialistic and prudish, yet at the same time also something immensely seductive, alluring, almost irresistible, thus providing fertile ground for *ressentiment* in the most pronounced Nietzscheian or Schelerian way. Freud's ambivalence and *ressentiment*, it seems, were quite similar to those expressed by European intellectuals and elites for the past 230 years. And Heidegger frequently mentioned 'Americanism' as a soulless, greedy, inauthentic force that undermined Europe.

Unique among Europeans was the Germans' inordinate extolling of native Americans as 'noble savages' whom the Germans regarded as their true soul mates in the defence of authentic culture against the onslaught of America's materialist and venal civilisation. Nowhere does this theme become more visible than in the writings of Karl May, whose pulp fiction was staple reading fodder for middle-class German children – particularly boys – throughout the twentieth century. May's books feature a German (presumably the author himself) under the assumed name of Old Shatterhand who, together with his blood brother Winnetou, chief of the Apaches, fights the good fight against an assortment of evil doers comprising venal Englishmen, drunken Scots, cunning Jews, and excessively cruel Comanches and Sioux, their native American allies. May's books feature all the anti-American, anti-British and anti-Semitic tropes of Germany's middle class all the way to 1945, if not beyond. The concern with the fate of native Americans remains singular to Germans among Europeans' antagonisms towards America. The reasons are obvious: by constantly invoking the genocide of native Americans, Germans can readily point to the Americans' own Holocaust and thus experience some sense of expiation, particularly since they see America – driven by its East Coast intellectuals (a convenient code word for Jews) – as Germany's most unforgiving reminder of its Nazi past.[28] To be sure, there were a handful of German intellectuals, writers, poets and thinkers who were not particularly anti-American. Johann Wolfgang von Goethe exclaimed that 'Amerika, Du hast es besser' (America, you have it better) when in an unusual (for Goethe) quasi-Tocquevillian mood, he weighed the political advances of American democracy in relation to Europe's continued autocratic forms of government. Karl Marx and Friedrich Engels were great admirers of the Union and backed it wholeheartedly in its battle against the Confederacy. Indeed, Marx sent a congratulatory telegram to Abraham Lincoln upon his re-election to the presidency of the United States in 1864, to which Lincoln replied in a presciently Wilsonian tone by stating that countries do not exist on their own but rather are part of an international order to which they need to show commitment and respect for the benefit of humanity (pace George W. Bush).[29] But adding validity to my argument about European elites' disdain for America as the embodiment of modern capitalism is the fact that leading members of the political classes in France and Britain openly rooted for the Confederacy, which they rightly assumed to be more akin to their own aristocratic ways than the brash, capitalist, industrial North whose victory would inevitably make the United States a formidable political rival for global domination.[30] Lastly, it was not only the German elites and intellectuals of the nineteenth century who expressed a habitual disdain for America. I would like to mention Charles Dickens, Frances Trollope, Knut Hamsun, Evelyn Waugh, Joseph de Maistre and Stendhal as eminent representatives of other European cultures.[31] Indeed, it is quite clear that there exists only a European anti-Americanism as opposed to a German, a French, an Italian or a Russian one since the tropes that define this prejudice are totally common to (and interchangeable among) all European cultures. In his study of Austrian Anti-Americanism, Günter

Bischof gives us ample evidence that this *ressentiment* has been alive and well in that country throughout the twentieth century and – just like elsewhere in contemporary Europe – might indeed be happily proliferating in the current atmosphere of its perhaps unprecedented social acceptability. But, as the author writes in the conclusion of his paper, 'Austrian anti-Americanism today is hardly unique.'[32] Its acuteness might vary from country to country, but its essence has remained remarkably steady and similar.

The period after World War I began to highlight the often irreconcilable bifurcation between the European elites' disdain for America and the European masses' acceptance of it. While the latter's leaving Europe in waves of emigration to find a home in the New World always underscored a certain inadvertent attraction to the United States, new forms of mass communication have rendered this culture clash a constant presence in Europe's daily existence to this day. Whereas in the pre–World War I world, Europeans expressed their preference for America by voting with their feet, so to speak, now they could do so unabashedly by dancing the charleston, flocking to movie theatres, idolising film stars, grooving on jazz, in short by making key aspects of American culture part of European life. Needless to say, this, if anything, heightened the elite's *ressentiment* of America. It was not only jazz that was vilified as decadent 'Negermusik' promoted by profit-hungry Jews intent on undermining the very fabric of European life. All aspects of mass culture were decried as inferior, shallow and tasteless. As such, it should never have incurred the wrath of Europe's elites, since by exhibiting such 'qualities', American culture should never have posed any threat to something perceived as so greatly superior. But it did – or at least Europe's elites feared it as such – and this, in turn, only exacerbated their irritation with and anger towards America and American culture.

The Nazis' (as well as most European fascists') hatred of and contempt for America needs no elaboration. America embodied every single social and political dimension that the Nazis found antithetical to their very being. To them, America was a mediocre mongrel mass society devoid of culture, ruled by a Jewish-dominated East-Coast-based plutocracy whose mission was global domination in politics, economics and culture. In an irony that underscores the attraction of American popular culture for Europe's masses, the Nazis were forced to broadcast jazz, swing and ragtime to their troops during the war lest they turn their radio dials to US Army stations.[33]

In an earlier work on anti-Americanism in Europe, I developed a fourfold table that establishes categories along the lines of left and right on the one hand; and politics and culture on the other. These are the narratives that comprise the four fields:

Left/politics:
America, as the world's foremost capitalist country, is engaged in imperialism. It is the leader of world reaction. America is a predatory power which is bent on totally controlling the world.

Right/politics:
America, because of its essentially vulgar nature, is not equipped to be the much-needed leader of the free, White and Western world. Because of its lack of traditional elites and its permissiveness, America's political system is disorganized, confused, and completely inappropriate to govern the United States adequately, let alone the world. Thus, Europeans would do well not to trust the United States because it is structurally and historically incapable of furnishing serious political leadership. America ultimately is weak, shallow, naïve, inexperienced, and no match for the adversaries of the free world.

In a sense then, whereas the left fears America's power by virtue of its size and ubiquity, the right disdains American power for its wannabe *parvenu* character that pretends but fails to execute effectively.

Left/culture:
American culture is the expression of an alienated, brutal, capitalist society which has produced soulless, plastic, and inauthentic artefacts solely for the profit of huge companies. The American 'culture industry' produces cheap, essentially worthless things for a quick fix in a mass market populated by misguided, manipulated and exploited individuals who are stripped of their collectiveness by the inherent divisiveness of a capitalist society.

Right/culture:
American culture is not worthy of the name. The United States, because of its vulgar nature, has never been capable of producing anything of lasting value. Worse, it has used its newly acquired financial might to buy real, that is European, culture and/or imitate

it in a crass style behoving the nouveau riche that the United States will always remain. The danger of American culture, however, is its mass appeal which has made it so successful among Europe's masses as well. Thus, American culture is not only worthless and shallow, but also dangerous and corrupting by virtue of its universal appeal.

Hence, if the European left has feared American power more than has the right, it is exactly the inverse in the realm of culture: here, the right is much more worried than the left. But both merge in their dismissal of American culture as 'inauthentic', with the left seeing this mainly as a consequence of America's commodified essence, and the right seeing it as a result of America's alleged lack of history and tradition, thus of depth, sophistication and the requisite education.[34]

Conclusion: September 11, 2001

September 11 added a hitherto underdeveloped sentiment to this anti-American mix – that of *Schadenfreude*. One always hears on this side of the Atlantic how Europe's goodwill towards the United States immediately following 9/11 was squandered by the Bush administration's aggressive unilateralism. This may have been true for the masses, but it certainly was not for the elites, who had no such goodwill to squander. Never before was the cleavage between the views of Europe's elites and its masses concerning America clearer than in the immediate wake of that tragedy. While, on the whole, Europe's mass opinion was deeply sympathetic towards Americans (New Yorkers in particular) and empathetic with Americans as victims, Europe's elites – especially its cultural ones – were by and large neither. Ground Zero was still burning when the first reports in the quality media initiated all the arguments, objections, analyses, conjectures, conspiracy theories and open rejoicing that have become commonplace: that the Americans clearly had it coming to them; that this was justified payback for all American misdeeds of the past, from Vietnam to globalisation, from exterminating the Native Americans to Dresden (two often-voiced staples of the German reaction as expressed repeatedly in *taz*, *Der Spiegel*, *Frankfurter Rundschau*, radio and television talk shows, and the *Römerberggespräche* in Frankfurt to mention but a few venues); that this was no big deal since many more Americans die in yearly traffic accidents; that, if anything, the destruction of the Twin Towers improved New York's skyline; that the Israeli Mossad was behind it all since many Jews stayed away from work that day lest they be killed; that it was all a ploy by the American government to obtain a carte blanche for its imperialist endeavours, very similar to the burning of the Reichstag in February of 1933 that led to the consolidation of the Nazi dictatorship (again, often voiced in Germany, though not exclusively there); that George W. Bush and Osama bin Laden were identical in their mental makeup and their (mainly religious) fanaticism, basically mirror images of each other, just as the United States in its religious revivalism was not a real democracy but in fact resembled the theocratic fanaticism of the Islamists. Just as the Israeli psychiatrist Zvi Rex was completely correct in saying that the Germans will never forgive the Jews for Auschwitz, so, too, will they never forgive the Americans for being daily reminders that it was they – together with the Red Army – who defeated Nazism, not the Germans. By year's end, bookstores in Paris, Berlin and London were full of publications that basically rejoiced at the tragedy of 9/11. In France, Thierry Meyssan's *L'Effroyable Imposture* (The Terrible Fraud), which argued that the crime of 9/11 was totally committed by the American government, made it to the top of the charts and became a steady bestseller. Ditto a book with an identical theme by former *taz* editor Mathias Broecker, which sold 130,000 copies for a very small German publisher in less than eight months, and remained on various bestseller lists for many more. Examples abound wherein a significant section of Europe's intellectuals and elites expressed a virtually unveiled *Schadenfreude* in America's woes: for Baudrillard, the destruction of the Twin Towers was the fulfilment of a long-held dream; for Stockhausen, it was a great piece of art. The rhapsodisation by European intellectuals goes on and on. A close reading of Jean-Marie Colombani's editorial in *Le Monde* of September 12 entitled, 'Nous Sommes Tous Américains' (We are all Americans) which has been touted as a major statement of solidarity with the United States, reveals quite the opposite: Colombani accuses the Americans of being the progenitors of Osama Bin Laden and thus the godfathers of Jihaddist terrorism. Permit me to submit the following telling counterfactual: had the Air France Airbus A-300 Flight 8969 on December 24, 1994, crashed into the Eiffel Tower in Paris, as the Groupe Armée Islamique wanted it to, I doubt very much that any – let alone many – American intellectual would have written lengthy pieces in prestigious publications like *The New York Times* or *The Washington Post* by, say, December 26 and 27 all but exculpating this crime by invoking France's many military and political missteps as well as its atrocities, from the Vendée to the Paris Commune, from Indochina to Algeria. Nor would they have invoked all kinds of conspiracy theories involving the French government, the Israeli Mossad or any of the other agents so often mentioned in connection with 9/11. I doubt very much that books purporting that such a crime was actually planned and executed by the French president – had this terrible plan become reality – would have been written by American intellectuals, let alone become bestsellers in the United States. But all of this has indeed happened in Europe, particularly among social groups from whom one would least expect it by dint of their intelligence and education. Clearly, antipathy, as has often been the case, trumps either and both.

It was payback time for Mr Big's arrogant attitude and demeanour, for his general misdeeds like imperialism as well as specific ones like the bombing of Dresden, but above all, simply for his being big. To be sure, everybody hates Mr Big in any context, be it in politics or in the classroom, be it Manchester United, the New York Yankees, or Harvard.[35] Alas, *Schadenfreude* is a very human trait which in fact gains in respectability and legitimacy when it pertains to the suffering of a perceived giant. That the widely held and vocally expressed *Schadenfreude* and anger pertaining to 9/11 quickly shifted from Europe's intellectuals and elites to a significant percentage of the population is best demonstrated by opinion polls, which clearly reveal that by the summer of 2003, for example, one third of Germans under age thirty believed that the US government sponsored the 9/11 attacks on New York and Washington. About 20 percent of the entire German population agreed with this view, according to the same survey.[36] And when as serious a person as Andreas von Bülow, former state secretary in an SPD-led government, writes a very successful book touting these views and when conspiracy theories deeply steeped in anti-Americanism and anti-Semitism are entering the mainstream in Germany and France, then this clearly constitutes a serious matter.

Chapter 3

Americanisation and Anti-Americanism

Andrei S. Markovits

Europe's Elite Voices on America from January 1, 1992, until December 31, 2002: A Crescendo of Condescension, Ridicule, Irritation and *Ressentiment*

As part of a larger empirical project on European anti-Americanism, I collected nearly 1,500 articles written on the United States in seven key European countries: Germany, France, Italy, Britain, Austria, Spain and Portugal. In order to maximise America's 'is' dimension as opposed to its 'does' one for my study, I consciously excluded articles and reports that dealt with *overtly* political questions, particularly all those related to American foreign policy broadly construed, since it is via its foreign policy that America 'does' things most overtly to other countries. I concentrated my research on articles about film, theatre, food, and travel, along with human interest pieces, and descriptions of the iconography of particular events such as party conventions, car manufacturing, subway construction and the world of sports. Now, as a child of the 1960s, I realise that there is no realm of social or cultural activity – or any activity for that matter – that is not also political. But I tried as best as I could to eliminate the obviously political from my study, precisely to analyse a *ressentiment* against America by Europeans that one could call 'surplus' or gratuitous anti-Americanism. This is an anti-Americanism for its own sake so to speak, where the invoking of a generalisation about the United States added little analysis or description to the issue at hand but merely served to reinforce already present prejudices instead. My sample included elite as well as other publications in the seven European nations surveyed. The publications that I consulted and analysed were: from Great Britain, *The Guardian, The Times, The Independent, The Daily Telegraph, The Sunday Times, The Observer, The Financial Times, The Scotsman*; from France, *Le Monde, Le Figaro, Libération, L'Express, Le Point, L'Equipe, La Tribune*; from Germany, *Frankfurter Allgemeine Zeitung, Frankfurter Rundschau, Süddeutsche Zeitung, Die Welt, Der Tagesspiegel, Berliner Zeitung, die tageszeitung, Die Zeit, Der Spiegel*; from Italy, *Corriere della Sera, La Stampa, La Repubblica, La Gazetta dello Sport*; from Spain, *El Pais, ABC, El Mundo, 5 Dias, 20 minutos*; from Austria, *Kronen-Zeitung, Die Presse, Der Standard, Salzburger Nachrichten, Tiroler Tageszeitung*; and from Portugal, *Expresso, Jornal Record, Jornal de Noticias, Diario de Noticias, Publico, Jornal Regiao Sul, Correio da Manha.*[1]

Over two thirds of the collected and analysed articles included some form of irritation with, condescension towards or ridicule of the topic that was being described – well before George W. Bush became the convenient, and partly appropriate, caricature of the American cowboy for the European press. *Overall conclusion*: virtually all aspects of American culture – including its high-brow variant – experienced at least one derisive or dismissive comment, even in an otherwise positive review. The term 'Americanisation' of whatever the case may be (movies, theatre, universities, business practices, habits, etc.) was invariably invoked in a negative manner and conveyed an undesirable situation as in 'Wien darf nicht Chicago werden' (Vienna must not become Chicago), Jörg Haider's highly successful slogan in an Austrian electoral campaign. (Why Chicago? Why not Palermo? Liverpool? Or any number of troubled European cities.)? Or take Gerhard Schröder's constant invoking of 'amerikanische Verhältnisse' (American conditions) as a very powerful bogeyman for his successful electoral campaign in 2002. This campaign was the very first in Europe's post-war history in which a major – indeed governing – party structured its electoral strategy on the national level around an explicit negation of America. It would certainly not be the last. Indeed, my research, published in another context, clearly shows that the term 'amerikanische Verhältnisse' has become a standard phrase in German when one wants to describe something bad, undesired, inferior and also dangerous.[2] 'Amerikanische Verhältnisse' are conjured up by trade union leaders but also by businessmen; by lawyers and educators; by police officials and doctors; they exist in virtually every conceivable niche of German life, from soccer to films, from television to trade unions, from construction to education, from the courts to the animal world.[3] Tellingly, in virtually none of these cases does the reader learn what these conditions are truly like in the United States. But that, after all, is not the point. 'Amerikanische Verhältnisse' does not delineate actual conditions in the United States. Instead, it is constantly used to stigmatise something in Germany. And there is no better way to do this than to invoke American conditions. One hardly needs a more persuasive

example of the acceptability of anti-Americanism as a potent agent
of political mobilisation. Above all, America was damned if it did,
and damned if it did not. The negative judgment was almost automatically assured independently of the action's intention, process
or outcome.

The world of soccer offers a fine example for my point, precisely
because, whatever one wants to argue about this sport and its culture,
it is clear that the United States has been – at best – an also-ran in it
throughout all of the twentieth century, with no power or importance.
America simply did not matter – and still matters very little. When the
World Cup was awarded to the United States for the summer of 1994,
much of the European press was appalled. Instead of rejoicing that the
last important *terra incognita* for soccer was about to be conquered
by the 'beautiful game', the usual objections to American crassness,
vulgarity, commercialism and ignorance were loudly voiced by
Europeans[4] – in notable contrast to Latin Americans who, if objective
criteria and real injustices were to decide predilections and negative
opinions, have many more compelling reasons to dislike the United States
than do Europeans. Many Europeans argued that giving the tournament
to the Americans was tantamount to degrading the game and its
tradition. The facilities were denigrated, the organisation ridiculed, the
whole endeavour treated with derision. When the stadia were filled like
at no other World Cup tournament before or since, when the level of
violence and arrests was by far and away the lowest at any event of this
size, the European press chalked this up to the stupidity and ignorance
of Americans.[5] Of course Americans came to the games because they like
events and pageantry, but did they really enjoy and understand the
games? Could they ever learn to? When more than 60,000 people
crowded into Giants Stadium near New York City on a Wednesday
afternoon to watch Saudi Arabia play Morocco (surely no powerhouses
in the world of soccer), this too was attributed to the vast ignorance of
Americans regarding soccer. Indeed, five articles proudly pointed to the
fact that similar games in soccer-savvy Italy attracted fewer than 20,000
people in the 1990 World Cup held in that country. Those few European
journalists who bothered to write anything about American sports such
as baseball which, as always in the summer, was in full swing at the time,
had nothing but contempt, derision and ridicule for the game: no attempt
to engage its traditions, no endeavour to understand it on its own terms,
just merely yet another vehicle to confirm one's prejudices about

America. Michel Platini, the French soccer great of the 1980s and in charge of organising the subsequent World Cup in France, summed up his feelings and judgments in the vernacular of current Europe: 'The World Cup in the United States was outstanding, but it was like Coca-Cola. Ours will be like sparkling champagne.'[6] Surely Platini could not have meant to characterise the riots, the violence, the ticket scandals, the racial insults that occurred during the tournament in France as 'sparkling champagne'. And it is equally unclear what he meant by characterising the American tournament as 'Coca-Cola'. The code, however, is clear to all: regardless of its actual success and its achievements, the American event was by definition crude and inauthentic (like Coca-Cola), whereas the French – equally by definition – was inevitably going to be refined and profound (like champagne).

It was remarkable then how differently the European press reported on the World Cup 2002 in Japan and South Korea, even though both countries bore the same newcomer status as the United States. Rave reviews were accorded, contrasting sharply with the negative tone that had described the US-hosted games in 1994, even though FIFA, for example, and soccer officials had highly praised the American effort. What was viewed as kitsch in the American context (the opening ceremony, for example, and other pageantries accompanying the tournament) was lauded as artistic and innovative in the Japanese and South Korean equivalents. Lastly, the American team was first ridiculed as an incompetent group of players who barely deserved to be in the tournament. The huge upset over Portugal was attributed to sheer luck. When Team USA advanced to the second round and then defeated its archrival Mexico, the press corps who had rooted for the Mexicans during the game sat in stunned silence in the press centre. In notable contrast to the positive sentiment expressed towards the other Cinderella teams of the tournament, Turkey, Senegal and South Korea, only bitterness and derision was voiced towards the American team. When the mighty Germans narrowly (and luckily) beat the Americans in a quarterfinal, some European commentators were genuinely alarmed. Quipped one British journalist: 'This is terrible. Now they are getting good at this, too. They will steal our game. Imagine eleven Michael Jordans running onto the pitch at Wembley. That would be the end.' Damned if you do, damned if you don't – it could not be articulated more clearly: when the Americans play poorly, they irritate merely by doing so and because they are aloof from everybody. When they finally play well, they are disliked because they have joined everybody but in doing so have also become threatening.

This underlying irritation was further confirmed during my many lectures on comparative sports in Germany, especially on my two book tours in support of the German edition of my book *Offside*. In literally every forum in which I presented my book and work, from university campuses to book stores, from rented public halls to semi-private settings, from Saarbrücken in the West to Potsdam in the East, the question arose as to whether I did not find it arrogant that the Americans' sports culture centred on baseball, basketball and American football, and did not include soccer; whether indeed this was not yet another expression of America's self-anointed status as being better than the rest of the world. To many people, my response that this development reflected America's different history and its construction of its own modernity, which indeed entailed creating its own sports culture, did not allay their suspicions that underneath it all there lurked a normative dimension that somehow made America – in the Americans' eyes – better rather than just different. Fears along the lines that Americans might yet prove successful at soccer as well merely reinforced the constant malaise with and disdain for the United States regardless of what it actually did or did not do.

Lastly, one need only follow the British media's openly anti-American (and barely concealed anti-Semitic) tone in its opposition to the American Jewish businessman Malcolm Glazer's recent acquisition of Manchester United. The derision of Glazer as a poor dresser, as physically ugly, arrogant and greedy, and as being a total ignoramus of the world of soccer had no bounds.[7] But beyond that, the takeover of Manchester United – without any doubt the world's most capitalist football club and as globalised a business entity as one can imagine – is uniformly depicted as an undesirable intrusion by an ugly American Jew of a pristinely little and innocent local English club that has thus far never even encountered capitalism let alone become its most obvious poster child in the world of international sports. To be sure, the Glazer affair embodied a perfect storm: Glazer as the American Jewish capitalist who knew nothing about the game and traditions of soccer and who never hid his intentions of the acquisition as purely a business arrangement. An interesting counterexample is provided by the Russian Jewish billionaire Roman Abramovich's acquisition of Chelsea. That, too, was met by initial scepticism and some hostility but perhaps the most salient differences between Abramovich and Glazer were that the former hailed from a culture in which soccer was cherished and respected, and that he was a rabid fan of the game himself. In short, Glazer was a Yank. This already made him suspect among inveterate soccer fans (or football supporters, to use the proper wording in this context), who were further aggravated by his demonstrated indifference to the game. The tone and content of the British media in the Glazer–Manchester United affair parallel exactly in time and space the notorious 'locust' affair in Germany wherein Franz Müntefering, the Social Democratic Party's (SPD) chairman, explicitly singled out American firms with Jewish-sounding names that descend upon defenceless German companies, suck them dry of their profits and assets and then depart – like locusts.[8] Not to be outdone, *metall,* the monthly publication of IG Metall, Germany's – perhaps Europe's – most important trade union featured mosquitoes with American hats and Stuemer-style beaks who suck out the blood from upright and well-meaning German firms and then burp out their destroyed carcasses.[9] The link between Jews and America is obvious to all in the German and the British cases.

Although left-leaning publications like *The Guardian*, *Le Monde*, *Frankfurter Rundschau* and *die tageszeitung* featured on balance much more negative reporting about things American both in style and in content – as expected – compared to that of their centrist and conservative competitors, this was by no means always the case. Precisely because my sample was heavily skewed towards cultural topics and away from conventionally political ones, disdainful language towards and ridicule of America was often also quite eminent in such publications as *Le Figaro*, *Frankfurter Allgemeine Zeitung*, *The Times* and *La Stampa*. Notable was the increase in irritation as the decade progressed. Even during Bill Clinton's presidency, European newspapers became noticeably more critical of the United States. After all, this was the decade in which the French foreign minister Hubert Védrine used every opportunity to inveigh against the United States, this new 'hyperpuissance' (hyperpower).[10] And with each passing year of the decade, more Europeans welcomed his message.

The negative predisposition ran so deep that even those few American innovations that one would expect European progressives to like were deformed into basically negative caricatures. Take affirmative action, multiculturalism, feminism and America's campaign against cigarette smoking. Rather than seeing these as impressive steps towards progressive reform, many European commentators – even on the Left – decried these as merely mutated expressions of American puritanism, collective control and hysteria. Many articles derided these reforms under the rubric of 'political correctness'. They warned that American universities had been taken over by zealous feminists who dictated a moral code that forbade flirting and punished men for complimenting women. Indeed, key French elites all but accused American feminism of deviously undermining the purity of the French language. When the French decided to introduce some neologisms such as 'directrice', 'conseillère' and 'Madame la ministre' that feminised hitherto male nouns for women holding such positions of distinction, the secretary of the Académie Française, among others, opposed these potential changes not only on the ground of tradition and linguistic aesthetics but by virtue of seeing this unwanted reform as a dark ploy by American feminists who, by way of Québec and the successful perversion of the French language used in that Canadian province, planned to surreptitiously undermine the purity of the French language in France proper. The prominence of women in America's soccer world was to Europeans yet another *prima facie* case of the American penchant to subvert, distort and essentially sully a sacred European tradition.

Article upon article warned of the decline of American universities whose curricula were allegedly hijacked by ideological commissars whose task it was to replace Western civilisation with politically correct multiculturalism. Once again, damned if you do, damned if you don't. If one of the standard staples of European complaint against American universities consisted of their alleged elitism, now the alleged opposite was held against them: somehow they seem to have degenerated into institutions wherein standards of achievement were completely forfeited for measures governed by political correctness dictated by the unqualified. To many European commentators – and their high-brow audiences – America had degenerated into a quasi-Orwellian society, following the dictates of a puritanical culture supervised by increasingly rigid governmental rules on the one hand, and succumbing on the other hand to the exigencies of an uncontrolled market with no social consciousness whatsoever. America the prudish and the prurient, home of unbridled individualism and collectivist conformity, progenitor of Harvard and Hollywood, the former representing the very best education that only lots of money can buy, the latter embodying shallow schlock. In a sense, ever more Europeans began to view America as a different civilisation from Europe's, and surely an inferior one.[11]

European labour's anti-Americanism, usually confined to vocal opposition of American capitalism and foreign policy, also manifested itself in a clear disdain for American workers. In a detailed study of Daimler workers' attitudes in Stuttgart towards their presumed fraternal colleagues in the Daimler-Chrysler plants around Detroit, there were no attempts made to hide the contempt and disdain. Chrysler workers were characterised as lazy, incompetent and inferior. The Stuttgart crew did not want its allegedly superior products 'contaminated' by the shoddy American ways of the Chrysler workers. The contempt did not remain confined to the factory gates. The home milieus and recreational habits of the Chrysler workers were also ridiculed and characterised as inferior.[12]

The overall conclusion is that virtually all aspects of American culture – including its high-brow variant – experienced at least one derisive or dismissive comment, even among the minority of articles that featured a positive view towards the issue reported. More than 75 percent of the articles were overwhelmingly negative in the presentation of their topic. Most of these exhibited what I have called 'gratuitous' or 'surplus' anti-Americanism, meaning that there were objections lodged that were not immanent criticisms of the issue at hand but rather catered to a pejorative generalisation of America or Americans that had little bearing on the immediate topic. Even beyond the United States itself, many adversities in Europe are conveniently associated with America. When a crazed teenager gunned down his classmates and teachers in Erfurt in 2002, much of the subsequent German debate blamed an alleged 'Americanisation' of German youth, society and culture for this tragedy.[13] When an extreme heat wave tormented Europeans, articles appeared decrying the 'Americanisation' of Europe's climate.[14] Americans were to blame when the dollar was high, just as they were to blame when the dollar was low. Thus Gerhard Schröder's constant invoking of 'amerikanische Verhältnisse' as a negative icon for effective political mobilisation made perfect sense for his successful electoral campaign in 2002. 'Americanisation' of anything has in the meantime developed such a solid basis of pejorative connotations in Western Europe that it pays for politicians to use this sentiment as an agent of mobilisation and legitimisation. Above all, it elicits virtually unanimous contempt that crosses political allegiances, social positions, nationalities, age and gender. In short, 'America' has ubiquitously become a thoroughly negative trope in contemporary western Europe.

With Europe currently undergoing a fascinating, and, in a way, unique state-building process, the creation of a European identity is not only politically paramount but indeed the consequence of the creation of new sovereignty and the institutions supporting such. It is not by chance that precisely when America's power over Europe has massively diminished – particularly when compared to the 40 years after the end of World War II and during the Cold War – and when Europe's power in relation to America's is growing, the ideology of opposing America has gained political as well as structural currency. Not all European elites need be explicitly anti-American or hostile to things American, but opposition to America has for the first time in Europe's history attained a 'functionality'. It is no longer an opinion, a view, a *Weltanschauung*, no matter how emphatically experienced; rather, it has mutated into an ideology that *eo ipso* serves in the formation of a European identity. It is to a discussion of this phenomenon that the chapter now proceeds.

From *Ressentiment* to Rebellion? The Political Function of Anti-Americanism in Europe's State-Building Process

What does it matter that Europe's elites, particularly its 'chattering classes', disdain the United States? As this work has argued, there seems to be nothing new here. And yet, it seems to me, the spill over from elite to mass opinion delineated by the aforementioned examples does in fact represent a new situation at this particular juncture in Europe's political development. Whereas there was still a clear disconnect between elite and mass opinion in Europe following the 9/11 tragedy, there emerged a hitherto unprecedented congruence in opinion of all constituents concerning the war in Iraq. In no other instance that I can recall in Europe's post-war development did such a complete convergence of views emerge between elites and masses, between government and opposition, among voices on the left and the right, as occurred in France and Germany, in particular, during the four months of build-up to the war with Iraq. I would go so far as to characterise the public voice and mood in these countries, but in others as well, as 'gleichgeschaltet' (creating an atmosphere in which little, if any, dissent is desired). What

49

rendered this hegemonic consensus (a general state of consensus) so different from those that accompany most dictatorships was its completely voluntary, and thus democratic, nature. Everyone was united in their opposition to what America was about to do. While the thrust of this antagonism focused on America's actions, its amazing passion was deeply anchored in what Europeans perceived as America's very core, its identity. To many Europeans, even in the countries where the governing elites maintained the deeply unpopular position of supporting the United States in its imminent war with Iraq – Britain, Spain and Italy come to mind – America had become the 'un-Europe', a clear 'other'. This othering was, of course, not totally new and had many precedents. Well before the arrival of the Bush administration, even under the aegis of Bill Clinton, whom European intellectuals embraced wholeheartedly as a kindred spirit – particularly during the Lewinsky scandal and the ensuing impeachment proceedings – Europeans commenced the conscious construction of Europe being America's other. 'Europe: The Un-America' proclaimed Michael Elliott in an article published in *Newsweek International* in which he dismissed any semblance of a common transatlantic civilisation.[15] Many European intellectuals, particularly in France, Germany, Britain and Italy, basically appropriated Samuel Huntington's famous and controversial notion of the 'clash of civilisations', with which they characterised what they perceived as the increasing divergence between Europe and the United States and not – pursuant to Huntington's original – a clash between the predominantly Christian West and the Islamic world.[16] The widely voiced indictment accused America of being retrograde on three levels: moral (America being the purveyor of the death penalty and of religious fundamentalism, as opposed to Europe's having abolished the death penalty and adhering to an enlightened secularism); social (America being the bastion of unbridled 'predatory capitalism', to use the words of former German Chancellor Helmut Schmidt and of punishment as opposed to Europe being the home of the considerate welfare state and of rehabilitation); and cultural (America the commodified, Europe the refined; America the prudish and prurient, Europe the savvy and wise.)[17] Well before George W. Bush was close to running for president, French Foreign Minister Hubert Vedrine inveighed against the United States as a 'hyperpower' which needed to be brought down by an 'un-American' Europe obviously led by France. To Vedrine, the clarion call of Europe's rise against the United States centred on the following American ills that all good

Europeans had to fight tooth and nail: 'ultraliberal market economy, rejection of the state, nonrepublican individualism, unthinking strengthening of the universal and 'indispensable' role of the United States, common law, anglophonie, Protestant rather than Catholic concepts'.[18] Among European intellectuals and elites, overt hostilities in language and attitude that are still taboo against any other culture or country have become acceptable against America. As I stated at the outset of this work, overt anti-Americanism has become a badge of honour in certain European circles, and in Germany, the word '*Kulturkampf*' (literally 'cultural struggle') has been revived as a rallying cry by German intellectuals and cultural elites in their battle against the United States. Thus, a well-known German director said: '*Kulturkampf*? Count me in. I deeply detest America.'[19] Or take the British novelist Margaret Drabble, who wrote: 'My anti-Americanism has become almost uncontrollable.'[20]

To be sure, the Bush administration's actions intensified this *Kulturkampf* and legitimated it among European publics to a degree unimaginable before. Max Scheler reminds us that *ressentiment* can linger and fester, thus becoming ever more consuming of the subject who holds this sentiment. It thus remains solely a negative and destructive force. Or, conversely, it can transform itself into rebellion which, as Scheler says, always necessitates the affirmation of counter-values as the first positive step towards the construction of a new identity.[21] No mobilisation around these European counter-values could have been more emphatic than the huge demonstrations on Saturday, February 15, 2003. As never before in Europe's history – not in the days of August 1914 when Europe's armies marched into slaughter against each other, nor at the end of World War II, nor the fall of communism – did so many millions of Europeans unite in public on one day for one purpose. From London to Rome, from Paris to Madrid, from Athens to Helsinki, from Berlin to Barcelona, Europeans across most of the political spectrum united in their opposition to the impending American attack on Iraq. And sure enough, a number of European intellectuals proclaimed this day as the one that historians will some day view as the true birthday of a united Europe precisely because, like no other day in European history, it united Europeans emotionally and not only by fiat of a faceless bureaucracy issued in impenetrable language from Brussels.

At least to my knowledge, the first and most emphatic interpretation of February 15, 2003, as Europe's nascent national holiday was offered by Dominique Strauss-Kahn in a lengthy article in *Le Monde*. Strauss-Kahn could not have been more explicit from the outset of his piece: 'On Saturday, February 15, 2003, a nation was born on the streets. This nation is the European nation.'[22] Every facet of Strauss-Kahn's article makes it unmistakably clear that the only commonality of this nascent nation lies in its opposition to the United States. Lest there be any misunderstanding that this pertains only to policy interpretations, political rivalries or differences in interest, Strauss-Kahn leaves absolutely no doubt that he sees the chasm between Europe and the United States as a matter of values, identity and essence. While these might be negotiable on a superficial level, they are deeply irreconcilable dimensions that obviously clash with each other. Barely two months later, Jürgen Habermas entered the fray with a hitherto unprecedentedly coordinated endeavour: as a number of commentators remarked, only a man of Habermas' stature could have pulled off a Europe-wide publication event of this magnitude. On May 31, 2003, Habermas published an article on Europe's rebirth following the war in Iraq in Germany's one of two papers of record, the *Frankfurter Allgemeine Zeitung*. Co-authored with the world-famous French intellectual Jacques Derrida, a French version of this piece was also published in *Libération*. On the very same day, Habermas' friend, the American intellectual Richard Rorty, published a supportive piece in *Süddeutsche Zeitung*, Germany's other paper of record and the *FAZ*'s main rival. Adolf Muschg wrote in the eminent Swiss paper *Neue Zürcher Zeitung*, Umberto Eco in *Repubblica*, Gianni Vattimo in *La Stampa*, and Fernando Savater in *El Pais*. Excepting the Habermas–Derrida article in *FAZ* and *Libération*, all other contributions were completely independent articles united only by one common theme: the war in Iraq was to be the auspicious beginning of a European nation. While all pieces dwelt on the United States being Europe's 'other', Eco deviated from this accusatory tone by arguing that the United States – far from being this hotly desired 'other' – was merely different, just like it had always been, and was always going to be. Exhibiting a sobriety in tone that none of the other contributions possessed, Eco warned the Europeans that the major problems awaiting the continent could never be solved merely by rallying around the negative moment of opposing the United States, as was increasingly the case in many European circles among intellectuals, the political class and – for the first time – increasingly the public as well. Particularly disappointing to me was the obviously conscious exclusion of intellectuals from Britain, the Scandinavian and Low Countries, and – most of all – Eastern Europe. Indeed, even a cursory reading of the Habermas–Derrida text which – by the authors' own admission – was largely penned by Habermas alone, reveals how much this allegedly European vision is little more than an undisguised advocacy of a Franco-German core that is to lead Europe away from its tutelage to the United States. Habermas speaks openly about a core Europe that would be a vanguard. Apart from the text's haughty dismissal of other options and its complete disregard for East Europeans and their five-decade-long experience under Communist rule, it is remarkable how German-centred this manifesto is, particularly given its author's *bona fide* standing as a genuine *Weltbürger* (citizen of the world). Tellingly, the only European politician whom Habermas mentions explicitly by name is Joschka Fischer, Germany's foreign minister. Habermas centres his entire argument on the alleged hegemony of the following clearly preferable European values that he juxtaposes – implicitly, though obvious to any reader – to their naturally inferior American counterparts: a large dosage of scepticism towards the market combined with an acceptance of the state as a major social actor; a cautious attitude towards technology; and a secular conviction that rejects any kind of religiosity in public life. These alleged European virtues have been the staples of Europe's debate about America and Americanism at least since 1945, if not before. Many European intellectuals – like Hubert Vedrine, as mentioned above – have listed them well before Habermas. But as Jürgen Kaube in a brilliant critique of Habermas points out, many of the values that Habermas claims for Europe do not pertain: few entities are more market-driven than the European Union; the French, Swedes and Belgians certainly do not share the Germans' fears of technological progress; and religion in Poland, Spain or Ireland certainly continues to play an important role in public life. Kaube concludes that Habermas really refers to mainly German values, which he then blithely extrapolates to the rest of Europe.[23] Jan Ross, another of Habermas' critics, correctly observes that Habermas' view of European values closely resembles those of the old Bonn Republic and of the old EU before the fall of the Berlin Wall.[24] This indeed is eerily true but with one major exception: after all, it was Jürgen Habermas more than any other German intellectual who always argued that the greatest achievement of the old Bonn Republic was its uncon-ditional acceptance of the West in all its forms: cultural, social, political. And it was obvious to anybody who listened at the time that the West for Habermas not only included but actually featured the United States. For Habermas too, apparently, one aspect of 'othering' the United States in the current European development is to claim a strong affinity with the 'genuine' United States that over the past decade or so seems to have lost its way. Thus, for liberals of Habermas' normative predilections at least, the new Europe is not only the 'un-America' but actually a sort of 'ur-America'. In the context of being awarded the prestigious Bruno-Kreisky-Prize awarded by the Karl-Renner-Institute of the Austrian Social Democrats in March 2006, Habermas once again reiterated that Europe needs to become a counter-America. For this purpose, it was also essential for Habermas that Europe establish its very own armed forces that can defend the continent and clearly establish Europe's independence from – and open opposition to – the United States.[25]

Conclusion

Fifty years ago, in a 1954 lecture at Princeton University dealing with the European image of 'America' (that is, of the United States), the social theorist Hannah Arendt warned of a political–cultural undercurrent that she conceptualised as a rising 'pan-European nationalism'.[26] Its very basis, she claimed, was neither a common European history and experience, nor a pre-existing European identity. It was first and foremost anti-Americanism; that is, a general hostility towards 'America' and the citizens of the United States, to which this European 'pan-nationalism' is intimately related. In the European image, Arendt argues, America now (1) becomes emblematic for the (European) problem of totalitarianism, (2) represents all the negative aspects of socio-cultural and technological modernisation and, most importantly, (3) serves as a common foe, a counter-image with an identity-creating function for Europe herself.

Based on empirical observations, Arendt fears that the political institutionalisation of a European body politic and government and Europe's integration, which she strongly endorses in principle, is in danger of being approached as an act of liberation from America's democracy and culture and America as a symbol of modernity at large:

> If it is true that each nationalism (though, of course, not the birth of every nation) begins with a real or fabricated common enemy, then the current image of America in Europe may well become the

beginning of a new pan-European nationalism. ... Since Europe is apparently no longer willing to see in America whatever it has to hope or to fear from her own future development, it has a tendency to consider the establishment of a European government an act of emancipation from America.[27]

While Arendt observes that America always remains a symbol of radical modernisation, she argues that the view that the United States is simultaneously a European project and thus strongly affiliated with old European history and civilisation, as Toqueville and many other European writers believed in the nineteenth century, is now conspicuously missing in Europe's image of America. All the other dreams and nightmares have somehow survived, though in Arendt's words, 'they have degenerated into clichés whose triviality makes it almost impossible to consider seriously the constantly increasing literature on the subject'.[28] However, in the post-war constellation of today, Arendt states that the United States is considered to have no more relations with Europe than with any other country, if America is not generally constructed as a counter-image of Europe.

Arendt points out that in the dominant European perception, America is no longer intermingled with but largely split off from the European self-image of her development and civilisation. After World War II, Arendt argues, America is increasingly constructed in the framework of a fundamental binary opposition that substitutes the notion of an intrinsic linkage between Europe and America, and more and more replaces the notion of the latter's ambiguity. America, according to Arendt, now only seems to represent all the *evil* aspects of modernisation: modern technologies of mass destruction and destructive potentialities in general; a new conformism of mass society; an 'inferior' consumer and money culture that is combined with a lack of communal tradition, history and 'essence'; a nation of individualised immigrants and blended cultures instead of 'rooted' cultural communities; and a foreign policy solely based on economic imperialism and power interests instead of diplomacy and mediation. To the contrary, in the image of most Europeans, says Arendt, their continent is positively redefined and valued by the sheer opposite of everything that is identified as American. Indeed, the political unification of Europe and a new supra- or pan-national European nationalism seem to be built on, and ideologically mobilised by, this binary construction.

It is Arendt's intention to expose this European construction as false
and distorted. According to Arendt, this image mainly reflects European
rather than American issues and problems. However, it needs to be
noted that she also tries to *understand* the European view and partially
identifies with some of the issues raised. Arendt, hence, also intends to
stimulate self-reflection on actual dangers within contemporary America
and modern society as such. It seems that she tries to 'deconstruct' the
anti-American perception and underlying European identity models
while at the same time presenting this misperception as a sort of convex
mirror: instead of fully rejecting anti-Americanism as a mere ensemble
of projections, she analyses it as completely out of proportion, but she
simultaneously views it as a stereotypical ticket that bears some truth or
somewhat reflects the modern condition. Be that as it may, Arendt also
uses the critical discussion of the European image of America to address
an American audience, which she wants to become aware of problematic
tendencies within America and modern societies in general, such as
McCarthyism, modern conformism or the use of new military technology
such as atom bombs. She also addresses a 'growing Americanism at
home', which 'expresses a more general mood than traditional isolationism or the limited appeal of America First movements'. Therefore
Arendt thinks that 'Americanism' oddly corresponds with the dangerous
anti-Americanism abroad.[29] For Arendt, hence, the peril of anti-
Americanism is mirrored and 'reinforced' by 'Americanistic' attitudes
and ideologies in the United States (which she doesn't really specify),
though not so much by a globally oriented foreign policy. And while the
'image of America which exists in Europe may not tell us much about
American realities', Arendt argues, if we are willing to learn, the
European fears may point to justified 'fears of the whole Western
world, and ultimately of all mankind'.[30]

At the end of the day, the debate about America and the various views
of and attitudes towards America by Europeans have little to do with
the 'real existing America' itself and everything to do with Europe.
It is far from certain in which direction the anti-Americanism analysed
in this work will proceed, since it remains equally uncertain where, how,
perhaps even if and whether Europe will develop. But one thing remains
quite telling: nobody ever spoke of Europe's birth being the fall of the
Berlin Wall or the dissolution of the Soviet Union and its communist rule
over the eastern half of the continent. And true enough, none of those
events attained the popular enthusiasm that February 15, 2003, clearly

did. Then, in 1989–1990, while Berliners danced in the streets, Londoners and Parisians fretted in their homes. And nobody in Europe's West thronged any public place in support of the celebrations in Warsaw and Prague. Whether Strauss-Kahn, Habermas and their friends will prove correct in their predictions that this day will indeed become Europe's national holiday, only future historians will be able to ascertain. One thing is clear, though: the long tradition of a deep ambivalence towards and a constant preoccupation with America in Europe clearly set the intellectual stage for the powerful symbolic presence of this potentially fateful day. History teaches us that *any* entity – certainly in its developing stages – only attains consciousness and self-awareness by defining itself in opposition to another entity. All nationalisms arose in opposition to others. While at the moment it remains unclear what positive sentiments and identifications unite Swedes and Greeks, it is quite clear what negative dimension does: that of *not* being American. This need not at all necessitate an active anti-Americanism but it certainly requires a clear delineation in opposition to America. Today, one is primarily European by dint of not being American. Whereas the European flag has obviously become an important symbol of a new sovereignty, I have yet to see it identified with any positive emotions and pride the way national flags of conventional states do with regularity. Only once have I seen the European flag being an object of pride and obvious emotion – and not surprisingly, it was in the context of a contest between the United States and Europe: the Ryder Cup match between Europe and the United States in September 2004 in a suburb of Detroit, Michigan. Sitting beside me on one of the greens was a portly Englishman sporting an England T-shirt, not a British one. When the Irish player Padraig Harrington won the hole with a superb putt defeating his American opponent, the Englishman jumped up with unfettered enthusiasm, waved a European flag widely all over the place and screamed at the top of his voice, 'Go Europe'. Indeed, when the superbly playing European team humiliated the poorly playing Americans, the ensuing celebration featured many European flags that draped the players hailing from England, Northern Ireland, the Irish Republic, Sweden, and Spain. They were coached by a German. Lest I be misunderstood, the last thing I want to do is accuse any of the players of being even in the vaguest way anti-American. They certainly were not. But their unity was defined as 'European' merely by dint of their playing against Team USA. With the entity of 'Europe' now on the agenda, anti-Americanism may well serve a useful coagulating function for the establishment of this new entity and become a potent political force on the mass level, way beyond the antipathy and *ressentiment* that has been a staple of elite European intellectual life since July 5, 1776, if not before.

Chapter 4

Guns, Capital Punishment and Anti-Americanism

Robert Singh

Like Americanism, anti-Americanism relies powerfully on an imagined community. But whereas in Americanism, the community epitomises the inspiring foundational ideals of the United States, in the case of anti-Americanism, that imagined community is populated by a decidedly eccentric and not always appealing collection of individuals. Of the many putatively dystopian features of the United States that currently animate popular antipathy to that community abroad, however, few are as reliably noxious as the subjects of guns and capital punishment. As a teacher of American politics, I find few subjects that so forcefully capture student imaginations about America – and so readily and reliably reveal the emotive, disdainful and on occasion morally superior and censorious attitude towards the United States common outside its borders – as these questions of life and death. Few subjects, moreover, are so lacking in comprehension, accuracy and balance in the manner in which they are typically treated in popular non-American commentaries where emotion, cartoonish stereotypes and symbolism rather than reason predominate.

There are three reasons why firearms and the death penalty invariably elicit critical and even condescending comments from non-Americans. First, both vividly capture a deep-seated sense of America as essentially and irredeemably violent, not only in its domestic life but also in its foreign relations. The 'dark' side of the American Dream – something that anti-Americans treat as the unholy grail that proves beyond reasonable doubt the deep degeneracy of America – is to be found here in all its gothic horror. A nation awash with firearms and Death Row inmates awaiting their murder by the state, 'AmeriKKKa' stands alone among industrialised liberal democracies in the twenty-first century in its unapologetic maintenance of deeply illiberal practices. Secondly, but relatedly, the abandonment of such practices by more 'civilised' nations in America's 'western' peer group confirms the essentially repugnant and barbaric nature of the 'first new nation' and its manifest failure to reach international maturity. European elites, especially, are apt to be antagonised to the point of indignation by an American society that is 'too unilateralist, too religious, too warlike, too laissez faire, too fond of guns and the death penalty, and too addicted to simple solutions for complex problems'.[1] Thirdly, that millions of Americans are not simply tolerant of these ancient practices today but actively campaign for their retention, spread or protection testifies to the civilisational gulf separating the United States even from erstwhile European allies such as the United Kingdom. Thus a British professor of American history could, apparently in all seriousness, describe the United States in 2005 as 'a more unattractive model than it has ever been' and suggest that America 'offers only a dubious answer' to the 'urgent' question of whether democracy can work.[2]

In one respect, the political controversies surrounding firearms regulation and judicial killings are unsurprising, since they direct us to some of the most fundamental existential issues concerning the value of individual life, the nature of collective security, and the propensity of humankind to violence, murder and crime. For such issues not to provoke passionate concern would, in some ways, be perverse. But precisely because these issues generate so much heat, it is especially important that some reasonable light is shed upon them. At the outset, it is therefore worth noting that the degree to which either guns or capital punishment can be seen as holding out certain eternal verities about America in general is at least questionable. In the case of guns, for example, most Americans do not own firearms, most who do possess them use them responsibly, and – far from being a lawless enterprise echoing 'frontier' traditions and 'wild west' values – the entire chain from production and sale to ownership and use of guns is governed by thousands of laws and regulations, from federal and state statutes to local ordinances. Similarly, in the case of capital punishment, the legality of the penalty is a matter of autonomous choice for the individual states (twelve, plus the District of Colombia, choose not to allow the ultimate penalty) and, even among the majority of the thirty-eight for whom it is legal, it is practiced with declining regularity. At best, the penalty occupies a peripheral place in the American criminal justice system. For all their international newsworthiness, then, the facts support neither the sensationalist notion that Americans are 'gun crazy' nor the claim that 'America' practices judicial murder with an equal amount of zealousness and indifference to the value of individual human life.

Notwithstanding the relative lack of critical clarity about these complex and nuanced empirical realities, however, the differences that exist over these issues within America as well as between Americans and non-Americans are far from inconsequential. In the case of the death penalty, in particular, the conflict has become a significant irritant in the transatlantic relationship and a genuine obstacle to full, frank and speedy cooperation on international counter-terrorism efforts. European states have had to confront the issue of how to respond to American requests for extradition of terrorist suspects to the United States when these suspects could subsequently be sentenced to death. The United States, in turn, has often sought to circumvent this problem by undertaking to European authorities not to press for a capital sentence in the cases of extradited suspects even in the event of their successful conviction for the crimes for which they were charged. In a few cases, Europeans and other non-American citizens convicted of capital crimes in the United States have been sentenced to death, and been executed, despite the protests of national governments, international human rights organisations such as Amnesty International, and pleas from religious leaders such as the Pope. In the most powerful sense, then, these are indeed literally issues of life and death for many Americans and non-Americans alike.

In this chapter, rather than treating the two subjects in turn as entirely distinct analytical concerns, I attempt to address certain common themes that appear to underpin the marked antipathy that both evoke among many, if not most, non-Americans. I argue that the vehemence with which denunciations of American practices are invariably made is especially forceful because the contrast with other nations is seemingly much starker and – to its proponents – more clearly in the moral favour of non-Americans than is the case with other contentious issues such as abortion or gay rights, religion in public life, and race relations. The censure that Americans face, however, is one that is frequently misguided, partial and suggestive of a particularly elitist and Eurocentric conception of liberal democracy, one in which the governing class is there to lead the people as much as to represent them. Whether a genuine civilisational gulf is identifiable through the prism of these two issues depends on how representative one believes both American and non-American images of the United States are. At minimum, however, the presence of criticisms of guns and capital punishment in European critiques, especially, testifies to the inherent ambiguities in the construct of anti-Americanism, since these concerns are markedly less conspicuous in many other – Islamic, Middle Eastern, and Asian – anti-Americanisms.

Armed, Dangerous and Democratic Worlds Apart?

The fact that discussions of anti-Americanism frequently treat certain commonly held notions about the United States, and attitudes to American practices, as self-evident requires careful examination and qualified scrutiny. The particular cases of gun ownership and capital punishment represent two of the most prominent instances of this phenomenon, whereby European elites especially – not least in the academy – treat as unproblematic the received wisdom that the two practices are viewed at large in the non-American world with a mixture of disdain, incomprehension and rejection. That Americans should approve the death penalty, in particular, and thereby share a punish-ment with brutally undemocratic regimes and even some of their most implacable enemies such as Iran is especially galling, but only marginally more than their seeming tolerance of high-school mass murders by school children armed with semi-automatic pistols and rifles. The remarkable critical and mass popularity of Michael Moore's partial and polemical attacks on America – not least the 'documentaries' *Bowling for Columbine* and *Fahrenheit 9/11* – are illustrative of the central but peculiarly ill-informed discussions of America in European public life. That the mass of Americans carry out daily lives much like those of people elsewhere – taking children to school, holding down stressful jobs, attempting to secure adequate health care, paying their taxes – is apt to become lost amid the unrelenting focus of mass media outlets and figures such as Moore on the most sensational aspects of America. The latter have helped to ensure that Robert Kagan's famous distinction receives eloquent expression not only in the field of international relations but also in terms of the perceived domestic orders of Martian America and Venusian Europe. Guns and capital punishment, especially, serve to compound popular conceptions of a neanderthal America in opposition to 'Renaissance Man' Europe.

One obvious expression of such a perceived divergence can be discerned in the extraordinary condescension, scorn and vitriol with which President George W. Bush has been regarded outside America since 2000, which has relied in large part on his zealous support for both gun rights and, especially, judicial killings. As governor of Texas from 1995 to 2001, Bush signed legislation allowing the concealed carrying of firearms by individual Texans, including for pastors in places of prayer. Bush also presided over the execution of 152 Death Row inmates and the largest number in a single calendar year in American history (40). During the 2000 election campaign, the British mass circulation tabloid, *The Daily Mirror*, printed photos of all those executed in Texas under Bush while asking: 'Do we really want a man like him making snap decisions on whether to drop bombs or go to war? Do we really like the idea of his finger on the big trigger? No ... [Bush] is a thoroughly dangerous, unpleasant piece of work who shouldn't be let anywhere near the White House.'[3] Jack Lang, one of France's most well-known politicians, even labelled Bush a 'murderer'.[4]

While the linkage of themes of US domestic and international violence is a familiar trope, reference was rarely made to the fact that Al Gore, John McCain and Bill Bradley had all supported both capital punishment and the right to gun ownership. Nor, in the dissensus over extraditing terror suspects to the United States, had much notice been given to the fact that it was Bill Clinton, not George W. Bush, who presided over the most dramatic increase in judicial killings of any modern American president. During the 1990s, the number of executions increased almost fivefold, while the number of states conducting executions more than doubled, from thirteen to thirty-two. Clinton had very publicly flown back to Arkansas during the primaries of 1992 to refuse to grant clemency to Ricky Ray Rector, a mentally retarded black Death Row inmate, and used his support for the death penalty to signal clearly to 'middle America' that he and Al Gore were New Democrats, not old-style liberals. After the Oklahoma City bombing of 1995, Clinton also signed the key punitive legislation of the 'Anti-Terrorism and Effective Death Penalty Act' of 1996, which expanded the number of crimes eligible for a capital sentence while simultaneously reducing both the number of appeals Death Row inmates could make and taxpayer financial assistance for such appeals. Yet it remains Bush who is invariably linked in the popular mind with judicial killings. Indeed, in a pellucid illustration of the familiar litany of perennial American failings, one account even recorded that Bush was berated at Chequers in 2001 by Cherie Blair, the wife of the British prime minister, for his egregious support for the death penalty and his opposition to the International Criminal Court.[5] One doubts whether Clinton had received similar censure previously from the then occupants of Number Ten Downing Street.

The empirical evidence confirms the distinctive divergence between the United States and Europe. In the case of gun ownership, most EU member states prohibit private legal ownership of firearms by their citizens. While illegal guns circulate widely in Europe, the legitimate legal use of coercive power remains confined to the state. As for capital punishment, eighty-six countries, including all twenty-five members of the European Union, have abolished the practice and another thirty-five rarely use it. Most West European states moved steadily over the 1970s and 1980s to prohibit the legality of the death penalty. Membership in the EU is now incompatible with the use of capital punishment, a requirement that forced Turkey to revoke the death penalty in its thus far futile quest to join the EU. Of those nations that do allow for capital punishment, only China, Iran, Saudi Arabia and the Congo execute prisoners on the scale of the United States. It is hardly surprising that, as two influential observers of America put it in a fairly representative example of the views of most Western critics' views, 'In most of the civilised world support for the death penalty is the prerogative of the lunatic fringe (and the lunatic Right at that).'[6]

That being so, what are we to make of the 'lunacy' of Americans' continued support for the penalty and their continued use of firearms, a practice that many Europeans see as equally dangerous, outmoded and ludicrous? One clue lies in the comparative nature of the political systems as well as the preferences of the mass of citizens for, as Stuart Banner observes:

> In most of the United States, popular support for capital punishment translated quickly into government policy. Many other countries, by contrast, abolished capital punishment despite considerable popular support for it . . . The difference between the United States and other wealthy democracies with respect to capital punishment may simply be that the United States is more democratic, in the sense that elected officials find it more necessary to implement policies supported by a majority of the voters.[7]

While the argument that elected officials either do, or should, attend to voters' preferences seems a rather quaint notion in much political theory, it nonetheless receives substantial empirical support in the American instance. According to public opinion surveys, for example, from 1977 to 1998, some 66 percent to 76 percent of Americans supported capital punishment for murder, a position taken by majorities in every region of the nation and across every ethnic group. By 2005, this support had declined somewhat to roughly two thirds of the public. Gallup, for example, recorded a decline from 80 percent support in 1994 to 64 percent in October 2005. That proportion decreases still further if the alternative is life imprisonment without parole, an option now available in almost all death penalty states. Despite the decline, however, majorities tend to support the death penalty on principle. By stark contrast, the United Kingdom abolished capital punishment when a majority of the population favoured it and refused to re-institute the penalty during the 1970s and 1980s when some 80 percent of the population supported it.[8]

For many Europeans, particularly in academic and commentariat circles, the American example exemplifies all that is worst about the domestic arrangements of the United States, not least the slavishly Pavlovian, plebiscitary-style responsiveness of American elected officials to a mass of citizens irredeemably unenlightened about the wrongs of capital punishment (such an attitude has ready comparisons with broader European critiques that, at least implicitly, seem to suggest that the main failing of contemporary America is that it is populated by Americans). But as Jonathan Freedland, a progressive British journalist has observed, remarking on a MORI opinion poll that put British support for the death penalty at 76 percent in 1996:

> Opponents of judicial killing have hardly won the argument among the British people. Instead our political system has simply failed to express the popular will … what is often a cause for self-congratulation – with progressive Britons imagining ours to be a more civilised society than the US – should perhaps be a trigger for self-doubt. American democracy ensures that the public get their way, even if the result is not always pleasant. The British system cannot say the same.[9]

As the US federal judge and prolific scholar, Richard Posner, rightly observes, if such a strong popular British preference 'cannot get translated into government action, this suggests that democracy is not working; and so it is ironic that many deliberative democrats would like the Supreme Court to declare capital punishment unconstitutional, even though there is no solid basis in the Constitution for such a declaration'.[10] Whether American democracy is working is a subject to which we shall return but, before doing so, it is worth examining why firearms and capital punishment so reliably stoke non-American antipathies.

Exceptionalisms and Constitutionalisms

For most American constitutional scholars and political scientists, there is no doubt that both the legal right of private citizens to gun ownership and the rights of the individual states to sanction judicial killings are protected by specific provisions of the Constitution of the United States and, in particular, the Bill of Rights. The right to own firearms is protected by the Second Amendment. Capital punishment is protected, subject to certain procedural guarantees, in the Fifth, Eighth and Fourteenth Amendments. Although numerous articles and books have contested the relative versus absolute nature of these constitutional guarantees, their comparative weight against competing constitutional clauses, and their 'incorporation' through the Fourteenth Amendment to apply to state and local – as well as the federal – governments, the basic issue of constitutional protection is settled and unremarkable.

Such an historical and constitutional pedigree provides much of the sharpness to non-American censure of these practices. Not only are these seen as uncivilised today in terms of their merits and demerits as public policy, but this also – in part – reflects their relationship to a long bygone era when such barbarism was then accepted practice both within and outside the United States. America may have partially sanitised its regime of death by having largely replaced the noose with the needle as the main method of execution, but it remains triply flawed in the eyes of its many critics: in allowing such practices today not only in the abstract but in actually practicing them; in not having rejected them as outdated and discredited expressions of a barbaric era in the way that other comparable nation-states have; and in still defending them by reference not simply to statute but also to constitutional law. To allow these is repudiation enough of the republic's credentials as a properly functioning liberal democracy. To relate them to the nation-state's foundational and most revered document – and thereby accord them the ultimate legitimacy of constitutional protection – is eloquent expression of a degenerate outlook.

Firearms and judicial killings powerfully reflect and reinforce American exceptionalism but in ways that point to profound doubts as to the rationality of American difference. Their integral relationship with the Constitution, especially, serves a reciprocal function. The fact that these practices have constitutional protection compounds their international uniqueness and disfavour. But, in turn, these also amplify the defects of the founding document more broadly. As such, since the base upon which the entire edifice of America is built upon is at fault, so too, necessarily, must be the broader structure. The inherent contradictions in the American project are thus glaringly exposed, the constitutional guarantees running directly against the Declaration of Independence's promise of the universal right to 'life, liberty and the pursuit of happiness'. Perversely, in many international eyes, America entered the twenty-first century in a doubly unique fashion: in being governed by a document designed in and for the eighteenth century; and, by virtue of that fact, in committing judicial murders and allowing the most heavily and legally armed civilian population to carry all manner of lethal firearms more than two hundred years later. That most Americans could not only tolerate such practices but simultaneously revere that founding document cast them in an ever more strange comparative light.

For admirers of the European 'social model', such clear and consistent constitutional protections have mired Americans in a static anachronism: a 'frozen' republic whose eighteenth century practices have somehow escaped the forces of enlightened progress and – paradoxically but tenaciously – retained their salience to the most technologically advanced and economically successful society of the twenty-first century. Thus it is that the Constitution, as well as the American people, is castigated for preserving outmoded and inappropriate practices. Of course, only rarely is the mixture of monarchical, autocratic and democratic elements that make up the constitutional design considered in conventional criticisms. The Second Amendment no more imposed an obligation to purchase firearms on Americans than did the Eighth compel states to legislate for the ultimate judicial punishment in 1791 or 2001. Millions of Americans purchase guns of their own free will, psychologically secure – rightly or wrongly – in the conviction that this will enhance the personal safety of themselves and their families, against criminals and government alike.

A clear majority of individual states enacted capital punishment statutes – in the case of New York as late as 1995 – willingly, and in the light of public campaigns for punitive and retributive justice (Mario Cuomo had vetoed such bills, as governor of the state, no less than twelve times prior to his defeat in 1994). Such is the breadth of American acceptance of their constitutional rights that, in the case of gun control, few advocates of tighter controls propose abolishing gun ownership or repealing the Second Amendment, instead framing their appeals for new firearms regulations in terms of these not affecting citizens' Second Amendment rights. Similarly, even federal courts that have sought to overturn the constitutionality of the most egregious forms of death penalty regulations (such as executing the mentally ill and juveniles) have not tackled the basic premise of the punishment's constitutionality head-on (no doubt chastened by the Supreme Court's unsuccessful effort to do so in 1972). Attempts at reform of the machinery of death – such as mandating use of DNA evidence in capital trials – appear more destined to preserve than dismantle the death penalty in America. That both practices are settled constitutional features of American public life only reiterates the apparent distance – politically as much as physically – from Europe that the United States is at now.

Violence

If the Constitution's imprimatur leads many non-Americans to treat the two practices with bemusement, an additional key current in non-American criticism of firearms and judicial killings focuses on the broader nature of American society. Central to this is the image of a rapacious capitalism and a Hobbesian dystopia, an America in which life is 'nasty, brutish and short'. An American proclivity to violence as part of the national and international narrative of American history, identity and influence is an inextricable element here. The settling of the nation, the securing of independence, the annexation of other states and the westward expansion of the continental frontier are complemented abroad by the tendency towards violence and America's apparent faith in military solutions to a range of problems. The charge that Americans were extraordinarily violent was a common theme of commentaries during the nineteenth century. The familiar litany of how many murders a child witnesses on a typical diet of American television is an additional element in this seemingly desensitised populace. Such depictions often draw on, or are linked to, American militarism, with the US military being regarded as 'cowboys' – albeit of the John Wayne rather than *Brokeback Mountain* ilk – untroubled by the loss of innocent (non-American) civilian lives. The marked reluctance of Europeans to endorse firearm ownership and judicial killings can be regarded as confirming the views of those such as Kagan, who identify a transatlantic gulf as having arisen with the end of the Cold War – one that encompasses more than specific disagreements such as Iraq, pointing instead to such differences as artefacts of a much deeper conflict in worldviews.

The depiction is, as with regard to other animating features of anti-Americanism, highly selective and lacking in self-referential balance. The notion that Europe is an oasis of peace, equity and order need not detain us at all. In certain respects at least, the self-image of Europeans as enlightened and pacific urgently needs recalibrating in the light of the assassination of Pim Fortuyn in the Netherlands; desecrations of synagogues and Jewish cemeteries in France; race riots in northern English towns of Burnley and Oldham in the summer of 2001 and Parisian suburbs in 2005; the London terror attacks of July 7, 2005; nativist attacks on immigrants in Italy; and communal violence across the Balkans. In the 'West', after all, it was on the European continent, not the continental United States, that ethnic cleansing and genocidal impulses found malevolent expression during the 1990s. Similarly, the levels of crime, violence and 'anti-social behaviour' reached a plateau sufficient to feature in election campaigns, such as that of the United Kingdom in 2005. Part of the success of New Labour from 1997 through to 2005 relied on a projection of the party as 'tough', imitating Clinton's New Democrats, not only on the social and economic causes of criminal behaviour but also on the criminals themselves. In the UK case, even official government statistics on violent crime showed British lawlessness to be on the increase in the later 1990s and 2000s. Only in the case of homicide was the American case worse by 2005. By contrast, most of the main indicators of American social dislocation – from divorce rates and crime to births outside marriage – saw striking declines during the 1990s. The case of New York City's remarkable success in combating high crime rates was the most well known of a much broader set of successes across the United States.

Nonetheless, the motif of violence has retained a powerful currency. Although America is not the only democracy to retain the death penalty as a legal and constitutionally sanctioned punishment (Japan, India and Taiwan also retain the ultimate penalty), its rates of execution place it in the uncongenial company of states such as China, Iran, Saudi Arabia and Vietnam. Unlike the latter, the emphasis accorded to human rights and individual dignity in the official speeches of American politicians seems to sit uneasily with the fact that the state can exercise the ultimate power of government to take the lives of its own and other citizens.

Moreover, if state-sanctioned killing poses one type of violent motif, so does the privatisation of security to the individual that is represented by legal access to firearms. Since 1933, more Americans have died through gun violence than were killed in all the wars that America has fought combined. During the 1990s, approximately 38,000 Americans died each year through gun-related deaths, with gun suicides the principle cause. Moreover, contrary to the 'good guy/bad guy' myth, the Justice Department's official statistics suggested that almost half of gun murders were committed by people whom the victim knew: friends, relatives or lovers. When combined with the more high-profile gun massacres, such as the Columbine High School killings of April 20, 1999, and the spate of killings by the Washington sniper in the fall of 2002, the international image of America as a primordially violent society is one that seemingly has ample support. Even the strongest opponent of gun bans in the United Kingdom or Australia would be unlikely to support carrying firearms concealed on the person as a deterrent to crime, yet laws allowing for these were passed in the majority of American states by the end of the 1990s.

But the more objective realities of American violence are not always easily captured by graphic and deeply disturbing images of school sieges and shootings. The difficulty of gleaning accurate and generally accepted statistics makes this debate highly politicised, but what is clear is that the vast majority of gun owners use their weapons responsibly. Most estimates suggest that approximately eighty million Americans – of some 280 million in total – own firearms, with guns being present in almost half of all American households. Some 300 million guns are in circulation in the fifty states. What is perhaps surprising, in this light, is not so much the severity of gun violence but the relative lack of victims thereof, given the scale and usage of firearms. Much depends on the lens by which the public health costs of gun ownership are viewed. Indeed, the gun control issue is partially so fraught because, as Jacobs observes, it is frequently but falsely depicted as a choice between a pandemic of violence and a panacea of a gunless nation – which is a utopian, not a feasible, prospect that distorts the current terms of the gun control debate in America.[11] None of this mitigates the scale and seriousness of the public health and criminal costs of illegal gun usage. But as Dizard, Muth and Andrews observe, 'As terrible as our national rates of violence are, as tragic as the murders are, the facts make it hard to support the notion that we are in the midst of an epidemic of gun violence.'[12] Only critics whose primary source of information is video games, film and gangsta rap can venture such a critique, which is simply uninformed by the brute realities of American life.

But those perceptions of primordial violence have a powerful and persistent force in crafting anti-American sentiments. The contradictions here are notable, but not unusual. Americans are frequently seen or depicted by their critics as gung-ho, eager to shoot wildly and unrestrained by the sensibilities of other nations. Yet simultaneously they are often portrayed as wimpish cowards, unable to accept the 'Dover effect' of returning body bags, to engage in too lengthy a foreign venture that involves the commitment of American ground forces or to accept the 'blood price' that this entails. Americans are depicted as cosseted by a consumerist nirvana, driven by material ambition and surrounded by technological devices of every type, yet somehow at the same time being persistently animated by a latent tendency to violence that is barely below the surface. Americans are seen as hyper-legalistic, erecting a Byzantine web of laws, precedents and judicial structures that govern every aspect of life from the safety of children's toys to the regulation of smoking. Yet they are also regarded as rapacious individualists, intent on a frontier-like challenge to established boundaries and disrespectful of authority, hierarchy and tradition. Imperialists who do not intervene enough, reluctant warriors who wage war via unmanned predator drones, Americans' apparent propensity to violence likewise sees a populace whose principal occupations comprise watching television, playing computer games and eating food and drink of poor nutritional value while also being health and fitness obsessed. If such contradictory charges starkly undermine the coherence of the anti-American case, they nonetheless fuel the sense of America as a land of irredeemably irrational passions.

Rationality and Public Policy

Non-Americans may have more respect for American domestic order than progressives typically evince – especially those of more conservative and libertarian persuasions. Such non-Americans might possibly concede the legitimacy of constitutionally protected practices were there a rational public policy explanation or justification for them. But in the case of gun control and the death penalty, that support is often forfeited by the empirical evidence of their ineffectual criminological rationale. The case against America in the dock of enlightened world opinion – *j'accuse!* – is thus strengthened even further on the basis not only of the symbolic barbarism and cruelty but also on more neutral and scientific public policy rationales. That is, neither private legal ownership of firearms nor state executions are seen by their critics to 'work'. That this is a widely shared perception can be gleaned from the fact that even those analysts who adamantly criticise anti-Americanism frequently make exceptions on these particular issues. Jean-François Revel, for example, whilst being highly critical of the French approach to criminal justice policy and French attitudes to the United States more generally, stated unequivocally that, 'Europeans are right to criticise the freedom to sell firearms that prevails in the United States.'[13]

Even for those of us who self-consciously subscribe to being 'anti-anti-Americanism', the case in regard to capital punishment has undeniable force here. The staunchest American supporters of judicial killings offer – if they do at all – only the most modest empirical evidence of their beneficial effects on crime rates. The deterrent effect of capital punishment is minimal – with states without the penalty having no higher rates of homicide than those that retain it – while the proportion of convicted murderers receiving the penalty is miniscule. The nature of the crimes typically eligible for a capital sentence virtually precludes a deterrent effect from being operative, since these conventionally entail such brutal behaviour that no rational, balanced individual – at the time of committing the crime, at least – would engage in such an act. Even if that was so, deterrence rarely forms a dominant part of the rationale for capital punishment. As noted later in the chapter, retribution and the expression of shared community values form more influential bulwarks of the pro-death penalty case. But if the sole purpose of the penalty is retribution alone, then the penalty is surely, as critics allege, inhuman. As *The Economist* argued, 'Even when it is carefully administered, America's machinery of death still seems cruel and unusual.'[14]

Moreover, whatever the criminological purposes that the death penalty does or does not serve, it is clear that, at best, the administration of the punishment is badly broken. Neither due process nor the equality of the laws is guaranteed in a system that is more capricious than even-handed. A Texan or Oklahoman criminal is far more likely to receive a death sentence, and see it implemented, than a Californian criminal, for example. The system is institutionally biased against the poor, who are invariably likely to receive inadequate counsel from the limited public coffers available. Stories of incompetent, venal, sleeping, prejudiced and drunk defendants' lawyers are legion. Perhaps most tellingly, more than 100 Death Row inmates since 1976 have been exonerated of the crimes for which they were originally convicted.[15]

If the empirical evidence is wanting in the capital punishment case, the evidence is markedly more complicated in relation to firearms. As Robert Spitzer notes, pro- and anti-gun control advocates are rarely able to agree even on what the evidence indicates, and the criminology surrounding the issue is highly politicised and contested by both sides.[16] The intensity with which the authors of even profoundly historical revisionist and statistically dense criminological treatises can be treated is a gauge of the polarised nature of conflict over the issue.[17] Certainly, as Jacobs soberly notes, the issue for Americans to address is not the possibility of a 'no guns' America – which is an impossibility – but rather a cost–benefit analysis of the kinds of laws and regulations that can achieve 'violence control' rather than gun control.

On that topic, analysts disagree strongly, but two features of the empirical evidence are especially noteworthy and relatively clear-cut in terms of the rationality – or otherwise – of America's gun-regulatory regime. First, it is clear that many of the fatalities and accidents that are gun-related are perpetrated by individuals who are intimates rather than strangers. As such, pro-control forces have powerful support for the case that guns exacerbate situations that would otherwise be resolved with less, or without, violent confrontation. The extent to which there is a 'displacement effect' – when an assailant intent on a crime carries it out with an alternative choice of weapon – is simply unknowable here. But, secondly, since there are no reliable records, it is equally unknowable how many criminal acts were deterred by the use, or threatened use, of a gun. To the extent that tens of millions of Americans own guns, we can be reasonably confident that at least some incidents have indeed been addressed in this manner. Whether through deterrence or usage, the non-sporting, self-defence rationale for gun ownership has some merit and is one that millions of Americans sincerely share. Could it be that they are all so woefully, and enduringly, mistaken?

The contrast with Europe also reveals a paradoxical aspect. On the one hand, 'small state' America vests the greatest possible coercive power in the hands of the state: that of taking the life of its individual citizens (and non-nationals). This is a power now denied to all 'big government' member states, and prospective member states, of the EU. On the other hand, one of the central purposes of the state – domestic order and national security (guaranteed as a motivation for the founding of the United States in the preamble to the Constitution) – is in effect privatised to the level of individual citizens. Even if this is not taking the law into their own hands as such, it is certainly implementing the law without recourse to legitimately sanctioned and properly trained state officials. Within America, an anti-federal government attitude plausibly supports the locus of capital punishment as primarily a state matter, and the widespread ownership of guns – and lack of federal laws on them – also reinforces this otherwise odd endorsement of state power.

Such curious approaches to crime control and public health invariably elicit bafflement and derision outside the United States. As the popular success and critical acclaim of Moore's *ouevre* suggested, the audience for sensationalist treatments of the more esoteric aspects of American life remains impressively broad. But, typically, certain basic facts were not allowed to intrude on the vivid story. Four, in particular, stand out. First, it is worth reiterating the earlier point that the overwhelming number of gun owners use their weapons responsibly. On a conservative estimate, some eighty million Americans own firearms. Given that, of the 30,000 or so annual deaths from firearm usage during the 1990s, over half of these were suicides, and around 15,000 deaths annually were homicides. The majority of these were related to drug-centred gang disputes. Without minimising the tragedy of each and every death, these figures suggest that some 98 percent to 99 percent of gun owners treat their weapons with the attention, respect and caution that they merit. The common image of Americans as quick on the draw is one that owes its provenance to Hollywood, not historical fact.

Second, far from lacking regulation, the ownership, use, production, distribution and transportation of firearms are governed by a myriad of some 20,000 federal, state and local laws. It is true that the federal dimension of regulation is relatively modest, with only nine pieces of national legislation enacted between 1934 and 2004. But the centrality of federal arrangements to policy outcomes on this issue is no different from those on most others in America. That is, the states are the key players in regulating most aspects of the firearms regime. Third, opponents of gun-rights groups are yet to demonstrate decisive empirical evidence that repudiates the claims made for private legal ownership in terms of its effectiveness in deterring and resisting crime. Even though considerable debate ensued over the veracity of his methodology, for example, John Lott's research into the effect of concealed-carry laws powerfully suggested that these had a major depressing effect on most crime rates. Fourth, treating the absolute figures as self-explanatory is no more persuasive on firearms than on road accidents, where the latter indicates a much higher level of fatalities.

Beyond these important qualifications, it is also useful to examine whether non-American claims to superior rationality in policymaking stand the test of scrutiny. Revel, for example, noted that while firearms cannot be freely bought and sold in France, the illicit black market in lethal weapons has been growing in almost unchecked fashion. In the United Kingdom, similarly, levels of gun violence have increased dramatically despite the ban on private handguns enacted in 1997. None of this is to claim that an American model would have been preferable, nor is it to suggest that a different statutory regime would have mitigated the illegal market for firearms. But claims by critics of the inherent irrationality of the American approach to regulation can only be taken seriously if the relative state of criminal justice policy can be meaningfully compared, and the comparative merits and demerits of distinct national policies evaluated realistically, not by reference to utopias.

Politics

The more overtly political dimensions of both issues offer two alternatives that have typically proven tempting for anti-Americans. The first is that the American people are directly to blame – through a combination of ignorance, naivety and barbarism – for the dismal facts and figures of gun violence and state executions. The second, however, partially exculpates the citizenry and instead charges American democracy as a sham and American politicians as cowards, unable to practice true 'leadership'. As Revel characterised the critique, it was the 'unpardonable cowardice – coupled with venality, obviously – that has prevented political elites from banning the sale of firearms results in periodic, appalling bloodbaths when teenagers mercilessly gun down their teachers and fellow students in the classroom'.[18] Lacking both the opportunity and will to challenge the mass of an ignorant citizenry to confront their own flaws and failings, Washington leaders allow popular prejudices to sonorously echo rather than be decisively silenced in the halls of power.

Nowhere is the contrast with Europe so poignant and pronounced. Prohibition of the death penalty – while enjoying active support among some interest groups and social movements – was overwhelmingly an elite-led phenomenon, in which enlightened European parliamentarians took up the cause 'in advance' of their own electorates. Despite opinion surveys indicating significant, and in several instances majority, support for the restoration of capital punishment in the United Kingdom, parliament has never come close to such an initiative. Such a move would entail the United Kingdom's departure from the European Union, since prohibition is now a condition of membership.

While the regulatory context differed in relation to firearms, the momentum for change was again centred upon elite initiatives. In the United Kingdom again, for example, the complete prohibition of private legal access to handguns enacted in 1997 was a response to the child shootings in Dunblane, Scotland. The cross-party consensus was so overwhelming, and so rapidly constructed, that no meaningful alternative was even countenanced. Subsequently, the number of crimes and murders committed with (illegally acquired) handguns in the United Kingdom increased. Yet while America is often depicted as a lawless nation of unrestrained firearms enthusiasts, some individual American states – New York, Massachusetts, the District of Columbia – have tougher gun laws than European states such as France.

As Posner has argued, the architecture of America's governing institutions combines elements of the democratic, the autocratic and the oligarchic. This robust combination is one that has proven reliably irksome not only to non-Americans but also to many American scholars, whose views about the true nature of democracy render the existing system suspect. European censure of the weakness of America's elected politicians not only depicts them as 'running scared' but also as pusillanimous where matters of 'leadership' are to be considered. In this conception, the enduringly vulgar mass public needs to be 'led' – educated and enlightened – rather than followed slavishly by their elected representatives. This Burkean conception stands in marked contrast to the plebsicitary and delegatory features of American democracy, even though it finds echoes in some parts of America. (Justice Thurgood Marshall, for example, relied on the partial ignorance of the American citizenry in arguing in *Furman v Georgia* [1972] that, were the public to have substantive knowledge of the facts of the death penalty, they would assuredly side against it.) These are rather ironic and selective judgements, of course. That certain European governments ignored the preferences of their anti-war publics over Iraq in 2003–2004 was a cause of censure, not celebration, from many of those least trustful of the 'wisdom of crowds'. Nonetheless, they reflect a more settled suspicion of the dangers of mass democracy, ones – ironically – shared by many of the founding fathers of the United States themselves.

Perhaps what is most galling to non-American critics, then, is that the policies that they find so reprehensible on guns and the death penalty cannot easily or convincingly be dismissed as merely being the product of inattentive mass publics. Politicians cannot reasonably be accused of 'pandering' to base sentiments when most Americans hold them to account more regularly than their counterparts in Europe and when they retain clear and deeply held views – however unpalatable to non-Americans – on matters of criminal justice policy. As Mickelthwait and Wooldridge note, 'Executions are such good vote-getting issues that states are 25 percent more likely to conduct executions in years when gubernatorial elections are held than in other years.'[19] Whatever the trends in popular opinion surveys, the on-the-ground experience of most risk-averse elected American officials is to endorse, not to oppose, capital punishment. The defeat of the Democratic Party's most outspoken abolitionists – Michael Dukakis in 1988, Cuomo in 1994 – was a stark reminder of this electoral reality. After surveying twenty-four Democratic governors in 2003, Mickelthwait and Wooldridge concluded that 'we have struggled to find any who oppose the death penalty'.

It is ultimately the fact of popular support that simultaneously accords these policies their political legitimacy in the United States while discrediting the nation in the eyes of its more 'advanced' critics. What is often lost here is the fact that both issues are immensely complex, nuanced and pervaded by questions of rights, liberties, individual and collective interests and the relative powers of distinct tiers and levels of government. In the case of firearms, for instance, most opinion surveys show the public as consistently and decisively favouring stronger federal controls such as waiting periods and police registration or permits, only to see the achievement of these regulations frustrated by the influence of gun rights groups such as the National Rifle Association. But even proponents of gun controls do not generally challenge the right of private legal gun ownership, much as even supporters of certain exemptions to capital punishment (juveniles, the mentally retarded) still uphold the legitimacy of the basic principle. The fact, then, that millions of Americans sincerely believe in the efficacy of these policies appears to some the strongest indication of a divide that is truly continental in scope and civilisational in scale.

Civilisation and Morality

In the early hours of December 13, 2005, Stanley 'Tookie' Williams, convicted murderer and founder of the Crips street gang, was killed by lethal injection in San Quentin State Prison, north of San Francisco. Despite a campaign featuring Jamie Foxx, Winnie Mandela, Jesse Jackson, Susan Sarandon and Joan Baez, Governor Arnold Schwarzenegger rejected a clemency appeal from the born-again Christian who had advocated a philosophy of non-violence to gang members from his Death Row cell. In refusing to grant clemency, Schwarzenegger wrote that 'the one thing that would be the clearest indication of complete remorse and full redemption is the one thing Williams will not do', namely, to apologise for the murder of four people in two separate armed robberies in February and March 1979. In response, the leading cartoon on the opinion pages of *The (London) Times* on December 14 featured a gurney in the shape of a cross, with a syringe resting in its centre, under the headline 'Christian Values …'.[20]

The cartoon captured much of the broader consternation in which America is viewed because of its sanctioning of capital punishment and its gun culture. In this respect, the headline 'Christian Values' served a double purpose. First, it suggested the marked distance that the United States now occupies in comparison with Europe. The implication here is that only a society fuelled by mindless violence and religious faith rather than enlightened rationality could endorse such a heinous practice.

The fact that the governor's former celebrity career was itself predicated mostly on films featuring plentiful killings added piquancy here, as did the execution occurring in supposedly 'liberal' California rather than the Deep South. But the cartoon's second purpose was to level the charge of hypocrisy at America. Thus, a purportedly Christian people – at least, the majority of Americans – could endorse such an un-Christian act. In speaking of its erstwhile value system at home (as well as abroad), once again the United States bore eloquent witness to its own hypocrisy.

The irony here – secular Europeans charging Americans with irrationality for believing in their faith and then hypocrisy for getting the appropriate interpretation of the faith wrong – should not obscure the broader significance of the criticism(s). For at base, the antipathies on the death penalty and firearms point to (or, at least, are invoked to imply) a much broader, deeper and abiding structural gulf in the rudimentary features of American and European 'civilisations'. Politically, in the case of Williams's execution, the refusal to grant clemency was a less risky choice for the governor than granting it. Williams was only the twelfth person to be executed in California since the Supreme Court reinstated the death penalty in 1976, of a total of 1,003 executions nationwide. By contrast, Texas had executed 355 Death Row inmates over the same period. American sentiments, like those elsewhere, ebb and flow. In the case of the death penalty, abolitionist arguments have had some impact, leading to not only falling rates of support for the penalty but also a growing reluctance to sentence capital crimes. The number of death penalty sentences has dropped from approximately 300 per year in the mid-1990s to fewer than 100 in 2005, the lowest level of such sentencing in three decades. But despite the growing concerns about miscarriages of justice and doubts about its efficacy, most Californians supported the penalty (54 percent of Democrats and 87 percent of Republicans, according to a Field poll in 2004) and the leading Democrats competing to challenge Schwarzenegger in the 2006 guber-natorial election did so as well.[21] The existence of such broad-based support, even in a supposedly liberal state such as California, made the invocations of a shared value system by American politicians and their British and Australian allies ring hollow to many European ears.

In a curious but consequential sense, then, such a gulf points to the confirmation of analyses such as Kagan's, and the refutation of those of Huntington. It is as much within, as between, 'civilisations' that we now can see conflict and division and, in terms of that notoriously problematic construct of 'the West', firearms and capital punishment are Exhibits A and B. To move from Europe to America is, to all intents and purposes, to inhabit an entirely different moral universe. While European and American death penalty abolitionists therefore find some solace in the current trends in US public opinion, there is good reason to question how influential these may prove to be. The adverse electoral consequences of opposition, for Republicans and Democrats alike, suggest that the penalty remains a touchstone of mainstream American opinion. Peremptory efforts at abolition, such as Illinois Governor George Ryan's commutation of 167 Death Row sentences to life imprisonment in 2003, were repudiated by his successor and helped to galvanise victims' rights movements in the state. For many Americans, whatever the flaws in the system, the error of abolitionist campaigners is too often to romanticise convicted criminals who, in the majority of cases, were guilty beyond any doubt of especially heinous and foul murders. Europeans, for whom life imprisonment is a sufficient punishment for any crime, in this view, are the ones who have lost their moral compass.

To suggest that such an interpretation of a civilisational rift is primarily a European one, however, would be misleading. It receives expression in America, too. The warm reception accorded to Kagan's thesis in Washington and Brussels alike was itself suggestive of a broadly held agreement on the disjuncture. An additional indication from the United States as to the significance of this seemingly widening gulf can be gleaned by the recent divisions among leading constitutional law scholars and Supreme Court Justices over the role and appropriateness of 'civilisational' comparisons in the Court's rulings. By the early 2000s, an increasingly heated judicial sparring occurred over the role international norms should play in appearing in, much less influencing, American judicial rulings. Gay rights and capital punishment were the main focus of this conflict, which aptly captured the long-standing polarisation between American nationalists and American cosmopolit ans (the former would perhaps term the latter an oxymoron – among other things – but let us leave that aside for the moment). On the one side were Justices such as Antonin Scalia, for whom international conventions and the examples of foreign courts and legislatures were informative academic exercises but entirely inappropriate in assessing the constitutionality of distinctively American practices. Whether on gay rights, the death penalty or firearms regulation, American traditions and the original meaning of the US Constitution were all that were necessary or appropriate to consider. On the other side were Justices such as Stephen Breyer, proponents of 'active liberty', for whom appeals to 'western civilisation' necessarily entailed and legitimated comparative assessments of which particular nation-state was the outlier – or the out-of-sync entity – in terms of contemporary Western norms.

Beyond this narrowly legalistic conflict are profoundly varying conceptions of the role of morals and values in public life and constitutional law. Scalia, for example, had chastised Breyer in a debate at the American University for his invoking non-American standards in Court decisions:

> You talk about how it's nice to know we're on the right track, that we have the same moral and legal framework as the rest of the world ... But we don't *have* the same moral and legal framework as the rest of the world, and never have. If you told the framers of the Constitution that what we're after is to do something that will be just like Europe, they would have been appalled.[22]

Scalia had written previously that capital punishment is easier for American Christians to abide by than for secular Europeans because Christians tend to 'regard punishment in general as deserved' and to consider death 'no big deal'.[23] Religious belief may be neither a necessary nor a sufficient condition of a moral populace, but the relative secularisation of European societies since World War II has manifestly reduced popular support for capital punishment. The civilisational contrast can perhaps most usefully be gleaned by comparing the most religiously and ethnically diverse nation-state – America – with the European Union, a self-consciously secular entity whose Judaeo-Christian credentials have recently been exposed by Turkey's application for membership and the broad opposition it has generated. Combined with low infant-mortality rates, declining fertility rates and longer life expectancy, the value that Europeans place on life – at least in terms of prohibitions on state killings – may indeed be comparatively greater.

Similarly, in a typically combative parry at Harvard's Lawrence Tribe on the issue of the Second Amendment, Scalia invokes both law and history to maintain a nationalist position as a mainstay of his originalist constitutional approach:

> Dispassionate scholarship suggests quite strongly that the right of the people to keep and bear arms meant just that. In addition to

the excellent study by Ms. (Joyce Lee) Malcolm (who is not a member of the Michigan Militia, but an Englishwoman) ... It is very likely that modern Americans no longer look contemptuously, as Madison did, upon the governments of Europe that 'are afraid to trust the people with arms', *The Federalist* No. 46; and the travelling Constitution that Professor Tribe espouses will probably give effect to that new sentiment by effectively eliminating the Second Amendment. But there is no need to deceive ourselves as to what the original Second Amendment said and meant. Of course, properly understood, it is no limitation upon arms control by the states.[24]

Perhaps then, ironically, American nationalists and anti-Americans abroad are reaching an unintended but clear convergence. Critics of capital punishment and firearms invariably view the distinct transatlantic practices as symptoms of a pronounced and growing civilisational difference. Whether or not the historical derivation of these American practices is even known or mentioned, this theme is sometimes explicit but more often implicit in the critiques. Indeed, on some accounts, these two practices represent the only significant gulf. Laurent Cohen-Tanugi, for example, identifies use of the death penalty as 'the only truly ethical question that separates Europe and America', albeit 'a regrettable archaism that is a product of the sovereignty of American states, over which neither Europe nor even the US federal government has any control'.[25] Cohen-Tanugi may not, perhaps, view firearms usage as a truly ethical question but one could reasonably add this to capital punishment as the cases where 'American' and 'European' opinions do sharply diverge. Most gun-control advocates in America do, after all, share more in common with gun-rights groups – both, overwhelmingly, recognise the constitutionality of private firearms possession and usage – than they do with Europeans.

But, in an additional irony, it may even be that the very dominance of the 'European' view in America's academic establishment has itself bred a brand of robust resistance. The invocation of western standards has, as the Scalia riposte above shows, itself produced a reaction in America. Similarly, as two commentators wryly noted, one contemporary form of 'professor baiting' in America has been to set up gun clubs:

The Harvard Law School's gun club boasts some 120 members, 5 percent of the student body. Alexander Volokh, who founded the club in 2001, takes members shooting on a range in New Hampshire – a journey not just across the state line but also across a cultural chasm. Guns are banned on the Harvard campus; the New Hampshire range displays a sign saying 'Children under 13 shoot for free.' Volokh has also held a wide range of gun-themed events on campus, including screenings of films that 'feature regular people using guns as a force for good.' Another student wrote an article in the *Harvard Law Record* entitled 'Discovering the Joy of a Semi-Automatic.' Over at Mount Holyoke, an all-women's college more readily associated with Betty Friedan than with Charlton Heston, students have formed the first college chapter of the Second Amendment Sisters, a national organisation of pro-gun women.[26]

That the breadth and depth of anti-Americanism would partially be eroded were firearms somehow to disappear from American public life and judicial executions to cease is perhaps a valid proposition. But the extent of the change would likely be slight. As John Peterson and Mark Pollack have rightly noted:

> In a contest to determine the 'biggest threat' to the transatlantic relationship, American unilateralism and European disarray would probably finish tied in a dead heat. However, the transatlantic 'values gap' that was often alleged to have surfaced after Bush's election – over the death penalty, the environment, abortion, religion and gun control – would appear only much further down the list of threats. Whatever their quarrels, it remains clear that norms, values and culture bind the EU and the US together far more strongly than either party is 'bound' to any other part of the world.[27]

Conclusion

Cohen-Tanugi, a distinguished and dispassionate observer of American–European relations, argues that, however disturbing it may be to some, 'the existence of the death penalty cannot seriously be used as a justification for characterising the United States as a barbaric nation disrespectful of human rights nor to substantiate the argument of an ethical gulf between the two sides of the Atlantic'.[28] Nor can the exercise by several million Americans of their constitutional right to own firearms be taken as an indication of some altogether alien people, strangely oblivious to their own backwardness and barbarism. The ubiquity of references to these issues in critiques of America arguably reveals more about the shallowness than the sharpness of their analysis – for in reliably focusing on these two practices, critics typically select the most emotive, sensationalist areas where American life is most easy to depict as dramatically distant from that of Europe. While they both undoubtedly reflect and reinforce American difference, to treat guns and the death penalty as somehow emblematic of American public life is to treat the exceptions as the norm.

If the controversies over guns and the death penalty shed critical light on the phenomenon of anti-Americanism, it is perhaps in power illustration of how anti-Americanisms derive their ubiquity from deeply divergent sources of antipathy towards the United States. I have argued elsewhere that the sole unifying thread in anti-Americanisms is ambivalence: admiration of aspects of America co-existing with disenchantment.[29] Those chanting 'death to America' in Tehran and Cairo rarely view capital punishment as an element in the Great Satan's long list of vices. Similarly, while lax gun regulations may occasionally elicit public concern in the United Kingdom, they lag far behind other foci of animus in most of Latin America, Asia and Africa. Indeed, one rarely – if ever – hears of popular antipathy in Europe towards Brazil because of the latter's permissively lax gun regulations. It is primarily in Europe that the two phenomena represent mainstays of critical sentiment against America of varying degrees of stridency, because – with the exception of American military power – they represent the most visible and easily digestible signs of (apparent) intra-western difference. In this respect, the shrill censure they typically occasion resembles the mass protests that condemn Washington's international actions but that rarely ever appear in relation to those of Beijing or Moscow, Harare or Caracas. In an ironic sense, for Europeans, American approval of firearms and judicial executions are the exceptions that testify not to how far apart the continents are, but rather how close they remain.

Chapter 5

George W. Bush, Religion and European Anti-Americanism

D. Jason Berggren and Nicol C. Rae

The pattern of American religious affiliation and the popular level of religiosity have been consistently exceptional features of American society. Even in the colonial period, America had an extraordinary number of contending Christian denominations, with none being predominant or 'established' by the state, as in most emerging European nation states. The United States has also always been conspicuous for the extent of popular support for evangelical Protestantism and recurrent evangelical revivals from the eighteenth century 'Great Awakening' onward. Alongside Enlightenment thought, evangelical pietism has been designated as the other principal source of influence for the founding of the United States.[1] The United States was born not from reason alone, but also 'out of religious zeal'.[2]

By the same token, religion has been a contributory factor to anti-Americanism throughout US history. Calvinistic Protestantism and evangelicalism have allegedly contributed to the so-called 'messianic' element in American political culture: the belief that America must not only be an example to other nations in the way it conducts its affairs but also occasionally must play a 'redeeming' role in a fallen world.[3] As David Chidester has written, a key component of American identity has been a pervasive sense that the United States is 'the locus of God's agency in the world', endowed with a 'millennial role' to work towards 'the regeneration of the world' and 'the salvation of humanity from the demonic domination of an absolute evil'.[4] The durability of this evangelical influence on American society and politics is undoubtedly a distinguishing feature of contemporary America that engenders anti-Americanism, particularly in the now highly secular advanced democracies of Western Europe.

In this chapter, using qualitative and quantitative sources, we explore these issues in more depth.[5] Two major themes emerge from the analysis: (1) Contemporary American religiosity is a denominational and regional phenomenon driven largely by the strength of evangelical Protestantism in the South and its environs. (2) This religiosity generates particular animosity in largely non-evangelical Europe and to a great extent explains the strong adverse European reaction to the persona and policies of President George W. Bush.

Contemporary European Anti-Americanism

Immediately after the terrorist attacks on New York and Washington on September 11, 2001, the French newspaper *Le Monde* ran an editorial titled 'We are all Americans now'. At that time, the US ambassador to the European Union declared that the 9/11 attacks 'will drive the US and the EU together ... Our common values will take precedence'.[6] Post-9/11 solidarity between the United States and the other Western democracies, as demonstrated by the successful campaign to overturn the Taliban regime in Afghanistan, apparently provided further proof of the oft-cited liberal maxim that democracies do not fight one another, but instead coalesce in opposition to non-democratic regimes.

Yet, even if contemporary liberal democracies appear unlikely to wage war on one another, serious rifts between and among them certainly do occur from time to time. Since the collapse of its common adversary in the Soviet Union and the end of the Cold War, the transatlantic alliance between the United States and Europe no longer appears to be a given in the international system. Western democracies do not necessarily have to be friends; but they do not have to be enemies either. They could become estranged or separated partners, maybe even competitors.[7]

During the Clinton presidency, the United States was very popular among European publics. The foreign policy of the Clinton administration was roundly approved among the powers of Western Europe: France (68 percent), Germany (86 percent), Italy (71 percent) and Great Britain (66 percent), and the image of the United States was strongly positive in Poland (86 percent), Great Britain (83 percent), Germany (78 percent) and Italy (76 percent).[8] Only in France (62 percent) and Spain (50 percent) was the image of the United States less impressive. Since George W. Bush became the president of the United States in 2001, however, transatlantic relations have sunk to their lowest levels since the turn of the last century. According to Andrew Kohut, director of the Pew Research Center, 'anti-Americanism runs broader and deeper than ever before. And it's getting worse'.[9] By 2006, favourable opinions of the

United States had dropped to all-time lows in Germany (37 percent) and Spain (23 percent).[10] Moreover, support for the US-led 'war on terror' had fallen for the first time below 50 percent in Britain (49 percent), France (43 percent) and Germany (47 percent). In Spain, from a high of 63 percent in 2003, support has plummeted to a meagre 19 percent.[11]

Among European leaders, George W. Bush has been compared to Caesar Augustus and Adolph Hitler.[12] A 2003 *Eurobarometer* survey ranked the United States along with Israel, Iran, North Korea, Iraq and Afghanistan as the greatest threats to world peace.[13] More than half of Europeans surveyed (53 percent) identified the United States as a threat, the same as Iran and North Korea. In the 2006 Pew survey, a majority in Spain (56 percent) and pluralities in France (36 percent) and Russia (45 percent) ranked the US war in Iraq as the greatest danger to world peace.[14] In Britain, a plurality (41 percent) identified the US war in Iraq as the second greatest danger, just behind the Israeli–Palestinian conflict. In contrast, more Americans identified the threats posed by Iran, the Israeli–Palestinian conflict and North Korea as greater threats to world peace than continued US involvement in Iraq. The 2006 Pew report also found that European confidence in Bush's leadership had reached all-time lows in Spain (7 percent), France (15 percent) and Germany (25 percent).[15] In Britain, confidence in Bush's leadership had returned to exactly what it was before September 11, 2001 – only 30 percent. Compared with British Prime Minister Tony Blair, French President Jacques Chirac, German Chancellor Angela Merkel and Russian President Vladimir Putin, the leadership of President Bush evoked the least confidence in Europe.

Of course, anti-American feeling in the Old World is nothing new and stems from multiple sources. The French commentator Jean-François Revel has offered many reasons for 'Europe's anti-American obsession': American obsession with money, its comparatively small welfare state, its higher incidents of violent crime, its tendency 'to elect mental defectives as presidents', its two-party system, its tendency towards unilateralist foreign policies, its lack of a 'mature culture', its history of racism, and 'simple jealousy of American power'.[16] In an interview with *Time* magazine, French President Jacques Chirac added credibility to that last assertion: 'Any community with only one dominant power is always a dangerous one and provokes reaction. That's why I favour a multipolar world, in which Europe obviously has its place.'[17]

Conventional wisdom holds that given widespread European opposition to the Iraq War, Bush's European 'problem' is due to his post-9/11 foreign policy and his 'arrogant' style of leadership.[18] But Bush's problem with Europe, or rather Europe's problem with Bush, antedates September 11, 2001. One editorial piece in the *Miami Herald*, dated August 21, 2001, captured pre-9/11 European feelings towards Bush: 'Europe not thrilled with Bush.'[19] Europeans were generally displeased by Bush's opposition to the Kyoto Treaty on global warming, his decision to pull out of the Anti-Ballistic Missile Treaty, and the execution of Oklahoma City bomber Timothy McVeigh.[20] One British paper was quoted as describing Bush as 'a bloodthirsty, ignorant Texas oilman'.[21] Bush's support for the death penalty and the fact that he was the former governor of Texas, the state that has executed the most people in the Western world in three decades, further contributed to his negative image in Europe.[22] As President Bush readied for his first visit to Europe, the *Miami Herald* reported, 'When George W. Bush goes to Europe ... he will face the most sceptical, if not downright hostile, reception ever to greet an American leader there.'[23] More specifically, however, his problems with Europe began shortly after Al Gore conceded.[24] The typical European had Bush caricatured as a gun-slinging cowboy, a happy executioner and a religious zealot, even before he took office.

What this suggests is that the sources of anti-Americanism cited by Revel and others are not the only ones, and maybe they are not even the most important. We suggest in this chapter that religion – or perhaps more accurately religiosity – is also a major source of anti-American feeling in Europe. There appears to be a widening religious – cultural gap between the two sides of the Atlantic. Some have said this is because much of Europe is 'becoming a very secular place', 'sunken progressively deeper into moral relativism'. With 'empty pews, aging believers, indifference', the post-Christian era in Europe is well under way. 'Almost everything about Western Europe's religious life conveys the sense of exhaustion and defeat.'[25] The United States, in contrast, is still, to use Peter Berger's words, as 'furiously religious as it ever was'.[26] What we may be witnessing is the emergence of a contest between two 'exceptionalisms', religious versus secular, American versus European.[27]

While Europe appears evermore secular, the condition of religion in America is one of continued vitality. Jeffery Sheler of US *News and World Report* observed that the United States is a place where 'there are more churches, synagogues, temples, and mosques per capita ... than in any other nation on Earth'.[28] Also, Europe has 'nothing comparable to the American religious right', evangelical Protestantism and politically influential evangelists such as Billy Graham.[29] By contrast, in the United States, Christian conservatives represent a core constituency of the Republican governing majority and 'religious tinged rhetoric' is much more common. Former European Commission President Jacques Delors also believes that transatlantic religious differences may complicate relations.[30] 'The clash between those who believe and those who don't believe', he said, 'will be a dominant aspect of relations between the United States and Europe in coming years. This question of a values gap', he continued, 'is being posed more sharply now than at any time in the history of European – United States relations since 1945.'

George W. Bush's 'Axis of Evil' Rhetoric

During his first term, Bush's rhetoric about evil, his public display of religious certitude, and frequent use of tough-talking cowboy imagery combined to make Europeans bristle. Generally, such expressions are 'alien to Europe' and reflect a 'pre-Enlightenment' disposition.[31] 'The biblical references in politics, the division of the world between good and evil, these are things', said one European analyst, 'we simply don't get.'[32] But such language and imagery comes quite naturally from a White House inspired and influenced by 'the culture of modern evangelicalism'. 'To understand the Bush White House', former Bush speechwriter David Frum explained, 'you must understand its predominant creed'.[33]

'America is a nation with a mission', Bush said, endowed with a 'special calling' to bring God's gift of freedom 'to every man and woman who lives in this world'.[34] But for Bush, the mission is not only to spread democracy, but also to exact Texas-style justice. 'The mission is to rout terrorists, to find them and bring them to justice … in Western terms, to smoke them out of their caves, to get them running so we can get them.'[35] He made it clear that 'we will not be intimidated by thugs and killers'.[36] Like the 'old poster out West', Bush said he wanted Osama bin Laden 'dead or alive'.[37] 'Justice demands that those who helped or harboured the terrorists be punished – and punished severely. The enormity of their evil demands it.'[38]

To the Taliban leaders of Afghanistan, he bluntly said, 'hand over the terrorists' or 'share in their fate'. This demand is 'not open to negotiation or discussion'.[39] To the world, he challenged, 'Every nation, in every region, now has a decision to make. Either you are with us, or you are with the terrorists.' And in this fight – civilisation's fight – 'God is not neutral' and Americans can be confident in 'the rightness of our cause'. In the end, he promised, like Nazism and communism, Islamic terrorism will be buried in 'history's unmarked grave of discarded lies'.[40] For Bush, the war on terror is 'a war between good people and evil people'.[41] Later, when asked about insurgent attacks on US forces in Iraq, he said, 'Bring them on'.[42] Using a poker image, 'an old Texas expression', to tell fellow members of the UN Security Council that the time for decision is at hand, Bush told members to 'show your cards'.[43]

But what got Europeans particularly apoplectic was Bush's 'axis of evil' comment during his 2002 State of the Union Address. Bush explained that the rogue states of Iraq, Iran and North Korea 'constitute an axis of evil', because together, they 'pose a grave and gathering danger' to civilisation by their pursuit of weapons of mass terror, and their potential to arm terrorists who could 'attack our allies or attempt to blackmail the United States'.[44] Though 'some governments will be timid in the face of terror', Bush added, 'make no mistake about it: if they do not act, America will. I will not wait on events, while dangers gather. I will not stand by, as peril draws closer and closer'. While he emphasised that he believed in coalition-building and working through international institutions, he let be known that on his watch, 'America will never seek a permission slip to defend the security of our country'.[45] Whether at home or abroad, Bush pledged to lead 'the armies of compassion in America' to victory.[46] Bush hoped the world would follow him, but he would not wait for them.

This is a president who made it clear that he will speak plainly and with certainty. 'My job isn't to try to nuance. My job is to tell people what I think'.[47] With calmness and confidence, Bush says, 'I know who I am'.[48] After 9/11, President Bush said, his mission became one to 'rid the world of evil' and in this mission, 'neither death nor life, nor angels nor principalities nor powers, nor things present nor things to come, nor height nor depth, can separate us from God's love'.[49] He believed that he could lead the United States because God was with him and the country. Though 'evil is real', Bush said, 'God is near'.[50] In his address to the nation on the night of 9/11, he quoted Psalm 23: 'Even though I walk through the valley of the shadow of death, I fear no evil, for You are with me'.[51] Such words were generally popular at home, but divisive abroad.

Polling data at the time revealed that Americans liked the 'axis of evil' rhetoric, while Europeans hated it (Table 5.1). According to the Pew

Table 5.1
Bush's 'Axis of Evil' Rhetoric.

Country	Support	Oppose
United States	56 percent	34 percent
Britain	32 percent	55 percent
Italy	29 percent	60 percent
France	27 percent	62 percent
Germany	17 percent	74 percent

Source: 2002 Pew Global Attitudes Project.

Research Center, 56 percent of Americans approved of the rhetoric, whereas majorities in Britain, France, Germany and Italy disapproved. Figure 5.1 shows that there appears to be a correlation between individual religiosity and support for 'axis of evil' rhetoric. Using figures from the 2002 Pew Global Attitudes Project, 59 percent of Americans said religion is very important in their lives and 56 percent supported Bush's 'axis of evil' rhetoric.[52] Meanwhile, 33 percent of Britons said religion was very important in their lives and 32 percent approved of Bush's choice of words. In Italy, 27 percent said religion was very important personally and 29 percent said they approved of Bush's words. Not

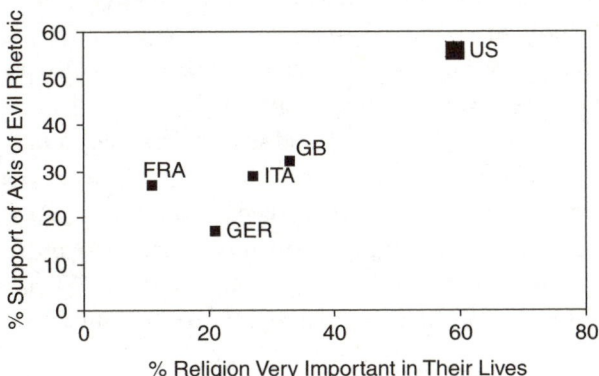

Figure 5.1
Individual Religiosity and Support for 'Axis of Evil' Rhetoric in America and Europe.
Source: 2002 Pew Global Attitudes Project.

surprisingly, France and Germany, the two most secular states among the five, were the least supportive of Bush's 'axis of evil' reference.

What many Europeans have failed to understand is that the 'axis of evil' rhetoric is rooted in an American context. In the United States, such rhetoric is popular. While 'the trend in Europe is generally towards the secularisation of politics', a supermajority of Americans (70 percent) in 2004 claimed it was important to them that their presidents possess 'strong religious beliefs'.[53]

'Bush's public piety is not unique or extreme among [American] Presidents', says Joe Klein. He noted, for instance, that it was President Woodrow Wilson who initiated an American tradition of 'diplomatic ostracism' when he refused to recognise the Soviet Union in 1917. 'The US', Klein continued, 'is the only major country that indulges in diplomatic ostracism'.[54]

What troubled Klein, like many Europeans, was Bush's certainty, his simple, unquestioning faith. During the Iraqi crisis, he lamented, 'it does not discomfort him enough; it does not impel him to have second thoughts, to explore other intellectual possibilities or question the possible consequences of his actions ... George W. Bush's faith offers no speed bumps on the road to Baghdad; it does not give him pause or force him to reflect. It is a source of comfort and strength but not of wisdom'. He's 'always bathed in the blinding glare of his own certainty'.[55] That was said of Jimmy Carter too, another evangelical Christian from the American South who possessed the 'blessed assurance' of being born again and a sense of doing the work of God in the political world. Wilson, a native of Virginia, who was raised in Georgia and whose father was a Confederate chaplain, also provoked European elite resistance and antagonism with his mix of religion and foreign policy. Put simply, 'Wilsonian presidents drive them crazy'.[56] Martin Marty, a church historian at the University of Chicago, remarked, 'The implication is that once you've worked [salvation] out, once you've been born again, you don't have to be fearful or tremble so much anymore'.[57] This is what Bush, Carter, and Wilson share.[58] This is what lies at the heart of European anxiety and antipathy towards Bush and America.

American or 'Southern' Religious Exceptionalism?

We question the commonly expressed argument that a transatlantic rivalry is emerging because America is 'religious' and Europe is 'secular'.

First, Europeans are not necessarily irreligious. As Grace Davie explained, they tend to be 'differently so'.[59] Andrew Greeley explains that Europeans by and large hold many religious beliefs, such as believing in God and life after death. He forthrightly proclaimed, 'Europe is hardly godless'.[60]

Davie presents data that describes Europeans as 'believing without belonging', showing that while Europeans no longer 'belong' to or participate in formal religious institutions as they once did, they still 'believe', many personally holding on to many religious beliefs.[61] She also notes that while many Europeans no longer attend religious services on a regular basis, they still want religious institutions to be available for others, and to them when they need them, such as at momentous life-cycle events, like marriage or death, or during national crises.[62] In other words, she explained, European churches have become 'public utilities'. Europeans may not regularly attend church, but they want them in case they need them. Many Europeans, she claims, have a 'vicarious religion'. They participate through the activities of others or the few who do attend take care of the religious well being of the greater majority.

Second, we contend that Americans are not necessarily exceedingly religious, either. Certainly, by many, if not most, survey measures, Americans are typically more religious than Europeans in their behaviour and belief. It is also true that in the United States, religion remains, as it has historically been, a public and consequentially political phenomenon. Unlike the French ideal of *laïcité* – the general desire and expectation of 'the absence of religion from public space and public affairs' – the general American ideal has been 'the freedom to believe', not 'the freedom from belief', and in finding a careful balance between the separation of church and state and the inclusion of religious expression and discourse in public life and affairs.[63] However, the religious divide between the United States and Europe can be, and often is, exaggerated.

The real religious divide is between Europe and a section of the United States – 'the South' broadly defined – rather than the United States as a whole. What is often overlooked in comparative studies between the United States and Canada and Europe is that the United States is an amalgam of states and regions that may be said to be very religious, and states and regions that are much more secular. As Peter Berger explained, 'the caricature of a "religious America" and a "secular Europe" ignores the fact that there are major differences within America itself.'[64] Survey data for the United States aggregates responses from parts of the country pushing towards greater secularisation (and more 'Europeanised' faith patterns) and parts of the country pulling in a more traditional (or 'exceptional') religious direction. Pew researchers may be right when they conclude that 'it may be more geography than nationality that divides' Americans from other Western publics.[65] Mark Silk, too, in his preface to *Religion by Region* series, writes that 'geographical diversity is the hallmark of religion in the United States' and 'region has not ceased to matter in national politics'.[66] It is his belief that 'whatever the virtues of compiling … a national narrative … they obscure a great deal'. He claims, in fact, that the American regions are not homogenising, but 'charting ever more distinctive courses' politically and religiously.

By examining the constituent parts of the United States, we argue that the religious style of President George W. Bush and the European unease with his presidential style can be more completely explained. If religion or the lack thereof is a contributing factor to anti-Americanism in some quarters of Europe, we believe that it is insufficient to merely say that 'American religious exceptionalism' and 'European secular exceptionalism' are the culprits. It is argued here that Europeans who are turned off or angered by Bush's religious style and tone are not actually reacting to 'American religious exceptionalism', but instead to a southern one.

What some commentators tend to overlook in their analyses of transatlantic relations and religion is that the presidency of George W. Bush has not only been divisive in terms of transatlantic relations, it has been divisive within the United States.[67] The Americans and areas of America that have been the least supportive of the Bush presidency are far less exceptional in terms of religion and culture relative to Europe than the areas that have strongly supported him. In terms of their politics, if some Europeans say 'we don't do God', the reality is that many Americans 'don't do God' either or are at least less comfortable 'doing God' than some of their fellow citizens.[68] One only has to recall, for example, that in 2003, the Democratic presidential frontrunner at the time, former Vermont governor Howard Dean, in effect said that he did not do 'guns, God, and gays'.[69] Even earlier, Garry Wills described another New England governor, Michael Dukakis, the Democrats' 1988 presidential nominee, as perhaps 'the first truly secular candidate we had ever had for the presidency'.[70] Without being hostile towards religion, he was someone, Wills continued, who was 'entirely free from religion'. He was simply unmoved by the spirit and spiritual things. For Dukakis, politics was not about finding monsters to slay or evil to root out, but cold, rational 'competence'.

The *Washington Post* columnist E.J. Dionne once noted, that in terms of values, there are many 'similarities between the Kerry states and European attitudes'. Europe 'is just a big blue state', he said.[71] More directly, Dionne suggested that a great deal of the difference between 'us and Europe' may be attributable to 'the peculiarities of Southern culture in the United States'. Though he did not explain what those 'peculiarities of Southern culture' were, we argue here that what Europeans often find discomforting or upsetting about Bush are features of 'Southern religious exceptionalism', not American exceptionalism. In this respect, we pick up on the regional arguments – with specific reference to the South – made by commentator Kevin Phillips and former New Jersey Republican governor Christie Todd Whitman.[72]

Phillips, a former GOP strategist, noted, to his dismay, that the old North – South rivalry has not only re-emerged, but this time, 'the South, more than the North, speaks with the voice and carries the insignia of national command'.[73] For Phillips, this development has had, and will have, seriously negative consequences for American politics, church – state relations, the future of the Republican Party, and American foreign policy. For Whitman, the southernisation of her party, as evinced by the inclusion of southern Democrats and 'religious leaders, mostly from the South', has uprooted the party and led to an abandonment of Abraham Lincoln's legacy.[74] In their own, yet similar, ways, Phillips and Whitman are troubled by the seeming fact that during the 1980s and 1990s, as one prominent journalist described, it became 'hard to know these days where the Confederacy ends and the Republican Party begins'.[75]

According to various survey data sources, the greatest religious – cultural gap in the Western world is not necessarily between the United States and Europe, but between the American South and Europe. In contrast, the American Northeast and West are closer (and may be moving closer still) to European levels of religious belief and behaviour. As such, we conclude that transatlantic relations will likely wax and wane depending upon the extent to which the occupant of the White House reflects this gap. Religious-styled or values-driven presidents, such as George W. Bush, or Jimmy Carter and Woodrow Wilson before him, will generally have more troubled, tense relations with Europe than more secular-oriented presidents (at least in terms of political style and rhetoric) such as the first Bush, Bill Clinton or 2004 Democratic candidate John Kerry had he won.

The American South: Bible Belt of the Western World

According to a 2002 Pew Global Attitudes Project brief, the United States 'stands alone in its embrace of religion'.[76] Using the single religious variable of personal importance of religion, the *Pew* brief concluded, 'Americans' views are closer to people in developing nations than to the publics of developed nations.' This conclusion reinforces age-old claims of American religious exceptionalism going back to at least Alexis de Tocqueville.

However, the American South, too, has long had its own claims of religious exceptionalism. Though it does not receive the same degree of popular coverage domestically or internationally, an entire body of scholarly literature on Southern religious exceptionalism coexists with the more widely known and cited American corpus. The other American regions, the Northeast, the Midwest, and the West, lack this independence. Commonly, their regional narratives are virtually indistinguishable from the wider national American narrative. In fact, it has long been argued, from the Southern perspective at least, that the story of the Northeast became the story of America. Georgia native and former president Jimmy Carter holds this view.[77]

By most religious indicators, the American South is the most traditionally religious, churchgoing and Protestant region of the United States.[78] It is a region where religion is said to constitute its 'soul', where even the sceptic 'is very much afraid that he may have been formed in the image and likeness of God'.[79] As will be shown below, when compared with other American regions, Canada, and Europe, the South may be said to be the 'Bible Belt' not only of the United States, but also of the Western world. To a greater degree than most other Americans and Westerners, Southerners believe in God, have negative views towards atheists and attend religious services weekly. Additionally, on many religious and cultural issues, the opinions of Southerners and Republicans tend to overlap and are often indistinguishable from each other.

Europeans are disturbed by the religious characteristics of President Bush and his willingness to publicise those traits and speak in religious terms, but what really underscores their unease is the regional context from which Bush has politically emerged and from where he has garnered the most support throughout his political career – the South and his home state of Texas.

Transatlantic Belief in God and the Personal Importance of Religion

American Southerners are among the most 'God-believing' and religious peoples in the Western world (Table 5.2). Though the data here does not show the American South having the highest levels of belief in God in the West, it should be noted that the figures for the United States and the American regions do not measure mere belief in God. They measure the *certainty* of theological belief. Thus, it may be stated that 88 percent of

Table 5.2
Western Belief in God and Personal Importance of Religion.

Belief in God		Religion 'Very Important'	
Region	Percentage	Region	Percentage
Malta	95	American South	73
Turkey	95	Turkey	65
Cyprus	90	United States	61
American South	88	American Midwest	59
United States	81	Mexico	57
Greece	81	American West	53
Portugal	81	American Northeast	52
Poland	80	Poland	36
American Midwest	77	Ukraine	35
Italy	74	Great Britain	33
Ireland	73	Canada	30
American West	71	Slovakia	29
American Northeast	70	Italy	27
Croatia	67	Quebec	23
Canada	64	Germany	21
Slovakia	61	Russia	14
Spain	59	Bulgaria	13
			(continued)

Table 5.2
(continued)

Belief in God		Religion 'Very Important'	
Region	Percentage	Region	Percentage
Austria	54	Czech Republic	11
European Union	52	France	11
Lithuania	49		
Switzerland	48		
Germany	47		
Great Britain	46		
Luxembourg	44		
Hungary	44		
Belgium	43		
Finland	41		
Bulgaria	40		
Iceland	38		
Latvia	37		
Slovenia	37		
France	34		
Netherlands	34		
Norway	32		
Denmark	31		
Sweden	23		
Czech Republic	19		
Estonia	16		

Sources: For belief in God for European countries, 'Social Values, Science & Technology', Eurobarometer 225 (2005), 9; for personal importance of religion for European countries and Canada, 2002 Pew Global Attitudes Survey; for belief in God for United States and regions, Albert L. Winseman, 'Americans Have Little Doubt God Exists', *Gallup Poll News Service*, December 13, 2005; for personal importance of religion for United States and Americans regions, 2001–2003 Pew Religion and Public Life surveys, the 2002 Pew Global Attitudes survey, and the August 2004 Pew News Interest Index.

Southerners do not just believe in God, but believe in God 'without a doubt'.[80]

Furthermore, the American South has a higher percentage of respondents claiming religion to be 'very important' (73 percent) than any other Western country or region. The country nearest to the American South in claiming the personal importance of religion is Turkey (65 percent). In this respect, Turkey, on the interface between the Islamic world and the West, is closest to the South than any other American region or Western country. On both indicators, the American West and American Northeast, Kerry's strongest regions in 2004, were the furthest away from the South. In terms of believing in God with certainty, the West and Northeast trailed the South by 17 percent and 18 percent respectively. On the personal importance of religion, responses in the West and Northeast were 20 percent lower than the South.

Regional Attitudes Towards Atheists

Though Americans have long been nearly unanimous in their belief in God or a higher being, Americans differ in their attitudes towards those who do not. Tables 5.3A and 5.3B shows that Southerners have the highest unfavourable views towards atheists and they are more likely than any other regional group to reject out of hand 'a generally well-qualified person for president' who does not believe in God. While respondents in the other regions are not generally fond of atheists either, majorities in the Northeast (58 percent) and the West (52 percent) would not necessarily hold it against presidential candidates who did not believe in God. Midwesterners, though they tend to share the South's general

Table 5.3A
National and Regional Favourability of Atheists.

Region	Favourable	Unfavourable	Gap
West	42.9	41.8	+1.1
Northeast	40.1	42.0	−1.9
Non-South	38.1	46.9	−8.8
United States	33.3	52.7	−19.4
Midwest	32.8	54.5	−21.7
South	25.4	62.2	−36.8

Sources: Aggregated data from the Pew 2000 Campaign Typology Survey and the 2001–2003, 2005 Religion and Public Life Surveys.

Table 5.3B			
Would Vote for 'A Generally Well-Qualified' Atheist for President.			
Region	Yes	No	Gap
Northeast	57.9	38.1	+19.8
West	52.1	43.3	+8.8
Non-South	52.3	44.2	+8.1
Midwest	48.7	49.1	−0.4
United States	47.0	49.5	−2.5
South	37.9	58.6	−20.7
Source: 2003 Pew Religion and Public Life Survey.			

antipathy towards atheism, are evenly divided on whether that alone would, or should, disqualify an otherwise 'well-qualified person' seeking the presidency. The evidence here suggests, then, that the South is the only region where there is both a general antipathy for non-believers and a general expectation that presidents should believe in God. Regarding the latter, the South, Bush's home region, and the Northeast, Kerry's home region, are virtual polar opposites.

Weekly Church Attendance

In measuring individual and societal religiosity, church attendance is one of the oldest and frequently used measures. It is also a measure more readily available for cross-national comparisons. Table 5.4 reports church attendance figures for the United States, forty-eight of the fifty American states, the District of Columbia, Canada, Mexico, Turkey and nearly every country in Europe.[81] Based on this measure, it is clear that compared with the United States, most European countries lack religious 'belonging'. But that is not the whole story or even the most important or most interesting. Though commentators and scholars talk of an all-encompassing 'American' religiosity, what in reality they are referring to is the religiosity of certain regions of the United States.

Based on the figures reported here, it may be said that a greater proportion of Americans 'belong' to religious communities compared to their European counterparts. In 1990, according to Davie, the European weekly church attendance average was 29 percent.[82] By the end of the

Table 5.4
Weekly Church Attendance Rates in the Western World.

Most Churchgoing (46 Percent+)		Churchgoing (31–45 Percent)		Secular (16–30 Percent)		Most Secular (1–15 Percent)	
Region	Percentage	Region	Percentage	Region	Percentage	Region	Percentage
Malta	75	South Dakota	45	Rhode Island	28	Great Britain	15
Poland	59	Virginia	44	Nevada	27	Lithuania	14
Alabama	58	Minnesota	44	Canada	26	Switzerland	14
Louisiana	58	Delaware	43	Greece	25	Luxembourg	13
South Carolina	58	Wisconsin	43	Cyprus	25	Hungary	12
Mississippi	57	Idaho	43	Belgium	25	Germany	11
Ireland	56	Pennsylvania	43	New Hampshire	24	Bulgaria	10
Utah	55	North Dakota	43	Spain	23	Georgia Republic	10
Arkansas	55	Ohio	43	Croatia	22	Moldova	10
Northern Ireland	54	US Midwest	43	Netherlands	21	Ukraine	10
Nebraska	53	Turkey	43	Romania	20	Czech Republic	10
North Carolina	53	Illinois	42	Slovenia	19	Armenia	8
Tennessee	52	Michigan	42	Austria	19	France	8
Georgia	52	United States	42	Australia	16	Montenegro	7
Oklahoma	50	Maryland	41			Serbia	7
US South	50	New Mexico	41			Belarus	6
Texas	49	Florida	39			Latvia	6
Kentucky	48	Connecticut	37			Norway	5

(continued)

Table 5.4
(continued)

Most Churchgoing (46 Percent+)		Churchgoing (31–45 Percent)		Secular (16–30 Percent)		Most Secular (1–15 Percent)	
Region	Percentage	Region	Percentage	Region	Percentage	Region	Percentage
Kansas	47	Wyoming	36			Finland	5
West Virginia	46	US West	35			Sweden	5
Indiana	46	Arizona	35			Iceland	4
Missouri	46	Colorado	35			Estonia	4
Iowa	46	Italy	35			Denmark	3
Mexico	46	New Jersey	34			Russia	2
		Montana	34				
		DC	33				
		New York	33				
		Slovakia	33				
		US Northeast	33				
		Oregon	32				
		California	32				
		Washington	32				
		Maine	31				
		Massachusetts	31				
		Portugal	31				

Note: Southern states in bold.

decade, the European average had dropped to 21 percent.[83] In contrast, according to the 1995–1997 *World Values Survey*, 44 percent of Americans attended religious services at least once a week. A decade later, little had changed. According to aggregated Gallup polling data from January 2004 to March 2006, 42 percent of Americans were attending at least once a week or almost every week. On the whole, the church attendance gap between Europe and the United States is growing, not narrowing.

The data here show that very few of the European nations have their polities attend religious services on a weekly basis. The only countries with attendance rates above 45 percent are the Catholic countries of Malta (75 percent), Poland (59 percent) and Ireland (56 percent). The only Protestant area of Europe with a strong religious attendance rate is Northern Ireland (54 percent). What is of further interest is that the American states with church attendance figures above 45 percent are nearly all from the South. In all, eighteen American states fall in this category. Of these, eleven, or 61 percent, are Southern states. This additionally means that of the thirteen Southern states, with the exception of Virginia and Florida, eleven states, or 85 percent, are found among the most religious publics in the Western world. The figures reported here confirm findings in other qualitative and quantitative reports and touch upon a line of inquiry suggested in several texts.[84]

The American South remains the Bible Belt, as measured by the reported frequency of church attendance, not only in the United States, but throughout the Western world. It may be said then that much of the claims of American religious exceptionalism are actually based on Southern-American religious exceptionalism, joined by pockets of high religiosity in geographically adjacent areas of the Midwest and the Mormon-majoritarian areas of the Mountain West, such as Utah. Outside of the American South and the religiously and culturally similar or adjoining areas of the Midwestern, Plains, or Mountain states, there is no other large, contiguous land mass of frequent churchgoers found anywhere else in North America or Europe.

Overlapping Southern and Republican Party Values

What may explain the comparatively higher church attendance rates in the South and adjacent areas is that this region is home for most of

America's evangelicals. With these states also the base for the Republican Party, it is no surprise that, of America's two major political parties, the Republicans are more likely to say they are 'born again'. According to Gallup, based on aggregated data for 2003 and 2004, 52 percent of Republicans say they are evangelicals compared to 36 percent of Democrats.[85] According to the same Gallup report, the South was the only region where a majority of respondents claimed to be 'born again' (58 percent). In contrast, less than 30 percent of respondents in the Northeast (26 percent) and the West (27 percent) claimed to be. 'Midwesterners', Gallup reported, 'are in between these two extremes', with 44 percent claiming to be born again. In comparative terms, being an evangelical in contemporary America is much more of a Southern trait than a non-Southern or generally American one.

Southerners and Republicans share many additional religious beliefs and cultural values.[86] Identical percentages of Southerners and Republicans believe in the existence of Heaven (90 percent), Hell (83 percent) and the Devil (79 percent).[87] The views of Southerners and Republicans are similar on claiming religion to be personally 'very important' (73 percent, 67 percent), believing the Bible to be the actual Word of God (39 percent, 33 percent), making homosexual relations illegal (46 percent, 42 percent), supporting a constitutional ban on same-sex marriage (65 percent, 71 percent), and owning guns (50 percent, 53 percent).[88] Few Southerners and Republicans consider abortion morally acceptable (27 percent, 30 percent) or believe that Charles Darwin's theory of evolution is well supported by scientific evidence (27 percent, 29 percent).[89] In contrast, 'with few exceptions, US Democrats are closer to Canadians in their views on many moral issues than to non-Democrats in their own country'. 'With few exceptions, Democrats' and Republicans' views radically diverge.'[90] Large numbers of Democrats and Canadians, for example, believe abortion (49 percent, 53 percent) and homosexuality (50 percent, 60 percent) are morally acceptable.

Religious Americans, mostly in the South, not only supported President Bush at the ballot box and regularly provided him higher job approval ratings than less religious Americans, they were also more likely to support the Iraq War than other Americans.[91] In a February 2003 Gallup poll, a month before the war began, self-identified members of the Religious Right were the most supportive of the war. Seventy percent of them said they would favour regime change in Iraq. Self-identified evangelicals were the second most supportive group, with 64 percent favouring the removal of Saddam Hussein. Those least supportive of the impending war were those who claimed that religion was not personally important in their daily lives. Only 49 percent of this group supported the war at the time. After the war became increasingly unpopular during Bush's second term, those least likely to say that the war was a mistake were Protestants and frequent churchgoers. Americans most likely to say the war was a mistake were non-Christians, those who 'never' attended religious services and those who claimed no religious affiliation.[92]

It is also noteworthy that of all the major religious denominations in the United States, the Southern Baptist Convention (SBC) was the only one to endorse Bush's war in Iraq. Shortly after the war began, SBC President Jack Graham, pastor of a church in Dallas, Texas, said, 'Removing Saddam Hussein from power is a just and necessary action after twelve years of lies and deception'. 'This war', he continued, 'is "just" because its cause is liberation not occupation, protection not aggression, peace not appeasement'.[93] For Graham, it is the duty of the United States 'to respond to threats of evil with courageous resolve', and for their part, 'Southern Baptists will embrace and engage this global challenge with faith and renewed commitment to evangelism and missions'. According to a 2003 SBC resolution, the denomination proclaimed that the Bible 'commands civil authorities to restrain evil and to punish evildoers through the power of the sword' (Romans 13:1–5).[94] It was resolved that 'the messengers [delegates] to the Southern Baptist Convention meeting in Phoenix, Arizona, June 17–18, 2003, affirm President George W. Bush, the United States Congress, and our armed forces for their leadership in the successful execution of Operation Iraqi Freedom'. Later, President Bush would count Southern Baptists among 'the soldiers in the armies of compassion at home and abroad'.[95]

If many Europeans and Canadians are troubled by Bush's religiosity, their discomfort is not merely with Bush, but more specifically with a specific regional subculture within the United States: the American South.

The Texas Factor

Religiously, one finds that George W. Bush's home state of Texas is like much of the rest of the South. Texas is a mostly Protestant and churchgoing state. It is a state where the Christian Right has had 'dominant' influence.[96] It is the home of several prominent Christian

Right leaders, including W.A. Criswell, James Robison and John Hagee, and the birthplace of prophecy writer Hal Lindsey. Politically, the Lone Star State 'has always been fertile ground for a mixture of religion and politics' and it is a state with a constitution that proclaims that there shall be no religious tests for public office provided candidates profess 'the existence of a Supreme Being'.[97]

This is Bush's home. It is where, Bush says, 'my first memories are', where he claims his values of family, community and faith were born, and where his political program of 'compassionate conservatism' was first implemented.[98] It was in Texas, the most populous state in the South and the largest state won by the Republican presidential candidate in the last four elections, that Bush learned and became fluent in the 'Biblical and political language of the evangelicals'.[99] Unlike his father, Bush rejected what he perceived to be the liberal elitism of the Northeast, and 'made the conscious choice to be a Texan through and through'.[100]

The true regional identity of Bush's father, President George H.W. Bush became much clearer after he left the presidency in 1993 and made the family home in Kennebunkport, Maine 'their true home'.[101] In remarkable contrast, the son's home in Crawford, Texas, is a ranch, 'a symbol of the cowboy populism he likes to convey', and his frequent vacationing there provides him 'the chance to show his macho side'.[102] But most importantly, said Bush's first press secretary Ari Fleisher about Bush going to his Crawford ranch, 'It's Texas and that's very important to him. One thing about Texans – they all want to return home. It's real America. It's outside the [Washington] Beltway.'[103]

According to aggregated Gallup polling data (2000–2004), like almost the entire South, Texas had a supermajority (60 percent+) of survey respondents who identified themselves as Protestant/Mormon (Table 5.5). Of these eighteen states, eleven of which are in the South, Bush won seventeen in 2000 and all of them in 2004. In 2004, the most Protestant/Mormon states accounted for 180 of his 286 electoral votes, or 63 percent.

In another Gallup report, in which data were aggregated over a two-year period (2004–2006), Texas was among eleven other Southern states in the country's 'top thirteen' most churchgoing states (Table 5.6). The only non-Southern states among the thirteen highest were the Mormon-majority Western mountain state of Utah and the Midwestern Plains state of Nebraska. In 2000 and 2004, Bush swept these states. Without these states, the South particularly, Bush could not have won the presidency.

Table 5.5
Most Protestant US States and 2000–2004 Statewide Winners
(States Ranked by Percentage of Protestant/Mormon Affiliation;
60 percent Minimum).

State	Percentage of Protestants/Mormon	2000	2004
Utah	79	Bush	Bush
Alabama	76	Bush	Bush
West Virginia	76	Bush	Bush
Mississippi	76	Bush	Bush
Tennessee	73	Bush	Bush
South Carolina	72	Bush	Bush
Arkansas	71	Bush	Bush
North Carolina	71	Bush	Bush
Oklahoma	69	Bush	Bush
Georgia	69	Bush	Bush
Kentucky	66	Bush	Bush
Wyoming	66	Bush	Bush
Iowa	64	Gore	Bush
Kansas	62	Bush	Bush
Virginia	62	Bush	Bush
Texas	61	Bush	Bush
Indiana	60	Bush	Bush
Missouri	60	Bush	Bush

Note: Southern states in bold.
Source: Jeffrey M. Jones, 'Tracking Religious Affiliation, State by State', *Gallup Poll News Service*, June 22, 2004.

Table 5.7 lists the fifteen least Protestant states (<50 percent). Of these states and D.C., the Democratic presidential candidate won eleven in 2000 and twelve in 2004. Nine are in the Northeast, the region Michael Lind identified as the essential core of the Democratic Party.[104] Since 1960, the least Protestant state in the country, Massachusetts, has been the home state for three Democratic presidential nominees (John Kennedy – 1960, Michael Dukakis – 1988, and John Kerry – 2004) and two nomination runner-ups (Edward Kennedy – 1980, Paul Tsongas – 1992). For the past four decades, few states rival the Democratic loyalty

Table 5.6
Most Churchgoing US States and 2000–2004 Statewide Winners
(States Ranked by Weekly Church Attendance Rates).

State	Percentage (Weekly Attendance)	2000	2004
Alabama	58	Bush	Bush
Louisiana	58	Bush	Bush
South Carolina	58	Bush	Bush
Mississippi	57	Bush	Bush
Utah	55	Bush	Bush
Arkansas	55	Bush	Bush
Nebraska	53	Bush	Bush
North Carolina	53	Bush	Bush
Tennessee	52	Bush	Bush
Georgia	52	Bush	Bush
Oklahoma	50	Bush	Bush
Texas	49	Bush	Bush
Kentucky	48	Bush	Bush

Note: Southern states in bold.
Source: Frank Newport, 'Church Attendance Lowest in New England, Highest in South', *Gallup Poll News Service*, April 27, 2006.

of New England's largest state in presidential politics. In 2004, twelve of the fifteen least Protestant states not only voted for Kerry, but together they represented 169 electoral votes or 67 percent of his electoral total. The least Protestant states gave Bush only 24 electoral votes or 8 percent of his re-election total.

Table 5.8 shows that the thirteen least churchgoing states are key parts of the Democratic presidential base, including nearly all of New England, New York, New Jersey, the nation's capital, and three Pacific coast states. In 2004, Kerry won eleven of them. At the beginning of the twenty-first century, it may be concluded that Democratic presidential candidates have thus fared best in the *least* Protestant and *least* churchgoing states, while President Bush has done best in the *most* Protestant and *most* churchgoing states.

Table 5.7
Least Protestant/Mormon US States and 2000–2004 Statewide
Winners (All States Below 50 Percent).

State	Percentage of Protestants/Mormons	2000	2004
Massachusetts	27	Gore	Kerry
New Jersey	30	Gore	Kerry
Connecticut	31	Gore	Kerry
Rhode Island	32	Gore	Kerry
New York	33	Gore	Kerry
District of Columbia	34	Gore	Kerry
New Hampshire	37	Bush	Kerry
California	41	Gore	Kerry
Nevada	44	Bush	Bush
Vermont	46	Gore	Kerry
Wisconsin	46	Gore	Kerry
Maine	47	Gore	Kerry
Arizona	49	Bush	Bush
Illinois	49	Gore	Kerry
Colorado	49	Bush	Bush

Note: Northeastern states in bold.
Source: Jeffrey M. Jones, 'Tracking Religious Affiliation, State by State', *Gallup Poll News Service*, June 22, 2004.

A Southern Evangelical President

Religiously, the two Bush presidents could not be more different.
President George Herbert Walker Bush is a member of what Bill Clinton
jokingly, yet tellingly, referred to as 'the frozen chosen'.[105] He is a life-
long Episcopalian for whom faith is largely a private matter between a
human being and God, a quiet, solitary spiritual reflection devoid of the
emotional enthusiasm, expressiveness, and certainty characteristic of
American, particularly Southern, evangelical Christianity.

George H.W. Bush has said that he has not 'always found it easy to
discuss [religion] in public, since my faith has been a very personal thing
to me'.[106] When it came to knowing what God expects believers to do in

Table 5.8
Least Churchgoing US States and 2000–2004 Statewide Winners (States Ranked by Weekly Church Attendance Rates, Starting with Lowest).

State	Percentage (Weekly Attendance)	2000	2004
New Hampshire	24	Bush	Kerry
Vermont	24	Gore	Kerry
Nevada	27	Bush	Bush
Rhode Island	28	Gore	Kerry
Massachusetts	31	Gore	Kerry
Maine	31	Gore	Kerry
Washington	32	Gore	Kerry
California	32	Gore	Kerry
Oregon	32	Gore	Kerry
New York	33	Gore	Kerry
District of Columbia	33	Gore	Kerry
Montana	34	Bush	Bush
New Jersey	34	Gore	Kerry

Note: Northeastern states in bold.
Source: Frank Newport, 'Church Attendance Lowest in New England, Highest in South', Gallup Poll News Service, April 27, 2006.

the public square, he wrote, 'I'm not sure what God wants of us'.[107] In his 1988 campaign autobiography, Bush rarely mentioned his faith.[108] We found only two instances. In the first reference, Bush mentioned his Episcopalian upbringing, his family's weekly church attendance, and his parents' practice of reading a Bible lesson daily at the breakfast table. In the second, Bush noted his private reliance on prayer and how his faith sustained him and Barbara when their daughter Robin died.

Compare this to the son's campaign autobiography where on the very first page, he mentions the importance of his faith and his life-long involvement in religious life. The autobiography of George W. Bush was entitled *A Charge to Keep*, a title that comes from a famous Methodist hymn written by Charles Wesley.[109] For Bush, the words are a source of inspiration; they invoke a duty 'to our highest and best' and speak of 'purpose and direction'.[110]

A charge to keep I have,
A God to glorify,
A never dying soul to save,
And fit it for the sky.
To serve the present age,
My calling to fulfill;
O may it all my powers engage
To do my Master's will!

Bush wrote that he was also given a painting with the same title that hung 'across his desk' in the Governor's Mansion and later hung in the Oval Office. The central image is a determined and confident, charging horseman leading a band of followers to some unknown purpose, to some unrevealed destination. He told his Texas staff, 'When you come into my office, please take a look at the beautiful painting ... This is us.'[111]

In the book, Bush discussed being called, in the religious sense, to run for president.[112] At a time when he was 'struggling with the decision about whether to seek the Presidency', he recalled a sermon his pastor gave about Moses, who was not 'a very good speaker', being chosen by God to lead the people of Israel. After that, Bush acknowledged that his pastor's words 'spoke directly to my heart and my life'; he 'was challenging me to do more'.[113] In an unusual confession for a presidential aspirant, Bush attributed his decision to run for president to his pastor, the one who 'had prodded me out of my comfortable life as Governor of Texas and towards a national campaign'.[114]

George W. Bush also mentioned the personal influence of Billy Graham, twentieth-century America's greatest evangelist and perhaps the greatest evangelist ever to come from the American South, on his decision for Christ. 'Reverend Graham planted a mustard seed in my soul, a seed that grew ... He led me to the path, and I began walking. And it was the beginning of a change in my life ... It was the beginning of a new walk where I would recommit my heart to Jesus Christ'. Continuing, Bush explained that his time with Graham humbled him. In Graham's presence, he learned 'that God sent His Son to die for a sinner like me. I was comforted to know that through the Son, I could find God's amazing grace'.[115]

Given the greater ease George W. Bush has in expressing his faith, it is not surprising that during the 1988 campaign, with great effectiveness, he represented his father before evangelical communities, particularly in the South.[116] Unlike his father, George W. Bush's testimonies of faith were 'strong and believable'.[117] Such efforts would later serve him well in his 1994 campaign for governor of Texas and his subsequent rise to the presidency. By 2000, for many within the Christian Right movement, George W. Bush would come to be seen not merely as an advocate of their agenda, but indeed the leader of their movement.[118]

This is the great difference between the two Bush presidents, wrote Phillips.[119] The father remained tied to and emblematic of 'the staid church of New England', Episcopalianism. Evangelicals never saw him as one of them. The son, however, had a full immersion into 'the emotional church of evangelical Texas'. Though both were residents of Texas, the son much more thoroughly than the father went 'GTT – Gone to Texas' politically, religiously and culturally. The father, Phillips recounted, 'always had one foot' in Texas and 'the other' in New England. But George W. Bush 'planted himself firmly in Texas and evolved a temperament to match'.[120] Bush embraces and promotes this interpretation as well. 'He was raised in New England', Bush explained about his father. 'I was raised in Texas. Texans are less reserved'.[121] However, Bush said 'we need to be mindful of that old Southern phrase, "You can talk the talk, but you need to walk the walk."' For many supporters, Bush has talked and walked his faith Southern-style.

Conclusion

The arguments presented in this chapter are not meant to deny the many other factors that contribute to European anti-Americanism, both in the past and the present. Many factors can affect transatlantic relations and the behavioural variance among European leaders in their relations with each other and American presidents. But we argue that transatlantic religious and political cultural differences are critically important – particularly in recent times. Even before the terrorist attacks on September 11, and before US forces invaded Iraq, Europe had a negative view of President Bush. His 9/11 decisions and rhetoric did not cause, but rather confirmed and deepened, the initial impressions Europeans had of him.

Under Bush, the United States once again undertook a messianic mission, another opportunity to be the redeemer nation. Historically, Americans tend to view their wars as crusades or 'holy wars'. If the country must go to war, it has been said, it 'must go for moral reasons', not for oil or power as primary motives, but because it is right.[122] It must go to war to make a fallen world right and to prevent the contamination of the world from coming to its shores.[123] Bush has embarked on a crusade, if you will, that represents, according to some, 'the biggest gamble' by a president in living memory and part of his effort to leave behind a 'consequential' presidency.[124] And he brought the American people, at least initially, along with him. This is what Europeans find puzzling and discomfiting. Europe is largely a post-modern, post-Christian continent that considers the rhetoric and policies coming from the other side of the Atlantic worrisome and repugnant to its sensibilities.

Henryk Broder, a writer for *Der Spiegel*, may be accurate when he observes, 'It's America, not Bush, that is the problem for Europeans.'[125] We would add that it is Southern, evangelical American values that are really the problem for Europeans, although many Europeans – who generally lack a sophisticated knowledge of American society and regional differences – might not realise it. Bush is only a reflection of the wider political culture of the 'red states' he carried in the 2000 and 2004 elections, states predominantly in the greater South that still affirm the creedal passions of God, the flag and traditional family values. Many Europeans may be uncomfortable with the cultural expressions and exports of the American South, but they are not the only ones. Cultural unease is also pronounced in the 'blue states' of New England and the Pacific coast.

The South is not only the most religious and conservative region in the United States, it is also the largest electorally, and, with continued North-to-South demographic shifts, the region's electoral weight will likely continue to grow. Republicans cannot win without solidly winning the greater South and, since the 1960s, Democrats have not won the presidency except when they ran Southerners (Johnson, Carter, Clinton) who were able to win at least some Southern states. As to which party controls the White House and Congress, increasingly, the South has become the 'vital South'.[126] Consequently, Europeans can regularly anticipate American presidents who are not only from the South, but whose political success relies upon solid and steady Southern support. Put differently, the greater a president's political fortunes rest upon the South or those who closely identify with Southern conservative religious and cultural values, the greater the tensions will be with much of Europe.

If this is indeed the case and many Europeans continue to assume that their version of secularism is the Western civilisational norm, believing, as Grace Davie explained, 'that what they do today everyone else will do tomorrow', then we should not expect to see any diminution in widespread European anti-Americanism based on religion and religious observance.[127]

Chapter 6

Anti-Americanism and the American Personality

Richard Boyd and Brandon Turner

The American Personality

America has been heralded as the 'first new nation', distinguished by a lack of the feudal baggage that plagued her European ancestors.[1] Almost from the moment they set foot on the new continent, America's inhabitants took pains to distinguish themselves from the European society they left behind. John Winthrop's providential vision of the American Puritans as God's chosen people was among the first and most enduring of these exercises in self-definition.[2] However, this was only the beginning of a long tradition of hypothesising America's exceptionalism. More than a century and a half later, Thomas Paine argued in his pamphlet *Common Sense* that the circumstances of the new continent had given America her own unique character and interests that marked her as distinct from Europe.[3] Thomas Jefferson similarly premised his revolutionary claims in the Declaration of Independence on the fact that the Americans were already 'one people', deserving of a separate and equal station in the eyes of the world.[4]

Some have argued that America's distinctiveness arises from her dedication to common civic principles, as Jefferson suggested in the Declaration. What makes America 'one people' in this view is an assent on the part of its inhabitants to 'certain self-evident truths', namely, the fundamental postulate that human beings are all equal in their inalienable rights to 'life, liberty and the pursuit of happiness'. More often, however, the United States has been defined, both by itself and by others, in terms of its unique cultural or sociological attributes. And yet to say that America is defined by some essential quality above and beyond its strictly political identity does not answer the question of what that essence consists of. Nor does it explain why that same American personality – however constructed – has so consistently evoked such strongly anti-American sentiments.

It is important to touch briefly on the different ways America has understood her own exceptionalism, because this self-understanding is surely related – both implicitly and explicitly – to the motivations of a whole tradition of anti-Americanism. Andrei Markovits has posited the helpful distinction between critics who focus on what America 'is' as opposed to those others who are angered by what America 'does'.[5] For the particular group of nineteenth-century social theorists we will be concerned with in this chapter, the former question of what America 'is' – her altogether original character or personality – is absolutely central. This question is all the more pressing because America's present has commonly been linked with Europe's future. Instead of regarding America's condition as alien to and disconnected from the fate of Europe, America is often seen as tied up with broader narratives of historical progress or decline in which Europe is also implicated. 'The faith of the American is becoming the faith of the European as well', Nietzsche warned.[6] America's restlessness, its constant sense of innovation and progress and its impatience with the past are beacons for European societies destined to be dragged along the path trod first by the United States.

While Alexis de Tocqueville, Frances Trollope and Karl Marx all share the conviction that America is the vanguard of commercial individualism, political democracy and cultural homogeneity, what is striking about these nineteenth-century visions of the American personality is their apparently contradictory nature. How could such astute social critics have looked at virtually the same American society and yet come to such widely different conclusions? One is tempted to say that the American personality is like a Rorschach test: nebulous and amorphous, and that these criticisms of the American personality tell us more about the observers themselves than the empirical realities of the American scene. Even so, there are patterns not so far beneath the surface of the disagreements, and the primary task of this chapter will be to bring to light underlying commonalities between the arguments of these three celebrated critics of America. The following analysis will be organised around three tightly linked sets of themes, namely, the political, economic and religious dimensions of the American personality.

With respect to the first of these variables, it is widely accepted that America personifies the values of democracy and equality. What may be less well known is the degree to which critics of America differ over whether this commitment to equality is a good or a bad thing.

Tocqueville and Trollope seem to concur, empirically at least, about the extent to which democratic equality has taken hold in America. Even so, they disagree about whether this should be seen as an accomplishment or a tragedy. For Tocqueville, the rise of democratic equality must be tolerated as ushering in a new phase in human relations, whereas for Trollope America's republican revolution brings an intolerable disordering and intermingling of naturally higher and lower elements. Particularly for critics on the Right, then, America's democratic and egalitarian political culture leads to mediocrity, the lowering of standards and a lack of cultivated sensibilities.

Second, and notwithstanding their acknowledgement of the unprecedented degree of equality in American society, all three of these critics regard America's commitment to democratic equality as potentially adulterated by its obsession with commerce and the naked pursuit of wealth. This is especially true for Karl Marx. Although he grudgingly concedes (with Tocqueville and Trollope) the equality of social relations in the United States, Marx complains about those residual economic inequalities such as slavery that remain and are only likely to compound in the future. Whereas more conservative observers like Tocqueville and Trollope are wary of the cultural costs of American materialism, Leftish critics like Marx protest that, although the universal pander of money may indeed level out traditional hierarchies and status relationships, the workings of the marketplace give rise to altogether new dependencies in civil society. Thus, as we will see, America can be simultaneously faulted for its political equality and its economic inequalities.

Finally, all three are struck by the potentially explosive amalgam of sacred and secular elements in American culture. On the one hand, the United States purports to be the apotheosis of secular Enlightenment ideals of natural rights, reason and scientific progress. Yet, at the very same time, America's providential sense of itself as a chosen nation – entrusted by God with a special mission, divine calling or destiny in the world – stems just as much from messianic ideals of Christianity as from the secular ideals of the Enlightenment. While critics complain that America is one of the most rationalistic nations in the world, it can also be ranked amongst the most puritanical.

America's apparent schizophrenia on these points has drawn the attention of a long and distinguished list of European critics. Our goal here is not to take sides in these debates but rather to bring out the main lines of agreement and disagreement between these three celebrated nineteenth-century critics, revealing how certain constitutive features of the American personality struck Tocqueville, Trollope and Marx as morally, aesthetically and politically objectionable. As we will see, not only are there surprising points of consensus amongst thinkers on the Right and the Left, but their criticisms of nineteenth-century America presage some of the most common complaints levelled by latter-day critics of the American personality.

Tocqueville on Democratic Equality

While Alexis de Tocqueville found much to praise in the civic life of America, he was also wary of the democratic value of equality. *Democracy in America* is written under the influence of a kind of 'religious dread', provoked by his recognition of 'this irresistible revolution advancing century by century over every obstacle'.[7] The most striking fact about America is how an 'equality of conditions' pervades almost all social relationships. By this, Tocqueville presumably had in mind America's overall, substantive equality. Americans by and large are more equal to one another than the polarised European society with which he is familiar. American society has neither serfs nor aristocrats. However, this vaunted 'equality of conditions' seems to be as much about what we would call today 'equality of opportunity' as an actual, substantive equality. 'It is not that in the United States, as everywhere, there are no rich', Tocqueville observes. The difference is that 'wealth circulates there with incredible rapidity, and experience shows that two successive generations seldom enjoy its favour'.[8] The fact that Americans are not fixed by birth in any particular social position but can advance themselves by their own talents and initiative is just one example of a universal, indeed providential, tendency of human history that has reached its peak in America.

One by-product of this rapid social mobility is America's palpable energy: 'Everyone is on the move, some in quest of power, others of gain'.[9] However, by virtue of being in perpetual motion, Americans are never content with their accomplishments. 'There is something astonishing', Tocqueville notes, 'in this spectacle of so many lucky men restless in the midst of abundance'.[10] Because of their relentless obsession with 'the things of this world', Americans pursue economic prosperity with a 'feverish ardour', forever 'tormented by the shadowy suspicion that they may not have chosen the shortest route to get to it'. Americans are constantly rushing, striving, clutching, grasping and snatching for the next economic increment or physical pleasure.[11] There is 'always a slight but troublesome restlessness, a sort of continual jostling ... which distracts or disturbs the mind without stimulating or elevating it'.[12] Even by the first decades of the nineteenth century, America already displayed the single-minded materialism and greed so roundly condemned today by anti-American critics.

Perhaps the most direct consequence of this rapid social mobility – both upward and presumably also downward – is the way it blurs lines between social classes. Rather than being stifled by the conventional social roles of master and servant, noble and peasant – even to the point of thinking about themselves as different kinds of human beings – social mobility in America encourages people from different social classes to treat one another as rough social equals. 'There is nothing degrading about the status of a domestic servant, because it is freely adopted and temporary and because it ... creates no permanent inequality between master and servant'.[13] All honest callings are honourable.[14] All of this is to the good, because it allows for the ascendancy of natural sentiments of friendship and fellow feeling. The bands of a democratic society are looser or more relaxed than those in an aristocracy and also extend more widely to all of humanity.[15]

The flip side of American social mobility is a dangerous kind of democratic levelling. As Tocqueville observes, in no other nation has he seen so few totally ignorant persons as in America.[16] Social mobility has made basic literacy accessible to almost everyone. The problem is that nowhere else are there so few truly educated individuals. Raising the bottom means dragging down the top. 'A middling standard has been established in America', Tocqueville complains: 'All minds approach it, some by raising and others by debasing themselves'.[17] The insatiable love for equality in a democratic society breeds *ressentiment* towards those who are truly exceptional or successful. Both the relentless practicality of the Americans and a lack of a hereditary cultivated class means that great artists, poets and philosophers will always be rare.[18] Worse still, the theory of 'equality applied to brains' implies that if everyone is of roughly equal intelligence – and thus no one can be expected to know more than anyone else – the right side of an issue is generally found on the side of the majority.[19] Thus the rise of tyrannical majoritarianism and the oppressive sway of public opinion are endemic to an egalitarian society like the United States. Although this 'elitist' critique of the United

States has to some degree been eclipsed by more egalitarian complaints, contemporary anti-Americanism seems, ironically, to have incorporated these more 'conservative' laments about the mediocrity, lack of taste and vapid homogeneity of American culture.

America's religiosity is another of Tocqueville's great preoccupations. Unlike France, where religion and liberty have proven incommensurable, America has managed to harmonise them in a way that promises the best of both worlds.[20] Even so, all is not perfect with American religion. America's practicality and rationalism guarantee that the religious instinct will sometimes express itself in bizarre and extreme forms.[21] Illiberal and enthusiastic religions take root in the midst of an otherwise secular and materialistic society, making America appear one of the most puritanical nations in the world. The 'ridiculous and tyrannical laws' that the New England Puritans imposed upon themselves are long since past, but the Puritan spirit remains alive and well in American culture.[22] The moderating and harmonising function of religion comes at the cost of formidable social pressures towards modesty, chastity and moral conformity. This 'spiritualised despotism' is more formidable than any generated by laws alone.[23] With respect to domestic politics, how strange it seems to Tocqueville that Americans should swear off alcohol *en masse* and then bring their collective moral force to bear on their fellow citizens to do likewise.[24] How different is the self-imposed chastity of American women and men from the hypocrisy of European sexuality.[25] And maybe more significantly in the case of foreign relations, America's messianic impulse is not so much a by-product of its intellectual origins in Enlightenment universalism as of its Puritan self-understanding as a moral beacon to the world.

Tocqueville's most lavish – and most often cited – praise of America has to do with its spirit of civic association.[26] No cause is too small, no occasion too trivial, for Americans to join together in civil associations. However, the darker side of this avid spirit of collective involvement and ubiquitous associations is the possibility of illiberal and undemocratic social movements. Although Tocqueville acknowledges that the spirit of association operates very differently in America than in Europe – where associations are like little armies – this laudable spirit of civic association might just as easily give way to the 'fatal results' of nativism, McCarthyism, nationalism and other undemocratic mass movements.[27] Once public opinion has made up its mind on an issue, the dissenting individual is liable to be crushed by the tide of popular mobilisation.[28]

Sympathetic commentators have long been struck by the centrist character of American politics – what Arthur Schlesinger, Jr. lionised as its 'vital centre' by way of contrast to the fascist and communist political extremism of other nations.[29] However, critics have just as often taken note of the nativist, populist and nationalist currents running just beneath the seemingly tranquil surface of American liberalism.

Notwithstanding Tocqueville's admiration for the spirit of civic association in America, he divines a long-term threat to the public spiritedness of the average American. In a society that values the individual as much as the United States, there is always the danger that persons will turn their backs on public life. Because they value their own independence and take pride in their ability to care for themselves, they assume that their neighbours ought to do likewise. This misguided sense of 'individualism' is not born of malevolence or even a narrow sense of selfishness or 'egoism'.[30] Unlike many subsequent critics, Tocqueville concedes that Americans are probably no more or less selfish than other nations. Rather, this spirit of individualism is born from the considered habit of taking care of one's own affairs and immediate circle of family and friends. All the rest of the world, in this view, can be left to its own devices. This misplaced sense of individualism is like a poison at the heart of a democratic society, throwing each individual back into the 'solitude of his own heart'.[31]

Subsequent critics inspired by Tocqueville have made it clear that the dynamic of individualism can have two very different but equally pernicious consequences. Abdicating public responsibility and living an exclusively private life lead to a 'mass society' where political life falls into the hands of charismatic leaders, concerted powers or special interests. Withdrawal into private life gives rise to what the Frankfurt School dubbed the 'authoritarian personality', at one extreme, or the kind of 'soft' or 'bureaucratic despotism' Tocqueville thinks is much more likely in America.[32] Either way, by forsaking public life and the spirit of civic association, Americans squander the liberty that is ultimately most valuable. The second danger is more purely individual and psychological. Neo-Tocquevillean critics like David Riesman and Robert Bellah have argued that the psychological consequences of such an atomised mass society leave individuals feeling despondent and powerless, robbed of meaningful relationships with other people and tragically 'lonely in the midst of a crowd'.[33]

Lastly, Tocqueville puts his finger on one of the most consistent and enduring complaints about the American personality, namely, what he calls the 'irritable patriotism of the Americans'. Because of the investment, the average American feels in his or her nation national pride 'descends to every childishness of personal vanity'. While it is difficult enough, according to Tocqueville, for the average American to express opinions different from those settled by public opinion, this privilege is absolutely denied the foreigner.[34] Visitors to the United States are expected to praise every aspect of life in the United States, from its government down to its climate and food, and any hesitation in conceding the superiority of the American way of life and its political institutions is greeted with hostility. Tocqueville's experience was shared by Charles Dickens and countless other European visitors to America.[35]

This hypersensitivity and childish patriotism stand out even more dramatically when Americans travel abroad.[36] Every inconvenience is taken as a national insult, which returns us to the paradox with which we began. Despite the peculiarities, even pathologies of the American character, the attitude of the American is that American principles are universal, whereas the customs and cultures of others are merely particularistic. So, on the one hand, as Tocqueville and others have complained, the 'ugly American' is rude and insensitive abroad because of his unbounded confidence in the superiority of all things American. And yet at the same time, confronted by a society rife with class differences and hierarchies that he finds inscrutable, the American experiences every misunderstanding as a slight: 'The American leaves his country with a heart swollen with pride. He comes to Europe and at once discovers that we are not nearly so interested as he had supposed in the United States and the great nation that lives there. This begins to annoy him'.[37]

Mrs. Frances Trollope on Republican Rudeness

Tocqueville is struck by the irritable patriotism of the Americans, because this trait seems to run contrary to their generally easygoing nature. However, for a long line of critics, the unmannerliness, rudeness, cultural insensitivity and intolerance of Americans are the rule rather than the exception. Even for Tocqueville – otherwise so impressed by the authenticity, spontaneity and transparency among democratic citizens – the lack of manners on the part of the Americans is irksome. In a democracy like the United States 'manners are often vulgar, as thoughts have little occasion to rise above a preoccupation with domestic interests'.

Manners undoubtedly suffer because 'there is too much mobility … for any definite group to establish a code of behaviour and see that it is observed'.[38]

Although she was not the first to identify this aspect of the American personality, nowhere has this characterisation been developed so fully and acerbically as in Mrs. Frances Trollope's *Domestic Manners of the Americans*. In 1827, after failing to receive an inheritance from an uncle that would have relieved her family's financial troubles, Trollope and her husband settled on a plan to establish a glorified department store in the West of the United States. When the outlandish structure she built to house her grand 'Bazaar' in Cincinnati, Ohio led to yet another failure, she returned to England to write *Domestic Manners*, which was published in March 1832 to popular and critical acclaim. Despite her fascinations with mercantile successes, throughout the book one is as struck by her sense of being an apostle of the values of an aristocratic society as by her palpable insecurity about her place – as a member of the downwardly mobile gentry – within such a society.[39]

Trollope was appalled by the 'total and universal want of manners' in America.[40] Although she professes not 'to decide whether man is better or worse off for requiring refinement in the manners and customs of the society that surrounds him', she clearly sides with Edmund Burke and other conservatives in defending the importance of manners as 'that polish which removes the coarser and rougher parts of our nature'.[41] Nonetheless, her description of such a 'total and universal want' of manners belies the fact that the 'manners' she encounters in the United States are in fact clearly defined and ever present. It is not that Americans lack a coherent system of 'manners'; Trollope just disapproves of the forms they take.

One of Trollope's most consistent grievances about America is the lack of privacy. Whether she is travelling by steamboat or coach, or eating meals in common in the various inns – all of which she pronounces unliveable – she is confronted by a society where familiarity and publicity are the norm. As much as American liberalism preoccupies itself with the idea of privacy, Trollope discovers much to her chagrin that social norms demand a certain degree of transparency on the part of republican citizens. There is a general suspicion if not antipathy to those like Trollope who seek to be left alone, to eat or enjoy her tea in her own room, to guard her personal affairs from the prying and importunate questions of those she meets. From the point of view of her republican hosts, her desire to remain aloof or reserved is interpreted, perhaps correctly, as reflective of a pretended sense of superiority.[42]

> In fairness, taking her meals in private is at least in part a reaction to what she experiences as: The total want of all the usual courtesies of the table, the voracious rapidity with which the viands were seized and devoured, the strange uncouth phrases and pronunciation; the loathsome spitting, from the contamination of which it was absolutely impossible to protect our dresses; the frightful manner of feeding with knives, till the whole blade seemed to enter into the mouth and the still more frightful manner of cleaning the teeth afterwards with a pocket knife.[43]

Such a scene would be unappetising enough for anyone. But her quest for privacy is interpreted by innkeepers and other travellers as a signal that she thinks herself better than others. She demands special privileges for herself and her family. 'Then, madam', an innkeeper declares, 'I cannot accommodate you on these terms; we have no family tea-drinkings here, and you must live either with me or my wife, or not at all in my house'.[44] There are undoubtedly inflections of social class to Mrs. Trollope's complaints. The vagaries of travel have long been responsible for flinging different social groups into proximity with one another. But rather than being consigned to travel and eat in shared public space by virtue of her inability to pay for something better, she is shocked to discover that the 'decent dignity of a private conveyance' was not even 'deemed necessary for the president of the United States'.[45]

Above and beyond the levelling and disordering effects of travel in the United States, even the so-called 'private' life seems liable to invasion:

> [T]he point where this republican equality was the most distressing was in the long and frequent visitations that it produced. No one dreams of fastening a door in Western America; I was told that it would be considered as an affront by the whole neighbourhood. I was thus exposed to perpetual and the most vexatious interruptions from people whom I had often never seen and whose names still oftener were unknown to me.[46]

Locked doors and private coaches may go some distance towards blunting the perfect transparency expected among democratic citizens.

However, above and beyond norms applying to physical space, one of the most significant ways in which cultures preserve distance is through forms of verbal address. Physical proximity need not in and of itself lead to moral proximity, but in a democratic society like the United States, Mrs. Trollope discovers, the battle lines are drawn at the level of language itself. The 'violent intimacy' and 'uncouth advances' of Mrs. Trollope's 'poor neighbours' consist not only of unannounced visits to her home but in their 'extraordinary familiarity' of addressing her children 'by their Christian names, excepting when [they] substituted the word "honey"', a 'familiarity of address' that was 'universal through-out all ranks in the United States'.[47]

Democratic forms of address not only blur the line between public and private she seeks rigidly to maintain – as when she is addressed by a complete stranger by her first name, or described as 'the English old woman' – but also serve to blur distinctions of breeding and birth. 'Generals', 'Majors', 'Governors' and 'Judges' are ubiquitous appellations among the seedy riverboat gamblers who populate American steamboats, thus degrading the entire aristocratic notion of titles as reserved to the eminent and worthy. Virtually any miserable soul will be described as a 'gentleman' or a 'lady'. Americans, she complains, see no incongruity in speaking of '"the lady over the way what takes in washing", or as "that there lady, out by the Gulley, what is making dip-candles"'.[48] If a scrubwoman or a candle-maker is entitled to be treated as a lady, then what can true gentility consist of? While her husband Mr. Trollope was referred to generally as 'the old man', an entire procession of 'draymen, butchers' boys and the labourers on the canal was invariably denominated "them gentlemen"'.[49] Forms of address that seek to communicate, generate or preserve difference – whether they be European titles of birth, significations of superior eminence or good breeding, specialised authority or the general respect one owes to strangers – are confounded by their ironic application everywhere and nowhere, without any regard for the naturally higher and lower elements of society.

Not only does the American language confound public and private, but it denies the distinction between higher and lower elements. The existence of poverty and ill-breeding troubles Trollope less than 'the useless meeting of incongruities that prevails all over the Union', that is, when the rigidly maintained boundaries between the upper and lower classes to which she is accustomed are transgressed. 'You are not startled', she notes (although she clearly is!), 'by a man reeking of work and whiskey approaching to take your hand'. That customary sense of deference or 'air of respect, elsewhere assumed by tradesmen, is wanting'.[50] Even the 'common courtesies of salutation are abridged, as if every one was afraid of compromising his dignity by being too condescending'.[51]

Manners may reflect underlying political values, and thus Trollope's more fundamental complaint is that the American doctrine 'all men are born free and equal' is nothing more than a 'phrase of mischievous sophistry'.[52] If taken literally, as ignoring natural inequalities of talent, intelligence or beauty, then certainly the doctrine of democratic equality rests on a patent falsehood. Some are obviously more beautiful, intelligent or talented than others – not to speak of conventional distinctions brought about by birth, breeding and acculturation. As Henry James surmised, 'Nature and industry keep producing differences as fast as constitutions keep proclaiming equality, and there are always, at the best, in any really liberal scheme or human view, more conscious inaptitudes to convince of their privilege than conscious possibilities to remind of their limits'.[53]

Trollope's way of thinking is premised on a society where eminence in some quality – good breeding, high birth and eminence of learning – entitles one not only to the respect of one's inferiors but indeed to special privileges that have no necessary relationship to this particular quality or excellence. She cites with horror the case of the German Duke of Saxe-Weimar's stagecoach ride during his travels in America. This man of ostensibly 'unaffected and amiable manners' is outraged when, after having tried to engage a 'monopoly on the vehicle' for himself and his luggage, he must share the carriage space with another traveller who has had the temerity to 'secure his seat by payment of the customary charges'.[54] When the Duke protests against this indignity and threatens to report the stagecoach driver to the Governor, he learns 'his first lesson of republicanism' by being beaten savagely and thrown back into the carriage next to the other traveller. Rather than an object lesson about the vices of putting on airs, Trollope regards 'this brutal history' as not only 'distasteful to the travelled and polished few', but also the very '*possibility* of such a scene ... a national degradation'. The broader problem is to be explained by the American inability to recognise and defer to others. 'The American people', she complains, 'have no more idea of what constitutes the difference between this "Prince of a five acre patch", and themselves, than a dray-horse has of estimating the points of the elegant victor of the race-course'.[55]

Trollope's otherwise anti-democratic narrative seems to be redeemed by her deft criticism of the peculiar institution of slavery. Like Tocqueville, Beaumont and other European visitors of the era, she is struck by its injustice as well as its pernicious moral effects on slave and slave owner alike. In the case of an accidental poisoning of a slave child in a house where she is visiting, she is horrified by the grotesque indifference of the young white girls of the house to the predicament of the child: 'the idea of really sympathising in the sufferings of a slave, appeared to them as absurd as weeping over a calf that had been slaughtered by the butcher'.[56] However, one of the ironies is that she seems incapable of generating the same degree of empathy for the lower classes who hold analogous domestic positions in the North, and her criticism of slavery focuses largely on its distorting effects on the deference of the lower orders of American society.[57] Despite slavery's abomination, 'its effect will appear less injurious to the country than the false, futile and preposterous tone assumed by the white population when compelled by necessity to sell their labour in domestic service'. If only the blight of slavery were removed, 'the gradation of ranks INEVITABLE in the progress of all society would take place naturally, and of necessity, leaving tranquillity and leisure for the progress of refinement'. This and this alone might bring 'civilisation' and 'order' to the United States.[58]

Describing a particularly wretched family in her village, Trollope alludes to an 'air of *indecent* poverty' that presumably marks the family for special opprobrium.[59] This poverty is less 'indecent' because of the squalor that accompanies it than for the refusal of the family so afflicted to personify the kind of deference and shame that Trollope expects from them. Residents of this village whom Trollope describes as the 'peasants of the United States' refuse to be designated as such.[60] They refuse to accept the 'alms-giving' of the Trollopes with the proper sense of deference, always insisting, much to her chagrin, that they will pay something for the hand-me-down clothes or perform some reciprocal labour in return for the milk they 'borrow'.[61] She duly notes, but seems unmoved by the fact, that they accept her charity 'in a form that shewed [showed] their dignity and freedom'.[62] Moreover, the kind of industry and ingenuity by which they attempt to raise themselves from their misery are rejected as the 'hard, dry calculating' of the 'Jew', which Trollope regards with an 'involuntary disgust'.[63]

Democratic equality implies 'any man's son may become the equal of any other man's son', and she acknowledges that 'the consciousness of this is certainly a spur to exertions'. Nonetheless her broader complaint is 'it is also a spur to that coarse familiarity, untempered by any shadow of respect, which is assumed by the grossest and the lowest in their intercourse with the highest and most refined'. Although the 'theory of equality may be very daintily discussed by English gentlemen in a London dining-room, when the servant, having placed a fresh bottle of cool wine on the table, respectfully shuts the door', it is abhorrent 'when it presents itself in the shape of a hard, greasy paw, and is claimed in accents that breathe less of freedom than of onions and whiskey'.[64] In this respect at least Trollope seems a keener observer of the nuances and social dynamics of democratic equality than Tocqueville. Or at least her own social insecurity and aristocratic pretensions lead her to be more attuned to the countercurrents and backwaters of aristocratic pretension that run against the powerful democratic currents Tocqueville discerns in American political culture.

In one of her rare 'democratic' moments, Mrs Trollope affects surprise that while 'recognising in almost every full-dressed *beau*' to pass her at a society ball the very same merchants and shopkeepers with whom she is accustomed to doing business, she is surprised not to find 'among the many very beautiful girls ... one more beautiful still, with whose lovely face I had been particularly struck at the school examination'. Inquiring about her conspicuous absence, she is told that, 'You do not yet understand our aristocracy ... the family of Miss C are mechanics'. Unlike the other equally prosperous families in attendance, her father 'assists in making the articles he sells; the others call themselves merchants'.[65] This instance of snobbery strikes her as false not so much because of the natural excellence of beauty and grace that is unjustly excluded, but rather because of the minute distinctions upon which these invidious distinctions are premised. What is more ridiculous: a gang of shopkeepers and merchants putting on society airs; or that such an unpolished bunch would actually have the audacity to slight someone because her family performs a trade?

The American passion for equality may lead us to try to pull down those who are above us, but it does not prevent others from trying to instantiate some new grounds of distinction to make themselves stand out from the crowd. In comments applying equally well to Tocqueville and Trollope, Henry James sagely observes: 'So beset' is the '"European" mind on the question of "differences" and the practicality of precautions for maintaining these' that it tends to overlook the fact that 'discriminations are produced by the mere working of the machine'.[66] Or as Tocqueville himself qualifies: 'The surface of American society is covered with a layer of democratic paint, but from time to time one can see the old [and new!] aristocratic colours breaking through'.[67]

Karl Marx on Capitalism and the American Spirit

Notwithstanding these and a few other isolated comments, Tocqueville and Trollope can both be faulted for ignoring elements of inequality and social class prevailing in nineteenth-century America.[68] So captivated are they both by the social mobility and equality of conditions they find in American society that traces of economic inequalities seem by and large to escape them. This theoretical oversight is amply filled by a third prominent nineteenth-century critic of the United States, Karl Marx. Like Tocqueville and Trollope before him, Marx viewed the United States with both restrained optimism and apprehension.[69] Unlike Tocqueville and Trollope, Marx never set foot on the other side of the Atlantic. His plans to emigrate to Texas at the age of twenty-seven never materialised, and subsequent trips were unlikely due to his perennial financial woes.[70] Perhaps as a result, Marx produced nothing approximating the kind of sustained characterological travelogue that one finds in Tocqueville, Beaumont or the Englishman Thomas Hamilton, though he was familiar with all three.[71] Marx did, however, write a substantial number of newspaper and journal articles dealing with the United States. Between the years 1851 and 1862, Marx authored a steady stream of opinion pieces for Horace Greeley's *New-York Daily Tribune*.[72] The American Civil War ended his association with the *Tribune*, but Marx spent the remainder of 1862 contributing pieces on the war to the Vienna daily *Die Presse*.

For Marx, unlike Tocqueville and Trollope, the source of any distinctively American 'character' is not to be found in its citizens but in its underlying material conditions. This is to say that whatever 'personality' Marx ascribes to denizens of the United States should be understood as flowing from their historical circumstances and certainly *not* from some intrinsic, cultural or ethnic source.[73] That being said, Marx does offer some incredibly illuminating criticisms of American society. Initially sympathetic, then gradually more critical, his thoughts on America all spring from a fundamentally materialist historical observation, namely, that the United States is the 'most modern form of existence of bourgeois society'.[74] America simultaneously embodies the greatest virtues (few as they may be) of the bourgeoisie as well as the most unsavoury aspects of capitalist exploitation.

Like Tocqueville and Trollope, the young Marx was well aware of America's commitment to moral and political equality.[75] He praised the absence of franchise property qualifications and proclaimed the United States in 1861 as 'the highest form of popular self-government till now recognised'.[76] In contrast to the Prussian state, America's freedom of the press, independent education and democratic principles stood out as admirable steps towards democratic equality. Concerning fiscal responsibility, for example, Marx criticises Prussian policy by first valourising the post-Mexican-War United States government as the 'courageous bourgeoisie, conscious of its power and determined to use it'. American prudence and determination are antidotes to the stagnant, fiscally wanton Prussian nobility: 'the two budgets are already sufficient proof … of the cowardice, narrow-mindedness and philistinism of the one country and of the self-reliance, intelligence and energy of the other'.[77]

Even at his most optimistic moments, however, Marx never loses sight of how America falls short of his egalitarian ideals. In 'On the Jewish Question', for example, Marx lauds the American republic's separation of church and state, for such 'political emancipation' of religion from the state is a praiseworthy and necessary development in modern history. However, as in much of what he wrote about America, Marx considers this accommodation or emancipation as not going far enough in the direction of a more fundamental 'human emancipation'. The American republic succeeds only in separating the 'rights of man' from the 'rights of citizens', leaving the self-interested private individual – the 'member of civil society' – alienated from his political self and the larger political community. Worse still, Americans exercise the rights of citizens with the rights of the self-interested individual in mind, so much so that the 'the citizen is declared to be the servant of egoistic "man", that the sphere in which man functions as a species-being is degraded to a level below the sphere where he functions as a partial being and, finally, that is man as a bourgeois and not man as a citizen who is considered the true and authentic man'.[78]

In fairness, this kind of alienation is endemic to any bourgeois society – France, the United States or England. And yet it is precisely because social classes are fluid in the United States that Americans behave like pure egoists, unchecked by larger class interests: '[I]n the United States of North America ... though classes, indeed, already exist, they have not yet become fixed, but continually change and interchange their elements in a constant state of flux'.[79] In part this is due to the colonial status of America, which momentarily spared its polarisation into the rigid social classes Marx otherwise believes are inevitable.[80] Rather than 'coinciding with a stagnant surplus population', as in Europe, the 'relative deficiency of heads and hands' in the United States gives some bargaining power to labour.[81] But instead of inspiring community, fellow-feeling or solidarity, America ends up being the most thoroughly selfish and purely atomised society in the world. The New England trader, Marx bitterly complains, worships at the idol of Mammon and behaves as though 'the world is no more than a Stock Exchange'.[82] Paradoxically, their crass concern to aggrandise themselves lends an inherently conservative, even reactionary dimension to American political culture: 'the feverishly youthful movement of material produc-tion, which has a new world to make its own, has left neither time nor opportunity for abolishing the old world spirit'.[83] Americans are so obsessed with economic well-being, innovation and the creation of new technologies that they have no motivation to question the status quo. America's dynamism and energy are tragically squandered.

Citing Tocqueville as one of his authorities, Marx concurs that 'North America is pre-eminently the country of religiosity'.[84] Rather than with-ering away when the support of the state is removed, religion instead takes on a *'fresh* and *vigorous'* potency in the United States.[85] The power of American religion, its diversity and vigour, however, stems from the fact that religion has 'become the spirit of *civil society*, of the sphere of egoism and of the *bellum omnium contra omnes'*.[86] Although vibrant – indeed sometimes fanatical – American Christianity is thoroughly profane, the very *'manifestation* of secular narrowness'.[87] Privatised and pushed out into bourgeois civil society, religion becomes a com-modity no different from any other good for sale and subject to the same crass competition. Despite the aura of religiosity that hovers over all of America, the American preacher is just another huckster, disguising a Jewish love of money in puritan garb: 'In North America ... the *preaching of the Gospel* itself, Christian preaching, has become an article of commerce, and the bankrupt trader in the church behaves like the prosperous clergyman in business'.[88]

Marx's analysis of antebellum American society, in conclusion, combined relative optimism (the political freedoms of the United States were undeniable advances) with legitimate criticism and concern (America's peculiar class structure prolonged material alienation and thus delayed full human emancipation). Even this qualified praise, however, withers away during the course of the Civil War. When war broke out in 1861, Marx predictably took the side of the Northern states. Antagonism between North and South was at bottom a matter of 'the *slavery question*' and the entire conflict was 'nothing but a struggle between two social systems and between the system of slavery and the system of free labour'.[89] Marx's preference for the latter was obvious. The North – the land of industry and freedom – represented the next stage in human development, for better and worse, while the South – 'oligarchy of 300,000 slaveholders' – represented the last gasp of an outdated feudal mode of production and human enslavement.[90] The North did in fact prevail, as we know, though not in the fashion expected by Marx and Engels. As the war dragged on, Marx complained to Engels in 1862, 'I see, of course, the repulsive side of the form the [war or anti-slavery] movement takes among the Yankees; but I find the explanation of it in the nature of "bourgeois" democracy.' A few weeks earlier he commented, 'In regard to the North's conduct of the war, nothing else could be expected from a *bourgeois* republic, where swindle has been enthroned for such a long time'.[91]

No American personified this bourgeois mediocrity as completely as Lincoln, for whom Marx reserved his most patronising scorn. Indeed it was Lincoln who 'never ventures a step forward before the turn of circumstances and the general call of public opinion forbid further delay', whose Emancipation Proclamation, despite its importance, 'seem[s] like the mean, pettifogging conditions that one lawyer puts to his opponent' and who disguises the '*revolutionary*' nature of the war with his '*constitutional*' rhetoric. Among an otherwise uninspiring lot of American statesmen, Lincoln best embodied the impotent, bumbling, *bourgeois* walk through history:

> Lincoln is not the product of a people's revolution. The ordinary play of the electoral system, unaware of the great tasks it was destined to decide, bore him to the summit – a plebeian … a man without intellectual brilliance, without special greatness of character and without exceptional importance – an average man of

good will. Never has the New World scored a greater victory than in the demonstration that with its political and social organisation, average men suffice to do what in the Old World would have required heroes![92]

Put into the framework Marx established in 'On the Jewish Question', what transpired in the North between the years 1861 and 1865 was the clash between the egoistic and political principles present in the American republic. The Civil War, which ought to have been fought on purely ideological – *political* – grounds, was being waged by a largely self-interested population moved only by economic interests. As Engels criticised, 'The *people* have been bamboozled, that is the trouble, and it is lucky that a peace is a physical impossibility, otherwise they would have made one long ago, merely to be able to live for the almighty dollar again'.[93]

Marx's sundry comments on the United States after the Civil War are almost totally preoccupied with the egoistical national character of the Americans. In post-bellum America, the alienation of product from worker was nearly complete, as 'nowhere are people so indifferent to the type of work they do ... nowhere are people so aware that their labour always produces the same product and money and nowhere do they pass through the most divergent kinds of work with the same nonchalance'.[94] Greed and the desire for self-advancement taint all aspects of American society. Correspondingly, American politics suffers from the inevitable result of politicians seeking to balance their egoistic and communal selves: namely, corruption. Marx, partly quoting Engels, writes in *The Civil War in France*:

> Nowhere do 'politicians' form a more separate and powerful section of the nation than precisely in North America. There, each of the two major parties which alternately succeed each other in power is itself in turn controlled by people who make a business of politics, who speculate on seats in the legislative assemblies of the Union as well as of the separate states, or who make a living by carrying on agitation for their party and on its victory are rewarded with positions ... We find here two great gangs of political speculators, who alternately take possession of the state power and exploit it by the most corrupt means and for the most corrupt ends – and the nation is powerless against these two great cartels of politicians, who are ostensibly its servants, but in reality dominate and plunder it.[95]

Although written in 1871, this polemic anticipates the by now familiar assessment of how the pursuit of wealth motivates the behaviour of American politicians, drives the conduct of American foreign policy and generates a dissonance (if not outright hypocrisy) between professed American ideals of equality and liberty and its underlying economic realities.

As we have seen, Marx is not alone in thinking that as America goes, so goes the rest of the world. Whether inspired by an elitist revulsion at the tacky nature of mass consumption (*à la* Tocqueville and Trollope) or by egalitarian misgivings about the inequalities and disruptions of global capitalism (*à la* Marx), this conviction has done much to shape the contours of latter-day anti-Americanism. Whereas Marx saw the nineteenth-century United States as both peripheral to the capitalist industrialisation already well advanced in Europe and as the archetypical bourgeois society, contemporary anti-Americanism regularly vilifies the United States as the unquestionable locus of global capitalism. The global hegemony of McDonald's and fast food, Hollywood films, American music, sports and fashions – all of these give rise to the idea, real or imagined, of America as dictating the nature of *consumption* around the globe. Likewise, America is linked to the capitalist forces of *production* necessary both to whet and to satisfy the tastes of global consumers.

The Italian Marxist Antonio Gramsci described the discipline of capitalist production in terms of an American-style 'Fordism' and 'Taylorism', which sought to remake the workers of the world in their capacity as producers as well as consumers.[96] In order for capitalism to prosper, workers must be made every bit as interchangeable, regular and predictable as the machines on which they labour and the goods they strive relentlessly to consume. This 'American phenomenon', Gramsci complains, is the 'biggest collective effort to date to create, with unprecedented speed, and with a consciousness of purpose unmatched in history, a new type of worker and of man'.[97] Contemporary critics echo similar complaints about how American consumer goods are weapons of globalisation threatening to displace authentic and particular traditions with one universal and homogenising consumer culture.

Conclusion

We have seen that Tocqueville, Trollope and Marx are simultaneously attracted and repelled by nineteenth-century American society.

In addition to the historical and sociological importance of their writings, these three commentators may also cast light on paradoxes at the heart of contemporary anti-Americanism. First, as we have argued throughout, America's critics have more often targeted aspects of its culture or 'personality' than its strictly political institutions. Tocqueville's analysis does make it clear that there is a mutually constitutive relationship between American society and its political institutions, but he is just as preoccupied with explaining the former in terms of the latter. Similarly, while Marx monitors and intervenes in the American political scene of the 1850s and 1860s, his analysis likewise seems to reduce American political development to underlying economic forces. And finally, while it is not hard to see the relationship between Mrs. Trollope's revulsion to republican manners and her own Tory predilections, she avers not to be interested in American politics or political institutions. Thus the force of their criticisms, as well as the brilliance of their analyses, stems from their attention to sociological variables that are best understood as part of American 'society', 'character' or 'personality'.

Second, while all of these thinkers reckon with the United States as a phenomenon that is captivating precisely because of its differences from European society, all three of them see America's present as linked inexorably with Europe's future. In the case of Tocqueville, France can profit from the lessons of how America has managed to come to terms with the democratic revolution sweeping through the world. For the early Marx, at least, American society offers hints of the revolutionary potential and sweeping economic changes to which a global civil society is leading. And, perhaps most unambiguously critical, for Mrs. Trollope, the republican manners of America are a harbinger of similar democratic transgressions soon to befall her beloved British society. Given this ubiquitous assumption that America is the vanguard for Europe, it is remarkable how many of the criticisms and observations unearthed by Tocqueville, Trollope and Marx in the nineteenth century have become part of a permanent trope of anti-Americanism (on both the Right and Left). That is to say that anti-Americanism has a long and distinguished genealogy, and looking at many contemporary criticisms of American greed, imperialism and the mediocrity of the mass culture America spreads throughout the world reveal both the precocious insights of these nineteenth-century thinkers and the archaeology (and sometimes, alas, unoriginality) of contemporary criticisms.

Third, given how explicitly these three commentators relate their thoughts on America back to the fate of their own nations, it is tempting to say that anti-Americanism has as much to do with the situation of the critics themselves as with the empirical realities of American society. Anti-Americanism is often dismissed as peculiarly (and pejoratively) 'French', 'European', 'non-Western', 'anti-Enlightenment', etc., as if the identity of the critic determines the nature of the shortcomings they identify within the American character. This consideration of Tocqueville, Trollope and Marx suggests both the partial truth and necessary limitations of this thesis. First off, it is obvious that the particular observations, commentary and criticisms levelled by these celebrated nineteenth-century observers have something to do with their own presuppositions and vantage outside of America. That said, given their radically different social backgrounds (downwardly mobile gentry, native-born aristocrat and abject intellectual); their different national traditions (England, France and Prussia) and political commitments (Tory conservative, ambivalent liberal and Communist), it is remarkable just how much their respective accounts and criticisms overlap. Even for such a trenchant critic as Marx, America is charac-terised by a *relative* equality *vis á vis* Europe because of its colonial status, the shortage of labour and the corresponding ability of unskilled labourers to command tolerable wages and some degree of control over their own labour. So the fact that these and other critics of the American personality have something at stake in their commentaries does not necessarily mean that their analyses and criticisms are biased or misguided.

On the other hand, undeniable differences between these critics underscore the difficulties of speaking of the American personality in monolithic terms. While there can be little doubt that critics of the United States are often well founded in highlighting real, palpable tendencies in the American personality that are sometimes lost on Americans them-selves, anti-Americanism is prone to a kind of monolithic rhetorical generalisation. In addition to the surprising areas of overlap mentioned above, readers of Tocqueville, Trollope and Marx should be as struck by the *differences* in their criticisms, by the ways in which their portrayals seem on the face of it to be mutually incompatible. Notwithstanding a common perception of America as materialistic, progressive and characterised by a high degree of social mobility, their criticisms vividly diverge. Tocqueville and Trollope both see democratic equality writ large in America, even while disagreeing about its desirability. Marx, on the other hand, sees the possibility of revolution stamped out by the presence of the ultimate inequality of slavery and an obsession with money making that frustrates any real possibility of social change. This paradoxical vision of America as heralding both the advent of a formal equality of rights even while generating new forms of material inequality – as simultaneously taking its inspiration from Enlightenment liberalism and Puritan fundamentalism – have provided ample fodder for these and subsequent critics of the American personality.

Chapter 7

The Environment and Anti-Americanism

Navraj Singh Ghaleigh[1]

If the intellectual landscape allows for 'respectable prejudices',[2] then anti-Americanism regarding the global environment has as sound a claim as any. Of course every prejudice, every 'feeling towards a person or thing, prior to or not based on actual experience',[3] is presumptively objectionable. But when we think of contemporary environmental challenges, the predilection of anti-Americanism can be stripped of its dubious character – made 'respectable' – on the basis that there is a solid foundation for our objection. Indeed, there are few areas of international governance where our 'actual experience' leads so strongly to an unfavourable feeling as in respect of America and the environment. Whether pertaining to patterns of American consumption, the failure to ratify the Kyoto Protocol or the actuality of extreme climate phenomena, ill dispositions to the United States are not entirely absent 'actual experience'. If we were looking for proof of (in)activity in the realm of the environment, any informed global citizen would be able to point to evidence of American conduct that reflects ill on that polity.

The meeting of the environment and anti-Americanism is a pressing and novel issue in the early years of this century. This is not due so much to the fact of American economic hegemony and its environmental consequences (a matter we've had the better part of a century to acculturate to) as to the belated cognisance of anthropogenic global climate change, its causes, its effects and the steps taken to combat it. When analysing the why and what of climate change, the singular position of the United States is a recurrent theme – America's contribution to the production of green house gases and its reluctance to engage in international efforts to tackle climate change are merely the better known charges laid against America. Be that as it may, the question remains whether such conventional wisdom is sufficient to justify a feeling of anti-Americanism, which, in turn, revolves around our understanding of that term itself.

Definitions of anti-Americanism must be sensitive to a number of dimensions, not least those of breadth and essence/conduct. Regarding the former, one might adopt the view of Rubinstein and Smith who see anti-Americanism as any hostile action or expression that becomes part and parcel of an undifferentiated attack on the foreign policy, society, culture and values of the United States.[4]

Such an approach is attractive in its embrace, capturing diverse aspects of American activity, the opposition to them, and critically, the weakness of criticism that is essentially unreflective or 'undifferentiated'. Nonetheless, the analytical utility of such an approach can be sharpened if we keep in mind, as do both Toinet and Zeldin, the slightly hysterical notion of an opposition to a whole nation.[5] The weight the term must bear in order to serve any useful end is well put by the former's insistence that the term 'is only fully justified if it implies systematic opposition – a sort of allergic reaction – to America as a whole'.[6] This is indeed a weighty burden, or to put it another way, a high hurdle for the concept to clear in order to serve any useful purpose. Is the bar set too high? By adopting such a standard do we become apologists, merely ensuring that no criticism can 'justifiably' be termed anti-American, and so neutering the term from the start? It is the argument herein that this definition can indeed be satisfied, that there are circumstances in which the case can be made for a 'systematic opposition ... to America as a whole', and indeed that the global environment is just such a realm in which that claim can plausibly be made.

The second dimension of the definitional work is the is/does dyad, that is, can we impugn America for what it is – its values, beliefs, foundational myths, etc. – or only for its conduct? The 'essentialist' approach certainly chimes with popularly shared ideas of America, namely, a society consumed by commerce, uncritically convinced of the notion of progress, overly religious and so on. Less appealing from a scholastic perspective is the chimerical quality of such an approach. For every perception of American religiosity in the form of tele-evangelism, there would be an equal and opposite perception of rampant secularism in MTV. Attempts at pinning down what America 'is' will invariably be subverted by the task of speaking generally and accurately about a diverse polity of 300 million people. As pertinently perhaps, the view might be taken that an 'allergic reaction' to the values of a society is a form of discrimination akin to racism (excepting the *de minimis* case of societies that hold to National Socialist or other fundamentally repugnant beliefs). Value-based societal objections of this sort seek to classify a vast swathe of humanity not on the basis of what they do but who they are and what kinships they hold. Accordingly, condemnations (or lionisations) move off from a sounder footing when they focus on the conduct of America rather than its being. As we shall see, criticising American environmental policy on the basis of its capture by corporate concerns that enjoy a disproportionate sway over governmental decision-making will have greater moment than assertions that 'Americans don't care about the environment'. Care must certainly be taken in ensuring that the evidence of 'doing' is evenly selected and deployed, but notwithstanding this modest methodological stricture, the focus on American *conduct* in respect of the environment yields a convincing account of claims of anti-Americanism in this realm.

The issue of global climate change will loom large in this analysis. Whilst not downplaying threats to biodiversity, river pollution or even zoning regulation, climate change as a focus of study has a pre-eminence in contemporary environmental discourse. Moreover, as an issue of regulatory and intellectual concern, the potential of human intervention to bring about climate change and airborne pollution has long commanded the attention of American governments and other actors. Indeed, from as early as the foundational period of the Republic, there has been an awareness of the capacity of human agency to alter the environment.

Environmental Thought in the Early American Republic

As early as the eighteenth century, there was a prominent debate in America surrounding questions of climate change and particularly the role that humans played in that process. Figures of no less standing than Thomas Jefferson – a man who claimed greater pride in his Presidency of the American Philosophical Society than that of the Nation – engaged with European thinkers in a transatlantic debate that linked climate with culture and civilisation. Ideas of this sort have origins in the ancient world,[7] but for present purposes, the debate sprang from enlightenment Europe, sections of whose elites viewed the New World with some disdain. Noting the struggles of the early colonists with the novel climate – its harsher storms and colder winters – European *philosophers* took the view that North America was a frozen, primitive and, therefore, degenerate continent. The foremost European protagonist of this school was Abbé Jean-Baptiste Du Bos whose *Critical Reflections on Poetry and Painting*[8] was praised by Voltaire as 'the most useful book ever written by a European on these matters'.[9]

Du Bos's work was principally concerned with aesthetics, making the argument that artistic genius could only flourish in countries with suitable climates. These propitious climates could be identified scientifically – they were all to be found between 25° and 52° North – and the changes in climate that took place over time accounted for the fluctuations in artistic achievement of cultures over time. Thus, Du Bos was able to arrive at a theory of climate (airs, waters and places) and culture that was able to explain the cultural highpoints, or 'Illustrious Ages', of Greece under Philip of Macedon, Rome under Julius and Augustus Caesar, sixteenth-century Italy at the time of Popes Julius II and Leo X and, of course, his own era in France under Louis XIV. Borrowing from the language of viniculture, Du Bos argued that just as the grapes of one particular year produce a characteristic vintage, so the inhabitants of a given nation at a particular time represent a cultural vintage distilled from the quality of the air and soil. Only the most favoured nations coinciding with the most favoured times would produce superior cultural distillations. Those less graced, either in terms of air or water or time, will produce table wines. The unlucky will produce vinegar.[10]

Predictably some European elites saw America as a somewhat vinegary place. However, within the terms of Du Boss' critique were the seeds for a counter argument. What distinguished his argument from his predecessors was that he wrote not merely of the linkage between culture and climate, but between culture and climate *change*. In this Du Bos was followed by luminaries such as Edward Gibbon, Johann Gottfried von Herder and ultimately the man whose candidacy for a position at the *Academie Française* he sponsored, de Montesquieu, who opened up the political implications of his ideas in the phrase, '[t]he empire of climate is the first of all empires'. By this, Montesquieu sundered the notion that European-type civilisations could not prosper in the North American climate, as it was too extreme. If moderation was possible, then Europeans could in fact colonise the New World as the climate became closer to a 'civilised' standard and, importantly, less suited to the natives.

To the generation of the Founding Fathers, the view of their nation as a substandard locus was an affront to their nascent sense of patriotism and as such strongly provocative. The upshot was a literature of apologetics in which Jefferson himself played a key role and can be seen as the catalyst for what is almost certainly the first transatlantic debate on climate change.[11] In response to Comte de Buffon's speculation that because of the cooler and more humid American climate, its flora and fauna were degenerate,[12] Jefferson launched a patriotic defence of the natural phenomena of the New World. In his *Notes of the State of Virginia*, Jefferson argues *à la* Du Bos and Hume, that the American climate is ameliorating and improving as a consequence of settlement, 'A change in our climate … is taking place very sensibly. Both heats and colds are becoming more moderate within the memory even of the middle-aged. Snows are less frequent and less deep … [t]he rivers, which then seldom failed to freeze over in the course of the winter, scarcely ever do so now'.[13]

In this and subsequent writings, Jefferson engaged in two intellectual enterprises. One was a literary debate concerned with climate and culture and change, conducted with European scholars, in the tradition of natural philosophy deploying the language of literary argument. Simultaneously, he talked about these same issues in a distinctly scientific voice, with that discipline's concern for measurement and the accumulation of statistical data.[14] Standing then at the crossroads of these traditions, Jefferson was pivotal as a prominent interlocutor in a transatlantic conversation concerning the very nature of the New World, developing a national sense of pride in not just what America was, but how it could be shaped by human agency, principally through changing the climate such that it would provide the conditions for the new nation to flourish. The related achievement of Jefferson's work in this area was his ensuring that measurements of American climate were taken before the climate changed. Both through his writings, and his example,[15] Jefferson ensured that networks of individuals developed across the nation dedicated to the accurate observation of the environment. The hope, unrealised in his lifetime, was that Federal funds, under the supervision of the American Philosophical Society, would allow such a nationwide meteorological system to develop. Nonetheless, the Society did lend its enthusiastic support to surveys of various sorts, most famously the seminal expedition of Lewis and Clark. From this point onwards, surveys, expeditions, studies and so on proliferated at the local, state and national level throughout the nineteenth century.[16]

There is little doubt that the catalyst for the systematic observation of the American environment was the dim view taken of it by European natural philosophers of the enlightenment. A combination of scientific enquiry was coupled with patriotic affrontedness to generate a distinctly American response – one that advanced the argument into the new territory of empiricism away from literary argumentation. By the commencement of the nineteenth century, a complex of meteorological systems and surveys had provided scientists with a volume of data such that new views of the climate could be arrived at.

To the extent that this episode subverts the trope of anti-Americanism that makes the claim that Americans 'don't care', the early discourse of the environment is of significance. Not only was the climate a matter of concern to intellectuals of the Foundational period, but it attracted and held the attention of figures no less than Jefferson and Madison who, in turn, spurred the development of the science of climatology.[17] Related developments in the nineteenth century such as the protection of areas of outstanding natural beauty[18] and the subsequent development of the National Park Service[19] similarly undermine the notion of American indifference to the environment. The argument might even be made that 'America's instinct for conservation has been a longstanding domestic concern'.[20]

Certainly, there is ample evidence to be had of the devastating environmental impact of the nation's industrialisation, but in this respect, it was not entirely distinguishable from other nations engaged in the same project.[21] Accordingly, 'systematic opposition' to America on the basis of this early period would either be over-inclusive (as one would then be compelled to be opposed to every other industrialised polity) or under-inclusive (as failing to account for the sophisticated debate and action on the environment). Either finding would be suspect. However, as American economic hegemony extended, the oppositional argument became easier to sustain. In terms of generating opposition to American policy, few administrations can have been as effective as those of Richard Nixon. Best known for his foreign policy exploits and domestic disgrace, there is a strong (though scarcely known) argument that Nixon's was the most environmentally significant administration in American history.

The Accidental Environmentalist – President Nixon in America

Owing to their perceived closeness to business, Republican administrations are rarely seen as environmentally progressive. In this respect, Richard Nixon could be expected to have been an exemplar. Despite hailing from San Bernardino, California, the young Nixon had an improbably fleeting relationship with nature. Academia was obviously central to the young man who won a full fee scholarship to Harvard (which he could not take up because it did not cover living expenses), but it is somewhat startling that he never ventured to the mountains and only rarely to the ocean.[22] From his brief career as a lawyer, and then his early experiences in the House of Representatives (where he made his name in the House Un-American Activities Committee) and then the Senate, there was no indication of the slightest interest in environmental issues. Nixon was, of course, the consummate politician and to the extent that substantive policy issues concerned him, they were those for which his Presidency became famous – foreign affairs. Nonetheless, on one view Nixon ranks amongst the great environmental presidents. The basis for this claim comes from the record established in the 1969–1971 period in which the institutional framework for modern environmental governance at federal level was created. Not only was this an innovation of some moment in American policymaking, but it was considerably ahead of developments taking place in comparable polities such as Japan or the European Union (EU), and it also established a regulatory approach that has gone on to have global influence.

The commonly attributed source for the Nixon administration's focus on environmental matters is the groundswell of opinion that led to the original 'Earth Day' of April 22, 1970. This outburst of democratic participation and ideological politics was created by widespread public demand for environmental protection. With over seventy million Americans participating in a variety of public events, there seemed to be a 'genuine republican moment', indicating a remarkable degree of willingness on the part of individuals to undergo sacrifices to promote the public good.[23] A political animal as astute as Nixon simply could not fail to respond to such popular sentiment. Spurred by the risk of being outflanked by Democratic congressional leaders such as Senator Muskie of Maine, Nixon moved decisively to embrace environmentalism, and the first full year of his Presidency saw him pass a comprehensive raft of environmental regulation. Nixon unfurled his new approach in the following terms:

> It is particularly fitting that my first official act of this new decade is to approve the National Environmental Policy Act ... I have

become convinced that the nineteen-seventies absolutely must be the years when America pays it debt to the past by reclaiming the purity of its air, its waters and our living environment. [The administration is] determined that the decade of the seventies will be known as the time when this country regained a productive harmony between man and nature.[24]

This message was buttressed later in January 1970, with Nixon's first State of the Union address, which stressed the importance of environmental quality and appeared to place the White House at the forefront of environmental activism. The success of this rhetorical strategy can be judged by the (largely approving) debate that followed in elite, policy, religious and other circles.[25] It would be unduly cynical, however, to see this as only so much window dressing. Following the passing of the National Environmental Policy Act, in July 1970, the Environmental Protection Agency was created and, just as importantly, new amendments to the Clean Air Act were signed into law, establishing the nation's first sweeping pollution control law. Collectively, these measures were nothing less than a revolution in environmental policy-making. As far as the latter instrument is concerned, the innovation came not from the legislative incursion into this area of activity – after all, these were amendments to the previous Clean Air Act. What was so striking about the new regime was the policy of Congress setting a national ceiling or cap for SO_x and NO_x (sulphur and nitrogen oxides) emissions, allocating a share to every major polluting plant and allowing these pollution entitlements to be traded – a model known as cap-and-trade regulation. By contrast to the traditional 'command and control' mode of pollution regulation, in which volumes of emissions are limited by administrative fiat (with all the inefficiencies that this entails), the market-based approach of cap-and-trade claims to reduce emissions in the most economically efficient way by leaving the question of allocation to the market. Under either mode, the aggregate quantity of emission saving is identical. The difference lies in the cost of abatement, with the market-based mechanism claiming significant allocative efficiency.

Notwithstanding the *accomplishment* of this legislative effort, there is ample basis on which to doubt the motivations behind these newfound environmental credentials. Nixon himself was no environmental radical and was later to describe environmentalists as advocates for 'ecological perfection at the cost of bankruptcy'. To the extent that he was energised by the issue, the popular momentum generated by Earth Day was too great even for someone of his policy dispositions to ignore. Further, much of the substantive energy for the initiatives came not from the president himself but from a group of advocates within the White House (principally John Whitaker, William Ruckelshaus, Russell Train and Walter Hickel) who operated autonomously and often in open conflict with more Conservative elements in the administration and the Republican Party as a whole.[26] However to the above-mentioned legislative record, one should also note the banning of dichlorodiphenyl-trichloroethane (DDT) and the passing of the Environmental Species Act – both against powerful corporate interests – as well as Nixon's own decisive contribution to the establishment of the United Nation's Environment Program in 1972.[27]

The fragility of this opportunistic compromise became apparent with unseemly haste. With the same speed that heralded its advent, the conviction of the environmental argument dissipated markedly in 1971. In a conversation with his Chief of Staff Bob Haldeman, Nixon said of the environment, '[it] has to be done but it's not worth a damn ... I have an uneasy feeling we're doing too much ... it's not a good political issue ... it's only a good defensive issue. We're catering to the left in all of this ... Don't play up the idea of destroying the system'.[28]

Nixon's feeling that he had milked all the potential political juice from the issue was repeated in various noted conversations throughout the spring of 1971.[29] It did not take long thereafter for the President to move decisively away from acceptance of environmental reforms. In July 1971, it was decided to examine all political bills in terms of their economic effects, which was of course a device to slow down the environmental juggernaut without 'getting caught'. Haldeman himself noted, 'economics is more important than cutting [Senator] Muskie'. The sentiment was put even more strongly one year later when Nixon himself stated, 'All the ecological arguments we hear today are for the privileged, not the underprivileged. The disadvantaged don't get the benefits of ecology. Only rich people and [Supreme Court] Justice Douglas do'.[30]

Thus, having decided that the political numbers were not stacking up in his favour on environmental matters, Nixon did not so much change gear on policy as perform an abrupt U-turn, as highlighted by his veto of the Clean Water Act in October 1972. The timing of that decision, a matter of weeks before voting began in that year's presidential election, indicates just how Nixon's calculation of the politics of the environment had shifted since the heady days of 1970. Given his landslide victory over George McGovern in the 1972 election, it is certainly arguable that Nixon read these runes accurately.

Any analysis of this period is bound to balance the record of substantive accomplishment with the low politics that gave the environmental cause its initial momentum and just as quickly undermined it. What should not be forgotten is that whatever the president's own approach, the manifestation of popular opinion in favour of stronger environmental awareness and protection in the Spring of 1970 is significant for the light it casts on the attitudes of large sections of the American population. As such it cannot be lightly dismissed nor can the fact that the Democrats held majorities in both chambers during Nixon's first term and formed a powerful pro-environment faction in the legislature.[31] Seen in these terms, and coupled with the infrastructural achievement of the brief moment of environmental activism, the charge of anti-Americanism sits ill with this period. The dubious motives of the administration are beyond argument,[32] but both the popular and constitutional structures of America were concerned with environmental protection to such a degree that the social movement environmentalism was firmly installed in the American polity by 1973.

The Development of International Environmental Agreements

At the same time as the Watergate Scandal unfolded during the Nixon government's second term, an even more momentous story, in environmental terms at least, was brewing at the University of Berkeley. In a paper that would two decades later earn them a Nobel Prize in Chemistry, Mario Molina and Sherwood Rowland argued that stratospheric ozone could be destroyed by releases of chlorofluorocarbons (CFCs).[33] Since their discovery in 1928, the use of CFCs expanded rapidly. The non-toxic, highly stable and cheap chemical answered any number of industrial production questions, from the propulsion of aerosols to refrigeration and cleaning microchips. Notwithstanding its apparently boundless uses, Molina and Rowland discovered that after release, CFCs make their way into the stratosphere, break down after exposure to solar radiation and then release chlorine, which destroys ozone. In turn, ozone depletion creates a risk to planetary survival that is difficult to overstate.

The press and television reporting of this scientific paper was considerable in the United States, generating much popular concern.[34] The United States National Academy of Sciences responded quickly with a follow-up study to the Molina-Rowland paper, predicting that CFC releases could deplete the ozone layer by up to 7 percent – a substantial risk. Of particular importance for our later discussion, even though a casual link between stratospheric ozone depletion and CFCs was at that point still unproven, the United States moved decisively (and unilaterally) to restrict the consumption and production of CFCs.[35] This lead was followed by Belgium, Canada, Norway, Brazil, Australia and the EU.[36]

As welcome as these essentially uncoordinated national measures were, the recognition of the ongoing risk from CFCs to the global climate led to international efforts to address the problem, culminating in the Vienna Convention for the Protection of the Ozone Layer in March 1985. Sands notes that, '[t]he United States led international efforts to address the problem, and in 1985, after five years of tortuous negotiations, much delayed by sceptical Europeans, more than 130 countries adopted a global convention to protect the ozone layer'.[37]

The Vienna agreement is a 'framework' convention, that is, one which does not require any specific timetables or targets of abatement from signatories but rather creates a forum within which monitoring can take place, with appropriate action being coordinated and more concrete measures pursued in the future. The Vienna Convention was no sooner than agreed upon than new scientific evidence emerged that more demanding action was required to safeguard the environment.[38] The resulting Montreal Protocol on Substances that Deplete the Ozone Layer (1987) imposed obligations of hitherto unknown stringency. The production and use of many ozone layer hostile substances was banned, including CFCs as aerosol propellants and in domestic refrigeration. For developing countries, who argued that they had not caused the problem and so should be treated less strictly, permission was given to continue to use CFCs for a decade, and financial assistance was given to develop chemical alternatives. In the view of the distinguished commentator Jim Hansen, 'The result [of the Vienna Convention and Montreal Protocol] is that the use of CFCs is now decreasing, the ozone layer was damaged but not destroyed, and it will soon be recovering'.[39]

Again we see a narrative of American environmental activism, this time in the international arena, which is inconsistent with claims of American indifference to matters environmental. Certainly, as Jim Hansen notes, the impetus for action came from domestic public concern arising from the Molina-Rowland paper, not from enlightened government. From the perspective of grassroots or bottom-up politics, this episode reflects well on the capacity of the American constitutional system to act as a conveyor belt that transmits popular interests and concerns to the government that then feels compelled to act. As to the specifics of the landmark international environmental agreements at Vienna and Montreal, a number of points are noteworthy. Firstly, discussions of America and the environment frequently juxtapose the virtue of the EU with the self-serving attitude of America. In respect of the domestic environmental achievements of the Nixon administration, it is notable that these preceded any action taken by the then European Community. This is unsurprising given that until the Single European Act of 1986, the European Community had no express environmental competence,[40] making such comprehensive environmental action outwith its legal authority until relatively recently. Of course, this did not prevent individual member states from taking action on their own, and many did, but the Vienna/Montreal negotiations again reveal that European attitudes towards the environment were far from uniformly principled.

Away from comparative assessments of transatlantic environmental virtue, one of the key issues in contemporary environmental law and policy is what is known as the 'precautionary principle'. This phrase reflects the recognition that scientific certainty often comes too late to design effective legal and policy responses for preventing many potential environmental threats, and so the principle addresses how decisions should be made in the face of scientific uncertainty. It is notable that this is very much the approach adopted by the United States negotiators in respect to the Montreal Protocol, whilst 'it was the European Community members who balked at the science and the economic and lifestyle consequences of international actions'.[41]

In a similar vein, mention might be made of the approach taken to developing countries by the United States in the Montreal negotiations. By taking a demanding approach to the issue of CFC use and production, there would evidently be asymmetric impacts on developed and less developed nations. The better off nations and economies of the world will always be better able to adjust to the demands of a new CFC regime, by developing their own alternative chemicals, technologies or processes, or simply by absorbing the cost of forgoing from such conduct. However hard such impacts are on wealthy nations, they are always doubly so for the poor. Additionally, such limits would impose burdens on developing countries that developed economies did not have to labour under at the equivalent stage of their economic histories. The failure to deal with these issues is not merely one of moral import but also of negotiating significance. International legal compacts are, at their base, agreements and in order to achieve buy-in from poorer nations, these nations need an incentive to participate. Larger nations such as India, China and Brazil, with burgeoning economies, aspirational citizens and a leadership function amongst their peers would need to be convinced that a treaty that made refrigeration more difficult was in their interests. In this respect, the United States again played an important role. In 1990, amendments were made to the Montreal Protocol, which allowed developed countries to join in by giving a ten-year grace period to meet targets and a timetable for the phasing out of production and use, as well as financial compensation towards facilitating that end.

An indication of the significance of the United States' role in these negotiations can be seen in the remarks of a prominent critic of American legal action.

The United States played a major role in brokering rules that would allow India and China to sign [the 1990 Amendments]. The Montreal Protocol has now been ratified by almost every country in the world [and] is frequently hailed as an international instrument that will be effective: American legal creativity and political muscle helped to make it a truly global instrument.[42]

Global Warming and Climate Change – New Challenges, Approaches

Concerns about climate change and calls for international action began in the 1970s and continued in the 1980s. By 1990, the spectre of global warming loomed so large that the United Nations authorised an Intergovernmental Negotiating Committee on Climate to begin discussions on a global treaty. Simultaneously, the Intergovernmental Panel on Climate Change was charged with assessing the scientific, technical and economic basis of climate change policy in preparation for the 1992 Earth Summit.[43] The Intergovernmental Panel on Climate Change (IPCC)'s first interim report was published in May 1990[44] and provided what was then the strongest evidence that atmospheric concentrations of green house gases (including CO_2) had increased significantly as a result of industrialisation and that these concentrations were contributing to increases in climate temperatures and subsequently sea levels. On a 'business as usual' basis, the report predicted rises in global temperature of about 2°C by 2025 and 4°C by 2100, and sea levels rising by 20 centimetres by 2030 and 65 centimetres by 2100.

A plethora of unilateral target setting[45] followed in the wake of the IPCC's report, with America's approach heavily shaped by President Bush Sr's Council of Economic Advisers.[46] The Council argued that the costs of reducing green house gases would be between 35 and 150 times more expensive than compliance with the Montreal Protocol and concluded that,

> the highest priority in the near term should be to improve understanding in order to build a foundation for sound policy decisions. Until such a foundation was in place, there was no justification for imposing major costs on the economy in order to slow the growth of greenhouse gas emissions.[47]

Such was the basic approach of the United States when entering the negotiations that led to the UN Conference on Environment and Development (UNCED) (or the 'Earth Summit') in Rio de Janeiro in June 1992. Negotiations opened in February 1991 just outside Washington DC. Already by this time, the major global players had set their basic positions. The European Community was committed to reducing its joint greenhouse gas emissions to 1990 levels by the year 2000, with financial assistance to help developing nations respond to climate change. The Japanese suggested that 'emissions of CO_2 should be stabilised on a per capita basis in the year 2000 and beyond at about the same level as in 1990'. The Group of seventy-seven developing countries proceeded from the position that 75 percent of energy-related CO_2 emissions were attributable to industrialised countries but acknowledged that developing countries ought not to proceed down the same path. To that end, industrialised countries should transfer environmentally sound technology to developing countries on preferential and non-commercial terms. Further, they called for the creation of a differentiated regime under the climate convention for developing countries, along the lines of the Montreal Protocol.

The American negotiating stance could scarcely have been more distinct, with its outright rejection of targets and timetables of the sort mooted by the EC and Japan. Described as a 'no regrets policy', the stance was that any new energy technology would only be considered if it produced benefits in addition to those related to global warming. Thus, initiatives would only be supported by the United States if they could also be shown to be more cost effective or to reduce urban pollution.[48] America also urged for further research to resolve scientific uncertainties and for a comprehensive approach to the reduction of all greenhouse gas emissions.

The bulk of 1991 was consumed with transatlantic diplomacy as the EC sought to persuade the United States to accept targets and timetables. All such advocacy was robustly resisted. There were hopes in December 1991 that the hard line position might be ameliorated with the resignation of the White House Chief of Staff John Sununu – one of the most committed opponents to greenhouse gas controls. However, in Goldberg's analysis,

> there was simply not enough time to make large scale revisions … The commitment section of the Chairman's text acknowledged the fact that a legally binding commitment to reduce greenhouse gases was beyond reach if the US was to be a signatory … The Chairman blamed the weak and ambiguous GHG commitment language squarely on the US …
> … the difference a constructive US approach might have made should not be overstated … a firm commitment to any targets and timetables would have been a significant improvement and might have accelerated the entire process of negotiating an effective global warming agreement by a year or more.[49]

Whatever the disappointments arising from the United Nations Framework Convention on Climate Change (UNFCCC), it did establish an international and legally binding mechanism for future progress to be made in combating climate change. Most significant in this respect was the new institutional framework for the continued implementation of the Protocol and the progressive development of the regime through protocols or amendments. Following the model established by the Vienna/Montreal agreements, the UNFCCC vested policymaking authority to a 'Conference of the Parties', with day-to-day monitoring of implementation being undertaken by a permanent Secretariat.

Putting these undoubted accomplishments to one side, it is clear that the first Bush administration can extract little credit from it. In contrast to earlier agreements, the United States adopted an approach that was decidedly inward looking. Whereas the effort to tackle ozone depletion was marked by repeated and successful attempts to ensure significant international comity, the UNFCCC negotiations exhibited almost the opposite tendency. The primary reason for this appears to be the question of cost and its capture of the United States agenda. Supported by the principal oil producing countries, the United States was unwilling to allow a Convention that would fix specific targets and timetables for the stabilisation of greenhouse gas emissions. Further, the previous United States approach to scientific uncertainty, so critical to the success of the Montreal Protocol, was unceremoniously rejected. The precautionary principle, so influential at Montreal, was rejected wholesale by the Americans in Rio.

The Kyoto Protocol and the Clinton Administration

Five years separated the ambiguous achievements of the UNFCCC and the next and perhaps most significant of all international environmental agreements, the Kyoto Protocol of 1997. These years were marked by decisive scientific and political developments, with the IPCC's report of 1995 being the greatest of the former. Described as 'one of the most significant milestones in the development of the climate change regime', the report for the first time reported a consensus amongst scientists that 'the balance of evidence suggests that there is a discernible human influence on global climate'. The polarising effect of such a statement can be imagined, with the bulk of scientific opinion endorsing the IPCC's findings and a small but well-organised minority disputing them.[50] On the political plane, the elevation of Bill Clinton to the White House was of no less significance to the shape of international environmental agreements to come.[51]

President Clinton wasted no time in distancing himself from his predecessor in environmental terms. Whilst President George H.W. Bush had signed the UNFCCC (making the United States the very first nation so to do) and the Senate had ratified it in October 1992, the incoming president broke from the path of limited policy ambition by committing the United States to reducing its emissions of greenhouse gases to 1990 levels by 2000 – the fabled target and timetable that had proved so elusive only months previously. Whilst the new administration's 'Climate Change Action Plan' of October was not materially different to that which would have been produced by a Bush administration (acknowledging that the United States would fall short of its greenhouse gas (GHG) emission goals by 50 percent), it was very different in tone.[52] The new view of the Democratic administration transformed the debate on climate change regulation at both the international and the domestic plane in a dramatic fashion.

At the second of the 'Conferences of the Parties' (COP) held in Berlin in July 1996, the new United States Head of Delegation (Undersecretary of State for Global Affairs, Timothy Wirth) announced the Clinton administration's *volte face* regarding timetables and targets, and its acceptance of the scientific findings from the IPCC's 1995 Report. Embracing the UNFCCC's commitment to 'common but differentiated responsibilities', Wirth's statement supported legally binding commitments for GHG emission reductions for thirty-four industrialised nations and no targets for 154 others, clearing the way for a new settlement which became known as the Berlin Mandate. At home however the new approach generated such hostility that in July 1997 the Senate resolved, by a vote of ninety-five to zero, that the United States should not approve any agreement at the upcoming third Conference of the Parties in Kyoto that would harm United States economic interests, and that did not impose binding emission reduction targets on all parties.[53]

With apparent agreement having broken down between all major groupings at the Kyoto COP, the Berlin Mandate formed the basis of the now famous Kyoto Protocol on Climate Change.[54] The industrialised nations made legally binding commitments to reduce their GHG emissions; in the case of the United States, it was agreed that it would bring its emissions to 7 percent below its 1990 levels by the compliance period 2008–2012. This was certainly a modest target, but it should be noted that the stated goal of the UNFCCC was to 'stabilise' emissions, not slash them radically. Further, on a business-as-usual scenario the 7 percent target translated to approximately a 30 percent reduction over a period.

The active participation of Vice-President Gore in the Kyoto negotiations is well documented, as is his support for the instrument. In addition to the symbolic importance of this stance for coalescing support around the Protocol, the United States delegation's contribution to the substance of the agreement is also significant. It will be recalled that the Clean Air Act regime in the United States had long deployed market-based mechanisms – in particular, an emissions trading scheme – to reduce acid rain in North America. The effectiveness of the scheme was remarkable,[55] and given this experience, it was not surprising that the United States was keen to export this mechanism to the international plane, with 'strong and unwavering support for cost-effective approaches' forming a 'key component of the Clinton administration's climate change policy'.[56]

It is these very market mechanisms (known as 'flexibility mechanisms' in the language of the Protocol) that have marked out the Kyoto Protocol as such an innovative legal instrument. Notably, the EU was long opposed to such a regulatory approach and fought a bitter rear guard action against their incorporation at Kyoto before yielding on the issue on the understanding that it was a necessary condition for America's participation in the agreement. It reflects well on the EU, that having set aside its long-held suspicions of emissions trading in order to facilitate a global compact, it then embraced the concept with considerable vim, moving quickly to establish the EU Emissions Trading Scheme – now the world's leading emissions trading market.[57]

The Kyoto Protocol can thus been seen as a qualified, but very real, success. It certainly did not end the need for further negotiations – further COPs at Buenos Aires, The Hague and Bonn followed quickly. Nor could the relatively modest emission reductions of Kyoto ever be expected to address and reverse the environmental challenges identified by the scientific mainstream. Technical problems relating to compliance could also be identified.[58] From an anti-Americanism perspective, the agreement is significant for the fact that it represents a firm US commitment to return to the mainstream in international environmental governance. This does not of course mean that the United States would be compliant in negotiations, but the acceptance of targets and timetables was a profoundly important step. As was noted in respect of the earlier Montreal Protocol, the engagement of the United States in this respect allowed it to deploy its diplomatic muscle such that it was able to create the Kyoto Protocol in its own image, by including the market mechanisms of emissions trading, the Clean Development Mechanism (which allows industrialised nations to offset their emissions by undertaking abatement with a developing country), and Joint Implementation (which allows industrialised nations jointly to reduce their emissions) into the agreement. President Clinton said of Kyoto that it was an

> historic agreement … to take unprecedented action to address global warming. It is environmentally strong and economically

sound [and reflected] the commitment of the United States to use the tools of the free market to tackle this difficult problem.[59]

Be that as it may, a pair of related issues remained to be resolved before the Kyoto Protocol could come into force. The first was the Protocol's own requirement of a 'double trigger'. To become legally binding, the Protocol would have to be ratified by at least fifty-five parties to the Framework Convention, and those ratifiers must account for at least 55 percent of all green house gas emissions of the industrialised nations. This meant that the first element of the 'trigger' could be easily satisfied, whilst the second required that at least two of the three largest emitters – the United States (36 percent), the EU (24 percent) and Russia (17 percent) – must join the Protocol in order for it to be binding. The Byrd–Hagel Resolution and bipartisan senatorial opposition to the Protocol saw domestic US politics present a significant barrier to the Kyoto Protocol's progress. This fact was of course not lost on President Clinton himself. Despite the United States becoming the 60th signatory to the Protocol in November 1998, it was never presented to the Senate for ratification – the then embattled President having no desire to become the Senate's whipping boy. (The official line was that, as the Kyoto Protocol did not meet the stipulations of Byrd – Hagel, the Clinton administration had no intention of submitting it for senatorial ratification.) In the absence of American ratification, Kyoto slipped into something of a legal limbo. As the American domestic scene became preoccupied with a presidential election, the pertinent question was what stance the Republican challenger, George W. Bush, would take on these issues.

The Decline and Fall of American Environmentalism

No story in contemporary environmental law and politics is better known than President George W. Bush's contrary attitude towards global warming, the Kyoto Protocol and international law generally. The quasicomical stereotypes of an oafish Texas oilman and stooge of the American corporate world did not fill environmentalists with confidence. Inevitably, the narrative is somewhat more complex, even if the ending is predictable.

Bush actually undertook to reduce America's CO_2 emissions during the presidential campaign, albeit without committing to Kyoto. Upon taking office, he appointed Paul O'Neill to the key post of US Treasury Secretary. At first blush, this sent a signal that environmental concerns were not at the top of the president's agenda. After all, O'Neill had for the past quarter century been the Chief Executive Officer (CEO) of Alcoa, the world's largest aluminium producer. Not only did heavy industry, as a massive energy user, not sit easily with stringent environmental controls, but the aluminium industry was exactly that sector of the economy most threatened by Kyoto. In this appointment though, Bush apparently had underestimated the independence of O'Neill and was likely oblivious to his environmental instincts.

As early as 1997, O'Neill had given great prominence to the issue of global warming in Alcoa's Annual Report, making the remarkable statement, 'We are environmentalists first and industrialists second'. Corporate statements need not always been taken at face value, but O'Neill's conduct as Treasury Secretary reveals those words to have had real substance. In his very first meeting with the new president, O'Neill raised the issue of global climate change and was asked to 'get [President Bush] a plan on global warming'.[60] The resulting plan, communicated to the President in February 2001, overtly aimed to knit United States policy within the timetables of the ongoing COP,[61] proceeded from a rigorously scientific basis and rather ambitiously sought to link environmental policy with an energy policy review then being undertaken by Vice-President Cheney.[62]

Simultaneously, Bush's senior administrator at the Environmental Protection Agency, Christine Todd Whitman, was testifying before a congressional committee and speaking from a script on global warming that few could have predicted. Her testimony, which enraged elements within the energy industry, stated 'there's no question but that global warming is a real phenomenon that is occurring. And while scientists can't predict where the droughts will occur, where the flooding will occur precisely, or when, we know those things will occur ...'[63]

The *Oil & Gas Journal,* citing both the testimony and the Bush's proposed energy policy, which acknowledged the importance of carbon dioxide limits, attacked the regulation of carbon dioxide as an air pollutant as 'a bad idea that belongs on the outer fringes of environmental extremism'.[64] Internationally however, the new administration's unexpectedly open-minded stance convinced the UN to delay the scheduled Bonn COP from May until the summer of 2001, at the administration's behest. Whitman herself won further international plaudits for the administration when on March 5, 2001, at a G8 Environment Ministers' meeting in Italy, she was reported by the *Financial Times* to have said, 'The President has said global climate change is the greatest environmental challenge that we face and that we must recognise that and take steps to move forward', a tone that 'pleasantly surprised' many delegates 'who feared that the United States would ignore the problem of global warming'.[65]

This appears to have been the high point of optimism that Bush would act on climate change in a scientific rather than self-interested manner, in accordance with the international community. Apparently sensing the precariousness of her position, Whitman immediately drafted a memo to the President that has been described as her 'laying down the gauntlet'.

> I would strongly recommend that you continue to recognise that global warming is a real and serious issue.
>
> While not specifically endorsing the targets called for in Kyoto, you could indicate that you are exploring how to reduce US greenhouse gas emissions internally and will continue no matter what else transpires.
>
> Mr President, this [global warming] is a credibility issue for the US in the international community. It is also an issue that is resonating here, at home. We need to appear engaged and shift the discussion from the focus on the 'K' word to action, but we have to build some bonafides first.
>
> We did win some issues at this [Trieste] meeting ... I'm available to discuss this further if you want.[66]

Even the modest position outlined by Whitman proved too much for what is now routinely viewed as the cabal surrounding President Bush. On March 8, a letter was sent to the president from a quartet of conservative Republican senators (including Chuck Hagel of the eponymous resolution and Jesse Helms) opposed to the Kyoto Protocol. It was a withering response to the messages that Whitman's diplomacy had been sending to the outside world and unflinching in its opposition to any regulation of CO_2 and other greenhouse gases.[67] The letter was devastating to Whitman and O'Neill, who had by now joined forces to co-ordinate on what they viewed as 'one of the few issues of current policy that is subject to rational thought [in the White House]'.[68] They were in no doubt that the real author of the joint letter was Vice-President Cheney.[69]

Any lingering hopes that the new administration would take a positive step on the global warming question were decisively crushed when Whitman met with the president on March 13, armed with an Environmental Protection Agency (EPA) report, 'setting forth the mountain of evidence already assembled, along with proposals for action both outside Kyoto and, if necessary, within the framework of the international protocol'. The meeting is recalled in O'Neill's memoirs and is worth setting out at length.

> [Whitman] started right in, talking about the importance of promoting international cooperation, the areas of scientific evidence that were indisputable, the issue of US credibility.
>
> Bush cut her off. 'Christie, I've already made my decision.' He had a letter all ready to send back to Hagel, Helms and the others. He read her portions of it.
>
> He would oppose Kyoto because it exempted 80 percent of the world, including China and India, and it was an 'unfair and ineffective means of addressing global climate change concerns'.
>
> … with the California energy shortages … we just can't harm consumers, he said. It only took a moment for Bush to recount the high points of what he'd be telling Hagel, Helms, and the rest of the world.
>
> Whitman just sat. It was a clean kill. She was running around the world, using her own hard-won, bipartisan credibility to add colour and depth to his campaign pronouncements, and now she ended up looking like the fool.[70]

Quite apart from its stark description of the Bush administration as one in which evidence, analysis and debate are rarely troubled with (a key point in O'Neill's memoirs), the above quotation clearly demonstrates the tensions that existed in the Bush White House, between officials, executive officers and even between the President and elements within his own office. It could scarcely be said that the president represented the views of his own advisors on this issue (except in the most formal sense), much less those of the nation. Over half of the states subsequently adopted their own emissions reduction plans.[71] Yet more surprising is the fact that many titans of corporate America such as Goldman Sachs, Intel and even Wal-Mart, are taking meaningful steps to 'green' their activities.[72] General Electric's CEO has even called for the Senate to ratify the Kyoto Protocol.[73] Whilst this was once a fanciful idea, the bipartisan Climate Stewardship Act 2003, sponsored by Senators Lieberman and McCain and containing much of the substance of the Kyoto Protocol, was only defeated in the Senate by a margin of forty-three to fifty-five. Quite how those numbers would play out in a post-Hurricane Katrina Senate is anyone's guess.

Conclusions

This chapter has sought to discern patterns and continuities in the way 'America' thinks about and acts in respect of the environment. To the extent that the notion of anti-Americanism was pinned down at the commencement of this chapter, it is not clear that such an attitude is justified by the above narrative. The claim that America does not care about the environment is too simplistic to detain us for long. Certainly, the Bush Presidency has not shown itself to be its champion, but there have been profound countervailing forces, both within and out with the administration. The early colonists proved themselves to have an anxious interest in this question, albeit not from a perspective that twenty-first century advocates might wish. Of President Nixon's own fleeting and political engagement, we might set aside our antipathy at his motives when having regard to the remarkable institutional apparatus (and global example) that he established.

To return to the definition of Toinet, can we claim that American environmental in/action is such that it fully justifies a 'systematic opposition – a sort of allergic reaction – to America as a whole'?[74] This seems doubtful. There is certainly no shortage of American conduct that we might disapprove of, that many Americans might themselves disapprove of, but in this respect, few polities are absolved responsibility. Whilst the Nixon administration was crafting a highly effective set of mechanisms to deal with acid rain, the EU lacked even the basic consti-tutional tools to take action of any sort. The intellectual leadership that the United States demonstrated in the development of both the Montreal and the Kyoto Protocols similarly cannot be gainsaid and has since been endorsed by the EU and its member states despite their opposition at the time.

However, to the extent that anti-Americanism is identified with anti-Bushism, there may be a case to be answered. When reading the account of an activist environmental lawyer lambasting Bush for intellectual weakness and acting with crass self-interest, we might be tempted to file it away as a hostile account from an implacable foe.[75] When a scion of corporate America and former aide to President Ford narrates an identical account (and was there at the time),[76] we cannot but take note. Contrary to the advice of his senior officials, the approach of a majority of the States of the Union, leading corporate actors and in the face of overwhelming scientific consensus,[77] President Bush has denied the fact of anthropogenic climate change. He has refused to engage with the rest of the world in tackling the problem and departed from a noble American tradition of accepting the precautionary principle as the basis of scientific decision-making and even withdrawn from the elementary precept of fairness in treating nations in different economic positions differently. Insofar as we might be able to justify an 'allergic reaction' to American approaches to the environment, they map closely to those taken by George W. Bush.

Chapter 8
American Democracy and Anti-Americanism Since 2000

Graeme Orr[1]

This chapter explores the role that perceptions of US democracy play in anti-American thought and rhetoric, particularly following the election of President George W. Bush. The focus on 'democracy' will be on electoral systems, though they are just one – albeit a cornerstone – feature of democracy, which also encompasses the public space and relations between citizen, government and media.

Bush's initial election in 2000 provided a volte, not because the cupboard of electoral history was free of controversies and scandals, nor because Florida 2000 lay bare any shocking truths. Rather, the high farce of Florida's 'hanging chads', and the spectre of an 'unelected' president emerging from the Supreme Court halting the recounting of disputed votes, became a lightning rod for disbelieving criticism of the gulf that sometimes exists between the dreams of democratic theory and the realities of electoral practice.

Most of the angst and introspection occurred within, rather than outside. The United States True international reaction was laced with *Schadenfreude* at the balloon of the 'world's leading democracy' bursting.[2] Often, behind diplomatic rhetoric and expressions of concern, lay the taunt, 'get your own house in order'. The United States, having supported, cajoled, hectored and occasionally invaded other countries in the name of democracy was wide open to accusations of hypocrisy. Even if it were not an 'exporter of democracy', the America's superpower status would ensure worldwide interest in its political shenanigans; so great is American influence that some foreigners almost expect to have a say in its political affairs. Whilst colouring ongoing rejection of his legitimacy abroad (where he is frequently portrayed as an accidental, even 'fictitious'[3] president, an aberration that continues despite the swing he enjoyed in 2004), the response to Bush's election in 2000 has proved muted and short-lived. Concerns about the health of US democracy are not an enduring catalyst for anti-Americanism, especially in contrast to US foreign and economic policy or its military and cultural hegemony.

Nonetheless, amongst all nations, politics in the United States sits in a uniquely liminal space. Politics elsewhere, except in egregious or revolutionary situations, is seen as an essentially internal affair, but US politics can be categorised neither as a purely internal affair nor as a truly international concern. The unique power and roles of the United States means that a significant percentage of the globe not only takes an interest in its politics but feels strongly enough to engage in an ongoing critique of it. Americans may be flattered or offended by this.

Whatever the level of international interest in the health of US democracy, interest within the United States is higher. This is as it should be. It is *their* democracy and, as we'll see, it is a democracy under numerous strains. But it is also quite a saving grace. In the United States, electoral reform is an ongoing agenda item – albeit one sometimes stifled by vested interests and institutional constraints – in a way that is rare amongst liberal democracies.

The 'Ism' that Isn't

Anti-Americanism is a protean concept. Undoubtedly there are parts of the world where it feeds political agendas, even violent ones. However, even there, the United States tends to be invoked as an emblem for opposition to western influence more generally. (Thus, from prison, Indonesia cleric Abu Bakar Ba'asyir makes the fatwa-like pronouncement, 'Muslims who don't hate America, sin.'[4] But his agenda is not the United States per se, but driving out 'infidels' and proselytising his brand of Islam, by force if necessary.)

To think of anti-Americanism as an 'ism' is a category error. There is no coherent body of anti-American thought, let alone a movement. There is nothing capable or deserving of being reified into an 'ism', even in the debased currency of that suffix captured in the chant bequeathed by John Lennon, 'Everybody's talking about … this-ism, that-ism, ism, ism, ism'.[5]

But there is such a thing as *Americanism*. By that term, I mean there are stereotypes of America, consisting of assumptions, claims and caricatures about US values and institutions. 'Americanism' is a bundle of perceptions of what distinctively defines America or being American.[6] Anti-Americanism, therefore, consists of knee-jerk responses to such stereotypes. It is a negative reflex or tendency.

Similarly, if we leave aside politically or religiously manufactured hostility, anti-Americanism, at least in its western manifestations, should not be conflated with prejudice, unless that term is leached of its pejorative connotations. Citizens and residents of the United States can be anti-American, at the same time as they enjoy living there and without being misanthropic towards their countrymen. (True prejudice can be identified through an indirect test. When Africans or Indians are mistaken for Aboriginal Australians, they invariably experience that as blind and invidious discrimination. In contrast, when Canadians are routinely mistaken for Americans because of the similarity in accents, they resent the mistake. Not because they fear being treated as an American, but because the shadow cast by their larger and brasher neighbour breeds a form of sibling rivalry.[7])

This understanding of anti-Americanism as a reactive manifestation of a stereotyping of things American, and not as an 'ism' or oppressive prejudice, is not just the most accurate way to appreciate the phenomena. It is also a fruitful and necessary one for reflecting on international understandings and misunderstandings of US democracy. US democracy is complex, and few outsiders have a coherent or contextualised appreciation of it. Instead, people are often hypercritical of failings in US democracy, based on perceptions, assumptions, claims and myths about American values and practices, that is, based on 'Americanisms'. Such Americanisms are both positive and negative. America is assumed and expected – because it claims – to be a model of individual liberty, free speech and formal equality; yet America is also seen as being controlled by vested interests and hierarchies of money and race. People are habituated to expect more from US democracy than is reasonable, and paradoxically, to be quick to find and condemn its flaws.[8] Between the idea and the reality, as Eliot said, 'fall such shadows'.

The International Response to the 2000 Election

The 2000 presidential campaign was unassuming: two lacklustre candidates trying to cast themselves in as moderate a light as possible. The 2000 presidential poll, in comparison, from the moment the networks prematurely called the decisive state of Florida for George W. Bush, was a compelling mix of administrative embarrassment, political gamesmanship and litigious warfare.

Under the microscopic scrutiny caused by the dead heat, various facts about US electoral practice came to be seen as dirty secrets. Some were presented as grounds for claims that Democrat Al Gore deserved, legally or morally, to be president. Many of these faults were attributable to the absence of any centralised electoral administration or even code of national rules for national elections. Electors were subject to different rules defining and enabling the franchise in different states and voted on different technologies and ballot designs in different counties. The confusion became symbolised by the 'hanging chad' – punch-card ballot papers that were imperfectly punched so that they were not counted by electronic card-readers, but subject to lengthy and contentious recounts relying on the naked eye. The election was thrown to the courts, where the Supreme Court ultimately stamped a conservative authority on the outcome by halting the Democrats' efforts to have a full recount of ballots in selected counties.[9] Mistrust in the process was magnified because election officials, all the way up to the Floridian Secretary of State, a Bush ally, were partisan in the sense of being elected or registered with one party or another.

In a nation used to an instantaneous verdict on election night, five weeks of confusion and high farce elapsed between polling day and Supreme Court verdict. From financial markets and world leaders issued the usual concerns that accompany any close or disputed election (ignoring the facts that democracy does not exist merely to provide stability for markets or diplomacy, and that the outgoing President Clinton still had two months to serve).

Governments in Africa, along with the Russian Duma, were soon gleefully echoing Cuban President Fidel Castro's teasing offer to send election observers across the Straits of Florida. The Cuban Foreign Minister chimed in, reflecting the sense of many American opponents that the America's democratic credentials had been exposed as hubris, if not hypocrisy: 'Those in the United States who have always tried to become judges of the elections that take place elsewhere must be receiving a lesson of modesty and humbleness'.[10] Official Iraqi media decried the elections as comic, and claimed wildly – especially since the result prevented Gore's running-mate, Joe Lieberman, from becoming the first Jewish vice-president – that 'the electoral strings are pulled by the Jews'.[11]

Whilst such complaints aligned foreign responses to the 2000 presidential debacle with broader critiques of the (inevitable) shortfall between US rhetoric and record, as reflections on US democracy they were either ironical or risible. Florida 2000 was almost an electoral meltdown.[12] But it was not evidence of any absence of democratic essentials so much as a system meltdown, caused in part through a chaotic *excess* of rules for democracy and institutional checks and balances.

For rulers of one-party states to taunt the United States on its internal democracy was so hypocritical that one suspects they spoke with tongues firmly in cheeks. Ordinary folk, craving greater democracy for themselves, were more likely to echo the Cameroon worker who said the election debacle seemed 'incredible' given that the United States 'is globally considered the father of democracy'.[13] His was a sentiment of lament rather than glee.

Amongst America's western stable mates, reaction was also mixed. Even friendly critics echoed the 'get your house in order' refrain with comments that 'Americans need to tend their own democracy before bothering themselves about the state of others'.[14] More egregiously flavoured media responses managed to mix apparent despair with bombastic condemnation:

> [At Bush's inauguration] there will be American-style pageantry and grand speeches about the best democracy in the world. But the myths have gone. The masks are off.[15]
> [N]obody could imagine that the citizens of a nation that once sent a man to the moon, would stare through punch cards for months to find out who could be its next president. After the pathetic procedures surrounding the counting of votes … America lost some of its authority.[16]

Such disorder, unimaginable in most democratic countries, does no honour to the United States. And it is worrying that the fate of the world hangs suspended upon such an archaic system.[17]

At the very least, this incident shows there is something rotten in Jeb Bush's Florida. More seriously it shows an operational defect in American democracy.[18]

But the general tone, when not showing sympathy, was one of finding, amongst the comic debris, cause to reinforce stereotypical Americanisms. This could be found even amongst newspapers otherwise wedded to their countries' alliances to the United States:

> From Baghdad to Belgrade, the world's only superpower has been the butt of jokes about its outdated vote-counting technology and archaic

electoral college system that denies whoever gets a majority from being elected to office, and, of course, that very American predilection for going to the courts when things don't go your own way.[19]

Invariably, of course, the jokes originated not abroad, but with the scriptwriters for US talk shows or American wags on the Internet.[20]

Not all of the criticism was tinged with suspicion of Bush or the Republican-leaning supreme court. The *Wall Street Journal Europe* attacked Gore's decision to initiate court-ordered recounts, invoking folk myths about American competitiveness descending into a win-at-all-costs mentality:

> It seems America has moved on from its mother's-milk adages to one of more recent vintage: Winning isn't everything, but losing is nothing. ... Mr Gore's team – as it shopped for the friendliest judges to hear its cases – updated Kennedy: 'Ask not what you can do for your country, ask what smart lawyers can do for you.' 'If at first you don't succeed, try, try again.' No statement is more American.[21]

Focal Points of Criticism of US Democracy

There is a litany of complaints about US democracy. In what follows, I group and briefly explore the key ones under seven headings. The first five are the roles of dynasties and celebrity, money, religion, lawyers and race. The last two are flaws in electoral systems and voter disengagement.

Whilst some are serious, and all have some basis in truth, many are caricatures – one-sided Americanisms or decontextualised assumptions. When understood in the context of both political and social culture, the picture of US democracy is made complex and seen three dimensionally. Only then can its truly unusual features be identified. On the whole, it will be found, the features of US democracy are not uniquely distinctive Americanisms but variants or accentuations on failings of modern, mass democracy generally.

Dynasty and Celebrity

For a republic that was born out of a rebellion against a hereditary monarchy, electoral politics in the United States can seem peculiarly dynastic. In this critique, George W. Bush and his brother, Florida Governor Jeb Bush, are the spoilt scions of a preppie oil millionaire, George Bush Sr. Thus the eminent British scientist, Professor Richard Dawkins, simultaneously declared his love for the United States and his flabbergast that a country that led the world in 'civilised attainment' could elect someone so catastrophically unqualified as the junior Bush:

> Would you do business with a company that devoted an entire year to little else than the process of choosing its new CEO, from the strongest field in the world, and ended up with Bush?[22]

The Bushes' alleged lack of intellect may explain why they receive more flak than the Kennedy clan, the Clinton ascendancy or for that matter George W. Bush's 2000 opponent, Vice-President Gore, who is the son of a former senator. Was the Kennedy family machine and treasure chest any less significant, or ruthless, than that of the Bushes?

However to point to Democrat lineages is only to intensify the critique that the narrowness of the political gene pool, in a country of nearly 300 million, belies the republican adage that any child in the United States can dream of becoming president. If we look further afield, however, we find that country size generally works in favour of, rather than against, familial succession. India is the world's largest democracy, but bred the Nehru/Gandhi dynasty. Politics is tough for women the world over, and Hillary Clinton will hardly be the first wife or daughter to benefit from her surname. Compare, in recent times, the Philippines' President Acquino, Pakistan's President Bhutto and Sri Lanka's President Bandaranaike Kumaratunga. Lest it be objected that these examples are all from Asian nations where family 'caste' may play a role that liberal democracies would prefer to sublimate, consider that in Australia, two of the past three Labour leaders have been sons of senior Labour politicians, and the last Liberal leader is a third-generation conservative parliamentarian.

What is going on here? Typically, two advantages accrue to a political lineage. One is the inevitably personalised nature of electoral politics. Character, whether measured in trust or charisma, matters to voters. Families serve as character 'brands'. Second, and related, is the machine factor. In non-parliamentary systems such as the United States, where the highest executive offices are filled by direct election, parties are less likely to act as filters of candidacies, and personality-driven machines have an upper hand. Even in parliamentary systems, such as Australia's, where parties determine their leaders, being born into politics is an advantage of acculturation, and not just of name.

A related accusation against US politics is that it throws up an excess of 'celebrity' leaders. B-grade actors and even pantomime wrestlers fill high office: witness President Reagan and Governors Schwarzenegger (California) and Ventura (Minnesota). Of course politics is in part theatre. But when the media reports on governmental decisions by the 'terminator' turned 'Governator' and Jesse 'the Body' Ventura, one senses one is witnessing a polity that, at best, is on the verge of vaudeville, and at worst, not far from the Caligulan option of nominating prize horses to cabinet.

The problem with such accusations is that they come with no statistical basis. A high profile gives a candidate a head start; but it also makes them more newsworthy, and hence memorable, *especially* to outsiders. Take Italy. It is no coincidence that Premier Berlusconi, who led its longest serving administration since Mussolini, is a media, footballing and all-round tycoon. Nor that, internationally, Italy's second best known politician in recent times has been a porn star known as La Cicciolina ('Little Cabbage'). But there are hundreds of dourer, hard-working politicians in Italy, of whom outsiders are ignorant, just as there are many hundreds of little-known Governors and congressmen in the United States. Besides, it would be undemocratic to make a high profile a disqualification for political office. Every country has examples of respected, even policy-wonk legislators who benefited from their pre-parliamentary incarnations: Senator Glenn (the first US astronaut), Glenda Jackson MP (a celebrated UK actress) and Peter Garrett MHR (an Australian rock star and environmentalist).

Money Politics

The core and most serious complaint about unequal access to US politics is money. Money politics, in the sense not of crude bribes, but of the cost of campaigning and risk of politicians becoming dependent on wealthy backers, is hardly a US phenomenon. But it is seen, worldwide, as reaching its zenith (or nadir) in the United States. George W. Bush, in particular, is depicted as a beneficiary. He overcame his primary opponent in 2000, Senator McCain, on the back of his war chest. This tale is reinforced by the fact that McCain's name now adorns the

McCain-Feingold Act,[23] the latest legislative measure in a thicket of laws regulating and constraining money politics.[24] The deeper accusation is that Bush is a mouthpiece for moneyed interests: hardly a new or even unusual accusation to level at a conservative politician, but a particularly problematic claim if his administration's ties to big oil conflict with its responsibilities in the energy, environmental and foreign policy portfolios.

None of this critique is new to US ears.[25] Indeed Americans have their own pejorative to describe the problem: 'special interests'. The United States, a century ago, was one of the first democracies to begin tackling it, when Republican President Teddy Roosevelt pioneered a ban on corporate and trade union donations to parties or candidates. Trading in legislative votes in the United States is also often quite explicit. But the fact that the metaphorical tag, 'log-rolling', is more openly discussed than in most other democracies is as much a sign of the openness of the practice as it is evidence that it is more endemic in the United States than elsewhere.

Worrying statistics, such as that 40 percent of US senators are millionaires, are also routinely cited as evidence of a plutocracy, if not kleptocracy, in action. Statistics like these are usually embellished with anecdotes of billionaire candidates, such as Ross Perot, Steve Forbes (both for president) and Michael Bloomberg (now mayor of New York). Here is not the place to resolve whether meritocracy in the United States is a myth or not. Rather I would make one observation and two caveats about the role of money in US elections.

The observation is that there *is* a distinct Americanism that tolerates or welcomes, rather than abhors, the sight of successful businessmen buying themselves a political profile. In a country where entrepreneurship and competition are valued more highly than egalitarianism, this should not come as a surprise. Politics reflects culture.

The first caveat is that money, whilst potentially corrosive of democratic values, is not in itself anti-democratic. '[T]he root of all evil is deeply rooted', as Daniel Lowenstein quipped,[26] because mass democracy relies so heavily, to the point of addiction, on expensive media to disseminate campaign messages, rather than town hall meetings and door-knocking. In US politics, this is accentuated by the 'primary election'. That is the widespread procedure whereby the right to stand for office under a party label requires one to win that party's 'primary', an election open to a large section of the public. Having to campaign twice or – in the case of a national election such as the presidency – fifty-one times, rather inflates the cost of a candidacy. The result, in political jargon, is 'the wealth primary'. But the primary, in intention and practice, was designed as a democratic initiative, ceding power that elsewhere is exercised behind closed doors by party activists or bosses to the electorate at large.[27] Primaries also may give supporters of the weaker party in a safe constituency some say over their representative.

The second caveat is that the importance of money is inflated in US politics due to the dispersed, even babbling nature of the media. There is no statist public broadcaster to keep political discourse on controlled and gentlemanly terms,[28] but rather a plethora of privately owned outlets. This is not an American-only phenomenon, though it is fair to say that the commercialisation of electoral politics first became institutionalised, to the point of becoming an industry, in the United States. Some of the dark arts of 'spin-doctoring', 'wedge politics' and 'negative advertising', perfected there, are imported into other countries, causing resentment proportionally to their success in displacing more time-honoured practices. We see much the same transmission with other US innovations, from the mass produced automobile to the Internet.

The role of money in US politics is also accentuated by the fact that politics competes with a cacophony of consumerism for attention. Money's prominence is secured by a strict First Amendment, a constitutional rule that gives priority to freedom of speech over other values. That rule is a double-edged sword for democracy. It ensures that all manner of civic groups are as free as possible to participate in debates, provided they can attract sufficient pecuniary support. But it also means that the United States cannot – even if it were culturally appropriate – legislate to cap electoral expenditure, unlike the contemporary United Kingdom, Canada and New Zealand.[29]

'Divine Providence' – Religion and Evangelisation in US Politics
Paradoxically amongst liberal western states, and in spite of possessing a rigidly formal constitutional separation of church and state, politics in the United States is saturated with religion. As with money politics, this Americanism is not a new phenomenon. But President George W. Bush is seen as an exemplar of how a pious individual blurs, and exploits a blurring of, the distinction between church and state. The contemporary Republican machine, under the guidance of Karl Rove, is depicted as pursuing a majoritarian wedge between evangelical/conservative

Christians and secular liberals/non-Christians. A sustained attack on the hypocritical nature of moralising in Bush's politics is given in Peter Singer's *The President of Good and Evil*.[30]

One accusation of hypocrisy is that the United States fulminates against the influence of foreign clerics, especially radical Muslim ones, yet tolerates and breeds the likes of popular televangelist, the Reverend Pat Robertson. Robertson recently urged his government, on national television, to assassinate President Chavez, the democratically elected leader of Venezuela, 'If he [President Chavez] thinks we're trying to assassinate him, I think we really ought to go ahead and do it. It's a whole lot cheaper than starting a war. ... We have the ability to take him out, and I think the time has come that we exercise that ability'.[31]

Of course there is no collective responsibility for randomly insane provocations such as Robertson's. The existence of double standards in this regard is of interest not because of any chauvinism it reveals ('extremist clerics are ok when they're *our* extremist clerics') but because such extremism does not exist in a vacuum. It depends, in part, on an unsecular political culture that integrates religious figures and values into politics precisely because God is omnipresent in mainstream political thought and life.

That US democracy does weave a distinctly unwestern blend of religious morality and language into its political discourse was illustrated in the wake of hurricane Katrina, which devastated the America's Gulf states in 2005. The invocations of the Almighty – which in other nations would have been short, scripted and either a token to those with religious sensibilities or made to accentuate a sense of pity – suffused responses from all sides of the US political divide. The Mayor of New Orleans, for example, warned that God would judge the federal administration if it failed to save affected people. President Bush, in turn, in an informal address to emergency workers, summonsed religious language six times in under a minute:

> lives are still being saved as we speak because thousands of people are taking in these *displaced souls* in their homes and *churches and synagogues and mosques* and providing love and compassion and food.

> This is – this is one of these disasters that will *test our soul and test our spirit*. And – but we're going to show the world, once again,

that not only we will survive, but that we will be stronger and better for it when it's all said and done, that *amidst this darkness, there is light* … .

God bless you and your families. May God bless the victims, and may God continue to bless our country [Author's italics].[32]

To top it off, some Christians asserted that the hurricane was divine wrath for New Orleans (home of the Mardi Gras). Such an outrageous claim is of interest not because it is representative, but because such discourse is protected by the First Amendment. Free speech is given an institutional priority, in a particularly American vision of democracy, and that liberty feeds such outrageous speech, because bilious sound bites titillate the media. Similar claims of divine wrath had been made by more senior US televangelists, such as Jerry Falwell, after 9/11. Such comment then scandalises international opinion, but out of proportion to its representativeness, perpetuating a crude perception of the role of religion in political discourse that feeds anti-Americanism.

Extremism aside, what part does religiosity really play in US democracy? A certain amount of it is humbug: openly atheist candidates are rare, but the closing of speeches with 'God bless America' is as much a ritual salutation as a sincere or holy gesture. What makes Bush's post-hurricane homily eye-opening to outsiders is that its preachiness is unaffected. There is neither irony nor soul-searching in his conclusion, 'may God *continue* to bless our country', when his country had just fallen victim to a brutal natural disaster. This could only happen in a democracy suffused with religiosity. When Americans elect self-proclaimed 'born again' leaders such as President Bush, they must expect to generate some anti-Americanism from less Christian nations. Reports that Bush proclaimed he was on a mission from God when he declared wars on Afghanistan and Iraq and pursued a two-state solution to the Arab – Israeli dispute undoubtedly will arouse concerns of messianic behaviour.[33]

We can recognise that the influence of religion on politics is more significant in the United States than in other western nations, and even enhanced during the Bush era, whilst admitting its influence is overstated. To appeal to the median voter, US politicians have to show or fake piety more than their counterparts elsewhere. Gallup in 1999 reported that only 49 percent of Americans would consider voting for an atheist (the true figure may be lower, since many believers would not admit to being discriminatory). US voters are also less likely to be averse to increased religious influence on political life than voters in Britain or Canada. On a variety of discrete issues, US opinion is decidedly less rationalist than elsewhere. For example, according to Gallup, 54 percent favour teaching creationism in science classes alongside evolution.[34] From a democratic – rather than a pedagogical – standpoint, the significance of that figure is that Bush's flirtation with 'intelligent design' can be read as his reflecting majority sentiment rather than leading it.

Yet on other issues, the US population is surprisingly tolerant. Take the iconic issue of prayer in public schools. For all their personal theism, Americans overwhelmingly prefer tolerance to enforced religiosity: by three to one they favour a moment's silence for private contemplation or unvoiced prayer over a public prayer. More Americans would prefer a reduced religious influence than an increased one,[35] and that majority has increased significantly during Bush's term of office.[36] Compared to the early 1990s, Americans believe that religion is having an increased influence on American life; yet the self-reported importance of religion in their lives, whilst high by western standards (around 55 percent of Americans say it is 'very important'), has been constant for more than a generation.[37]

Religious influence on politics is a perennial issue everywhere. What has made it headline news in the United States recently is the radical Islamic opposition to the west, coupled with the Republican mobilisation of evangelical Protestantism, previously a latent, even apolitical, force. Bush's ability to stoke and cook on this fire has generated concern about doctrinaire politics, a concern shared equally at home and abroad. This concern is partly the response of progressives to the pendulum of social reaction, and partly it is a concern with the professionalism – and potential for zealotry – with which American religious conservatives and their partisan associates are mobilising. In contrast, connections between progressives and religious movements that preached social justice attracted less concern when they were prominent from the 1950s to the 1970s.

Bush's 'compassionate conservatism', including his incorporation of 'faith-based' initiatives in the delivery of public services, has been derided on various fronts. First, as mere spin to soften his image in the 2000 election. Second, as a fig leaf for outsourcing governmental obligations, guided by an ideology of smaller government, designed to morph the welfare state into a society of charity. And third, as a concession of power to the religious. It may be all these things; but it is also consonant with

'third-way' politics; less a revolutionary desecularisation than a variant
of the trendy communitarian model of public–private partnerships and
preference for civic society over state agencies.

Meddlesome Lawyers: Litigiousness and Elections

The mess of Florida 2000 famously resulted in a partisan split in the
Supreme Court. In its 5–4 ruling in *Bush v Gore*, it halted the recounting
of votes and effectively awarded the election to George W. Bush. Electoral
lawyers were split between those who opposed the court's method and
reasoning and those who argued that it had no choice but to exercise
authority lest confusion billow into chaos. A predominant critique was
that the decision was deeply political, as the judges (on the outcome if
not the reasoning) split along lines of liberal-versus-conservative. Such
labels are based not just on judicial philosophy, but on cruder measures
such as which president appointed which justice, and whether they were
a registered Republican or Democrat in their pre-judicial days.

Bush v Gore will rank lowly in the pantheon of Supreme Court
opinions. In terms of precedent, that is, laying down rules to guide future
cases, it has quickly become in technical terms '*sui generis*' or, more
colloquially, 'a ticket good for one day only'. These are polite terms for
a ruling whose reasoning is fishy enough that it is ignored by confining
it to its peculiar facts. We have already noted that lawyer-phobia was
evident not just in attacks on Bush and his legal entourage for trying to
'shut down the count' but in attacks on Gore and his advisers for only
seeking recounts in pre-dominantly democratic counties in Florida.
Outsiders were mystified why a single, statewide recount was not automatically mandated. But that ignores the devolved or 'hyper-federalised'
logic of the administration of US democracy. The irony for Gore is that
a study of the ballots later revealed that a *full*, manual recount of Florida
would probably have won him the election, but not the limited recount
his lawyers gambled on.[38]

Reports at the 2004 election that the parties had assembled a
combined army of more than 10,000 lawyers[39] only served to reinforce
prejudice about the extent of American litigiousness. The image of a
lawyer-driven society derives much from de Tocqueville's famous analysis
of early nineteenth-century American democracy as a kind of liberal
meritocracy, where men of law fill the vacuum created by the absence
of European classes or castes and provide a bulwark against the excesses

of majority passions. This was achieved by ensuring that '[s]carcely any political question arises in the United States that is not resolved, sooner or later, into a judicial question'.[40]

As a lawyer, I do not want to be accused of being an apologist for litigiousness. In many societies the juridification of political and social issues is seen as pathological. And writing as an electoral lawyer, I do not want to be accused of self-interest. Electoral law, like campaign consultancies, form a veritable industry in the United States, when elsewhere they are merely arcane specialties. The tangles of US electoral law confuse not just outsiders, but sometimes the very people and officials they are meant to guide; and those tangles present the wealthy, two-party duopoly with the chance to play endless games in the courts.

But if there is truth in the dictum, attributed to Sir Thomas More, that planting a thicket of laws is a bulwark against subjective or oppressive rule, the least that can be said of US elections is that they are firmly subject to the rule of law, even if the rule of law sometimes descends into a confusion of lawyers. The best that can be said is that sometimes lawyers have been democratisers, instrumental in the abandonment of inimical practices and mindsets. For example, in a series of cases in the early 1960s, the Supreme Court carved, from the constitutional rule of 'equal protection', the principle of one-vote, one-value in the face of legislative malapportionment.[41] As we shall now see, similar legal impositions on a retrograde political culture were needed to ensure racial equality in the post-bellum South to ensure such fundamentals as access to the ballot.

Race

In a country that has welcomed more immigrants than any other in history, racial divides haunt the American body politic. The primal wounds of colonialism continue to marginalise both native Americans and African-Americans from full citizenship. As electoral law scholar Professor Lani Guinier argues, racial divides are reinscribed, indeed perpetuated, by the tyranny of majoritarian democracy.[42] Florida 2000 drew attention to a narrower but no less serious form of indirect discrimination – the denial of votes to people with felony convictions, who are disproportionately black. Dramatic claims of electoral theft were given oxygen because of two facts. The first is that residents of Florida with felony convictions, no matter how dated, could only be re-enfranchised if they received a gubernatorial waiver (i.e., from Governor Jeb Bush). The second was that partisan officials determine how lightly or heavily the rolls are purged.[43]

Prisoner disenfranchisement is not uncommon,[44] although in both Canada and the European Union, recent court rulings have decreed that a ban on prisoners voting whilst in custody is unlawful. Lifetime disenfranchisement, common in the United States, reeks of the ancient stigma of civil death. Yet to what degree are such rules simply rein-scribing deeper forms of economic deprivation and cultural exclusion? The United States has some of the harshest prisoner disenfranchisement rules in the 'first' world, but the symbolics – and political football – of the issue make reform difficult in most countries.[45]

In other respects, US reformers have been more successful in searching for ways to achieve the promise of democracy to redress injustice. In the 1930s, the battle was to remove barriers to black candidates reaching the ballot in what were then, effectively, one-party 'Dixiecrat' states of the south. The Texas Democratic Party, in particular, was the focus of litigation, as it sought to perpetuate the 'White Primary'.[46] To achieve a formal emancipation of candidatures, anti-discrimination law had to trump a competing tenet of democracy – freedom of association.

Similarly, practices to disenfranchise African-Americans had to be overcome through the federal *Voting Rights Act* of 1965. Even a conservative opponent of the Act's continuation heralded it recently as 'the twentieth century's noblest and most transformative law'.[47] Its effects lie not just in achieving practical enfranchisement for millions, but in shaping 'majority – minority' districts (i.e., constituencies with sufficient minority voters to give a minority candidate a fair chance of success). But as with much amelioration, even this legislation has been a double-edged sword. Since African-Americans overwhelmingly vote Democrat, their corralling into 'black' electoral districts, whether through ghettoisation or re-districting, may make it harder for Democrats to win legislative control, as large surpluses of their votes are tied up in safe, inner-city districts. Black politics would have more influence if it were spread more evenly between the parties. Yet the proportion of blacks supporting President Bush has gone from the risible to the negligible – from an estimated 11 percent at the 2004 election to 2 percent in one poll taken in the wake of hurricane Katrina.[48] Such polarisation indicates that Republicans face a permanent challenge in governing for all; nevertheless Bush has broken ground in appointing not one, but two African-Americans as Secretary of State.

Systemic Flaws – the Electoral College and Partisan, Localised Administration

At the heart of the Florida 2000 battle was the 'electoral college'. In this system, voters technically do not vote for candidates but indirectly for 'electors' who gather in state-by-state 'colleges' to cast their own votes for the Presidency. Each state receives college votes equal to its numbers of members of Congress. As a matter of principle, indirect election is rightly seen as an undemocratic throwback. It was designed out of mistrust of the masses. But for practical purposes, it is only undemocratic in form, since by a mixture of law and custom, electoral college members normally vote in accordance with their state's popular vote. Of course, normally is not always, but then parliamentarians sometimes renege on their party affiliations in deciding who will form government .

The broader critique of the electoral college in 2000, both at home and at abroad, was in how its winner-takes-all approach favoured President Bush, when Vice-President Gore received over half a million more votes. The rule of awarding, with two minor exceptions, the whole of a state to one side, even when the result is lineball (as in Florida) was seen as tilting presidential elections to the conservatives. The reasoning went that they always carried the 'heartland' of smaller states (for which read 'hick' country), whereas the Democrats piled up majorities in the more populous, but fewer, seaboard states. The debate of course was not new. The American Bar Association, in the debate after Richard Nixon scraped out a popular vote majority over Hubert Humphrey in 1968, described the college as 'archaic, undemocratic, complex, ambiguous, indirect and dangerous'. The angst in 2000 was accentuated by the fact that the United States clings to first-past-the-post voting, a simplistic system rejected throughout the democratic world, except, notably in the United Kingdom and Canada. In the outcome, nearly three million leftist votes for Green candidate Ralph Nader were wasted.

In truth, though Bush was indeed fortunate, over time the electoral college system has proven tolerable. It awarded the presidency to the candidate with the fewer votes in only three previous elections. Such results also arise in parliamentary systems, where the executive depends on winning a majority of constituencies, not a majority of votes. Even where, as in Australia, preferential (or 'instant run-off') voting is used, a truly proportional outcome is far from guaranteed.[49] All these typically anglophonic systems encourage candidates who appeal to a broad geographical spread. This is an important value in regionalised or dispersed countries such as the United States. The alternative of a purely national count would have unintended effects, such as directing virtually all campaigning attention to the most populous states. Also we have no way of knowing if the national vote would be the same if the rules changed: Bush supporters in large, liberal states such as California and New York – and Democrats in Texas – may be more inclined to vote in a close national election than under the college system.[50]

In awakening international attention to the peculiarities of US elections, Florida 2000 was more significant in focusing attention on the bizarre (to outsiders) localisation of electoral administration. Why were voters in adjacent counties in Florida voting on wildly different technologies? Why were officials with partisan affiliations, often themselves directly elected, running local and state electoral units? Why did the world's richest nation not have a single,[51] professional and independent body to register electors and run its national elections, rather than leaving the administration to many thousands of electoral districts?

Part of the answer is simple. The United States is a distinctly federalised nation (hence the constitutional entrenchment of the state-by-state electoral college). Alec Ewald describes US elections as 'hyper-federalised'. In his study of how such a 'system' survived the ballot reforms that swept the democratic world in the late nineteenth century, Ewald hypothesised that the answer might lie in values such as popular sovereignty and resistance to centralisation. Both are Americanisms. The first, a simple faith in the potency of the ballot, runs deep. Judges, after all, are elected in many US states. The second, perhaps even stronger value is a suspicion of governmental power, reflected in a plethora of checks and balances, intended to prevent large-scale abuses of power or fraud. Wed those two values together, and you have the unique, if paradoxical situation that all levels of governance are politicised, yet politics is mistrusted so much that top-down, efficiency-minded models of governance are avoided. Ewald concludes that the hyper-federalised system survived in spite of itself and is preserved because state governments continue to delegate power to local units.[52] The net effect, by 2000, was to leave electors in poorer counties relying on outmoded voting technology.

To electoral law scholar Professor Rick Hasen, the lesson is clear. The only way to avoid another 'meltdown', such as occurred in 2000 (and could have been repeated in 2004, given the closeness in the key battleground of Ohio), is institutional reform. Hasen advocates introducing non-partisan electoral officials.[53] But if the earthquake of 2000 was not enough to replace the fragmented system in the United States with a more rational and centralised one, no one should hold their breath for more than piecemeal reform, which will be a case of two steps forward and one step back.[54]

Low Turnout, Disinterest and Disengagement

The problems in US democracy are often summarised by reference to a single issue or rather number: voter turnout. American elections are routinely treated, even in friendly nations, as a byword for disengagement and concerns over the health of representative government. For example, in a debate about compulsory voting, Australia's shadow foreign minister (a strong supporter of the US alliance) simply proclaimed 'We don't want to Americanise our system' to make his case against voluntary voting.[55]

To define low turnout as a blight is to make a value judgment that democratic participation is always a good thing. Those of an anti-politics bent might counter that politics is pathological, a sign of problems or discord, and that many choose not to vote because they are happily lost in their families, their hobbies and their lifestyles. To those who believe that politics is inescapable, however, consumerism-as-the-opiate-of-the-people is inherently undemocratic. To the realist, turnout is important since without a sense of mass ownership of elections, representative government loses its legitimacy and, in a worst case scenario, its stability.

Accepting that it is a cancer, low or declining turnout, like money politics, is accentuated in, but far from confined to, US elections.[56] Worldwide, there is a drift away from party allegiances once defined by self-perception of class. Sharp ideological distinctions between parties are a fillip to turnout as they energise political debate and make electoral choice more meaningful. But much of the ideological sting was drawn out of politics as the right accepted the welfare state and the left the decline of socialism. That on many issues the Democratic Party and the Republican Party sound like tweedledum and tweedledee should be no surprise to readers in other two-party systems such as in Australia and the United Kingdom. On the other hand, no one wants ideology for its own sake, and it is an international (as well as domestic) critique of Bush that he ran in 2000 on a moderate platform, yet as president he panders to a hard-line conservative 'base'. If that is so, then he has reinforced ideological divisions over policy, and that, along with the reminder from Florida 2000 that each vote can make a difference, actually contributed to an increase in turnout in 2004.

Conclusion

Foreign criticism of a country's democratic practices creates a feedback loop. Inevitably it produces the reaction, 'What's it to you anyway?', which is then taken as head-in-the-sand insularity rather than as a claim of sovereignty. At one level, the rebuke 'Our political system, for better or worse, is a matter for us', is a statement of the obvious. Only Americans can cure that nation's democratic deficits. On another level, it contradicts the globalising liberalism underlying such instruments as the 1966 UN *International Covenant on Civil and Political Rights*, namely that civil and political rights everywhere are the concern of everyone.

The United States is peculiarly susceptible to foreign critiques of its internal democracy, given its status as the world's only superpower. Few foreigners think that the outcomes of US democracy are only relevant to the United States itself. To those living in the Middle East and Central America, US policies directly affect regional stability. To those living in the West, the affinity or divergence of their nation's foreign policies from the United States, and the susceptibility of their cultures to US influence, are perennial issues. And to all, US politics would be inescapable, even if it lacked any tangible effects. This is largely due to the global dominance of anglophonic media, especially US cable and Internet sources. But it has other causes. In Australia, for example, the debate about the replacements for US Supreme Court Justices Rehnquist and O'Connor overshadowed the debate about contemporaneous appointments to Australia's High Court, and Mr Murdoch's media empire is not solely to blame. The process of appointing judges in the United States is so much more open, and hence reportable (if not seemly) than in any comparable nation. In addition, the decisions of the US Supreme Court, although not precedent elsewhere, influence comparative legal and cultural discourse, by virtue of the US Supreme Court's power to decide social questions that in other lands are left to parliamentary compromise or evolving social norms.

Perceptions of the United States, pro- and anti-, and its international relations, have profound impacts on democratic debates and electoral events elsewhere. Witness the German elections of 2003 or the South Korean elections of 2002. Of course the impact may be overstated, in either of two ways. One is hubris by nationalistic Americans. Thus a *Wall Street Journal* opinion feature claimed that Chancellor Schroeder won re-election by 'playing the anti-American card', as if German voters just wanted to send the United States a message, rather than make their own stand.[57] A mirror form of overreach is committed by foreign nationalists. As Daniel Drezner noted, 'campaigning against the United States is one thing; governing against the United States is another matter altogether'.[58] Politics founded on opposition to the United States or its policies is inherently reactive. In any free society it is unlikely to sustain political agitation, unless resentment of the United States is organically refreshed by periodic overreaching of US power.

Jean-François Revel wrote that 'contrary to every lesson of real history' the European establishment and intelligentsia alike wrongly identify the United States as 'the singular threat to democracy'. Ignoring any hyperbole in it, that observation captures a significant strand in anti-Americanism. For as long as people the world over subscribe to Baron Acton's rule of politics and human nature that 'Power tends to corrupt and absolute power corrupts absolutely', then the United States, by virtue of its relative omnipotence, will be the target of at least heightened suspicion. Indeed Americans, if they were born in less mighty nations, would be the first to subscribe to such a reflexive suspicion of power. It mirrors a key aspect of the American vision of democracy, namely a quest to separate, balance and limit governmental power.[59]

Pro-Americans however decry suspicion of the United States based on its might alone as the 'tall poppy syndrome', the desire to belittle 'Mr. Big'. This reaction is revealing of an attitude – an Americanism – that is heightened in the United States, namely immodesty about conspicuous success. Foreigners often recoil at that attitude, especially when manifested in what they see as excessive self-promotion or statistics such as the infeasible percentage of Americans who claim to be millionaires. Understanding that attitude is important, however, to appreciating the razzmatazz and infectious optimism of American politics. The showmanship of conventions and campaigns hints at a bandwagon effect that is absent, say, from British and Australian elections, where claiming underdog status is more likely to attract votes.[60] US politics focuses intensely on individual politicians who may owe limited loyalty to a party machine. Their charisma, character and 'winningness' is often more important than their policy pronouncements. This focus on the manna of the individual has given the Westminster world the presidentialisation of politics, and the quest for the star politician's electoral coat-tail. Conversely, the optimism that imbues activists in raising money and gathering signatures – even for lost causes such as getting minor party candidates onto ballots, kick-starting unpopular citizens' initiatives or making a point through doomed constitutional litigation – is an aspect of civic and associational life in the United States that is less detectable in more statist political cultures where established party structures dominate affairs. In the United States, in contrast, party is often just a label, disguising significant ideological and regional differences. Thus a southern Democrat may be well to the right of a northern Republican.

Such differences aside, the core 'Americanisms' that drive foreign ridicule of US electoral democracy turn out to be far from unique. Rather, the United States is a convenient case study, its practices forming a kind of *lingua franca* since its political affairs are broadcast so widely. The advantages of family, celebrity and money; the uneasy interplay of religious and political beliefs; voter apathy; the marginalisation of minorities and disproportionate outcomes or failures of electoral systems are all ubiquitous phenomena. Perhaps the only factor we have broached, which is truly American, is the 'hyper-federalised' decentralisation of electoral administration. But that is a structural issue and, by definition, an un-nationalistic approach. It barely warrants the label 'Americanism'.

American democracy is hardly optimal, as Americans well know. International polling in 2005 found that Americans considered their elections to be 'free and fair' by only a 10 percent margin (the corresponding margin for Western Europeans was 37 percent).[61] But imperfection, introspection and dissatisfaction are conditions of democracy, and activism for reform is alive and well in the United States. To the (limited) extent that the failings in American democracy feed anti-American sentiments abroad, they should also be the source of self-reflection. If, as Lowenstein argued, the 2000 election was a classical comedy rather than a whodunit,[62] then we should all be wary of becoming the next plaything of the gods. A little *Schadenfreude* between *Freundes* was the order of the day in the wake of the German national election of 2005.[63] That election produced a stalemate, followed by much posturing and negotiations that culminated in a 'grand coalition' of the Social and Christian Democratic parties. Yet only weeks before, those parties had sold themselves to voters as diametrical and implacable opponents.

Democratic processes in the United States invite particular scrutiny since the United States uses its military and trading might and institutional influence to spread a particular brand of liberal, market democracy. Americans don't like to think of themselves as inhabiting an empire,[64] although even its strongest friends see it that way. (As a conservative Labour Premier in Australia and acolyte of US history and politics put it, 'if a nation state has got twelve aircraft carrier battle groups, it's an empire'.[65]) There's a long tradition, exemplified in Thoreau,[66] and labelled 'Jeffersonian', that wants American policy to fulfil the democratic promise of the 'self-evident' truths of liberty and equality at home before it concerns itself with exporting them. That position seems currently eclipsed by both 'Wilsonian' international idealism and 'Jacksonian' pre-emptive belligerence.[67] Ultimately, any critique of the US agenda should start in an account of the propriety of empire, not in finger pointing about electoral democracy in the Republic.

Chapter 9
Bush, the Iraq War and Anti-Americanism

Pierangelo Isernia and Sergio Fabbrini

Introduction: Anti-Americanism or Anti-Bushism?

The period between 2000 and 2006 represented a dramatically negative turning point in the relationship between Europe and the United States. The lasting nature of this critical state of affairs is debatable. Some observers point to the fact that the transatlantic crisis raised by the Iraq War is only the last in a long legacy of crises that have marred Euro–American relationships since the very inception of the Atlantic alliance, back in the late 1940s. Others, on the contrary, blame the flare up on the changed paradigm created by a new post-Cold War transatlantic context, in which Europe and the United States are divided by both the perception of threat and the preferred strategies to deal with it. Still others stress the importance of the contingent and idiosyncratic way the Iraq crisis blew up in the face of all participants, their good will notwithstanding. Whatever the reason, it is hardly debatable that the Iraq War has accelerated and starkly highlighted long-term trends that have been simmering away under the surface and that have only been obfuscated by the strenuous – as seen from today's perspective – efforts of the Clinton administration to accommodate European desires and wishes. The Iraq crisis melded together disparate controversies that ranged from growing concern about uncontested and uncontestable American leadership, to underlying and rapidly formed European antipathy towards Bush and his administration, to differing attitudes on the where, when and how of military force in international relations.

The transatlantic crisis around the Iraq War only helped to crystallise these different streams of Euro–American animosities at both the elite and the mass level, making the appearance of anti-Americanism as a topical issue in Europe no surprise. In this chapter, we will look at the evolution of public opinion attitudes towards America in the period between 2000 and 2006. Our aim is to show that European anti-Americanism was more about opposition to the Iraq War, and its handling by George W. Bush's administration, than about opposition to the United States more generally. In discussing the evolution of anti-Americanism in Western Europe, we will focus on the four most populous countries in the European Union: France, Germany, Italy and the United Kingdom. But before discussing the evolution of anti-Americanism in those crucial years, it is necessary to locate it in a larger historical context. Anti-Americanism was a significant component of European political culture in the twentieth century, although it presented itself more as an elite rather than as a mass public phenomenon. Indeed, social and political elites nourished this attitude even in the post-Cold War period through their criticism of the globalisation process that was interpreted as an American-led attempt to dominate the world. At the same time, after World War II, European mass publics appeared to have been much more positive towards the United States than their political elites. On September 11, 2001, this positive populist attitude was reaffirmed. However, the 2003 Iraq War seems to have signalled a radical change in both mass and elite attitudes towards the United States. While mass publics have become more anti-American than they have ever been, political elites appear to have become more sensitive to the need for US global leadership, albeit constrained by the rules of multilateral international institutions. It is this paradox that we wish to describe. We will begin by delineating the political culture of the European political elites in the twentieth century, in order to show why this culture was largely anti-American. Secondly we will focus on public opinion, showing mass attitudes towards America in the post-World War II period. Then we will discuss the crucial period of 2001 to 2006, in order to show the different phases public opinion has undergone in attitudes towards the United States and its foreign policy. Finally, in the conclusion, we will present some postulations from recent data: firstly from the *Transatlantic Trends* 2006 survey and secondly from a survey of the attitudes of European elites towards the United States conducted by the University of Siena Centre for Political Change in June 2006.

European Anti-Americanism in an Historical Perspective

Anti-Americanism is both an ambiguous concept and a loaded term. The term 'anti-American' is akin in its ambiguity to 'un-American', a term used to disparage and delegitimise domestic critics throughout American history.[1] Anti-Americanism is a loose concept, comprising criticism of both the American system (what America *is*) and the specific American policies (what America *does*). Of course, the two criticisms have different qualities and implications. There are also different implications according to whether the anti-Americanism predominately comes from above (elites) or from below (mass publics). More generally, the European experience shows that anti-Americanism also changes meaning and nature in different historical periods. It is thus not only a loose concept but also a concept constrained by specific empirical and time contingencies.[2]

Despite its ambiguity, anti-Americanism is a recurrent sentiment around the world, Europe included[3], with European governments expressing their resentment of US dominance[4] long before September 11. In Europe, America continued to be perceived as the country that resorts to military solutions for international crises. This perceived predisposition preoccupied many Europeans, as the Euro-Barometer of November 2003 indicates: 53 percent of Europeans considered America a threat to world peace. The same percentage was recorded for Iran and North Korea; only one country, Israel, rated higher, at 59 percent. One might thus argue that the reaction to the American invasion of Iraq in spring 2003 was the tip of a much larger iceberg, revealing an already deep-rooted anti-American mood[5] that was probably aided in its liberation by the end of the Cold War, at least in Europe. In fact, the presence of the Soviet Union at the heart of Europe constrained most political and cultural elites (apart from those of the radical Left and Right) from criticising American grand strategy, thereby confining debate to issues of its management.[6]

However, as our data surprisingly show, anti-Americanism, although prominent among the political elites, was in fact a limited phenomenon at the mass level in post-World War II Europe. The European political elites had historically expressed a strong refusal of America as a whole and not just specific American policies.[7] America was never to the liking of the twentieth-century European left. This dislike seems natural for the communist left,[8] whose very aim was to destroy capitalism and to supersede democracy, but it also spread to the socialist left, which looked for a third way between (American) capitalism and (Soviet) communism. For the communists, America was the capitalist system by definition: the kingdom of the market, the society of profit. Moreover, from the beginnings of the communist challenge onward, America stood as the alternative to the Russian route to social emancipation – in other words, Americanism was the democratic ideological alternative to communism, with Woodrow Wilson as the international leader alternative to Vladimir Lenin. Werner Sombart's question of 1906, 'Why no socialism in America?' crept into the European socialist conscience, keeping alive a sense not only of difference from, but also of refusal of, the American political experience.[9] The long Cold War confrontation only served to solidify revulsion for a country viewed as the spearhead of an anti-Communist coalition, intent (it was alleged) on subjugating the world to the dominance of the capitalist market and the hypocrisy of the democratic plutocracy.[10] This is why the European left as a whole, although more in the communist component than in the socialist, continued to be anti-American for a good part of the Cold War period. Giddens and Hutton[11] recently remarked 'all the things the traditional left says about the United States are still there, and even accentuated – the accumulation of fortunes, the vulgarity of new monied elites and so forth […] But I'm strongly against the knee-jerk anti-Americanism that so many of the European (and some of the American) left go in for.' Certainly, since the end of the Cold War, the post-communist left has reflected self-critically on its traditional interpretation of the 'American model' primarily by distinguishing between capitalism and democracy and by revaluing the importance of democracy and no longer viewing it as a mere proxy for the promotion of market capitalism. Today, some national leaders of the post-communist left (as in Italy or Spain) are acquainted with, or even admirers of, American democracy. And of course, some national leaders of the post-social democratic left (the new third-wayers of Britain and Germany) recognise the progressive side of the American political experience.

America was never to the liking of much of the European right either,[12] and throughout Europe's modern history,[13] the political right has constantly fostered an attitude of contempt towards America. Conservatives could not be sympathetic to a country born from a revolution that was not only anti-colonial but also, and especially, liberal-progressive,[14] and, which from the outset was connoted by a pronounced egalitarianism. For the European rightist parties, America's democratic origins and its egalitarian spirit coincided in the sense that the one nourished the other. For the right, America represented a challenge against the traditional hierarchies, a refusal to defer to constituted authority, the kingdom of the individual, the society that showed no respect for the past (nor wished to). The European right has traditionally regarded Americans as crude, uncouth, ill mannered and ingenuous, if not stupid[15] – in other words, lacking the sophistication and refinement that the representatives of that right believed they possessed either by birthright or as the result of long acculturation. The European neo-fascist parties shared this disdain for America with the conservative right. After all, in the 1920s and in the 1930s, fascist and authoritarian regimes presented themselves in Italy, Germany, Spain, Portugal and Greece as a response to Americanism and its purported crude materialism.[16] For the European conservative right, moreover, America represented also the passion for political participation, the organisation of party machines able to mobilise millions of voters, the ascent to power of ordinary people. When, during the course of the post-World War II period, the European right was forced to accept *liberal democracy* as a permanent condition, it nevertheless continued to conjugate it in paternalistic and hierarchical terms. That is to say it continued to give an interpretation of democracy diametrically opposed to that of America's, because that country made no secret of its intolerance of elites.[17]

But nor has America ever been to the liking of the European Catholic world, under the umbrella of which sit a large number of national political parties and groupings. Indeed, the higher echelons of the Vatican Church have never concealed their distance from, and rivalry with, America.[18] There are numerous underlying reasons for this attitude, but the main is America's status as the world's largest Protestant country. America, after all, was born from the wars of religion that devastated Europe in the seventeenth century, and which were followed by the Reformation and then the Counter-Reformation. America, therefore, has a religious origin unique in the world. It was colonised by communities of Protestant dissidents fleeing to the New World to construct (finally) 'the city on the hill'; dissidents, moreover, who were the dissidents of dissidents, the heretics of heresy, or in other words, the radicals of the Reformation.[19] Sectarian Protestantism is still today the hallmark of American identity and it is manifest, for example, in the American defence of the death penalty.[20] The difference between America and Europe, thus, is that the former has *sects* while the latter has *churches*.[21] Of course, with successive waves of emigrants, the other great monotheistic religions eventually reached the American side of the Atlantic.[22] However, once these religious groups established in America, as Walzer[23] remarked, the American 'expanding toleration regime tended to protestantise the groups that it included. American Catholics and Jews gradually came to look less and less like Catholics and Jews in other countries'. It is likely that America's religious *pluralism* fostered a more tolerant religious climate than elsewhere, although it has not prevented, at regular intervals, the birth of fundamentalist and illiberal religious movements, especially within the Protestant movement such as after 9/11.

Thus the left, the right and the centre have found themselves united in their rejection of America. While all sides were united in their radical rejection of so-called American individualism, the reasons for opposition differed; some have justified its rejection in the name of a social solidarity that would be threatened by individualism, while others have justified it in the name of an organic and communitarian state that would be undermined by individualism. After all, historically, European political elites have had a largely anti-liberal origin,[24] although that was gradually recast in the post-World War II period. What was not recast, however, was the uneasiness of the European elite relationship with the United States. Particularly after the end of the Cold War, new fears have helped to nourish anti-American attitudes among political and social European elites.[25] The first type of anti-Americanism that has emerged from these fears justifies itself as the reaction to globalisation, a process perceived as coterminous with the Americanisation of the world[26] by many authors. For instance, the British journalist, Will Hutton,[27] said '[t]here is a dimension of globalisation that is about opening up the world to American interests in particular and Western capitalism in general'. The same author has also stressed that the enforcers of globalisation are 'the US Treasury, the Federal Reserve, Wall Street and the International Monetary Fund (IMF). Its chief beneficiaries are US investment and commercial banks and the rest of Fortune 500', reminding his readers that 'it is not simply capitalist values that are being transmitted to the globe; it is American capitalist values'. For these critics, globalisation consists in the formation of a one-world homogeneous market dominated by America, a market able to reduce the relevance of specific local or national forms of production, regional peculiarities in labour markets or traditional national methods of mediating between the main social forces and their functional and political representatives. Moreover, globalisation is identified with the spread of socio-cultural, economic and political developments that had already been tested in the western world or in the American laboratory more specifically. The conflation between globalisation and Americanisation also results from the fact that widespread awareness of globalisation only really took hold in the 1990s, a period of undeniable American supremacy in world affairs. Since the end of the Cold War, the military and economic might of America has evoked the longstanding spectre of an imperial power capable of global control.[28]

A second type of anti-Americanism uses political rather than economic justifications. The post-World War II period saw America begin to use its power to promote American democracy worldwide, and this development has continued since the end of the Cold War. After all, with the demise of Communism, many observers rushed to celebrate the expansion of American democracy. The conservative thinker Francis Fukuyama[29] has observed that 'liberal democracy and capitalism remain the essential, indeed the only, framework for the political and economic organisation of modern societies', and there was no doubt (for him, at least) that America offered the best combination of the two. Clearly, America has a legitimate interest in prizing her democracy, although the exact nature of American democracy frequently remains unclear. For instance, many simply equate it with an electoral process based on highly personalised competition, largely driven by media interests, and strongly conditioned by advertising strategies.[30] However, this ignores the fact that any model of democracy is more than a media-oriented electoral process. In sum, the streams of anti-Americanism discussed above shaped in ways large and small Europe's political relations with the United States during the twentieth century.

A Comparative Perspective on European Anti-Americanism

Although elites have an inevitable influence on public opinion, the interaction between the two is much more complicated than usually assumed.[31] Moreover, no matter how deeply rooted historically and ideologically the anti-Americanism of the European elites was, in comparative terms, it was a much more limited phenomenon than the anti-Americanism of elites in Asian muslim countries and the Middle East. The stark contrast between these two groups of elites is evident in public opinion polls. Although a variety of answers have been given to the question of why Americans are hated,[32] a consensus exists on who the haters are: mainly the muslim fundamentalists in the Arab world,[33] while Europeans, including the traditional culprits of the French,[34] have 'mixed' feelings[35] rather than outright aversion for the United States. The American public seem to share this view. In June 2002, 61 percent of the American people thought that 'Anti-American sentiments in the Muslim world' were a 'very serious' (and 21 percent a 'serious') threat 'to the quality of life here in the United States'.[36]

That anti-Americanism is much more virulent in the Middle East than elsewhere in the world is also borne out by a quick glance at the available comparative survey data. Comparing average anti-American feelings in Europe with that in the Middle East (and Southern Far East) in a set of surveys conducted between 2002 and 2005,[37] we found that, in Europe, an average 47 percent of the public had favourable feelings towards the United States, while only 21 percent in the Middle and Far East shared these feelings. In France, usually considered among the least pro-American countries in Europe, a March 2003 Pew survey showed that 63 percent of the French had a favourable opinion of the United States, but by May 2005, the Pew survey showed this had dropped to 43 percent. A June 2002 Gallup poll showed that 41 percent in Turkey had a positive feeling towards the United States, but the Pew surveys in May 2005 revealed this had dropped to 22 percent. In Pakistan, favourable opinion was at 5 percent in June 2002 according to a Gallup poll, but in a Pew survey of May 2005, this had jumped to 23 percent, following America's significant contribution to earthquake relief. A Gallup poll of Islamic countries in 2002 (carried out in January–February and including Pakistan, Iran, Indonesia, Turkey, Lebanon, Morocco, Kuwait, Jordan and Saudi Arabia) showed that 6 percent had a very favourable opinion of the United States, and 16 percent a favourable opinion. By contrast, 35 percent had a very unfavourable and 17 percent a somewhat unfavourable view. Those with neither a favourable nor an unfavourable view of the United States accounted for 23 percent.

Moving to the evolution of anti-Americanism in Western Europe, we can rely on a long-standing series of polls on the four largest European countries of France, Germany, Italy and United Kingdom, considered in Figures 9.1 and 9.2.[38] The evolution of net general feeling towards the United States between 1948 and 2006 was obtained by subtracting the total of negative feeling from positive, and points to three main results. First, over time, sentiment towards the United States in all four countries has been predominantly positive. During the twentieth century, France was the only one of the four countries studied to have negative feelings

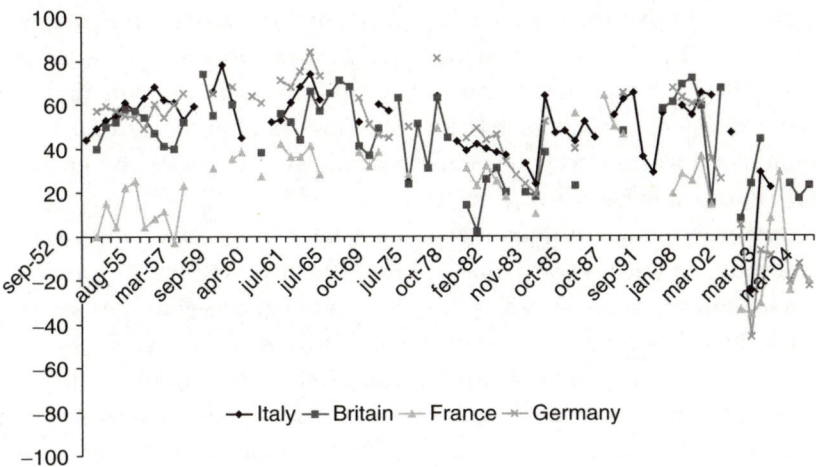

Figure 9.1
Trend in the Net Attitudes Towards the United States.

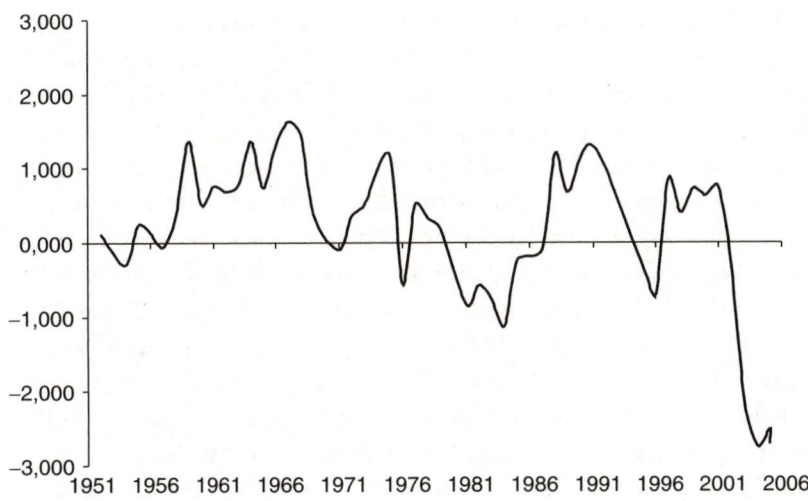

Figure 9.2
Mood of Anti-Americanism in Four European Countries.

outweigh positive and even then this was only for a very short period of time. In contrast, the post-Iraq War period represents a unique situation, in which negative sentiments prevail over positive ones for more than one year and in more countries than the usual suspect of France. Negative sentiment towards the United States became prevalent from 2004 on in *both* France and Germany.

Second, although substantially positive, the aggregate level of anti-American sentiment varies from country to country. The French public is systematically more anti-American in its orientation, while the German and Italian publics are less so than the overall average. Great Britain locates itself in the middle. The net average feeling towards the United States in the period 1952–2004 in France is twenty points, while Germany and Italy score fifty and forty-five, respectively, with Britain at forty-four points. This confirms the popular image of the French public as generally less pro-American than other European countries. Third, the figures show some fluctuations over time in the net level of anti-Americanism.

To examine more carefully these fluctuations of anti-Americanism over time, the four trend lines[39] need to be smoothed.[40] In plotting and evaluating the general movement of anti-Americanism over time, the differences between countries can be ignored.[41] Forced to vary around the same average and range of variation, the series of figures flattens somewhat and shows the starker picture revealed in Figure 9.2.

Analysing this figure led to three further thoughts. The first is that the fluctuating nature of anti-Americanism after World War II shows no clear trend either up or down. A long-time perspective at the level of the masses would lead us to conclude that anti-Americanism has not been on the rise. Rather the data indicate that anti-American sentiment shows a cyclical nature around a definitely positive mean. Each downward movement is very quickly followed by a reversal of the trend line towards the mean. Second, these fluctuations in anti-Americanism, as measured by the net favourability indicator, are not erratic, but rather appear to be related to the evolution of the international political environment. The increase in anti-Americanism (as measured by dips in net favour) is all connected with crises in transatlantic relations. The first spike in anti-Americanism recorded by the available data is in October 1954, due exclusively to the French data point. This spike followed the refusal of the French National Assembly to ratify the European Defence Community. A second increase, in the second half of the 1950s, is brought about by the Suez crisis and lasts until November 1957, as reported from the available survey data. The 1960s are a period of steadily declining anti-Americanism, as shown by the net favourability results. The third surge in anti-Americanism materialises between 1971 and 1976, as a likely consequence of the controversies over the Vietnam War, the monetary crisis over the termination of the dollar convertibility, and the economic drift brought about by the Arab oil embargo.

The next show of anti-Americanism manifested itself in the early 1980s, in connection with the collapse of détente, the controversial North Atlantic Treaty Organisation (NATO) Euromissiles decision and the acrimonious debate over Reagan's Soviet foreign policy. This began abating again in 1985, with the arrival of Gorbachev. The first post-Cold War spike in anti-Americanism occurs in 1994–1995, but it should be interpreted with caution, since it is based on only the one data point from Italy. It probably occurred as a consequence of the reluctance of the United States to be embroiled in the turmoil of the Balkans, and European uncertainty over America's willingness to intervene in support of European troops on the ground. Eventually, the deepest crisis takes place in 2003 when net favour in these four countries not only reaches its lowest ever level, but for the first time also becomes negative in Germany and Italy and reaches the bottom lowest +8 points for Great Britain.

As in the past,[42] sympathy towards the United States is quick to recover. Already by July 2003, positive feelings in France outmatched negative opinions. This upswing in positive feeling is quite characteristic of attitudes towards the United States over the entire 50-year period. However, contrary to the past, a diverging trend seems to separate French and German public opinion from that in Italy and Britain. Following the outbreak of the Iraq War and persisting over the last two years, sentiments towards the United States in Italy and Britain have recovered as quickly as in the past, while those of the French public remain ostensibly cooler than in the past. The real novelty is represented by Germany. While in the past forty years, German public opinion has always been among the least anti-American, from 2002, pro-American sentiment in this country has plummeted to an unprecedented low point and has remained so.

Figure 9.2 also emphasises a third dynamic in anti-Americanism trends. Although one of the characteristics of anti-American sentiment has been fluctuation, the range of fluctuation has become wider over time. In other words, while anti-American sentiment remains a minority view, it has also become more volatile over time. While this trend started in the early 1980s, the end of the Cold War may have contributed significantly to its increase. The demise of the Soviet Union made it easier to express anti-American feelings whenever international events put the United States at odds with her European partners. These greater oscillations might be interpreted as a consequence of long-term and, to an extent, inter-related structural changes in Euro–American relationships that, while they pre-date the Iraq crisis, have been catalysed by it. On the American side, two structural changes of relevance in the post-Cold War period are, on the one hand, the overwhelming power of the United States (the *hyperpuissnace*) and, on the other hand, the lack of any constraints, such as the Soviet threat, to its expression. America is now more powerful and more unilateral simply because it is the only remaining superpower. These changes were brought about by the collapse of the post-World War II system rather than by an intentional US policy. Clinton had managed to hold off anti-American sentiment by wrapping changes in his 'policy as usual' style, making him one of Europe's most popular American presidents. On the European side, the structural changes are also important and somewhat symmetric. The disappearance of the Soviet threat made the need to restore the status quo with the United States less urgent than in the past. At the same time, over the past thirty years and particularly since the end of the Cold War, Europe has been developing a unique and different view of the world system from the United States, with a more multilateral and 'soft' view on how to deal with world problems.

These changes have wrought two sets of conflicting consequences for anti-Americanism. While Europeans feel less and less constrained in expressing anti-American feelings, at the same time, Americans have become more sensitive to criticism of their nation than in the past. All this makes anti-Americanism a more topical issue.[43] The topicality of anti-Americanism for both the American public and elites is shown by Figure 9.3, which shows a monthly count of references to anti-American and anti-Americanism from Lexis-Nexis in the two influential newspapers, the *New York Times* and the *Washington Post*. This figure shows two things. First, references to anti-Americanism spike immediately after 9/11 and have a second upsurge when the Iraq War breaks out. Second, references to anti-Americanism in the post-9/11 period are more frequent in the two newspapers than before 9/11.

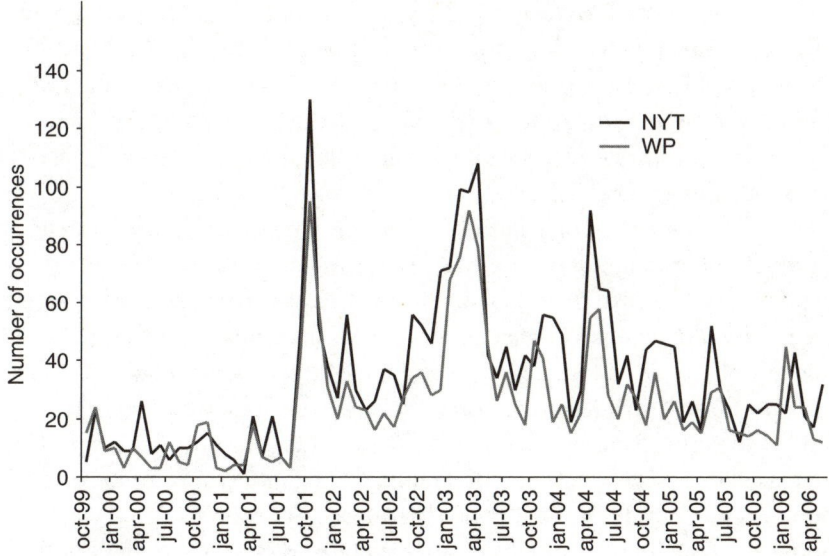

Figure 9.3
Anti-Americanism in American Mass Media.
Source: References to anti-Americanism and anti-American in the *New York Times* and the *Washington Post*, Lexis-Nexis.

European Anti-Americanism in the George W. Bush Era: The Year Before 9/11

To examine the trend of anti-Americanism over time in France, Germany, Italy and the United Kingdom during the Bush era, we examined three main areas: the general opinion of the United States, judgment of American leadership and evaluation of Bush. The responses to these questions capture the different elements that make up anti-American opinion. The first indicator of opinions towards the United States[44] reflects what we think is the true anti-American mood. We view anti-Americanism as a 'mood', whose main function is to act as 'a primary mechanism for altering information-processing priorities and for shifting modes of information processing'.[45] The judgment on American leadership, usually measured by a question asking, 'How desirable is it that the United States exert strong leadership in world affairs? Very, somewhat desirable, somewhat undesirable or very undesirable?' has been asked for many years now. It is generally considered a measure of evaluation of American foreign policy. The last indicator, the assessment of Bush, measures the job performance of President George W. Bush in foreign policy, using the same standard question usually asked in the United States: 'Do you approve or disapprove of the way the president of the United States George W. Bush is handling international policies? Very much or somewhat?'

A widely discussed topic in Europe and the United States is the extent to which things might have been different had Gore won the recount.[46] Pending an answer to that question, however, even the American public seems now ready to acknowledge Bush's negative impact on America's image globally. In March 2003, 56 percent of the American public thought that 'Bush administration policies and diplomatic efforts have … led to more anti-Americanism around the world'.[47] In July 2004, this had increased to 60 percent.[48] And two months later, in October 2004, the numbers had not diminished.[49] It is therefore important to assess whether opinion on the Iraq War might be affected by anti-Bushism rather than anti-Americanism and the extent to which the two are related.

Figure 9.4 compares assessments of Bush, sentiment towards the United States and the desire or not for strong US leadership in world politics between late 2000 and 2006. The data[50] show that, in the years

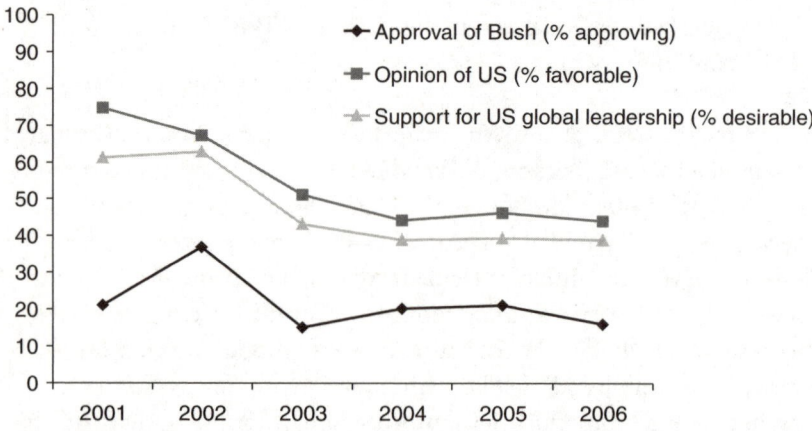

Figure 9.4
Approval Levels Among Supporters of Bush and the United States.
2001 data for opinion towards United States refer to the year 2000.
Sources: US opinion, Pew Surveys; Bush approval, Pew Surveys and Transatlantic Trends; US leadership, USIA and Transatlantic Trends Surveys.

preceding 9/11, the four European countries on average had both much stronger sympathy for the United States and support for strong US leadership in the world than sympathy towards Bush. 9/11 brought about an increase of sympathy towards Bush *and* towards the US leadership, which both declined with the Iraq War. Over the last four years, however, all three indicators show a parallel downward trend, with a persistent difference among the three. Favour towards the United States is consistently although only slightly higher than support for a strong US leadership and this in turn is on an average 33 percent points higher than approval of Bush's handling of foreign policy.

It is probably true that, 'As he took office in January 2001, George W. Bush's views on foreign affairs, and by extension, those of his administration, were not well known'.[51] But in six months his views were known and both the president and his administration were widely disliked in the four European countries considered here. In August 2001, the Princeton Survey Research Associates carried out a survey for the Pew Research Center in our four European countries and the United States. In that survey, a set of questions were asked that aimed at assessing Bush's image (Table 9.1). The results clearly show that Bush's image was quite bleak, especially compared to Clinton. Only 20 percent of the public in the four European countries surveyed approved of 'the international policies of President George W. Bush' (versus 47 percent of the Americans), while 56 percent disapproved (30 percent in United States) and twenty-four were uncertain or did not answer (22 percent in United States). On the contrary, 73 percent of the Europeans in France, Germany, Italy and the United Kingdom approved of 'the international policies of president Clinton', with only 14 percent disapproving and 13 percent not knowing. This negative 'retrospective assessment' of Bush's foreign policy was common through all four countries, but the British and the French results were systematically lower than those of the Italians and the Germans. Only 16 percent of the British and the French approved of Bush's international policies in August 2001. In Germany and Italy, these were 21 percent and 29 percent, respectively.

Looking at the 'prospective' assessment of Bush's foreign policy, the expectations were also low, although slightly less negative than the retrospective assessment just examined, with France and Britain again more critical than Italy and, especially, Germany. In August 2001, only 21 percent of the public in France, 30 percent in Britain and 36 percent in Italy were confident that Bush 'will do the right thing regarding

Table 9.1
Attitudes Towards Bush and American Foreign Policy.

	Britain	Italy	Germany	France	Total
Decisions solely in US interest	81	74	75	85	79
Understands Europe less than most other US presidents	77	53	77	75	70
Not confident Bush will do the right thing in world affairs	67	59	49	75	63
Disapprove Bush handling of foreign policy	50	47	69	59	50
Europe/US interests further apart	24	14	20	20	19

Source: Pew Survey, August 2001.
Wording: As I read some specific policies of President George W. Bush, tell me if you approve or disapprove of them. Rotate list items: Bush's decision that the US should not support the Kyoto protocol to reduce greenhouse gas emissions; Bush's decision that the US should try to develop a missile defence system even if it means withdrawing from the ABM treaty; Bush's support for the death penalty in the U.S.; Bush's decision to keep US troops in Bosnia and Kosovo; Bush's support for free trade policies.

world affairs'. Germany came in at a much higher 50 percent (but only 3 percent had a 'great deal' of confidence in Bush doing the right thing in world affairs). Dichotomising both variables and cross-tabulating them, we find that in all four countries a majority neither approved of nor had confidence in Bush. Those who both disapproved Bush and had no confidence in his ability to do the right thing in foreign policy reached 60 percent, and only 20 percent approved him and thought he would do the right thing; 13 percent disapproved his foreign policy but were confident he would do the right thing in the future, while 6 percent approved of his foreign policy but had no confidence that he would do the right thing in the future. Once again, there were some predictable differences among the four European countries. France and Britain had a bleaker image of Bush than Germany and Italy (66 percent in Britain and 73 percent in France did not approve of him and were not confident for the future, while in Italy and Germany, they were 54 percent and 51 percent, respectively). However, in Germany and Italy a robust minority (of 22 percent and 28 percent, respectively) both approved of Bush and gave him credit for the future. Equally interesting was the fact that in Germany a substantial minority of 26 percent was willing to give him credit even if they did not approve of him.

Two further questions (Table 9.1) explore what characteristics made Bush so unappealing to the European public. Two sets of arguments were suggested: his understanding of Europe and his unilateralist inclination. By August 2001, a two-third majority of the European public judged the Bush presidency as both unilateralist and indifferent to Europe. In all four countries overwhelming majorities thought that Bush was making his decisions based exclusively on American interests (on average 79 percent thought so) and that – with the partial exception of Italy (where only 53 percent thought so) – he understood Europe 'less than most other US presidents' (70 percent on average). And 77 percent of the public in the four countries shared the conviction that Bush both had only US interests in mind when making decisions *and* understood Europe less than other American presidents.

The survey also probed the degree of approval for specific policies carried out during the first eight months of the Bush administration (Table 9.2). The abrupt decision to abandon the Kyoto protocol on global warming – a decision communicated to European partners by Bush only hours before leaving for Europe – was the least popular one, followed by the decision to no longer abide unilaterally by the Anti-Ballistic Missile (ABM) Treaty of 1972. To further stress the degree of antipathy Bush had generated by August 2001, even those policy decisions in line with the wishes of European governments (such as the decision to keep troops in Kosovo and Bosnia) found more disapproval than approval. For example while 85 percent disapproved of Bush's policy on Kyoto, Bush's decision to keep troops in Bosnia and Kosovo still only met with 60 percent approval.[52]

However, the Pew survey also clearly showed that Bush's tarnished image had not spilled over into more general attitudes about transatlantic relations. In August 2001, the two issues – Bush and transatlantic relations – were not as yet strongly related. Although substantial majorities in all countries did not like Bush and his policies and nourished pessimistic expectations about the future of his foreign policy, majorities still believed American and European interests remained substantially the same or were getting closer. On average, only 19 percent thought that European and US interests were growing further apart.[53] The assessments, of course, varied across the four European countries, with the

Table 9.2
Attitudes Towards a US Attack on Iraq (June, 2002, in percent)
There has been some discussion about whether the United States
should use its troops to invade Iraq and overthrow the government of
Saddam Hussein. Which of the following positions is closest to yours.

	United Kingdom	Italy	France	Germany	United States
The United States should not invade Iraq	20	32	27	27	13
The United States only invade Iraq with UN approval and the support of allies	69	54	63	56	65
The United States should invade Iraq even if they have to do it alone	10	10	6	12	20
Don't know	1	3	3	4	2
Total	100	100	100	100	100
(N)	1000	1000	1001	1000	1000

Source: CCFR-GMF Worldviews 2002.

United Kingdom and France, as usual, the least optimistic and Germany
and Italy the most. In Britain and France, no more than a fifth of the public
(respectively, 15 percent and 19 percent) thought European and American
interests were growing closer. A fourth of the British sample (24 percent)
and 20 percent of the French sample thought that interests were growing
further apart. Majorities in both countries (56 percent), however, answered
that the interests had 'stayed the same'. Italy and Germany were more
optimistic in their assessment of the state of US–European relations.
Thirty-four percent of Italians and 39 percent of Germans thought the
interests were getting closer, and 45 percent and 36 percent, respectively,
thought that they had remained the same. Only 14 percent of the Italians,
the lowest percentage of the four countries, and 20 percent of the Germans
answered that the relationships were growing further apart. It is also
worth mentioning that a follow-on question, probing those who had
answered that there was a growing gap between Europe and the United
States, shows that the 'growing power of the European Union (EU)' was

the most frequently mentioned reason behind this growing differences, in all European countries except Germany, where it was second to the 'end of the Cold War' as a reason for Europe's decreasing importance.

European Anti-Americanism Between 9/11 and the Iraq War

In the wake of 9/11, sympathy towards the United States rose immediately in all the four countries examined here. In France, the country most often escoriated for its anti-Americanism, the terrorist attack produced an upward pulse of sympathy of more than 20 percentage points, from the 41 percent who had 'sympathy for the United States' in May 2000 well before the arrival of George W. Bush[54] to 65 percent in November 2001. [55] Similarly, in Germany 79 percent of the public said they felt 'solidarity with the United States' in November 2001.[56]

The increase in sympathy towards the United States in the wake of the 9/11 attacks not surprisingly led to support for the military action undertaken by the United States in Afghanistan starting October 7, 2001. The data on the degree of support for the United States action in Afghanistan in a set of sixty-three countries surveyed in November–December 2001 by Gallup International showed that France, Germany, Italy and the United Kingdom, together with most of the other NATO members, Albania, Israel, India and Kosovo, are the only countries in which a clear majority support the US military action in Afghanistan. In Britain, France, Germany and Italy, two thirds of the public were in support of the action. All other countries were either divided, with only a slim majority or a plurality in favour of the US military operation (e.g. Japan, Switzerland, Ireland and Sweden), or resolutely hostile to the operation (with Pakistan at the top and then in descending order: Greece, Azerbaijan, Malaysia, Argentina, Turkey, Mexico, Bolivia, Bosnia, Uruguay, Yugoslavia and Ukraine).

In another survey, carried out by IPSOS/REID in twelve countries during the same period,[57] a majority of the public in France (60 percent), Germany (60 percent), Italy (58 percent) and the United Kingdom (65 percent) supported 'US-led air strikes on Afghanistan', including 'military sites of the Taliban government, and training camps of the Al Qaeda group led by Osama bin Laden', while Argentina, Turkey,

China and Spain opposed such actions, and South Korea and Japan showed mixed feelings.[58]

While 9/11 greatly increased sympathy for America, it brought with it only a modest increase of support for Bush himself. Although sympathy for Bush never reached the peak of pro-Americanism, a Pew survey carried out in April 2002 in France, Germany, Italy and Great Britain shows an increase in positive assessments of Bush. An average 37 percent of the four European publics in April 2002 approved Bush, as compared to 23 percent in August 2001. In Italy and Germany, approval of Bush increased more (from 25 percent to 44 percent and from 10 percent to 33 percent) than in Britain and France, where it was more modest (from 34 percent to 40 percent, and 25 percent to 32 percent, respectively). This reflected harsh judgments on Bush's conduct of his 'war against terror'. Between August 2001 and April 2002, the percentage of those who described Bush as unilateralist ('He makes decisions based entirely on US interests') remained virtually unaltered: 78 percent in April 2002 and 79 percent in August 2001.

Some evidence suggests that support for the US war on terrorism in France, Britain, Germany and Italy stemmed from a show of support for a friendly country rather than from a shared diagnosis of the best way to deal with terrorism. Scattered but convergent evidence from survey data point to the fact that military force was not perceived by the Europeans at that time as the preferred option to deal with the terrorist threat. An Environics survey, the Global Issues Monitor Survey, carried out in late 2001 in sixteen countries asked whether the respondent agreed 'military force is the most effective way of dealing with international terrorism'. Of the French, 59 percent agreed with this statement, and these middling figures were also reflected in responses from the Germans (39 percent), Italians (36 percent) and the British (46 percent). On the contrary, in America, 76 percent subscribed to this view. In the Gallup International Survey during September 14–17, 2001, only India and Israel showed clear majorities in favour of a military option. In the United States, only a bare majority of 54 percent of the public said yes to the question of 'once the identity of the terrorists is known, should the American government launch a military attack on the country or countries where the terrorists are based?' Firm majorities in all the other thirty-four countries surveyed (and 30 percent of the Americans) would have rather seen 'the American government seek to extradite the terrorists to stand trial'. In France, only 29 percent would have approved an attack

rather than extradition, and lower figures were shown by Germany
(17 percent), Italy (21 percent) and Britain (18 percent). Extradition was
chosen as the best option by 77 percent of the Germans, 67 percent of the
French, 71 percent of the Italians and 75 percent of the British.

But the last question examined hints at even lower support for the
use of force. Apparently, the way in which the question was phrased may
have led to an overestimation of the degree of support for military action.
Whenever the question was not asked in the form of a simple 'yes' and
'no', but rather with alternative options including non-military ones,
the outcomes were often rather different and support generally went
down. Thus, for instance, in one German poll (EMNID), 58 percent
preferred to use diplomatic means in the struggle against terrorism,
with 40 percent saying that only military force could be effective. In an
SWG survey in Italy in September 2001, among the alternative options,
only 10 percent preferred 'bombing', and 20 percent to 'send ground
troops' while 49 percent preferred 'economic sanctions'. In one
YOUGOV poll in the United Kingdom, to a question asking 'Which
of the following do you think should be the main focus for action taken
against countries that knowingly harbouring terrorist organisations?'
33 percent preferred 'diplomatic negotiations', 26 percent 'economic
sanctions', with 'military action' coming in third at 34 percent. However,
when YOUGOV asked on two different occasions in the fall of 2001
if 'there should be no military retaliation and that any action should
be limited to economic and/or diplomatic sanctions against countries
knowingly harbouring terrorist organisations', a strong majority
answered that actions should include 'military retaliation'. And to a
Gallup/Daily Telegraph question asking 'should the United States and
its allies, or should they not, be prepared to take military action against
countries believed to be giving aid and comfort to last week's terrorists?'
70 percent of the sample interviewed during September 17–18, 2001,
answered they 'should'.

Feeling sympathy for America's situation and believing their
counteractions justified did not however automatically equate to wanting
the involvement of one's own country. But again, France, Germany, Italy
and the United Kingdom stand out, together with most of the NATO
members, Israel and India, in their willingness to go along with the US
military strategy in Afghanistan. To a Gallup International question from
September to October 2001 asking 'some countries and all NATO
member states have agreed to participate in the military action against

Afghanistan. Do you agree or disagree that [your country] should take part in the United States military action against Afghanistan?' 73 percent of the French, 53 percent of the Germans, 66 percent of the Italians and 79 percent of the British agreed. To a slightly different question, asked by EOS Gallup in the fifteen EU countries in the second half of November (November 13–23, 2001), in which an explicit reference to ground troops rather than to the more generic 'take part with the United States military action' was made, among the NATO members only France, Germany, Italy, the Netherlands and the United Kingdom gave majorities, with Belgium, Denmark, Portugal, Spain and Greece disagreeing. In France, 54 percent answered yes, national 'troops should be sent to fight with the US forces', in Germany 55 percent, in Italy 51 percent and in United Kingdom 66 percent.

Giving credit to the American stance however did not last long. By November to December 2001, those respondents in support of their own countries taking part still remained in the majority, but enthusiasm had already waned compared with when the identical question had been asked two months earlier (France went from 73 percent to 67 percent, Italy from 66 percent to 57 percent and the United Kingdom from 79 percent to 68 percent, with only Germany showing a slight increase from 53 percent to 58 percent). However by the time this second survey was carried out, the operations in Afghanistan were underway with the US government making it clear that it welcomed the allies as a cheer squad but not their active participation if it meant them claiming a say in the way the battle was being fought. This flagging support shows an erosion of the initial goodwill among these so far staunchest allies of the United States.

This slight, but unequivocal, decrease in support for – and presumably sympathy towards – the US position in the fight against terrorism indicates a re-emergence of differences between European countries and the United States in how best to fight terrorism. An April 2002 Pew survey compared attitudes across the Atlantic (the United States on the one hand and France, Germany, Italy and the United Kingdom on the other) on a number of issues related to the terrorist attacks and the problems of how to respond to them. It revealed a growing gap between the American and European views on a number of important aspects of the terrorist issue, an issue that would loom large in the following years due to the Iraq crisis. In 2002, a majority of the public in our four European countries approved of the US-led military campaign against

Afghanistan but the 'axis of evil' reference in the State of the Union speech by president Bush in February 2002 secured approval of no more than one third in France, Germany and Italy and slightly less than 40 percent in Britain. America's Middle East policy received similarly low approval. Conversely, overwhelming majorities of Europeans (but only a slight majority of Americans) approved of Bush's decision 'to increase US foreign aid to poor countries'.

This survey also revealed a further development in the months following the war in Afghanistan a growing sense of dissatisfaction with the state of transatlantic relations. In August 2001, only a fifth of the public in France, Germany, Italy and the United Kingdom were thinking that European and US interests should be further apart; by April 2002, the percentage of those who thought that Europe should have more independence in its partnership with the United States had risen to 55 percent (47 percent in Britain, 54 percent in Germany and 59 percent in Italy and France). Thus, available evidence on the support for the United States and its foreign policy in the crucial period between 9/11 and spring 2002 shows that the conspicuous endowment of sympathy and support for the United States generated in our four countries by 9/11 began to be eroded well before the Iraq War, for reasons related to both differing views on how best to deal with terrorism, and an increasing uneasiness with developments in US foreign policy following the war in Afghanistan. In this context of increasing wariness of and puzzlement about the general direction of US foreign policy, the Iraq issue was put on the agenda by the Bush administration.

European Anti-Americanism and the Iraq War

By April 2002, discussion inside the Bush administration had already begun on what to do in Iraq and the military option for dealing with Iraq had already been decided.[59] The intentions of the Bush administration contrasted sharply with the state of public opinion in Europe and, to an extent, in the United States as well. In France, Germany, Italy and the United Kingdom an average of 38 percent was in support of 'the United States and its allies taking military action in Iraq to end Saddam Hussein's rule as part of the war on terrorism', with 53 percent opposed and 8 percent uncertain or did not know. In the United States, 77 percent were in support of such an action, 22 percent opposed and 11 percent

uncertain or did not answer. A set of Pew and Transatlantic Trend
Surveys allow us to explore in further detail the evolution of European
public opinion in the crucial period between the 'axis of evil' speech
in January 29, 2002, and the outbreak of war in March 2003.

We start with an April 2002 survey, carried out by PSRA for Pew,
which allows us to gauge in greater detail what the Americans on one
hand and the Europeans in the four countries considered here on the
other thought of the prospect of Iraq as part of the war on terrorism.
Three questions in particular shed light on attitudes about Iraq among
the European public months ahead of the war. The first observation
is that the public view on this matter in April was quite diversified.
As shown in Figure 9.5, public opinion in the four countries was quite
different both between themselves and with the United States. The
American public was strongly in support (67 percent in favour) of
Saddam being removed 'as part of the war on terrorism'. In Europe, on
the contrary, only a plurality was in favour of this option in Britain and
France (46 percent and 45 percent, respectively), while majorities were
opposed in Italy and Germany (57 percent and 64 percent, respectively).
In other words, opinions on what to do about Saddam were quite differ-
entiated in Europe, with pluralities or strong minorities in France and the
United Kingdom ready to consider Saddam's overthrow as part of the

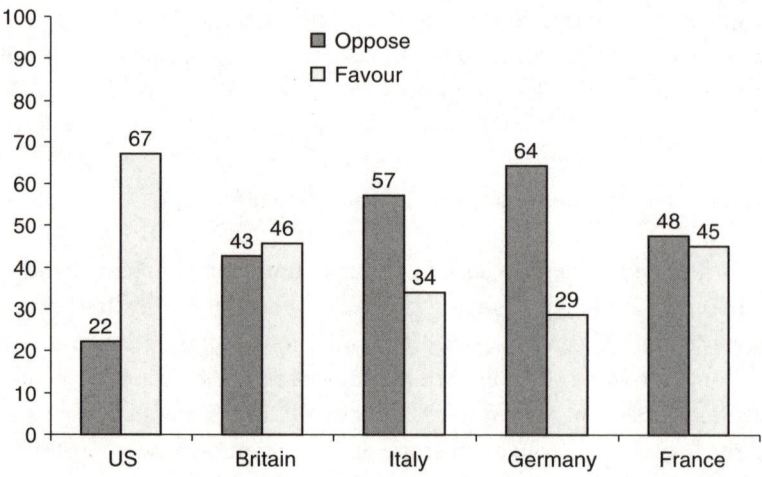

Figure 9.5
Support for the War in Iraq in April 2002.
Source: Pew Survey, April 2002.

war against terrorism, while the public in Italy and Germany were more inclined to opposition. It is also interesting to note that in Europe weapons of mass destruction (WMDs) were seen as offering a slightly stronger argument for supporting the war than Iraq's links to the al Qaeda attacks of 9/11, with 56 percent answering WMDs were 'a very important reason' to support the war, as compared to 47 percent considering Saddam's connection with the 9/11 attacks a 'very important reason' for attacking Iraq.

In June 2002, the situation was still fluid, with public opinion divided in both the United States and Europe. A new issue was also emerging with discussion of the need for UN intervention in Iraq. As shown in Table 9.3, by June 2002, a clear majority of the public in the four European countries (and in the United States as well) was in favour of attacking Iraq 'only ... with UN approval and the support of allies'. Only one tenth of the public in Europe, and one fifth in the United States would have approved it 'even if they (i.e. United States) have to do it alone'.

By November, however, opposition in Europe was beginning to crystallise with a clear divergence emerging between the European and US publics. In a November 2002 Pew survey that covered Britain, France and Germany and the United States, a majority in the United States was in favour of military action in Iraq to overthrow Saddam Hussein, but only 45 percent of the British, 31 percent of the French and 25 percent of the Germans were in favour of their own country 'joining the United States and other allies in military action in Iraq to end Saddam Hussein's rule'. Several reasons contributed to explaining this difference in view. Sympathy for the Iraq regime was not among them. Strong majorities in the three European countries (63 percent of the French, 72 percent of the Germans and 73 percent of the British) and the United States thought that removing Saddam from power was 'the best way to deal with the possible threat posed by Saddam Hussein'. Some differences existed, however, on how serious a threat flowed from Saddam Hussein's regime. A slim majority of the American public (50 percent) thought that 'the current government in Iraq' was a great danger to stability in the Middle East. In Britain and Germany about 40 percent thought the same, while in France only one fourth of the sample agreed. At the same time, French, British and US public opinion was on the same wavelength in assessing the risks of such an undertaking. Approximately one third of the public in these three countries were worried 'a great deal' about the risk that a war with Iraq 'might lead to an all out war in the Middle East'. Germany was the only country where a majority of the public – 57 percent – had these same worries.

Different perceptions of threat and risk were also joined by differences about what the most urgent issues in the Middle East were. A strong plurality of the public in Germany and France (45 percent and 49 percent, respectively) thought that the 'continued conflict between the Israelis and the Palestinians' was a 'greater international threat to our country' than Iraq, while only 35 percent of the British public and 24 percent of the American public thought the same. On the contrary, a plurality in both these latter two countries thought that Saddam was a greater threat to their country (46 percent and 47 percent, respectively) than the Arab–Israeli conflict.

Another issue, which revealed differences of opinion between Europeans and Americans, were the consequences of this war in the fight against terrorism. A majority of the European public was convinced that the war in Iraq would 'increase the chances of terrorist attacks in Europe' (Germans at 56 percent, French at 61 percent and British at 60 percent), but opinion in the United States was more divided. Only 8 percent, 9 percent and 9 percent, respectively, thought that the war would lessen this chance. Conversely 18 percent, double the number in Europe, thought the war would decrease such a chance of attack while a plurality of the American public (46 percent) thought the war would increase the chance of a terrorist attack against the United States.

The issue on which divisions became even sharper, as of November 2002, was on the real US motivations behind such a plan of attack. While 67 percent of the American public thought the Iraqi threats to stability in the Middle East was the better explanation for the America's use of military might, only 43 percent of the British, 37 percent of the Germans and 21 percent of the French thought the same. Majorities in all these three European countries thought, on the contrary, that the 'control of Iraqi oil' was the main motivating force behind such a plan of attack, with 45 percent of the British, 56 percent of the Germans and 76 percent of the French sharing this view.

Given the way the debate had evolved between November 2002 and early March 2003, it is not surprising that, a few days before the actual attack took place, Europeans and Americans were at arm's length. Support for either 'joining' the war, as in the case of Britain and, to a lesser extent, Italy, or favouring the US-led coalition, as in the case of France and Germany, was extremely low in all these countries. In Britain 39 percent of the public supported their country joining the United States 'in military action in Iraq to end Saddam Hussein's rule'. In Italy, this percentage was a low 17 percent, even less in favour than in France and Germany, the countries of 'old Europe' that had spurned the 'coalition of the willing' assembled by the American government. In Germany, 26 percent of the public was in favour of 'the United States and other allies taking military action in Iraq to end Saddam Hussein's rule', while those opposed were 71 percent. In France 18 percent were in favour with 77 percent opposed.

A remarkable fact, given the divisive transatlantic debate about Iraq to date, was the public belief in the European countries of the positive consequences an overthrowing of Saddam might have for the Iraqi people and, to a lesser extent, for the Middle East, in general. Between 61 percent in Italy and 76 percent in Britain (with France at 73 percent and Germany at 71 percent) thought that the removal of Saddam Hussein would make the Iraqi people better off. Pluralities in Italy (46 percent) and France (49 percent) and majorities in Germany (53 percent) and Britain (59 percent) thought that Saddam's removal would make the Middle East region 'more stable … in the long run than it is now'. As far as the public was concerned, the bone of contention seemed to rest not on the merit of the issue but on the procedural matters of how to reach the widely shared goal of the removal of Saddam; in sum, not on the nature of the threat but on the best way to handle it.

It is therefore probably not surprising that in June 2003, to the Transatlantic Trend Survey's question of whether 'the war in Iraq was worth the loss of life and the other costs of attacking Iraq, yes was the answer for' 41 percent in the United Kingdom, 26 percent in Italy, 15 percent in Germany and 13 percent in France. By that time, a majority of Europeans in all these countries, irrespective of the position taken by their own government on the issues, had made up their mind about the Iraq War. This negative trend has only worsened over time, both in the United States and in the Europe.[60]

The Iraq War has thus deepened the contrast, not only between the Bush administration and the public opinion of these European countries, but also between the European political elites (those of 'old Europe' and those of 'new Europe'). Meanwhile European public opinion has continued to be opposed to the US military intervention in

Iraq. More generally, as the post-2003 *Transatlantic Trends* surveys have shown, the Iraq War has also divided US public opinion, with a growing minority closer to the European critical view about the war. With this internal United States opposition tending to come from US Democratic Party supporters, one might conclude that the Iraq War has dichotomised two sets of opinion: one a US Republican-oriented public opinion, the other a European and US Democratic-oriented public opinion.

Conclusion: What Lies Beyond Anti-Bushism?

In this chapter, we have distinguished several stages in the evolution of both transatlantic relations and European anti-Americanism during the 2000s. A first stage opened with the arrival of George W. Bush at the helm of the American presidency and ended with 9/11. This was a period characterised by a growing resentment and uneasiness with the Bush administration and its policies; however, it was not matched by a rise in anti-Americanism or excessive worry for the state of transatlantic relations. As a matter of fact, the period spanning late 2000 to September 2001 was characterised by largely pro-American sentiments in most of the European countries and surely in the four considered here. The second stage opens with the air attacks in New York and Washington and lasts from 9/11 up to early 2002. This second period is characterised by a substantial upsurge in sympathy towards the United States and the American people, which also prompted a public softening towards Bush, making his image more positive as well. However, as time went by, the justifications for overthrowing the Taliban regime in Afghanistan gave way to the spectre of Saddam Hussein's overthrow, seeing sentiment towards both Bush and America take a turn for the worse. Although it is difficult to precisely demarcate the moment when the European public decided that the Iraq issue was paramount in their assessment of the United States, by the summer of 2002, the Iraq issue had control of the agenda, and a third stage had begun. This was a period of more intense transatlantic controversy with both opponents and advocates of the use of force against Saddam spending the summer and fall of 2002 mobilising their own domestic publics to support or to oppose the war. This period concluded with the attack on Iraq in March 2003. The fourth and latest stage began with the rapid overthrow of Saddam's regime and the protracted ongoing war following his demise. This has been a period in which anti-Americanism in Western Europe has been persistently high and steady. The Iraq War has ignited a new European anti-American attitude, especially because of the lack of international legitimacy for the American military intervention in Iraq.

However, such anti-Americanism has continued to have strong anti-Bush connotations. Moreover, contrary to historical precedent, the current wave of anti-Americanism seems to be more connected with mass opinion than with that of political elites. In fact, the *Transatlantic Trend* and the *European Elite Surveys* conducted in June 2006[61] both show a reversal of position between European elite and public opinion in their evaluation of the US global role: the former appears to be much less in favour of that role than the latter. Certainly, the majority of European public opinion now shows an opposition to the global role of the United States – this has grown significantly since 2002 when opposition was at 31 percent – by 2006 it was up to 57 percent. There has also been a significant decline in sympathy towards Americans and the United States after the Iraq War: from 64 percent in 2002 to 51 percent in 2006. The European public's view of George W. Bush had also become more negative: by 2006, positive evaluation of his role had plummeted to 18 percent after being at 38 percent in 2002. It is difficult to say whether this European attitude will change after the US presidential and congressional elections of 2008. Nevertheless, it would pay to take note of the evidence that shows that the Iraq War has deepened the distance between the two shores of the Atlantic. However, this increased distance appears less reflective of differing values than of differences in opinion over how best to deal with the new post-9/11 global scenario.

Chapter 10
The Washington Consensus and Anti-Americanism

Iwan Morgan

In the political lexicon of the late twentieth and early twenty-first centuries, the 'Washington Consensus' became synonymous with 'neoliberal globalisation'. What was initially devised as a technocratic policy agenda that contained some element of statism was transformed in political discourse into a label for a set of ideas identified with the most extreme form of Reaganomics. John Williamson, the World Bank economist who formulated the term, lamented its association in 'the populist definition' with market fundamentalism, but conceded that many people the world over could not speak its name 'without foaming at the mouth'.[1] Without doubt, the Washington Consensus, as it was broadly understood, became a potent source of widespread hostility against the agenda of economic globalisation promoted by the United States and, as a consequence, against America itself. Nevertheless, analysis of the anti-Americanism that the Washington Consensus generated also underlines the complexity of this phenomenon. The genesis of the reaction against American promotion of a free-market agenda was different in East Asia and Western Europe from the impulse that provoked antipathy to the same agenda in Latin America.

To understand the reaction against the Washington Consensus, it is important to consider the varieties of anti-Americanism. In spite of a widespread sense that there is universal understanding of the term, it is used inconsistently with regard to content – it can mean opposition to America's singular global power or to the policies of George W. Bush or to America's values or to Americans as people. From this imprecision stems an underlying and simplistic assumption that the opposite mani-festation, namely 'Americanism', has systematic coherence, and that the United States is a homogenous entity rather than a diverse one.[2] As political scientist Brendon O'Connor has argued, there are at least four possible understandings of how anti-Americanism as a term is deployed in popular and scholarly debates. It can be variously characterised as: a *tendency* (essentially a crude and imprecise dichotomy of being pro-American or anti-American); a *pathology* (an allergic reaction to all things American); a *prejudice* (an *a priori* belief that only bad intentions and selfish power concerns drive America's ideas and actions) or an *ideology* (the organisation of political thinking on the basis of antipathy to 'Americanism', namely, the symbols, attitudes and values that the United States itself represents).[3]

The anti-Americanism that emerged in Europe and Asia in reaction to the Washington Consensus was the *ideological* variety. Its animus was directed against this agenda as a liberal model of globalisation that rightly or wrongly was identified with core values of Americanism – namely the primacy of open markets, the sanctity of private property rights and the imperative of limited state involvement in the economy. In opposition to the ideas associated with the Washington Consensus, the Japanese in particular championed an alternative Asian model of economic development in the 1990s. In continental Western Europe, the French and Germans spearheaded the cause of the 'European social model' against the 'Anglo-Saxon model', the European synonym for the Washington Consensus.

By contrast, in many Latin American countries the Washington Consensus was initially greeted with open arms – at least by governing elites – as the blueprint for economic revitalisation. Reaction set in only as the problematic consequences of its policy recommendations became evident. Nevertheless, the resulting outburst of anti-Americanism primarily manifested the characteristics not of an ideology but of a *prejudice*. Owing to its experience of repeated interventions, both overt and covert, by the United States, Latin America had a historical animus against what it regarded as American imperialism. When faced with the downside of open markets – the volatility of foreign (mainly United States) capital inflows, foreign appropriation of formerly public-owned enterprises and the effect of free trade on domestic industry – Latin American countries began to view the Washington Consensus as a new mechanism to extend American domination over their region by means of undermining their economic sovereignty.

This essay, firstly, seeks to explain how the Washington Consensus evolved from a specific policy prescription into the symbol for the made-in-America model of neoliberal globalisation. It then examines the ideological anti-Americanism displayed in Asia and Europe in reaction to this. Finally, it explores the different brand of anti-Americanism generated by the Washington Consensus in Latin America and assesses whether this could develop into an ideological form of this phenomenon.

The Washington Consensus and 'Made-in-America' Neoliberal Globalisation

Devised in 1990, the Washington Consensus represented in John Williamson's words, 'the lowest common denominator of policy advice' proffered by three Washington-based agencies – the United States. Treasury, the International Monetary Fund (IMF) and the World Bank – to help rescue Latin America from the economic stagnation that afflicted the continent in the 1980s. The ten-point formula comprised fiscal discipline to combat inflation; a redirection of public expenditure from areas of low economic return (administration, defence and subsidies) to those of high return (primary healthcare, primary education and infrastructure); tax reform to broaden the tax base and lower marginal rates; interest rate liberalisation; competitive exchange rates to induce rapid growth in non-traditional exports; trade liberalisation to move towards low tariffs of between 10 percent and 20 percent; liberalisation of inflows of foreign direct investment; privatisation of state enterprises; abolition of regulations that impeded entry of new firms or restricted competition and legal security for property rights.[4]

As John Williamson has been at pains to point out ever since, the Washington Consensus was a policy-oriented agenda conceived by technocrats rather than ideologues to address the specific problems of Latin America. Furthermore, this blueprint was not intrinsically hostile to the state in the sense of recognising its utility for social and public investment while seeking to free the market from its strictures. This necessitates explanation as to why the Washington Consensus became in Moises Naim's words the 'global brand name' of market-oriented anti-statist economic policies in the 1990s and why it generated an ideological reaction, particularly in East Asia and Western Europe, against the United States itself.[5]

The universalisation of the Washington Consensus was a case of 'timing is everything'. The formulation of this agenda coincided with the advent of a new world order in which globalisation, privatisation and free markets dominated the terms of political discourse in the manner that class, capitalism and socialism had once done. By 1990, the initially chaotic and necessarily partial challenges of Reaganism and Thatcherism to Keynesianism and social democracy in the United States and the United Kingdom had endowed free-market economics with enhanced legitimacy. Meanwhile the communist challenge to the West was patently on its last legs, as the 'velvet revolution' in Eastern Europe manifested, and its driving force, the Soviet Union, was on the verge of disintegration. As David Harvey has noted, these monumental but somewhat haphazard developments 'really only converged as a new orthodoxy with the articulation of what became known as the "Washington Consensus"'.[6] Regardless of its architects' intent, the Washington Consensus gave expression to the growing belief that the tide of history was running inexorably in favour of market democracy. It therefore became the *Magna Carta* of neoliberal doctrine regarding the primacy of the market and the limitation of the state's purpose to ensuring law and order, macroeconomic stability and the adequacy of physical infrastructure.[7]

The Washington Consensus's linkage with neoliberalism was further strengthened by its instrumental role in gathering fresh converts to the new orthodoxy. The newly democratised governments of Eastern Europe enthusiastically adopted its free-market prescription as the fastest and surest route to post-communist economic development. To Polish economist Grzegorz Kolodko, the message of the Washington Consensus was as applicable to the former communist bloc as it was to Latin America: 'Liberalise as much as you can, privatise as fast as you can and be tough in monetary and fiscal matters'.[8] Many third world governments outside Latin America also seized on the Washington Consensus as a prescription for economic growth in the context of emergent globalisation. John Williamson himself later conceded that its policy agenda could just as well have been applied to Asia and Africa, making its broad acceptance as a manifesto of market liberalism valid for all places and all times unsurprising.[9]

If the confluence of historical forces explains the establishment of the Washington Consensus as the symbol of neoliberal globalisation, the explanation for its consequent generation of anti-Americanism reveals some of the problems associated with this concept. A succession of financial crises in East Asia, Brazil and Russia in the late 1990s and in Argentina in 2001 and 2002 provoked intense controversy about the applicability of the Washington Consensus as a universal model of development. Neoliberal ideas came under challenge from critics who insisted that the state had a social responsibility to redress the inequalities inherent in a market economy.[10]

Yet this was not an attack on ideas that were exclusively American. The neoliberal pedigree had a strong European strand that could be traced back through the proponents of Thatcherism to the Austrian philosopher Friedrich Hayek's writings in the mid-twentieth century and ultimately to Adam Smith's late-eighteenth century treatise on the wealth of nations and the magic of the market. Nor were the battle lines in the controversy a simple case of American supporters of the Washington Consensus being aligned against its foreign critics. There was considerable diversity of opinion within the United States about the merits of free-market doctrine. Among its American opponents could be counted most of the trade union movement and many congressional Democrats who retained their party's traditional affiliation with labour interests.[11] Support from influential American economists, particularly those associated with the so-called Chicago School and devotees of public choice theory, helped to endow neoliberalism with intellectual legitimacy, but there were also a goodly number of prominent sceptics in the profession. Most notably, former World Bank chief economist Joseph Stiglitz charged that 'the dogma of liberalisation' had become 'an end in itself, not a means to achieving a better financial system'.[12] Even the head of one of the founding organisations of the Washington Consensus expressed doubts about its prescription. From the late 1990s, World Bank chairman James Wolfensohn became publicly critical of the way his agency had promoted open market policies that had alienated the very people the reforms were originally intended to help – those living in economic deprivation.[13]

In spite of this, neoliberalism became increasingly identified as a quintessentially American set of values. The Washington Consensus brand name encouraged this association. As John Williamson later acknowledged, it was 'difficult to think of a less diplomatic label', and he expressed regret for not conceiving a different appellation such as 'universal convergence' or 'one world consensus'.[14] To many critics, the designation epitomised America's arrogant belief that it could remake the world in its own economic image without regard for or understanding of other models. As one expert on development put it, the name itself came clean about who called the shots in the unipolar era – 'not government, but Washington. "Washington" … embraced not only the IMF and the World Bank, but also their less than shadowy master – the US government, and behind it, its shadowy masters, the US economics profession and western business interests'.[15]

However, it was the association of the Washington Consensus with America's aspirations of global mission that was the primary inspiration for the anti-Americanism it generated. This sense of mission was nothing new, of course, for it reflected belief in American exceptionalism that had shaped America's distinctive identity as a nation since the founding of the republic. Benjamin Franklin had given perfect expression of this ideal in his avowal that 'America's cause is the cause of mankind'. According to the credo of American exceptionalism, the United States was a special place where individuals could enjoy freedom and equality to pursue their aspirations, but its 'specialness' also endowed it with responsibility to promote its values in the outside world. As one scholar has observed, there was a peculiar inconsistency in this posture, which was 'at once inclusive and exclusive, outward-looking and deeply chauvinistic internationalist and nationalist'.[16] Whatever its convoluted logic, America's sense of mission was an important ideological element in its Cold War commitment to save the world from the threat of communism. As one cheerleader of American exceptionalism put it in 1957, 'To be American is no longer to be only a nationality. It has become, along with communism and in rivalry with it, a key pattern of action and values'.[17] Once the red peril was seen off, however, America's missionary enthusiasm turned to promotion of market democracy. In the estimation, of *New York Times* columnist Thomas Friedman, the central aim of post-Cold War US foreign policy was to encourage worldwide acceptance of free-market capitalism in order to fulfil the material aspirations of people everywhere. In this regard, he proclaimed, 'America not only can be, it must be a beacon for the whole world'.[18]

Policy makers clearly shared this belief. The national security strategies of both the Clinton and George W. Bush administrations explicitly identified promotion of free trade and free markets as a core goal of their foreign policy and essential for the spread of democracy and prosperity.[19] President Bush reiterated this in an op-ed column commemorating the first anniversary of the 9/11 attacks. America's aim in the war on terror, he declared, was to achieve a 'just peace ... where repression, resentment and poverty are replaced with the hope of democracy, development, free markets and free trade' – the last two having 'proved their ability to lift whole societies out of poverty'.[20] Returning to the same theme in his 2004 state of the Union address,

Bush made an unambiguous affirmation of his country's messianic responsibility. 'America', he declared, 'is a nation with a mission and that mission comes from our most basic beliefs'.[21]

America's 'Western' allies, including its Asian ones, had welcomed its anti-communist mission because this addressed a common threat, but, for the most part, they did not share to the same degree America's enthusiasm for the promotion of open markets and the retrenchment of the state. However, they had to operate in a unipolar international order in which America had unmatched power to promote its values. Aside from its military supremacy, the United States was the prime mover and shaker in global economics, the dollar was the principal reserve currency and a significant proportion of the top 100 companies in the world were American. In a matter-of-fact statement that accepted the increasing liberalisation and integration of the post-Cold War international economy as inseparable from US power, one American analyst commented approvingly, 'Globalisation is Americanisation'.[22] Many commentators outside the United States agreed with this assessment but wholly rejected its desirability. British commentator Will Hutton observed that economic liberalisation had become 'the dogma of the expanding [American] superstate' intent on maximising its power rather than promoting the world public good.[23]

American advocates of open markets assumed that people everywhere would accept them as harbingers of prosperity. In their eyes, the successful example of the US economy operating in accordance with liberal values was the ultimate agent of co-optive soft power that would make others want what America had. For a true believer like Thomas Friedman, it was inconceivable that there could be 'a coherent, universal ideological reaction' against market liberalisation because appreciation of the benefits of globalisation 'emerges from below, from street level, from people's very souls and from their deepest aspirations'.[24] Almost as soon as these words appeared in print, however, mass protests against the third ministerial meeting of the World Trade Organisation in Seattle in November 1999 proved the seminal event in the development of an anti-globalisation movement. After the 'battle of Seattle', anti-globalisation protests became a common accompaniment of every major international financial conference.

The anti-globalisation movement carried a strong subtext of anti-Americanism because the United States was regarded as the principal driver of globalisation, but it also railed against multinational corporations and rich nations in general. However the leaders of some rich nations were already engaged in their own form of rebellion against the full-blown American economic model. It was the East Asian financial crisis of 1997 that dealt the first significant blow to America's advocacy of the universal applications of the ideals of the Washington Consensus.

Asian Animus Against the Washington Consensus

To its Asian critics, the Washington Consensus embodied the American failure to respect systemic diversity in global capitalism and to appreciate that sound economic policy could flow from strong public institutions. Throughout the 1990s, the Japanese government and the World Bank were engaged in intricate manoeuvrings to promote their differing interpretations of the rapid development of the newly industrialising economies of East Asia. While the latter sought to fit the so-called 'East Asian economic miracle' into the framework of Anglo-American liberalism, the former saw it as the product of state-led economic development. The World Bank gradually shifted position in a series of official and semi-official reports to an acceptance that government intervention had played an important part, which was instrumental in the development of its more sceptical approach to neoliberalism in general. However, the financial crisis of 1997 put paid to any prospects of reconciliation between the American and Asian models.[25]

According to Chalmers Johnson, this crisis resulted from a clash between the American form of capitalism, disciplined by the profit motive, and the Asian version, disciplined by the imperative of export-led growth. The United States had been instrumental, through its growing influence in the Asia-Pacific Economic Cooperation (APEC) forum, in getting the Asian Tiger economies to open up to global market forces in the shape of free trade and investment. From 1995 onward, unrestricted capital flows resulted in huge foreign lending to Asian countries, but the rapid growth of their indebtedness raised concern about repayment that in turn produced a capital flight. Coming to the 'rescue', the IMF provided Indonesia, Thailand and South Korea with substantial loans that were made conditional on the imposition of austerity budgets, high interest rates and sales of debt-ridden companies to foreign bargain hunters.[26]

In an insensitive commentary, columnist Charles Krauthammer, a cheerleader for neoliberal reform, declared that the crisis had shown up the shortcomings of 'Asia's paternalistic crony capitalism that so seduced critics of the American system during Asia's now burst bubble'.[27] However the crisis and its aftermath, far from persuading East Asian leaders of the virtues of the American model, fomented their resentment of it. They saw their countries as victims of America's championship of globalisation of to the benefit international – and particularly American – financiers.[28] This did much to torpedo APEC's embrace of free trade. When the forum met at Kuala Lumpur in 1998, Vice-President Al Gore openly denounced Malaysian Prime Minister Mahathir Mohamad for imposing capital controls that insulated his country's economy from gipsy capital and effectively encouraged his people to overthrow him. In response, the Malaysian Ministry of Foreign Affairs accused the United States of being in the possession of an 'evil spirit' in its determination to force open-market doctrines on East Asian countries regardless of the harm to their weak economies. Significantly neither of the two disputants sent representatives to the 1999 APEC meeting of trade ministers in Auckland.[29]

In the wake of the crisis, Japanese leaders, who had endured nearly a decade of American criticism that their country's rigid economic structures and institutional arrangements were responsible for its loss of competitiveness, grew increasingly assertive in their criticism of the American model. Washington's rejection of their proposal to set up a special Asian Bank, which would have rendered loan aid to crisis-hit East Asian countries without imposing IMF free-market conditions, particularly irked them as a naked display of US determination to control the agenda of globalisation.[30] In January 1999, Eisuke Sakakibara, a top-ranking finance ministry official, issued a rebuke in a rebuke at the Tokyo Foreign Correspondents' Club. Delivered in English to gain maximum international coverage, his address denounced the Washington Consensus as an ideology that amounted to 'the blind application of a universal model' and warned of its potential to create anti-Americanism in different parts of the world.[31]

In the early twenty-first century, however, there were signs that the People's Republic of China was set to replace Japan as the principal champion of an Asian alternative to the Washington Consensus. According to advocates of the American way, Japan's strong economic performance in the early twenty-first century was attributable to Prime

Minister Junichiro Koizumi's reforms that cut government-backed ties between banks and their corporate clients, thereby forcing the latter to become more competitive in order to survive.[32] Meanwhile, China's leaders pronounced their goal of developing democracy with Chinese characteristics. The five-year plan approved in March 2006 embodied this in its projection of a dual economy in which the private sector would spearhead liberalisation reforms and the public sector would promote social reforms. Some commentators heralded the emergence of a Beijing Consensus because many of China's neighbours – particularly India – increasingly saw it as a socio-economic model rather than as a threat. According to one enthusiast, the Chinese model could become a potent challenger to the American one in the developing world because it projected an alternative 'where integration of global ideas is first rigorously gut-checked against the demands of local suitability'.[33]

European Antipathy to the 'Anglo-Saxon Model'

In Europe, the debate over the American model was intensified by its identification as an 'Anglo-Saxon model'. Critics of the open market values of the Washington Consensus considered the United Kingdom a partner in crime with the United States because of its desire to replace the 'European social model' at the heart of the European Union (EU) project with this new liberal model. One of the clearest areas of agreement in the often-fractious relationship between Prime Minister Tony Blair and his putative successor, Chancellor of the Exchequer Gordon Brown, was their admiration for the American model of market democracy, which they considered to be in harmony with the New Labour drive for modernisation.[34] Thatcherism had also been drawn to it for the same reason, but the Conservative Party as a whole was more ambivalent because of its attachment to social hierarchies that the new openness would weaken. Seeking to explain why New Labour had fewer reservations, one critic observed, 'In the absence of anything else or anything better, the American model – or what is understood by the American model – increasingly serves as New Labour ideology.'[35] As a result, Europeans who were hostile to the American model vented their spleen on its British advocates just as much as on the United States itself, but their animus was fundamentally an expression of ideological anti-Americanism.

One of the most trenchant critics, Will Hutton, the British newspaper columnist and chief executive of the Work Foundation, attacked the US model of globalisation as pandering to the preoccupations of American conservatism and corporate greed. In his view, the United Kingdom had signed on in support of an economic prescription that could not cure global ills and would only export the income inequality and social dislocation that characterised America's own society.[36] Hutton called on European leaders to challenge the American version of globalisation and champion the reinvigoration of international society based on the best European values regarding the state's role to ensure equality, social solidarity and the public realm. In his view, the essence of 'the idea of Europe' to be achieved through the EU project was the development of 'a rational, universal infrastructure of justice built on complex trade-offs between liberty, solidarity and equality'. In an interesting reversal of missions, Hutton believed that Europe would thereby help America itself to rediscover its true values of liberal egalitarianism, which had been championed by the previous generation of US leaders under the aegis of New Deal liberalism but forsaken by the present one through its fixation on neoliberalism.[37]

Resistance within the EU to the American model was strongest in France and Germany, where social market ideas were far more deeply rooted than free market ones. When French voters decisively rejected the proposed EU Constitution in the 2005 referendum, some analysts ascribed this to their fears that the European project had been hijacked by Anglo-American liberalism.[38] French and German leaders grew increasingly exasperated at being lectured by New Labour leaders and spokesmen on the need for EU members to adopt reforms based on American values.[39] French President Jacques Chirac reportedly commented that 'ultra-liberalism is the new communism of our age' in declaring his unyielding opposition to the Blair-backed 'services directive' proposal that aped the Washington Consensus by allowing firms based in one EU nation to offer services in another.[40] In bowing out of public life after his defeat in the 2005 German general election, former Social Democrat chancellor Gerhard Schroder told a trade union audience that the new market-minded Christian Democrat chancellor, Angela Merkl, would do Germany damage if she sought to incorporate Anglo-American liberal reforms into her agenda. In a clear reference to the Bush administration's failure to act quickly on behalf of low-income African-Americans in flooded sections of New Orleans after Hurricane Katrina, he commented, 'I can think of a recent disaster that shows what happens when a country neglects its duties of state towards its people. ... People do not want the state in their faces, but they want it at their side'.[41]

The Latin American Exception

Nowhere in the world was the Washington Consensus embraced so readily as in Latin America in the 1990s. Anxious for assistance from global financial institutions, many of its governments implemented open-market reforms that promised economic revitalisation after the 'Lost Decade' of the 1980s. They also signed up to the Clinton administration's proposal at the Summit of the Americas meeting at Miami in 1995 for the development of hemispheric free trade within a ten-year timetable. However, a severe regionwide recession from 1998 to 2002 put paid to hopes that economic reforms and hemispheric free trade would provide a miracle cure. Growth in Latin America during the 1990s was barely half of what it had been in the 1950s, 1960s and 1970s. Chile was the continent's lone success story, but it had been selective in implementing the Washington Consensus, only partially liberalising capital markets, taxed capital inflows and increased social spending. More commonly, Latin American economies continued to be hampered by structural weaknesses such as poor education standards, low investment in new technology, paltry savings rates and divisive inequalities. Far from overcoming such problems, Washington Consensus reforms arguably made matters worse because they increased exposure to volatile capital flows, currency fluctuations that damaged trade and investment, and the transfer of national resources into foreign hands through privatisation. According to a 2004 World Bank report, Latin America was the world's most unequal continent in terms of income distribution. On average, the richest 10 percent of the population in each of its countries accounted for 36 percent of national income while the bottom 40 percent received less than 14 percent. An estimated 222 million people lived in poverty – up from 200 million in 1990, 185 million lived on less than $2 a day and unemployment exceeded 10 percent (without accounting for forced emigration).[42]

In spite of this, there was initially no dramatic ideological reaction against American-inspired neoliberalism at the elite level in Latin America. In contrast to East Asia and Western Europe, Latin America did not have a broadly acceptable alternative model of its own to rally around. Market reforms had undermined the traditional sources of support for a strong state role in the economy. The trade unions had been weakened by labour deregulation, the public sector workforce through privatisation and special interest groups via the elimination of subsidies. The new leaders who came to power in Latin America in the early twenty-first century, notably Luiz Inacio 'Lula' da Silva in Brazil, Nestor Kirchner in Argentina and Lucio Gutierrez in Ecuador, were populists rather than leftists in the conventional sense. They rose as outsiders by attacking the established political class and special interests in the name of those segments of the population who felt left out, but were pragmatists rather than ideologues in terms of economic policy. Believing that there was no real alternative to open markets as a path to growth, they sought only to soften the edges of the liberal model.[43] As *The Economist* put it, the new leadership generation hewed to 'a new "post-Washington" consensus, combining (more-or-less) sound macroeconomic policies with a greater emphasis on social spending, and some tinkering with further liberalisation'.[44]

The main exception to this trend was President Hugo Chavez of Venezuela. Buoyed by enormous oil revenues and lack of effective domestic opposition, he promoted a 'Bolivarian vision' that emphasised Latin American unity against the Washington Consensus and independence from the United States. To this end, he launched Petrocaribe to sell discounted Venezuelan oil to small Caribbean states and purchased $25 million of Ecuador's public debt and $986 million of Argentina's to lessen their obligations to creditors from outside the continent. Chavez also pursued full membership for Venezuela in the Mercosur free trade zone (comprising Argentina, Brazil, Paraguay and Uruguay), proposed a confederation of Latin America's state-owned petroleum companies and vehemently opposed the US-promoted plan for the Free Trade Area of the Americas (FTAA).[45] Chavez made world headlines with his attack on the FTAA before a large rally gathered to protest against hemispheric free trade when the Summit of the Americas met at Mar del Plata in November 2005. He made a ringing vow to bury US-style capitalism throughout Latin America, 'Each one of us has brought a shovel, a gravediggers' shovel, because here in Mar del Plata is the tomb of the FTAA'.[46]

The consequent failure of the summit to agree on restarting stalled FTAA talks was widely attributed in the US media to Chavez's anti-American influence. In reality, none of the Latin American leaders at the summit bought into Chavez's Bolivarian vision. All but five signified their willingness to resume negotiations, and four of the latter were the Mercosur members who preferred to await World Trade Organisation talks in the hopes of getting a better deal on contentious issues like agricultural subsidies ahead of hemispheric discussions.[47] However populist leaders were careful to assert their independence from the United States and to engage in some Yankee-bashing. One reason they did so was to assuage the anti-American nationalism that had surfaced in their domestic constituencies in reaction to the Washington Consensus.[48] They also sought to highlight their sense that the United States was taking Latin America for granted under the aegis of this agenda.[49]

Nowhere was popular anti-Americanism stronger in Latin America than in Argentina, which had been the 'A+ student' of liberal reform.[50] It had implemented free trade, capital-market liberalisation, privatisation and a fixed-convertibility rate tying the peso in equal value with the dollar to control inflation. From 1998 onwards, however, Argentina's economy buckled under the impact of a strong peso that rose parallel with the dollar, high interest rates and capital-flow volatility. In December 2001, unemployment was running at 20 percent, a banking collapse obliterated a large portion of the middle class's savings, and over fifteen million people were living in poverty. The IMF's refusal to make further loans brought the economy to the verge of meltdown and plunged the country into political crisis.[51]

The early success of the reform program helped to make 'American chic' cool in Buenos Aires. Some nightclubs painted their dance floors with the Stars and Stripes, and movie theatres adopted the alien custom of selling popcorn for customers anxious to display their affinity with American tastes. When financial crisis hit, however, the refusal of the US government and its client agencies to come to the rescue generated a strong nationalist reaction against what Peronist Senator Jorge Yorna called 'the return of big stick policy'. The symbols of hard and soft American power, respectively, US-owned banks and McDonalds' restaurants, became targets of popular revulsion and protest. Two leading newsmagazines, *Noticias* and *Veintitres*, ran cover stories alleging that the United States was intent on making the crisis worse to enable American companies to buy up pampas farmlands at a cheap price. American interests, declared leftist congresswoman Elisa Carrio, 'have already taken most of what we have, and now they are coming for our lands'.[52]

Argentina's downfall sent shock waves throughout Latin America at both elite and popular levels. The United States was widely condemned as selfish and unreliable for its failure to come to the rescue of the nation that followed its economic bidding more closely than any other. Many in the region saw this outcome as proof that the Washington Consensus only brought 'misery, sacrifice and the loss of national sovereignty'.[53] American officials made matters worse by blaming Argentina for the denouement. Secretary of State Colin Powell's remarks that Argentina needed to clean up 'institutional flaws', notably government corruption, to restore its economy provoked widespread outcry against the United States' lack of respect for Argentina's sovereignty. The same reaction greeted Treasury Secretary Paul O'Neill's rash public warning that the election of former trade union leader and now left-wing Worker Party candidate Lula as Brazil's president would result in economic chaos and send the country the same way as Argentina. His words were deemed an American effort to tip the election to Lula's opponent.[54]

This outlook melded with resentment of US unilateralism in invading Iraq, which was deeply unpopular in a continent that had historic antipathy to American interventionism and overbearing power.[55] The personal unpopularity of George W. Bush added a third ingredient to the mix of nationalistic anti-Americanism. The US President, observed Latin American expert Richard Feinberg, was widely seen as 'a heartless conservative', because his insistence on the benefits of hemispheric free trade ignored regional concerns about equity for Latin America in the arrangement.[56] America's determination to have its own way regardless of the cost to others was a common complaint voiced by anti-FTAA protesters at Mar del Plata. One of them told a *New York Times* reporter that Bush would destroy Argentina through hemispheric free trade just as surely as he had destroyed Iraq with American bombs. Another declared, 'Chavez defends our countries. We're looking for alternatives to the way the United States controls the world'.[57]

In this context, the new populist leaders of Latin America regarded it as good politics to demonstrate their independence from the United States. This reaffirmed their outsider status from the traditional establishment in the eyes of their supporters and also sent Washington the signal that their national interests would have to be considered in any future hemispheric or bilateral trade agreement negotiations. As the new Brazilian president, Lula, declared, 'Only in Latin America, where we have ruling classes with colonial minds, do we believe that if we are kind to others, they will be

kind to us. I will defend Brazil's interests first and foremost'. As a former
trade unionist and now leader of the Workers' Party, he promised to create
ten million new jobs and double the purchasing power of the nearly one
third of Brazil's 175 million people who live in poverty.[58] Compared with
the old leadership's broad willingness to embrace the United States and its
new economic agenda in the 1990s, the insistence of the new leaders in
asserting their independence in the next decade carried overtones of anti-
Americanism. It bespoke a belief that America's economic interests were
at variance with Latin America's aspiration for economic independence,
growth and prosperity.

No single act better demonstrated the new approach than Argentina's
decision in 2004 to offer its creditors just thirty cents per dollar
in repayment of its public debt of $102.6 billion. This was the greatest
default in history, but foreign lenders accepted it as the best deal they
were likely to get. The IMF could not risk losing all the money it had
loaned Argentina. Moreover, Wall Street investment houses had moved
out of the country long before the 2001 crisis hit, so the US Treasury had
no need to press for a tough line. President Kirchner called it 'the greatest
deal ever' for a debtor nation and boasted that Argentina had given its
creditors a 'haircut'. While acknowledging that his country would have
to rebuild international confidence to attract much needed foreign
investment, he remarked that this would not be done 'by satisfying a few
economic, financial or ideological powers'. Even though the main losers
in the default were French and Italian creditors, his words were clearly
aimed at the United States and its client agencies. In the words of one
commentator, Kirchner's message as understood throughout Latin
America was 'Wall Street, the IMF, the Washington consensus crowd
can go hang ... the global policy establishment can be seen off'.[59]

Before caving in, the IMF and groups of bondholders accused
Argentina of bad faith. Sympathetic coverage in the world financial
press drew comparisons with Diego Maradona's 'hand of God goal'
against England in the 1986 World Cup. This showed a supreme
misunderstanding of the Argentine psyche. Maradona's 'goal' had
only contributed to his popularity at home for putting one over on a
foreign power that had recently humbled Argentina (in this case in the
Falklands/Malvinas war). Moreover, Maradona became something of
a metaphor for the new Argentina. Having sunk into a very unhealthy
lifestyle and drug taking, he suffered a serious heart attack in 2005. Upon
his recovery he found a new career as a television presenter and fierce

critic of George Bush. Holding US policy responsible for the impoverishment of millions of Argentines, he was at Chavez's side during the anti-FTAA demonstrations at Mar del Plata.[60]

Argentina made its own remarkable comeback from economic collapse through the combination of a devalued peso, some monetary relaxation and increased social spending within the framework of fiscal soundness. Though by no means in robust economic health, it was strong enough to repay the final instalment of $9.5 billion on its debt to the IMF in early 2006. The substantive and symbolic significance of liberation from an institution perceived to be under American control was evident. 'With this payment', Kirchner declared, 'we are burying a significant part of an ignominious past'.[61]

Cosying up to Washington's hemispheric *bête noir*, President Fidel Castro of Cuba,[62] was another way Latin American leaders found of thumbing their nose at the United States. Lula, Kirchner and Uruguay's Tabare Vasquez engaged in friendly public commune with Castro, with only Mexico's Vincente Fox, a trenchant critic of Castro's human rights record, resisting the trend. Moderate governments in Paraguay and Uruguay also restored full diplomatic relations with Cuba in 2005. Even the most pro-Bush leader in South America, Columbia's Alvaro Uribe Velez, accepted Castro's offer to reopen peace talks in Havana with one of his country's leading Marxist factions. Commenting on these developments, Lula's predecessor as Brazilian president, Fernando Henrique Cardoso, justifiably downplayed American concerns that Latin American countries might look to follow Cuba's socialist example in reaction against neoliberalism. Moving closer to Cuba was more important for its symbolism. Despite prolonged American efforts to isolate it, Cuba retained an aura of independence that many in Latin America felt they had lost in the age of globalisation.[63]

Of more substantive significance was the new toughness that some Latin American governments showed in trade negotiations with the United States, exemplified by the Mercosur governments' refusal to renew FTAA talks in 2005. In their eyes, the United States was guilty of bad faith because it did not itself practice what it preached with the Washington Consensus. Since their predecessors in the 1990s had enacted reforms that offended important domestic constituencies, they expected Washington to follow suit and cease its deference to powerful American lobbies. In particular Latin American leaders expected it to cut its subsidies for US agricultural producers, which the Bush administration raised in 2002, and reduce its high tariffs and quotas on key commodities that are high-volume Latin American exports, including sugar, orange juice, and cotton. Argentina, for example, might have moderated its decline into economic catastrophe had it been better able to sell its main commodities in the US market, where it was disadvantaged not by the strong peso but by tariffs. Another source of regional ire was Washington's demands that trade talks should also negotiate tough new standards for intellectual property protection. This was grist to the mill for those who feared that the United States was bent on preserving its lead in scientific and technological knowledge over Latin America at all costs. Acceptance of this American requirement would also eliminate the possibility of distributing generic medicines at affordable cost to the many impoverished and non-affluent citizens of the continent and of boosting employment in local businesses involved in their production.[64]

As Lula remarked, Latin America was in favour of free trade as long as there was 'effective equality', but Brazil's twenty main product exports faced an average tariff of 40 percent in the United States while its twenty major product imports carried an average tariff of only 13 percent.[65] There was also deep resentment in Latin America that the United States appeared to be using the threat of exclusion from its giant domestic market as stick to beat them into submission over free trade. United States Trade Representative Robert Zoellick fuelled this when he publicly warned that if the newly elected Lula did not back the FTAA, he would find himself having 'to export to Antarctica'. Concern was consequently voiced in some circles in Brazil that the United States was out to deindustrialise the country by forcing through a free-trade model that only served its interests.[66]

Prospects of Ideological Anti-Americanism in Latin America

The anti-Americanism that initially characterised Latin American reaction against the Washington Consensus bore the hallmarks of nationalistic prejudice against what was perceived as the US threat to the national economic interest and consequently the economic sovereignty of the countries in this region. The open market agenda pushed by the United States and its putative client agency, the IMF, may have qualitatively altered the context of intervention, but it struck many in Latin America as another manifestation of American imperialism. Due first to the growth of its economic interests in the continent and then the development of its Cold War strategic concerns therein, the United States had seemingly become so fully integrated with Latin America in the twentieth century that, according to one scholar, it could 'no longer conduct its foreign policy with these states without interfering in their domestic affairs'.[67]

Nevertheless some commentators have perceived a danger that nationalist anti-Americanism could transmogrify into an ideological variant if Hugo Chavez's ideas for *Alternativa Bolivariana para las Américas* (ALBA) gains adherence as an alternative to the FTAA. After witnessing the hostile demonstrations against the FTAA in Mar del Plata, Cuban-born and Madrid-domiciled political columnist Carlos Alberto Montaner warned that anti-Americanism had become an ideology in Latin America where growing numbers of people 'reject the market economy as a way to create and assign wealth'.[68] As self-described, Chavez's ALBA advocated a socially oriented trade bloc rather than one based strictly on the logic of deregulated profit maximisation. It sought a 'genuine regional integration that transcends the prerogatives of transnational corporations' that would provide solidarity with the poorest Latin American countries like Haiti and Bolivia in their dealings with the hemispheric economic superpower. Among other things, Chavez wanted the ALBA to promote a regional agricultural policy that would prioritise member-countries' food self-sufficiency to protect the poor from unfair foreign subsidies, oppose liberalisation of public services and reject the Washington Consensus-FTAA label of 'Most Favoured Nation', which undermined sovereignty by forcing countries to give foreign and domestic firms equal footing.[69]

Until late 2005, Chavez's vision was bereft of support from his fellow regional heads-of-state. However, the stunning 2005 presidential victory of Evo Morales in Bolivia with 54 percent of the popular vote – the first time in modern history that the country had elected a leader by majority vote – suggested to some that, in Fidel Castro's words, 'the map is changing'. A number of analysts of differing political persuasions, such as Niall Ferguson and Richard Gott, saw this as an important development that could portend an ideological and geopolitical challenge to the United States from the energy-rich region situated on its southern flank.[70]

Morales, leader of the Movement to Socialism (MAS) party, called himself 'America's worst nightmare' in his last campaign address. On election night, following his defeat of former President Jorge Quiroga, a US-educated businessman, he declared, 'The people have defeated the neoliberals'. Shortly before winning the vote on a manifesto of natural resource privatisation and coca decriminalisation, he appeared at Chavez's side at the anti-FTAA rally in Mar del Plata. During post-election visits to Chavez and Castro, he poked fun at George Bush by referring to himself and his two political heroes as 'the axis of good'. Morales tapped into popular resentment that foreign-owned interests had denied Bolivia its rightful share of successive commodity booms in silver, tin and natural gas over the course of the previous century or more. He promised to reverse the privatisation allowed under previous regimes with a program of oil, gas and water supply re-nationalisation, even though foreign corporations have already ploughed billions of dollars into exploration and extraction.[71] An Aymara Indian (the first indigenous Bolivian to become president) and former head of the coca growers union, Morales also vowed that coca cultivation, the only source of income for many impoverished farmers, would be legalised despite US determination to eradicate it.[72]

There are other signs that Chavez's ideas may spread on the continent. Ecuador and Peru have large indigenous populations whose political mobilisation could have a significant impact on the left turn of the region. Chavez has also bankrolled the return to the political fray of Sandinista leader Daniel Ortega in Nicaragua. Bolivarian Committees have sprung up on university campuses all over Latin America, even in Mexico, where the Venezuelan leader had not hitherto been held in high esteem. Former Mexican foreign minister Jorge Castaneda warned that the trend had to be countered by lionising Chile as proof that reform could be made to work in Latin America.[73]

Without doubt, new forces did emerge in Latin American politics in the middle years of the first decade of the twenty-first century, but whether this trend will transform anti-Americanism in the region into an ideological force of opposition to liberalism is open to doubt. America's dedication to promoting international respect for private property rights may have led it to underestimate the redistributive reforms that Chavez has implemented at home. Yet in spite of its oil wealth, Venezuela's economic performance and the still high levels of poverty amongst its people have not yet made it a successful model for broad emulation. The challenge for any Latin American regime ideologically hostile to the United States is whether it can deliver a significantly better economic outcome for its people. How Morales fares as Bolivia's president will arguably provide important clues as to the future of Boliviarian ideals.

His country remains dependent, in the short term at least on annual US foreign aid of $91 million, which itself is conditional on coca eradication. Exploitation of the country's hydrocarbon and other natural resources requires continued foreign investment in exploration and extraction technology that would have to be taken into account when changing the rules of engagement with international corporations. It may very well be that he seeks a middle ground between the cautious, selective engagement of Lula with the US agenda and Chavez's alternative vision. At the time of writing, however, it is premature to suggest that there will be widespread development of a Latin American economic model with values directly opposite to the American free-market model.

Conclusion

The neoliberal agenda of the Washington Consensus has been the source of different varieties of anti-Americanism. In East Asia and Western Europe, it has generated an ideological reaction against its promotion of government disengagement from the market. In Western Europe, hostility to the American model has been intensified by the drive of Britain's New Labour government to promote the 'Anglo-Saxon model' in place of the traditional preference for the social democratic model within the EU. Both France and Germany have come to view the Blair administration's belief in modernisation along neoliberal lines as simply copying the American economic values inherent in the Washington Consensus. However, if the UK economy continues to flourish under the aegis of open-market ideas, and conversely if economies such as those of France and Germany in which the state is more strongly involved underperform, this resistance to change within the EU could well be worn down, leading to a decline in ideological anti-Americanism in Western Europe.

In Asia, too, Japanese antipathy to the American economic model seems to be in decline as the economy recovers from prolonged stagnation after reforms implemented by the Koizumi government. China may still well take up the championing of an economic model tailored to Asian needs, and if the United States pushes harder for open-market rules with Beijing, the growing superpower rivalry between the two nations could be tinged with an ideological anti-Americanism.

In Latin America's case, the shortcomings of the Washington Consensus agenda led neither to its wholesale abandonment nor to widespread development of ideological anti-Americanism. Antipathy towards the United States for promoting open market doctrines did intensify markedly in the region in the wake of the Argentine crisis of 2001 and 2002, but this was largely an expression of traditional nationalist resentments against the dominant hemispheric power. In other words this anti-Americanism was rooted not in ideology but prejudice – a belief that the United States promoted the Washington Consensus to feather its own economic nest rather than to help Latin America achieve real economic independence.

A number of analysts have warned that a Washington distracted by the Middle East needs to end the relative neglect of Latin America in its foreign policy agenda. Of necessity, this would require making some compromises to assuage regional concerns about its free trade agenda, particularly with regard to its own policies on subsidies, tariffs and quotas. The best hope to allay the anti-Americanism that has developed in Latin America as a result of the Washington Consensus is for both sides to recognise their mutual interests in developing productive economic ties. In 2005, America's exports to Latin America were valued above $150 billion, nearly on a par with its exports to the EU. Two thirds of this trade was with Mexico and Brazil; so the rest of the region is a relatively untapped market for the United States. Meanwhile Latin America needs to expand its foreign investment and trade, particularly in high-tech products, and its proximity to the United States can give it an advantage over the Asia Pacific in this regard, particularly if an appropriate hemispheric free-trade agreement can be negotiated. There is a danger, however, that if the United States continues to insist on full adherence to its open-market agenda, Latin America will move towards Hugo Chavez's Bolivarian model. This would be a more dangerous type of ideological anti-Americanism than the European and Asian varieties. Anti-Americanism against Washington Consensus liberalism developed incidentally in Europe and the Asia Pacific because of differing ideas about the role of the state in the economy. Moreover, both regions were partners with the United States in the global economy and had an interest in preserving it – even if they differed in opinion about the degree of market openness that should accompany this. If Latin America's anti-Americanism acquires an ideological dimension, this will have evolved out of nationalist antipathy and its *raison d'être* will be opposition to the United States. Such a development would pose a significant challenge in a region that Washington has neglected of late but that remains vital to its interests.

Chapter 11

American Popular Culture and Anti-Americanism

Cheryl Hudson

At the start of the twenty-first century, culture is cool and ubiquitous. In this culturalised climate, politicians rush to reframe political issues as cultural preferences, communities redefine themselves according to cultural heritage and many academic disciplines have taken a 'cultural turn'. You might expect popular culture therefore to be just as exalted and indeed in some post-modern circles it is. Yet popular culture is also the target of much derision and hostility, particularly if it emanates from the United States. The reasons for this widespread animosity are many and varied but before we explore them, the terms of the discussion need to be examined a little more closely.

In the realm of culture, definitions are notoriously difficult. Where and how then do we locate popular culture? The anthropological definition of culture as the loose complex of values, customs, beliefs and practices that constitute the way of life of a particular group obviously encompasses 'popular culture' within it but so much more beside. Perhaps it is popularity that is the key and the size of the audience or practicing cultural group that defines whether a cultural product or practice is 'popular'? The development of media technologies has had a bearing on the scale of distribution and audience size and thus the definition of popular culture. The penny press allowed for the mass production and circulation of newspapers, magazines and books in the nineteenth century. In the twentieth century, photography, phonography, film, radio, television and the Internet have all expanded the production and distribution of cultural products and helped to create a popular market for them. The United States, of course, was in the forefront of the development of these modern communication technologies.

With the emergence of mass cultural production, concerns about 'vulgarisation' arose, particularly among social elites. These concerns expressed the anti-democratic tendencies within the elite rather than any intellectual or artistic judgment about cultural products. Such elitist judgments about value based on audience size (less is more) rather than the quality of the cultural product continue into the twenty-first century. Popular culture is usually regarded as distinct from 'high' culture and is in fact often viewed more as entertainment than art. Of course, 'popular' and 'high' are not antonyms and in some societies, in some historical periods, they may even amount to the same thing. Shakespeare's plays, for example, tended to draw large audiences from across the social stratum. Historically, the lines between high culture and popular culture have often been crossed and boundaries blurred. The Waltz, for instance, was originally an Austrian peasant dance, but it went through a process of refinement in Viennese high society in the 1780s and subsequently spread worldwide.

Nevertheless, popular culture carries an aura of having some connection to the common folk and to traditions of folklore and folk art – most importantly, of carrying 'the authenticity of a collective past'.[1] This characteristic makes the distinction between 'popular' and 'mass' culture meaningful as well as differentiating the popular from high culture. While mass culture is said to be inauthentic due to its manufacture by the 'culture industry' through mass production and marketing techniques, elite culture might be seen as inauthentic due to its exclusivity and socially managed access. Only popular culture conjures spontaneous, vernacular or 'street' credibility and authenticity. Yet, as Rob Kroes reminds us, mass culture draws on and recycles repertoires of culture that have a folk character thus making the distinction between the two forms much less meaningful.[2]

In the terms of the discussion about American popular culture and anti-Americanism, there is little sense in making much of the distinction between 'mass' and 'popular' culture because they are often taken as synonymous. In any case, critics of American popular culture usually assume the dead weight of sterile mass production and distribution processes behind the cultural products not the energy of spontaneous and authentic creativity.

Although there are some real and obvious problems with the contemporary production of quality cultural goods, this essay will argue that American popular culture does in fact produce meaningful and tasteful cultural products rather than merely shallow, bland and stiflingly uniform ones as critics charge. Much of the reason it can do so is that the United States is an unashamedly modern nation – it is heterogeneous, energetic, dynamic and forward-looking. Much American popular culture reflects this freshness and fullness of possibility, but in fact the best of American popular culture critically engages with the modern condition and fearlessly explores it, warts and all.

After examining a few examples of the best American television, film, music and fashion, this chapter will review some of the forms that opposition to American culture and consumer products has taken over the course of the twentieth century before looking at the content of contemporary cultural anti-Americanism. I will then suggest some reasons for the increase in this particular type of anti-Americanism in the twenty-first century. Many critics of American popular culture are actually articulating a discomfort with modernity, which they project onto the United States as the representative of all that is wrong with modern life. There is much subterfuge within the discussion or at least a profound confusion between social and aesthetic values. While critics from the left project their political objections into the cultural sphere, critics from the right present and defend a historical view of culture, particularly from American encroachments. Both ends of the political spectrum arrive at a position of celebrating the past, or of attempting to escape from modernity. The United States offends them because it embraces the future and confronts the challenges of modernity head on.

This essay will conclude with a discussion of some alternative explanations for contemporary problems with cultural production, particularly the 'dumbing down' of culture and will ask whether a common global culture is either desirable or necessary. The focus of the essay will be on European cultural anti-Americanism, but I will offer examples from around the globe.

The Best of American Popular Culture

The rest of the world experiences America largely through its consumption of American popular culture – films, music, television shows, fashion, magazines, advertising, theme parks and other consumer goods. Cultural merchandise ranks high among American exports, and exported American movies, TV shows and pop songs dominate lists of top grossing cultural product in Europe and worldwide.[3] In 1994, in Germany, American films took eight of the top ten grossing film spots and in France, eleven of the top twenty films were imported from the United States. The percentage of American films dominating the top ten is even higher in English-speaking Britain; 90 percent of the most popular films were American imports (although one third of these were Harry Potter films, written by a British woman and jointly produced in Britain). The first non-American film in a list of the top box office successes worldwide appeared at number 27.[4] The sheer dominance of American film suggests that the success and popularity of American cultural products cannot simply be attributed to aggressive marketing or viewed as an unfortunate side effect of American military and economic domination – unless, of course, the choices of the global audience are entirely discounted. Without a doubt, the quality of the cultural products plays a role.

Although the primary purpose of this essay is to address and explain the criticisms of American popular culture, it is worth establishing at the start that American popular culture is in fact innovative, creative, dynamic and often highly deserving of its popularity. That is not to suggest that it is uniformly good any more than it is uniformly bad. Yet if we want to acknowledge the very best of global popular culture, our eyes must turn towards Hollywood, Motown and HBO.

On television, American writers, directors and producers have provoked and challenged the world with ground-breaking drama series such as the darkly comic *Six Feet Under*, the brutal and poignant *The Sopranos*, the frantically paced, morally charged *ER*, and the ironic post-feminist *Buffy the Vampire Slayer*. Offering penetrating insight into and an intelligent commentary upon the society that produced them, these shows also have global appeal due to their sophisticated dealings with the universal themes of love, death, family and friendship. They each approach these universal themes through rich specific contexts and environments, probing and exploring particular American experiences and through them addressing universal modern problems and issues.

The best example of this is perhaps *Six Feet Under*. The Academy Award-winning writer of *American Beauty* Alan Ball created, co-wrote and executive produced the dark show that grapples with the meaning of life by confronting the inevitability of death.[5] Following the story of the Fisher family who run a funeral home in Los Angeles and therefore deal daily with death and the process of grieving, the show was designed to challenge what Alan Ball called the American (particularly Californian) denial of death.[6] Production values are impeccable, the acting out-standing, and each storyline contains elements of dark comedy as well as haunting beauty. The diverse cast of characters provides someone for everyone to identify with, and as the series finale tells us 'Everyone,

Everything, Everywhere, Ends' (including the show itself which ended in August 2005), driving home the common human experience of life, loss and mortality. Like all good art, *Six Feet Under* challenges and confronts rather than comforts the audience.

Six Feet Under clearly earned its global success. Broadcast on both public and private television channels in thirty-eight countries on all five continents, the show gathered critical acclaim and audience numbers across its five seasons. The show also gathered industry awards: seven Emmys, three Golden Globes and two Screen Actors Guild awards. The quality of the acting, writing, directing and production suggests that the popularity of the show was the result of the preferences of a thoughtful and appreciative public.

American movies are, of course, a global phenomenon and again, the superior quality of the films goes a long way for accounting for this. Where would world cinema be, after all, without the directorial genius of Martin Scorsese, Francis Ford Coppola, Robert Altman and Woody Allen? Each of these directors has not only pushed the ceiling higher when it comes to technical film-making excellence, but they have brought insights both peculiarly American and universally human to their film direction. Their films are witness to their artistic ambition. Scorcese's gifts lies in his ability to articulate the violent tragedy as well as the intense excitement of modern urban life and in his empathetic treatment of masculine insecurities as well as the catholic themes of guilt and redemption; Coppola's and Altman's work overhauls the conventions of Hollywood film genres and challenges the 'star' system with the utilisation of illuminating ensemble performances in their films; Allen give the audience a wry and comic tour of both America's most modern city New York and the interior of the modern American psyche. All of them demonstrate intelligence and literacy in their filmmaking and importantly also assume these qualities on the part of the audience too.

American filmmakers have produced a mass of truly great films in the twentieth and twenty-first centuries: from *Casablanca* to *The Deer Hunter*; from *Taxi Driver* to *Donnie Darko*; from *Citizen Kane* to *Lost in Translation* and from *Gone with the Wind* to *Crash*. Many of these films and others of similar quality challenge and provoke the audience, sometimes to an unsettling extent. Sophia Coppola's searching examination of personal dislocation and loneliness in *Lost in Translation*, for example, works on a number of levels: the film asks the audience to find both tragedy and comedy in the plight of Bill Murray's ageing movie star cast adrift in a sea of bright Tokyo lights. It demands that the audience contemplate the feeling of alienation brought on by the experience of being alone in a strange and unfamiliar country, but it also asks us to recognise the similarities between Japan's most modern cities and our own fast-paced and anonymous lives. Finally, but not exhaustively, by introducing Scarlett Johansson's newlywed character, the film demonstrates that connections of friendship, trust and, ultimately, hope can be found in the most unlikely of places. *Lost in Translation*'s multiple and seemingly contradictory meanings reflect the complexity of the modern human experience. The film was made on a small budget, but it proved to be a box office success around the world, and it won an Academy Award for best original screenplay as well as three Golden Globes and three British Academy of Film and Television Arts (BAFTA) awards.

Americans have also defined and redefined the nature of popular music over the course of the last century. The blues of Robert Johnson, the jazz of Miles Davis and the rock and roll of Elvis Presley set the benchmark for popular music internationally. The Motown record label bought to the world the sounds of African-American musicians Marvin Gaye, The Temptations, The Supremes, Stevie Wonder and, of course, Michael Jackson. Beginning at Motown with The Jackson Five and going on to a spectacular solo career, Michael Jackson is the world's most successful pop superstar. His album *Thriller* is the largest selling album of all time with fifty-one million sales worldwide, and he was awarded the World Music Award's best-selling pop male artist of the Millennium as well as thirteen Grammies over the course of his career. Despite the shadows over his personal life, few people could deny Jackson's massive talent as a singer, songwriter, dancer and performer.

While the argument for the excellence and quality of American popular culture may not hold as strongly in the field of fashion, there is no denying that the invention of denim jeans by American immigrant Levi Strauss in the nineteenth century was a massive boon to the comfort and functionality of clothing. Although the material and dyes for blue jeans originated in Europe and Asia, Strauss added the metal rivets, which made jeans such a hard-wearing item of clothing. Initially used for work wear, denim jeans became a fashionable and mildly rebellious style statement by young Americans in the 1950s. When James Dean, Marlon Brando and Elvis Presley appeared on screen wearing jeans, they took off as an international fashion statement. Within a decade or so, denim jeans had become a wardrobe staple in the United States – with the average American owning seven pairs. In the former Soviet Union, blue jeans were an expensive import and associated with the good life and American culture. From Spain to China, jeans are known as 'cowboy pants', indicating their association with the American West and cowboy culture. Internationally, denim jeans remain a symbol of egalitarianism, and they are the supreme example of the casual, practical fashions that Americans export to the world in fashion chain stores such as Gap.

These few positive examples of American popular culture will hopefully serve to temper the prejudiced reaction against what is often portrayed as an unthinking, trite and commercialised American culture. They indicate the diversity of American cultural products as well as the varied cultural influences – many of them international – that go into making up popular culture in the United States. They also suggest positive reasons for the global embrace of popular culture beyond the destructive coercion of America's cultural marketing machine. The best of American popular culture combines a great respect for the intelligence and discretion of the audience with a democratic, even iconoclastic, irreverence for established custom and practice. As we shall see below, such a view of US popular culture contradicts much criticism of it and the American global role.

Forms of Cultural Anti-Americanism

America's global presence in the twentieth and twenty-first centuries has elicited a vast array of conflicting reactions from other nations that range from sympathetic emulation to caustic denunciation. The scale of the negative response to American influence, or 'Americanisation' in recent years, however, appears to have grown exponentially in both force and irrationality and become, as Todd Gitlin indicates, nothing less than a 'demonology' that kills all rational thought and discussion.[7]

While it is certainly true that negative attitudes towards America and Americans have grown in recent times – particularly among the educated and articulate – global views of the United States are still intriguingly contradictory. Around the world, peoples of various nations have admired America for its democracy, egalitarianism and social dynamism while others have loathed its lack of refinement, its stultifying conformity and its 'cultural imperialism'. Moreover, responses to processes of cultural Americanisation, both negative and positive, often say more about the nation under transformation than any real or imagined American influence.

Nevertheless, anti-Americanism has a long and enduring history. Indeed, James Ceasar claims that anti-Americanism is much more than simply a prejudice or stereotype, since it is rooted in and has been fashioned by the philosophies of some of the greatest European minds over the course of several centuries. From colonial degeneracy theories to nineteenth-century Romantic denunciations of enlightened and rational government to Nietzschean accusations of 'spiritual emptiness', anti-Americanism remains, according to Caeser, the 'lingua franca of the intellectual class'.[8]

Much of the current cultural anti-Americanism has indeed developed and evolved from intellectuals of both the political left and the political right at different times and for different reasons over the course of the last century. The most powerful influence on interpretations of the impact of American culture arguably comes from Marxist theorists Theodor Adorno and Max Horkheimer. In their deeply pessimistic 1947 work, *Dialectic of Enlightenment*, Adorno and Horkheimer outline the operational mode of the increasingly powerful 'culture industry'. Although their theory of cultural standardisation and commodification did not directly implicate the United States as a *cause* of cultural corruption, they did note that, since the monopolisation of culture was more advanced in the United States than in Europe, intellect and creativity were banished from American culture more completely and at an earlier date than in Europe.[9]

According to the theory of the culture industry, the industrial system of cultural production creates standardised products that can no longer be differentiated one from the other. Replacing the social order that was lost with the disestablishment of religion and the increasing differentiation of society, 'culture now impresses the same stamp on everything. Film, radio and magazines make up a system that is uniform as a whole and in every part'.[10] As art becomes a mere commodity for market exchange, all active engagement between cultural consumer and cultural product ends. Consumers are made passive both in being denied any creative or imaginative input and in the sense of being manipulated to enjoy that which they have no control over. Ultimately, the power and seduction of the culture industry results in the destruction of the individual and the triumph of monopoly capitalism. Since the United

States is the centre of the culture industry, it is not difficult to see how exponents of this theory draw negative conclusions about the impact of American culture on those of other nations.

Adorno and Horkheimer were both victims and critics of Nazism, which explains their own social pessimism, but not necessarily that of contemporary advocates of their theory. Besides its dour outlook, their theory is problematic, because it imagines that culture can sustain social cohesion as powerfully as religion once did – or in fact even more powerfully since society is, in their own view, becoming increasingly differentiated. Moreover, in its all-embracing pessimism, the theory denigrates the ability of ordinary people to engage with modern life and culture and reflects a deeply patronising view of the audience.

At the other end of the political spectrum, the philosopher Martin Heidegger – a supporter of Nazism – fashioned an even more damning critique of the United States and its culture. For Heidegger, America was nothing less than *Katestrophenhaft*, the site of catastrophe, and Americanism was in his view 'the still unfolding and not yet full or completed essence of the emerging monstrousness of modern times'.[11] Not feeling the pull of tradition and folk culture, the United States had little respect for authenticity or uniqueness resulting in a barren cultural landscape bereft of meaningful cultural goods and stocked full of uniform and ersatz cultural products.

In most historical periods, Heidegger's analysis of American culture would be questionable but never more so than at the time of writing. Between the world wars, the United States may have had intense social and economic obstacles to overcome, but culturally it was awash with innovation and creativity. From the art, music, poetry and literature flowing out of Harlem during the twenties to the modernist literature of Fitzgerald, Hemingway, and Faulkner, to the movies of Charlie Chaplin and Orson Welles, American culture was far from barren or superficial. Heidegger's problem was in fact more with modernity *per se* than with the United States. We shall return to the theme of America as a symbol of modernity, but for now, it is worth noting that the reasons Heidegger gave for his rejection of Americanism were strikingly similar to those adopted by the left in the post-war period.

It is useful to understand that the strands of modern cultural anti-Americanism have their origins in both sides of the political divide. In contemporary forms of cultural anti-Americanism – of which there are many – it is increasingly difficult to discern where the particular critic of

the United States sits on the political spectrum. Apparently progressive
critiques end with calls for a preservation of traditional cultures, while
apparently elitist critiques are revealed on closer scrutiny as being the
result of intense national insecurity and self-loathing.

The concept of cultural imperialism dominates discussions of the
negative impact of American culture on the rest of the world. Proponents
of the theory argue that powerful media organisations colonise and dominate the cultural content of the media transmissions in weaker or less
developed nations to the detriment of the local cultures. Coined in the
1970s by Herbert Schiller, the term 'cultural imperialism' initially applied
to the expansive cultural policies of both the United States and the Soviet
Union ('Russification'), but in the post-Cold War world, it generally refers
solely to media domination by American corporations.[12] Although the
term was most prominent in discussions about Latin America during
the 1970s, it has come to apply to all non-reciprocal American cultural
penetration whether in the 'peripheral' countries of the developing world
or in the more advanced nations of Europe and Asia.

The theory of cultural imperialism posits that it is the role and
function of American media organisations to transmit positive images
and the core values of the United States to the rest of the world both in
order to dominate the global media industry and in order to remake the
world in the American image. Many proponents of the theory hold that
American popular culture is ideologically inscribed with American
values, and that foreign consumers have no choice but to internalise these
values as they are exposed to an endless round of American soap operas,
game shows, web sites, movies and other media products. Sometimes the
process operates entirely through market domination but at other times,
the American state perceives a more politically urgent need to create
an expansionist cultural policy in order to win the 'hearts and minds'
of a foreign population through cultural propaganda tactics. Arguably,
initiatives such as the Fulbright exchange (established in 1946) and the
Congress for Cultural Freedom (established in 1950) were weapons
in the United State's anti-communist arsenal and have been understood
as a 'cultural Marshall Plan'.[13]

In the post-Cold War world, American cultural imperialism
apparently operates more through Hollywood's than Washington's
design and machinations. By whichever method American popular
culture is spread, however, proponents of cultural imperialism see
it as a pernicious and insidious influence. Indeed, in some of the more

rabidly anti-American literature, the global spread of American culture is compared to the spread of a virulent and deadly virus:

> American culture seems like a virus, a particularly pathological one at that. We might, not without some justification, compare American culture to the AIDs virus, HIV. Like that brilliantly adapted organism, US culture is endlessly self-replicating and alarmingly adept at co-opting the production machinery of its hosts ... American fast food culture, pop music, films and television infect the cultural body of other nations, co-opting local production machinery to focus their efforts on mimicry. This pattern of viral replication repeats itself the world over, with American pop cultural norms choking out and stifling native flora and fauna.[14]

Protest at the malevolent effect of American cultural influence on indigenous cultures comes from serious academic works and radical activist literature like Naomi Klein's *No Logo*, as well as populist tracts. In their best-selling book *Why Do People Hate America?* and its sequel *American Dream, Global Nightmare*, writers Ziauddin Sardar and Merryl Wyn Davies provide a populist critique of American popular culture. For Sardar and Davies, all of American popular culture is simply one enormous billboard advertisement for the goods, services and material endowments of the American way of life, which includes the apparently sinister goals of material affluence and consumer choice. The authors prefer the term 'bio-terrorism' to 'cultural imperialism' since this portrays the complicity of the host population in the blighting of their cultural and physical landscapes by American cultural imports.[15]

Sardar and Davies are particularly keen to defend the traditional cultures of developing countries from the encroachments of American popular culture and its attendant values. They outline the devastation wrought by the failure of Americanisers to demonstrate the proper respect for other cultures:

> The tsunami of American consumerist culture assimilates everything, exerting immense, unstoppable pressure on the people of much of the world to change their lifestyles, to abandon all that gives meaning to their lives, to throw away not just their values but also their identity, stable relationships, attachment to history, buildings, places, families and received ways of doing and being.[16]

The picture they present is not pretty. They argue that American multinationals occupy all available cultural space and place local cultures in a vice-like grip, making it impossible for developing countries to run their own local television programming or denying them the possibility of owning independent Internet content. Sardar and Davies even go so far as to blame the marketing of rap music, Nike trainers and baggy jeans for the crime, truancy, drug addiction, promiscuity and the breakdown in parental authority among Asian youth. This is supposedly due to the fact that they 'imbibe the representation of the psychological profile' of disaffected black urban youth in the United States along with their reversed baseball caps – and not, of course, because they share the experience of alienation, poverty and hardship with them.[17]

The real problem for Sardar and Davies is not so much popular culture itself but rather the ideals and values that are transferred from the United States to the rest of the world with the spread of that popular culture, particularly to the more traditional parts of the world. With the aim of demonstrating the corrosiveness of American ideals and ideologies, the two authors dedicate their sequel publication to an analysis of the Hollywood 'dream factory' that plays such a large role in promoting those ideals. Employing a painstaking analysis of a handful of movies – most of which were made in the first half of the twentieth century, incidentally – Sardar and Davies set out to unveil the myths propagated by Hollywood to the detriment of the rest of the world. From their analysis, they distil ten laws that shape the mythology of American democracy, culture and history: myths and laws that, in their own words, add up to a collective American 'psychosis', a grotesque and dangerous imbalance between fantasy and reality. The authors argue that making myths about their own culture and history prevents Americans from understanding themselves and their real relationship to the world as well as what kind of world is out there.[18]

Of course, the all-encompassing anti-Americanism espoused by Sardar and Davies goes a long way in preventing the world from really understanding America – or American popular culture – itself. As we have seen, it is simply not the case that all American cultural products triumphantly celebrate the 'American way' or propagate nationalistic myths abroad. The depth and quality of American self-examination and self-understanding are apparent in much popular culture. Since the 1970s, for instance, numerous American artists, singers, writers and filmmakers have engaged with America's involvement in the Vietnam

War in a critical fashion. In similar ways, Bruce Springsteen's song 'Born in the USA' and Michael Cimino's film *The Deer Hunter* both question the meaning of American involvement in the war and distrust the motivations of the American government, who 'Sent me off to Vietnam, to go and kill the yellow man'. Indeed, in the post-Vietnam period, it might even be argued that Americans have pushed the critical distance from national values too far and are not proud enough of their creed and birthright. American commentators like Michael Moore join in the anti-American attack on American ideals using popular culture as a vehicle. Yet, many of these ideals – of freedom, independence and democracy – are worth defending and, indeed, celebrating as well as scrutinising and questioning. Perhaps the democratising tendencies of American culture can offer more on the global stage than many Americans imagine. While Sardar and Davies seemingly lionise the pre-modern traditions of much of the developing world, many who live there understandably wish to escape them or at least be transformed.

It might be possible to dismiss Sardar and Davies's arguments as an irrelevant gnashing of teeth if not for the best-selling status of their books and for the echo that many of their arguments find in more serious academic treatments. For instance, although Benjamin Barber's understanding of traditional or anti-modern communities is rather less romantic, he is just as negative about what he sees as the 'dully insistent' and potent cultural imperatives of 'McWorld'. According to Barber, the world faces two equally undesirable cultural alternatives:

> The Enlightenment dream of a universal rational society has to a remarkable degree been realised – but in a form that is commercialised, homogenised, depoliticised, bureaucraticised and, of course, radically incomplete, for the movement toward McWorld is in competition with forces of global breakdown, national dissolution, and centrifugal corruption. These forces, working in the opposite direction, are the essence of what I call Jihad.[19]

On Barber's balance sheet, the advantages of the Americanisation of 'McWorld' are peace, prosperity and relative unity at the cost of independence, community and identity – Jihad or 're-tribalisation', by contrast, offers the virtues of solidarity and community but also guarantees parochialism and war as an emblem of identity. Neither option allows for the operation of democracy. It is not an optimistic vision of the future shape of global affairs.

The clinging to and recreation of local, tribal and other sub-national cultural identities that Barber describes might very well be a reaction against the forces of globalisation, a shrinking from the implications of modernity and a search for a smaller more secure world that will seal them off from the demands and impositions of the modern world.[20] This is often an understandable if regrettable reaction in parts of the developing world. It is clear, however, that more developed nations are certainly not immune from it.

Indeed, a primary source of contemporary cultural anti-Americanism in Europe is a fear of the new. Cultural Americanisation and anti-Americanism both operate, as Heinz Ickstadt has pointed out, as both fact and metaphor: 'In its largest, most inclusive sense [anti-Americanism] is a metaphor of resentment, nostalgia or regret – a regret for everything that has been lost in the process of modernisation.'[21] Older Europeans are obviously more likely to experience and feel the loss than younger ones. Cultural Americanisation is, after all, strongly associated with youth culture – it is the young who determine what is 'cool'. In a 2003 *New York Times* article, Nina Bernstein cited a poll that found young Germans two to three times more likely to hold positive attitudes about the 'American way of life' than those over forty-five.[22]

In the immediate post-war period, the generational divide in Europe was most acute. Ickstadt describes how, growing up in post-war Germany, he and his peers listened to American popular music (Rock and Roll and Jazz) simply because their parents so obviously disliked it – 'We punished their silence to our questions about the war and their past allegiances by embracing wholeheartedly what they abhorred: "Negermusik." '[23] Across Europe, young people sought independence and acted out their rebelliousness by adopting the music, fashions and even hairstyles of American popular culture.

While young Europeans embraced American cultural products in the post-war period, they also began to critique American power. The 1960s saw a jumbled flow of messages across the Atlantic, in both directions. Inspired by the liberationist rhetoric of the US civil rights movement but repelled by American actions in Vietnam, the youth of Europe adopted radical and revolutionary political positions both in support of Americans and against the United States. Some commentators suggest that anti-Americanism became a far more important factor in European politics after Vietnam, but this had less to do with American policy in Asia and much more to do with what was happening in Europe itself.

Heightened perceptions about the process of Americanisation – and resistance to it – have often sprung from deep-seated anxieties at home. When Baudrillard wrote, 'America is the original version of modernity. We are the dubbed or subtitled version', he told us more about French feelings of inferiority than any real truth about America.[24] Of the European countries, France has been particularly hostile to Americanisation and defensive about protecting its own culture. This is partly because of a national feeling that French civilisation is of universal importance and partly because of a relative decline in French global status – as Bruno Racine, chief advisor of the French conservative prime minister, Alain Juppe pointed out, 'America's hyper-power irritates us because it forces us to acknowledge our historical downgrading.'[25]

In his study of French responses to Americanisation, Richard Kuisel notes that most anti-Americanism during the Cold War was expressed by Parisian communist and leftists, but there was widespread unease among the French people about the coming consumer society (understood widely as 'Americanisation'). Once France began to feel the benefits of consumerism and modernisation, the response to American culture became more ambiguous. In 1992, when Euro Disney opened outside Paris, theatrical director Ariane Mnouchkine famously condemned it as a 'cultural Chernobyl', but thousands of French men, women and children flocked to the park. Insecurities about French national identity remain, and the French reaction to American culture is still often that of disdain – no less than civilisation is seen to be at stake.[26]

French defensiveness has led to attempts to preserve many aspects of French cultural identity from the impositions of American culture. For example, since the Internet is widely viewed as one of the most pernicious forms of US-led cultural imperialism and France has its own information highway, the Minitel, French users have been relatively slow to gain Internet access. In 1998, only around 420,000 used the Internet (less than neighbouring Switzerland whose population is one tenth of France's) compared with fourteen million users of Minitel. Although French usage had risen to twenty-six million (43 percent penetration of the population) by 2006, it still lagged behind that of many other European countries including Italy (48.8 percent), Germany (59 percent) and Sweden (74.9 percent). Maintaining the purity and integrity of the French language is an important factor in French avoidance of the

Internet; Jacques Chirac has objected to the fact that 90 percent of traffic on the worldwide web is in English. Insecurities about French national identity run so high that regulation has been introduced to prevent the dilution of France's Frenchness, with such laws as quotas on the import of non-European (read American) cultural products, requirements that advertising be in French, and stipulations about the percentage of French music played on radio. The *Académie française* has also tried to stem the Americanisation of language by suggesting replacements for English words, for example 'baladeur' for 'Walkman'.[27]

Anti-Americanism in Britain in the post-war period has also been driven by anxieties about the preservation of national identity but, unlike in France, it has for the most part and until relatively recently, been confined to political and cultural elites. British elites were forced to accept a junior role in the 'special relationship' with the United States in the post-war world; their inferior status was made painfully evident in the 1956 Suez crisis. However, the humiliations of Suez had little impact on the British public's reception of American popular culture. In the same year as Suez, John Osborne's *Look Back in Anger* first played British theatres, reflecting a sentiment of bitterness and nostalgia among the elite (Jimmy Porter laments that 'there aren't any good brave causes left') as well as a rejection of the older generation of Empire and the stiff upper lip by a new generation of 'angry young men'. Yet the year after Suez, American rock group Bill Haley and his Comets toured the country with their sell out 'Rock Around the Clock' tour and were greeted with screaming crowds of fans everywhere they went. The national identity crisis of the British political elite became more profound in 1968, following the IMF's devaluation of the pound, and since then anti-Americanism has become increasingly more generalised. In the 1970s, antagonism towards American popular culture began to appear in British punk rock, evidenced by the Clash's 1977, 'I'm so bored with the USA.' Rebellious youth were beginning to see the United States as a target rather than as a vehicle for their rebellion. Arguably, the Britpop revival of the 1990s was a symptom of a growing nostalgia for Britain's own empire of culture.[28]

Sensitivity to Americanisation and a growth in cultural anti-Americanism so often represents the projection of home-grown anxieties onto an external entity: whether they be British concerns about the loss of international status and influence, French defensiveness about the corruption of their national civilisation, or the German desire for rehabilitation from post-war guilt. The United States is an obvious and necessary scapegoat because it can be positioned as ignorant and arrogant; as both uncultured and dangerously powerful. As we have seen, the process of Americanisation can be more apparent than real. Americanisation is, as George McKay has it, 'perhaps more a signifier of one's own culture's place in the world rather than of American culture's. In effect, we project our own fears and weaknesses, and our cultural nostalgia, on to America, and by doing so, we construct it as the root of the problem'.[29]

Globalisation or Americanisation?

In order to understand the roots and the growth of prejudices towards the United States in Europe and around the world, the initial step is to examine the complexities of America itself, to try to understand what America is and what it is not; what it represents and what it does not; and thereby to discover what it is culpable for and what it is not. For many critics, America represents all that is wrong with modern life: conformity, deracination, rampant consumerism, standardisation, environmental destruction, individuation and the like. These critics tend to conflate processes of modernisation and/or globalisation with that of Americanisation. America often looks like the agent of modernisation and globalisation, but these processes have many sources and in fact often bring great benefits.

Among Western critics and protestors, anti-American rhetoric can start to look like self-loathing; modern culture is their culture, after all. It is certainly the case that most of those who condemn America for its cultural imperialism are not defending a universal humanist standard against American onslaught but rather have adopted a very Romantic, conservationist view of local cultures that must be preserved at all cost. Yet, culture is never static; it is dynamic and constantly changing in response to internal and external stimuli. Those who seek to portray traditional local cultures as unchanging but besieged usually have reactionary motivations. Of course, the more progressive political predecessor of this conservative cultural critique was a Romantic anti-colonialism, although even proponents of this view always did have a penchant for suppressed 'primitive' or exotic societies. As Terry Eagleton has noted, this posture resurfaces in the post-modern romanticisation of popular culture as expressive, spontaneous and quasi-utopian. Thus, paradoxically, perhaps, while those opposed to the spread of American popular culture want to preserve the 'exotic' cultures it apparently destroys, those post-modern celebrants of American popular culture who favour its spread, romanticise it exactly for its primitive features.[30] Both show discomfort with a universal humanist discourse and with the notions of progress and modernity.

Vibrant cultures continually borrow and adapt from other cultures and the transfer of behaviour and ideas is never a one-way process. As Richard Pells has persuasively argued, the United States has not transformed the world into a replica of itself but, rather, the ethnic, racial and cultural pluralism of the United States alongside its dependence on foreign cultural influences has in fact made the United States a replica of the world.[31] Indeed, American culture is so diversified and fragmented it seems implausible to identify it as a monolithic actor. Historically, the United States has been incredibly open to international cultural influences – Hollywood itself was established and built by immigrant European Jews and has always employed the talents of foreign film-makers, directors and actors.[32] In popular music too, the 1960s 'British Invasion' of bands like the Rolling Stones and the Beatles, transformed the American scene, bringing back into the mainstream sounds from black America that had already once traversed the Atlantic.

The point here is that globalisation affects America as well as the rest of the globe and brings to its shores an array of foreign cultural influences, in the shape of immigrants themselves and foreign cultural products, including some that originated in the United States but have since gone on to be modified and transformed abroad. The result of all of this global cultural exchange is that the world becomes more complex, not simpler and more diverse, not more standardised. Rather than globalisation creating a hegemony of US culture, Ron Robins suggests, there is instead 'an internationalisation of material culture throughout a world that has truly become a global village'.[33]

The global spread of modern technologies of communication may bring US cultural imports to other countries, but they also stimulate the production of local media and cultural production. Satellite television has opened up the market to stations like the Arab-language al-Jazeera, increasingly notorious for its independence from American influence or control. Many experts too predict that Chinese will soon compete with English as the Internet's dominant language. And, despite the French reluctance to use the Internet, some French producers have transformed it into a niche-marketing tool for French cheeses. Arguably, therefore, rather than stifling indigenous cultures, globalisation has exposed it to new influences and opened it to new avenues of creative exploration.[34]

Thus, local producers can thrive in the age of global communications, creating local, national, regional or global markets for their own products. The top grossing movies in Japan, Germany, Spain, France and India in 2002 were produced locally. In a 2001 survey of sixty countries, Charles Paul Freund found that, on average, 70 percent of the most popular television shows were locally produced. In India, domestically produced music makes up 90 percent of the market; in Egypt, 81 percent; in Brazil, 73 percent. Mexico and Brazil transmit their films and television soap operas to other countries in Latin America. Indeed, the Mexican-based Televisa, which produces 78 percent of its own programming, and the Brazilian Globo Network, which produces 80 percent, have managed to secure and dominate their domestic markets to a degree unmatched by any English-speaking market. The Hong Kong film industry dominates the East Asian market. India's film industry 'Bollywood' has a larger global audience than Hollywood (3.6 billion to 2.5 billion according to one estimate). In a 1999 BBC poll, viewers named Bollywood star Amitabh Bachchan superstar of the millennium ahead of Cary Grant and Laurence Olivier; the biggest film star in the world today is not Brad Pitt or Julia Roberts, but Bollywood superstar Shah Rukh Khan.[35] Of course, local control over production and programming is not in any way a guarantee of quality but neither is it clear that this is what critics of the 'domination' of American popular culture are actually concerned about.

Even where American popular culture does dominate international markets, there is little evidence to suggest that it alters, undermines or destroys local cultures. The impact of US culture and consumer goods on the customs and practices of local people is probably far more negligible than critics of cultural imperialism imagine. As Pells argues, people around the world listen, watch, wear and eat their cultural fare much more lightly than intellectuals, politicians and sometimes parents worry about: 'Sometimes, to paraphrase Freud, a hamburger is just a hamburger'.[36]

Moreover, to cast audiences of popular culture as victims of an all-powerful global media system and its messages is simply to patronise and underestimate them. Even if the messages were homogenised (which they are not), the audience still has the ability to interpret the messages in their

own context and to form their own meanings from the messages.
As Anthony Smith explains: 'Images and cultural traditions do not derive
from or descend upon mute and passive populations on whose *tabula
rasa* they inscribe themselves. Instead, they invariably express the
identities which historical circumstances have formed, often over long
periods'.37

A number of active audience theorists have conducted ethnographic
research into the cultural reception of Western media internationally
and discovered that different foreign cultures 'read' cultural products
in vastly different ways. Driven by the worldwide popularity of the US
television soap opera, *Dallas* in the 1980s, researchers set out to examine
the impact and reception of the show. Tamar Liebes interviewed four
groups of Israeli viewers – Israeli Arabs, Moroccan Jewish immigrants,
kibbutz members and new Russian immigrants – and found that the
message imparted by *Dallas* depended on the viewer's values and varied
according to the experiences of the particular group to which the viewer
belonged. Ien Ang found that Dutch women interpreted the program
through their own feminist agenda in opposition to the supposedly
embedded message of patriarchy. Finally, Eric Michaels showed how
Australian Aboriginals used their own notions of kinship to understand
the meaning of *Dallas* in ways quite contrary to that intended by
program producers. Not only do audience members actively produce
meaning while consuming media products, but they sometimes reject
them altogether. *Dallas* failed miserably in both Brazil and Japan,
suggesting that US cultural content does not have the power to overwhelm every other culture at will.38 The examples provided at the
beginning of this essay suggest that audiences will usually respond
positively to quality programming and to cultural products that carry
meaning for them.

Following from the assumptions that inform Adorno and
Horkheimer's analysis of modern culture, contemporary critics of the
American 'culture industry' take a dim view of the sensibilities of the
audience for popular culture. Stripped of agency and meaningful choice,
international audiences become mere dupes to the machinations of the
cultural imperialists in Washington and Hollywood. Contemporary
critics of American cultural imperialism combine just such a condescending attitude to global audiences with a Heideggerian romantic
attachment to traditional local cultures, with little or no appraisal
of what any specific local culture actually represents or signifies. This

merging of a disillusioned leftist outlook with a backward-looking conservative celebration of traditionalism defines much 'oppositional' political discussion today and the fusing of the two ideas – from left and right – is at the root of much contemporary cultural anti-Americanism.

The Fall of Politics and the Rise of Culture

The end of the twentieth century saw many changes in political life that helped to create a fertile climate for the growth of cultural anti-Americanism. The collapse of the Soviet Union, the disintegration of movements for national liberation and the decline of working class politics in the West signalled the failure of any alternative to triumphant capitalism. With the end of meaningful political alternatives, the traditional forms of politics became defunct.[39] As the political categories of 'left' and 'right' became increasingly meaningless, politics was emptied of any real contestation and therefore of any socially transformative content. When there are no political alternatives, there is little point for engagement and debate about how the future might look. Instead, it began to appear to many in Europe and around the world that the United States, the sole remaining global superpower, could determine the shape of all of our futures. Resentments about the unilateral power of the United States built steadily in Europe and elsewhere. Following the events of 9/11, a temporary rush of compassion and support for the United States was soon replaced with further resentments and anger at the Bush administration's aggressive foreign policy in Afghanistan and Iraq.

The current political climate helps to explain why critics of the United States tend to make that nation the metaphor for so many changes that are seemingly outside effective political control. The relative might of America does not, however, excuse us from the need to penetrate beneath the surface of the discussion about the domination of American culture globally, to explode the metaphor of Americanisation as modernisation, globalisation, alienation and deracination. Ultimately, participants on both sides of the debate about the Americanisation of culture endow the United States with too much power and weight in bringing about the changes they either abhor or celebrate. Perhaps even more troublingly, they also tend to give too much power and weight to the very concept of culture itself.

The end of politics has resulted in an elevation of culture and all things cultural. The 'culturalisation' process began in the 1960s when cultural relativists promoted culture as a signification and affirmation of specific national, ethnic, sexual or regional identities rather than the transcendence of these categories. Overturning the Enlightenment rejection of culture as a series of regressive attachments to tradition, identity, hierarchy or place, cultural relativists of the 1960s and since have embraced difference not as a negation of equality but as a mark of it. Yet, as Terry Eagleton points out, by insisting that all cultural worlds are as good as one another, Western relativists end up absolutising the concept of culture itself.[40]

Among the consequences of cultural relativism is the idealisation of primitive cultures as an apparent critique of the West (or America alone in the present discussion). Thus, much anti-American criticism attempts to shield local cultures in developing countries from American cultural intervention or domination without reference to the actual content of the political or cultural life of the particular developing nation. Again, as Eagleton notes, cultural relativism can come to ratify the most virulent forms of cultural absolutism: 'What may seem like the last word in epistemological radicalism in Paris can end up justifying autocracy elsewhere'. Or, as Meera Nanda has it, the post-modern doctrine that truth is culture-bound ends up 'providing theoretical grounds for, and a progressive gloss on, the fast growing anti-modernist, nativist and cultural/religious revivalist movements in many parts of what used to be called the third world'.[41] Anti-modernism in the West reinforces – perhaps even creates – it elsewhere in the world.

Cultural concepts have come to dominate our political understanding. Apparently progressive leftist critics target American popular culture as a substitute for meaningful political action. Where there is no robust anti-imperialist movement left, they celebrate indigenous cultures against modern impositions. Where there is no political language of opposition, they seek solace in cultural critiques and a politics of cultural identity. Yet, culture is not necessarily political and to try to make it so ultimately demeans both politics and culture. The point of a politics of culture should be to overcome conflict not to exaggerate or perpetuate it – or, as Eagleton argues, to return the Breton love song, African-American art exhibition or declaration of lesbianism to their innocuousness 'so that one can sing, paint or make love without the bothersome distraction of political strife'.[42] American popular culture exists within a highly politicised cultural context, and it is difficult within that context to judge it for what it is – on its artistic merits alone – but this is what we should strive to do.

Despite the high quality of much American popular culture, the proliferation of inferior cultural products seems undeniable. The question is whether this 'dumbing down' process can be attributed simply to American bad taste. I would suggest not. Many of the problems with the declining quality of cultural goods can be traced to changes taking place across the Western world, not solely in America. In the realm of popular culture, at least, the United States is as much the victim of contemporary trends as the perpetrator of them. To ask the question of what has caused such widespread cultural 'dumbing down' is a much more interesting and useful exercise than issuing a blanket condemnation of 'America'. Rather than pursuing a cultural crusade against American crassness, I would suggest instead that we would be better off investigating the impact of such phenomena as the relativisation of knowledge, the impact of increasing commercialism in all areas of life, and the consequences of the decline of the public sphere. Indeed, much of the dismissal of American popular culture as vulgar is rooted in a highly anti-democratic disdain for the mass of ordinary people, American or otherwise.

There is not enough space here to fully investigate the number of causes behind the 'dumbing down' of culture, as it is undoubtedly the result of complex social and political processes. Yet, it is far easier for critics to point the finger of blame at the United States for the explosion of reality TV shows and tacky talent contests (in fact, both *Big Brother* and *Pop Idol* originated in Europe and were exported *to* the United States) than to look beyond appearances. Rather than address the difficult issues that lie behind the discussion about contemporary culture, critics are far more comfortable simply attacking America.

The political values that the United States represents are often the real target of criticism when American popular culture is criticised. The American founding creed rests on Enlightenment notions of liberty, democracy, rationality and universalism. These are increasingly seen as out of date and some see them as arrogant and oppressive ideologies riding roughshod over global cultural diversity. Cultural relativists insist on the political importance of a plurality of global cultures, each with equal standing and recognition and thus deny the special status and emancipatory logic of the Western humanist tradition. A truly universal global culture would embrace not dismiss the best of humanity's achievements, whether that is in the field of political philosophy or in popular culture. For sure, a truly universal popular culture would be contributed to by nations around the globe – a gallery of the finest works of national cultures, if you will – but it would certainly include many of the best offerings from American television, film, music and fashion.

Chapter 12

Modernity, Resentment and Anti-Americanism

Michael Werz and Barbara Fried

In numerous discussions over the years, America has served as an almost universal point of reference with regard to how the world perceives political conflict and economic modernisation. The name itself can express both an engagement with and a reification of the complex cultural and social traditions that make up modern life.[1]

Although anti-Americanism is often treated as if it were a uniform reaction towards some undefined but somehow concrete experience, it should be analysed instead against the background of dynamic societies undergoing profound social, economic, political and cultural transformations. Contemporary expressions of anti-Americanism can be interpreted within the context of two historical watersheds: the fall of the Berlin Wall on November 9, 1989, and the terrorist attacks on the World Trade Center and Pentagon on September 11, 2001, events that – in terms of historical epochs – mark the end of the twentieth century and the beginning of the present era, respectively. At the same time, however, a concept of anti-Americanism must be developed that takes into consideration social and historical particularities, in order to be anything more than a form of reaction. The first part of this essay will highlight some of the attempts to understand this phenomenon and develop a preliminary framework in which anti-Americanism can be interpreted as a contemporary ideology. The second part focuses more specifically on the German case, reviewing the 1920s, the post-1945 period and united Germany after 1990. The post-unification period is the prelude to the remarkable ambivalence towards the United States that surged after 2001. Contemporary forms of anti-Americanism are not identical with older forms of anti-Americanism: although there are some continuities, recent expressions of anti-Americanism draw their strength from very different sources than the resentments towards the United States that were prevalent in Germany almost 100 years ago.

In that past phase of anti-Americanism, the most intellectually pronounced debates arose during the first decade of the twentieth century, when renowned European social scientists such as Max Weber, Ferdinand Tönnies and Joseph Schumpeter – responding in part to the European encounter with America occasioned by the St. Louis World's Fair in 1904 – argued that the kind of modernisation witnessed in America would soon come to Europe.[2] Since then, America has served as a metaphor for change and as a prism through which many Europeans interpret events lacking historical precedent.

It is too simple to conceive of anti-Americanism as merely a form of projection in which America serves as nothing but an empty canvas. Anti-Americanism can better be understood as a distorted perception of real, existent differences, interactions and asynchronies occurring in the formation of two modern societies that are at once similar and distinct. Uneven or differing developments often resulted not only in the shattering of putative certitudes within the European mindset but also in misconceptions, which over time coalesced into anti-American stereotypes. In the last century, during periods of rapid social change and profound modernisation processes, whenever people felt they were losing reliable means of orientation, they clung to simple reassuring explanations for the origins and causes of these transitions. The predominance of a competitive economy and the rationalisation of many aspects of daily life in the first decades of the twentieth century, for example, were often seen as American influences.

During the era of rapid industrialisation, growing metropolises, chauvinist nationalism and politicised cultural differences among the European peoples and vis-à-vis minorities, a gaze across the ocean was often the constitutive, if unacknowledged historical gesture. The United States had recently debuted on the world stage as a serious actor, home of a rival and more advanced system of Western-style modernisation. From the European vantage point, the future had already begun on the other side of the ocean: Americans had superseded (in the sense of Hegel's *Aufhebung*) the folkways, mores and customs of traditional society, even as – paradoxically – first-generation American sociologists like William Graham Sumner turned to anthropological rather than sociological terms to describe this change. The heterogeneous and unprecedented context in which a nation of nations had been established presented a serious challenge to national self-perception of European countries that were largely based on founding myths of ethnic homogeneity and century-old traditions. The self-declared 'land of the free and home of the brave' came to offer a framework of interpretation that allowed Europeans to shed their feelings of inadequacy and fears of losing their traditional points of reference in rapidly transforming societies and so cast them off on America. The concept of divergent paths of cultural modernisation offers an inadequate explanation of European attempts to 'reject' America's path into the twentieth century; far more often, the European impulse was largely an attempt to recapture a vision of clarity, hierarchy and cultural assuredness that the European past, rather than the American future, seemed to offer.

Thus, anti-Americanism established itself as the negation of the New World, which lacked aristocratic rituals and authoritarian rule; it was an attempt to repatriate modernity into a symbolic America, to give the ills of contemporary society a geographic point of origin. Modernity of course has no national origin; instead, it embodies the emergence of displaced and disoriented subjectivity. The power of the concept of America to symbolise this social abstraction meant that modernity in its anti-American appearance began to thrive during the first two decades of the twentieth century, when modernisation was being acutely felt in Europe. As a modern ideology, it was accomplishing sociological miracles, claiming to explain and translate experiences of increasingly abstract and alienated societies into concrete and local terms. With the appearance of a geographical locus for modernity, a surplus of anger and fear could be directed against the United States, supposedly the home of a barbaric, uncultured capitalism. Five centuries of shared history led into an abstract rejection of the past: the Atlantic Ocean came to symbolise the divide between a bad modernity and an idealised past. The philosopher Martin Heidegger revealed just how deeply felt such distorted world views were when he lamented, '[T]he surrender of the German essence to Americanism has already gone so far as on occasion to produce the disastrous effect that Germany actually feels herself ashamed that her people were once considered being "the people of poetry and thought." '[3] For him and many others, the development of modern mass culture in the United States epitomised all that was wrong with modernity.

Hollywood became one of the cornerstones of resentment vis-à-vis the United States. However, Hollywood was hardly an agent of worldwide manipulation; it was instead a response to the diverse American audience and in turn anticipated the global audience. At the turn of the century – the early years of movies and mass culture – American moviegoers represented an extremely diverse audience, a vibrant immigrant nation, where people often did not even speak a common language.

These circumstances forced editors, writers and producers to invent cosmopolitan techniques for reaching out to the largest possible crowd of readers, listeners and viewers. Hollywood made cultural products accessible to broader spectra of society. It therefore had an impact not only on the democratisation of culture, but also on the integration and Americanisation of millions of new immigrants.[4] The film industry provided a means of communication and entertainment to an audience that otherwise lacked common traditions or backgrounds, thus serving as a tool of orientation amid the unfamiliar living conditions of the New World. Unsurprisingly, cultural commodities successful in a country 'where custom had no time to solidify'[5] soon proved suitable for the world beyond. Many contemporary cultural products did not even originate in the United States but were only liberated from their national origin in Hollywood and broadcast back into the world's regions in a generalised version. This holds true for the metamorphosis of European working class dishes into fast food as an expression of increasing time constraints; and it holds true for Walt Disney, who found a model for his Anaheim Park in Copenhagen's Tivoli. Something similar happened to Stravinsky's polyrhythmic music, which was inspired by jazz and in turn influenced new jazz rhythms, or the achievements of the Bauhaus architects, which could be realised in the United States by means of advanced steel construction. In Hollywood, this fusion was more intense than in other places; after all, Hollywood was itself a community of émigrés, with the British-born Charlie Chaplin as its first superstar. Because it produced such universally palatable commodities, Hollywood remained the most important byword for cultural modernisation throughout the twentieth century. In turn, mass culture was henceforth perceived as American.

Obviously, not all criticism of commercialised movies and mass culture at that time was tainted by ideological distortions. It is striking, however, that European commentators often did not take into consideration the specific circumstances that led to Hollywood's success and the critical role of mass culture in integrating American society. Many critics continue to dismiss the egalitarianism and uniformity of mass culture as an expression of superficiality and a lack of refinement, but these phenomena were of profound significance for such a heterogeneous society as the United States – mass culture both mirrored and facilitated the integration of different immigrant groups. European observers of America rarely acknowledged this function, instead labelling the transformation and commercialisation of culture with the generally pejorative tag of 'American'. This perception not only obsessed on the supposedly destructive impact that Hollywood and the Americanisation of cultural expressions had on European high culture, but it also offered an ostensibly simple cause for certain patterns of social change.

9/11 and the New Intellectual World Order

Today, modern mass culture has penetrated almost every society and created a simultaneity of individual experiences. Accordingly, the cultural anti-Americanism of the 1920s is quite distinct from the ambivalence towards the United States found in present-day Europe. This ambivalence should not be conflated with the nihilistic rebellions that qualify themselves as Islamicist and anti-Western. Such differences are important, for ambivalence towards the United States is interwoven with legitimate criticism and is not identical with the paranoid world view that Theodor W. Adorno and Max Horkheimer once characterised as the 'dark side of cognition and perception'. It is true that only a few weeks after the devastating September 11 attacks one found an astonishing indifference on display. From Mexico to Europe to Asia, the search for rationalisations for the attacks set, in mostly led by public intellectuals and sometimes manifested in barely concealed, malicious joy. America, the alleged source of violence and all ills, finally had received its comeuppance for its historical role as a global power. Such authoritarian identifications were all too common. However, they are only part of the story.

The September 11 attacks and subsequent wars in Afghanistan and Iraq simply reinforced and deepened a new ideological constellation that did not develop in a historical vacuum but was a knee-jerk reaction brought on by the political and cultural disintegration after 1990. With the end of the Soviet Union, the alternative to Western-style modernisation (as unattractive as it may have been) had disappeared. Not only did the Soviet Union evaporate as a superpower, but the era of superpowers itself ended. The emerging political vacuum was filled with modern ideologies and distorted perceptions of a new world that had lost its stabilising point of reference of a bipolar world order based on the threat of mutual annihilation. With no other points of reference in sight, America became the codeword that gave meaning (and power) to a meaningless, disorderly world. Although it does not make much sense to speak of the sole superpower, the Cold War vocabulary does not provide a more differentiated term. The notion of a new imperialism is even less adequate. Sole superpowers are not as super as they think, as is currently being proven in a number of places around the globe. The very concept of an all-encompassing power structure was inextricably tied to the nuclear confrontation of the bipolar world, and with the passing of that epoch, the concept lost its significance. This is not to imply that such notions cannot outlive their reality. After the fall of state socialism, rhetoric concerning American *hyperpower* increased. It seemed inevitable that, after the loss of one of two superpowers, the remaining one would grow omnipotent.

The Soviet Union's demise not only changed politics but also economics in most parts of the world. Every region was to be integrated into the market economy, which for many countries was a difficult process. Furthermore, the contrast between the highly industrialised countries, on one hand, and countries of the Arab world, on the other, became much more obvious without the Soviets' alternative version of modernisation. These ruptures in turn tended to be seen as a threat to previously existing certitudes and social stability.[6] The repercussions of a globalised market with no limits were also felt in Western Europe. In the 1990s, globalisation and neo liberalism, as the contemporary phase of world economy is often labelled, started to affect most of the European welfare states. The subsequent restructuring of the systems of social security was widely perceived as Americanisation.

Such fundamental transformations in the world order and their respective political, economical and social conditions are intricate and not easy to grasp. People are therefore inclined to make sense of complex social changes by perceiving them in ontological terms. Social and historical dissimilarity between different parts of the world does not appear as uneven developments but are often interpreted as characteristics unique to given societies. For obvious reasons, the United States had emerged from the historical upheavals at the end of the 'short century' not only as the lone global player relatively untouched by the turmoil between 1914 and 1989 but as the most advanced economic force as well. Consequently, the divergences between more traditional and more advanced forms of modern society 'froze into geographic difference – between Europe and the United States'.[7] Such a simple and apparently reassuring set of oppositions seems to make sense in a fast-moving world.

Since integration into a global economy does not evolve at the same pace, time and manner everywhere around the world, the resulting asynchronies are often interpreted as essential cultural-geographical differences. Therefore, changes within one's own surroundings are not seen as social and political processes of modification but as outside influences, in this case from America. Emmanuel Todd's statement 'a single threat to global instability weighs on the world today: America, which from a protector, has become a predator'[8] is strong evidence for the confusion that reigns even in academic debates.

While expressions of ambivalence, resentment and hatred vis-à-vis America are seen as being essentially rooted in cultural difference, they in reality reflect asynchronous developments within modern societies. This makes it possible to understand anti-Americanism as an indicator of change. Inquiry into this modern ideology should therefore disregard essentialist categories in favour of expressions of social transformations.

1989–1990: The Return of Uncertainty

As mentioned before, the ongoing political impact of the changes that occurred after 1989 is seen in the transformation of the image of the remaining Cold War superpower, the United States, into the codeword 'America'. The latter inherited all the attributes of the former but not nearly as much of its world structuring capabilities. Without its opposite, the Soviet empire, political orientation was lost, and the cemented convictions of the Cold War – East versus West, communist versus liberal – coalesced into something even more metaphysical. Since no one was certain which principles arranged and defined the new, globalised world, how people *imagined* it was structured became much more important.

The lack of stability and clarity after 1989 led to the simultaneous emergence of a new, distinctly modern piety in many parts of the world. This encompassed not only radical Islam, but Protestant fundamentalism in the United States, Orthodox and Catholic revival in Eastern Europe and Africa (which is often combined with ethnic identifications), Hindu radicalism in India and even the Falun Gong in China. In Western Europe, the new consciousness was often expressed more in cultural and nationalist forms than in overtly religious ones. In political discussions about the future, people referred to pre-modern forms of community as if all the answers lay in the past. The fact that these perceptions and notions of belonging were themselves inherently modern, dating back to the initial emergence of an 'invention of traditions'9 in the late nineteenth century, has often been overlooked.

Early on, such religious, ethnic and nationalistic self-conceptions were often formulated in negative references to the United States. Being a country of immigrants whose citizens often did not even speak the same language and could hardly claim a common history, heritage or culture, the United States was the only society in the world, lacking the illusion of a past based on visions of ethnic tradition or homogeneous self-certainty. For that reason, it served and continues to serve to this day as the natural symbol of negative self-definition. In times of disorientation, it is easy to invent meaning by measuring one's own national aspirations and self-legitimisation against the experience of a society that in this sense is *per se* non-traditional. As a unique nation of nations and locus of successful diversity, the United States serves as an ideological opposite.

In the process, the all-important distinction between traditional societies with their respective modes of consciousness and modern ideologies has been completely blurred. Modern social organisation really does mitigate traditional structures of authority, while simultaneously pushing human beings towards forms of legitimisation that assume imagined communities, invented traditions and increasingly extreme fundamentalisms. Such modern ideologies only pretend to be remnants of something old; in truth, they are very modern modes of interpreting social reality. They are appealing, because certain religious and cultural traditions have been lost, not because they have been conserved and prolonged. One can understand them as an ideological upgrade, because traditional forms of belonging and communal cohesion are no longer valid. Such contemporary modes of consciousness bestow legitimacy upon themselves by intoning the trappings of cultural affiliations and heritage and transforming them into insignia of difference in an increasingly uniform society. They have no ties whatsoever to the traditional ensemble to which they arbitrarily refer.

Such consciousness cannot be identical with the nineteenth-century predecessors, which stemmed from an era when ideology still claimed aesthetic, logical and ethical objectivity. Neither the pressure to be consistent with reality, nor the projection of secret desires into the realm of ethereal gods, as described by Ludwig Feuerbach, suffices to depict these contemporary forms of modern ideology. They address neither real entities, nor transcendental objects, but are based on living individuals who are active in the process of forming a collective consciousness. The codeword 'America' is a crucial and convenient ingredient in the formation of these new ideological features.

Anti-Americanism and Ethno-Religious Ideologies

Although America can serve as a codeword in the course of many societies' economic and political transformation, not every form of this mystification is the same. Rather, each society, even as it defines its relation to America, retains elements of its own traditional identifications (religious or non-religious). These elements are sociologically legible. Whenever a community undergoes full-scale modernisation and re-organisation around the principle of economic competition, the self-perception of every individual is transformed. Following the breakdown of traditional religious orientations and patterns of behaviour, 'religion does not play such a decisive role within the frame of mind of most people as it once did; only rarely does it seem to account for their social attitudes and opinions'.[10] However, secularisation is rarely complete and the bipolarity of the believer and the non-believer persists in modernised forms. With regard to this transformation, Western and Arab societies underwent rather similar experiences during the first few decades of the twentieth century, when conventional ideologies and belief systems collapsed under the weight of the new. For example, the circumstances and consequences of modern Turkey's founding in 1923, after the upheaval of World War I and the break up of the Ottoman Empire, can be reasonably compared to the collapse of the Austro-Hungarian Empire a few years earlier. In both cases, these empires were challenged and ultimately destroyed from within, as new forms of national and nationalistic identification became more powerful. As in Europe, many parts of the Arab world experienced the first two decades of the twentieth century as times of overwhelming modernisation and cultural uncertainties. Individuals were suddenly deprived of their framework of orientation. The subsequent emergence of national independence and more radicalised local and regional groups, such as the Egyptian Muslim Brotherhood, founded in 1928 by Hasan al-Banna', were the direct result. The fact that traditional religion broke free from its dissolving communal ties and was privatised in more radical forms mirrored a crisis, rather than the power of religion.[11] Religious fundamentalism and nationalist de-historicisation went hand-in-hand. Comparable processes took place in Western societies: Anti-Americanism (among other modern ideologies) in Western Europe, but also the Nativism within America during the 1920s, assumed a religious character, because people saw it as a way to avoid coming to terms with enlightenment and modernisation.

At the end of the 'short century', similar forms of collective consciousness have emerged again. Modern ideologies that adorn themselves with religious trappings have developed in many parts of the globe as substitutes for more enlightened approaches to the world and as a countermodel to a new period of rapid modernisation. Coming after two world wars, decolonisation and the Cold War and amid an era of global communication, anti-Americanism mirrors these experiences. Increasingly, resentment against America is framed in broad categories of foreign policy. This is true for Europe as for other parts of the world. The impact of this modern ideology plays out quite differently though. Discussing the Arab world, historian Dan Diner describes this pattern of negative identification as an odd but logical reversal:

> Instead of engaging with the philosophical, social and civilising requirements of the Enlightenment, especially the secularisation of the world in which they live ... these requirements are substituted by a fundamental and sustained belief in God and are combated with an elevated religious zeal. Under such a perceptual horizon, the only imaginable way of triumphing over the West would be by adopting an ever-increasing rigidity and radicalism in following Islam's religious guidelines.[12]

The fundamental lack of a secularised social sphere and its rejection leads to a mystified idealisation of Western technology and economic superiority within the Arab world, Diner argues. This is because the complexity of modern reality is only to be understood against the background of an enlightened worldview. In contrast, anti-modern ideologies not only foster interpretations of world affairs in terms of conspiracy theories, but they also provide putative explanations for failed processes of decolonisation, dysfunctional politics and economic and technological inferiority vis-à-vis the West.

In this sense, ethno-religious and nationalist ideologies are the constant companion of anti-Americanism. As a habit of thought, they serve to separate individuals from their intellectual autonomy and so help legitimise authoritarian rule or nihilistic rebellion. Fantasies of rebellion against an almost imaginary entity, America, undermine credibility for addressing whatever real grievances they might otherwise have: the target of the revolt is detached from its local context.

This mechanism of displacement makes it possible to see how even the legitimisation of secular Baathism in modern Iraq often adhered to the same logic pursued by religious fundamentalists in their stance towards America.[13] Modern anti-Americanism in various parts of the world shares similar patterns and psychological dispositions, the political outcome of which may radically differ. Sociologist Detlev Claussen has coined the concept 'everyday religion' (*Alltagsreligion*)[14] to describe the similarities and differences of this modern ideology as the undercurrent of political Islam, ethnic nationalism and religious fundamentalism. He interprets everyday religions as distinct ways of reflecting a social transition at the end of the twentieth and the start of the twenty-first century. 'Everyday religions' enable modern individuals to feel they are victims and victors at the same time, as members of an elite and part of the master; they even feel as if they are acting autonomously. These 'everyday religions' serve to provide overarching principles of organisation, a link between men and historical contingencies and therefore prove that such contemporary ideological formations no longer represent an objective relationship but are invaded by moments of subjective arbitrariness. Such mindsets have a fanatical aspect to them, because they can be immune to real experience but at the same time constitute a part of it.

Distorted approaches to viewing the world easily translate into terms of religious or cultural-nationalist self-justification. This distortion can emerge from any corner of world society, as can the pseudo-historical gloss attached to it. The much discussed, largely Western notion of a 'clash of civilisations' or a global, historical, 'cultural conflict' typifies the kind of catchphrase that, in its categorical misrepresentations, reveals its emptiness and lack of reflection. Although it may now appear as if culture determines consciousness in the real world, consciousness must constantly re-adjust to reality. New cultural and ethnic collectivities, ranging from radical Islam to ethnic nationalism in the Balkans to milder forms in German, Italian or Turkish society, which are shaped contrary to the codeword 'America', are based not on knowledge but amnesia. Forgetting constitutes the core of their epistemology and helps unleash modern fantasies of political unification and cultural homogeneity, which then appear on the stage of world history cloaked in ancient garb.

Anti-Americanism in Historical Transformation: Germany

Conflating very different phenomena by diagnosing an all-encompassing anti-Americanism nullifies distinctions that are indispensable. It is crucial not to underestimate the genesis of modern consciousness, for ideologies also have a history and undergo transformations, not only in the Arab world but also in Western societies.

For example, during the turn of the twentieth century's Romantic revivalism, Friedrich Nietzsche's notion of cultural struggle was widely misunderstood and abused for mythologically inspired aesthetic and political illusions. This distorted version of Nietzsche's notion of culture was merged with fantasies of a future German world power and laid the foundations for the debate *Kultur* versus *Zivilisation*, which, in turn, was imposed on the United States. By 1913, the United States had become the world's biggest economy and therefore appeared to be a political rival. Economic power alone does not account for the tremendous increase in cultural anti-Americanism in the following years; it merely catapulted the United States into the world stage as a powerful actor. The idea, however, made it possible for an anti-modern, anti-socialist German bourgeoisie to manipulate class conflicts in European societies by invoking notions of superiority vis-à-vis the United States.

The abstract juxtaposition of a profound German *Kultur* with a profane American *Zivilisation* readily served as a framework of interpretation for a variety of social conflicts and fears. It was not only economic contention but also the lost World War, a widespread scepticism towards capitalist modernity and issues concerning the social distribution of wealth that found an ideological expression in that comparison.

However, this transatlantic opposition had other historical antecedents as well. Germany was a belated nation, unified only in 1871, and the hostile feelings towards the United States mirrored the anti-democratic sentiments of the Wilhelmine state. Anti-Americanism then migrated into the core of the German ruling elite's self-perception and became an integral part of nationalistic folklore and a source of anger towards the real world power – all of which was shared by many intellectuals.

A second important ingredient was the emergent mass culture before WWI and in the Weimar period, which further reinforced these forms of consciousness. It was an era for which Karl Kraus, looking to Chicago and Detroit, invented the delightful term '*Fordschritt*', a play on the German word for progress, *Fortschritt*. Cultural and political anti-Americanism merged in the hatred of Woodrow Wilson's internationalism, the League of Nations and other sentiments, anticipating the National–Socialist imperialism of have-nots. The image of a hypocritical Wilsonianism and a treacherous Treaty of Versailles became 'Siamese twins', as Ernst Fraenkel called them. Prejudice hardened during the following years, as the Nazi agitators combined this revanchism with their anti-Semitic rhetoric of German superiority, denouncing 'Uncle Sam as Uncle Shylock'.

Economic modernisation in the post-World War II period produced a sense of déjà vu as past tropes reappeared under a new set of circumstances. The increasing strength and social mobility of a broad middle class, something that had existed in the United States a generation earlier, became the universal standard in the Western world. Uneven developments thus led to the perception that West Germany – and the world in general – was being Americanised once again. It was true that economic reconstruction, fostered largely by the Marshall Plan, was welcomed by the West German population and celebrated as an economic miracle or *Wirtschaftswunder*. However, the fact that Germany had lost a World War to the United States for the second time in two decades and was guilty of what was even then considered the greatest crimes in modern human history was indigestible and nearly impossible to incorporate into national self-conception. The enormous crimes revealed by the US-led Nuremberg Trials, on the one hand, and the start of the Cold War, in which the United States was seen as the main protector against communist aggression, on the other, generated a new attitude of ambivalence towards America. Gratefulness towards the United States for bringing the country back to normality co-existed with a fundamental rejection and hatred towards the nation that had won the war.

Although de-Nazification and re-education were relatively successful in West Germany, nationalist attitudes did not die out in 1945. However, with the emergence of the myth of the 'Zero Hour' – the idea of a fresh start from scratch that became an important ideological feature of the new Federal Republic – outspoken nationalism was nearly impossible for decades. During most of the Federal Republic's existence, one could relate to national traditions solely in negative terms. In retrospect, it is fascinating and astounding to see how in 1952 – when former Assistant Secretary of War John McCloy was effectively running West Germany – nationalist-minded Germans re-defined victimisation by claiming Germany had been collectively persecuted by the Allies through the US-led tribunals at Nuremberg and the de-Nazification programs. An essay on 'German anti-Americanism' that appeared in *Commentary* in February 1953 offers striking evidence of just how long such sentiments have been around.[15]

At the same time, admiration for and orientation towards the United States appeared to be a painless way to distance oneself from the crimes of National Socialism. This constellation further contributed to an ambivalent identification with the United States, which frequently found an outlet in anti-American rhetoric. One theme that re-emerged in the post-war era was the criticism of America's alleged cultural superficiality. It was easy to highlight European and German cultural profundity without violating the anti-nationalist taboo or indulging in distinctly National Socialist rhetoric against America's 'degenerate modernity'.[16] The aggressive anti-Americanism of the late Weimar Republic and the Third Reich was thus transformed into an ambivalent identification with America, constrained by certain taboos that had emerged not only from the Nazi past, but also from the Cold War present.

This attitude entered mainstream culture only in the late 1960s, when the student rebellion transformed university and public life. With the 1969 general election, the era of Christian Democratic-led governments came to an end. The student rebellion with its American-style forms of protest – sit-ins, teach-ins, demonstrations and public debates – was important in the second democratisation of post-war German society. Legitimate criticism of the Vietnam War, much of which was shared by Americans, should not be misinterpreted as the flaring up of old prejudices, as some analysts suggested. However, the war in Southeast Asia, with more than two million Vietnamese victims, led to a shift of political identification from the West to the South. The protests against the United States, together with widespread enthusiasm and engagement for Third World causes, did much to foster democratic practices in the Federal Republic. Since leftwing students could not rally around German national traditions, many directed their criticism against the United States. This mechanism helps explain the revival of anti-imperialist rhetoric during the 1970s.

The fact that Germany's new place in the world developed along lines that appear almost pre-political was due to a unique quality of the Federal Republic. A good part of its success had to do with it being a society without a nation, an economic power without expressed national interests, a global player with few foreign policy responsibilities. Nestled in an awkward yet still comfortable position between the superpowers, Germany remained at the centre of world politics for several decades without playing an active role. In fact, in the context of the times, restraint and neutrality best suited and served Germany's capabilities and interests.

This extraordinary situation prolonged the attitude of 'determined neutrality', which Hannah Arendt had already observed during her first visit to the country in 1950. Arendt said she had the impression Germans thought it was 'as absurd to take sides in the [Cold War] conflict as it would be to take sides in an earthquake'.[17] At the same time, there arose an attitude of provincial pacifism, partly because violence and war had never played a progressive, liberating role in German history. This is one reason why current social and political challenges produce so much perplexity at various intellectual and emotional levels. It is not the fear of losing so-called 'cultural identity' that is expressed in anti-Americanism, but a collective and individual readjustment to massive social and political changes. These cannot be understood in abstract terms, wrapped in phrases such as the search for cultural self-awareness or dismissed by some academics as the confusion induced by imbibing too many 'second-hand notions of the Frankfurt School's critique of civilisation'.[18]

This current constellation of fading neutrality and ascendant provincialism not only fuels current ambivalence towards the United States and results in simplistic critiques of American unilateralism, but it also conceals one's own impotence and unwillingness to act. As difficult as it may be to accept, West Germany's tradition of neutrality was an important ingredient in democratising German society. It was the most radical negation of Nazi leadership. The politics of the will was replaced by the politics of unwillingness, as it were. This did not change with the unification of the two German societies in 1990, often misleadingly called re-unification, as if something old had been reborn. In fact, the Federal Republic's eastern enlargement helped sustain Cold War mentalities for another inward-oriented decade.

Carte Blanche: The New Germany

It was an impressive sight when 250,000 Berliners gathered on June 17 Street in front of the Brandenburg Gate a few days after the September 11 attacks to demonstrate their solidarity with the people of the United States. They saw almost the entire German government pay homage to the United States, heard mournful blues and gospel songs and listened to a speech by US Ambassador Daniel Coats. The most emotional moment came when many in the crowd started applauding before his remarks could be translated. Coats, a former senator from Indiana who had begun his tenure in Germany only a few days earlier, was at first puzzled by this reaction. He soon realised that his audience, which included many young people, wanted to prove just how much of a success story the re-education project had been in Germany and to show their own familiarity with the English language. Chancellor Gerhard Schröder's promise of 'unlimited solidarity' followed, and a few weeks later, the then government – a centre-left coalition of Social Democrats and Greens – narrowly survived a vote of confidence that in turn made it possible to send German troops to Afghanistan.

These bold statements and acts quickly came to be overshadowed by doubts and were eventually reversed. Then German President Johannes Rau, one of the speakers at the Berlin demonstration, murmured some of the first prominent reservations with regard to American 'self-victimisation' and expressed concerns about a possible over-reaction from the United States. Rau was promptly seconded by a number of church representatives as well as by Christian Democrats such as former Under Secretary of Defence Willy Wimmer and former Labour Minister Norbert Blüm, an icon of Rhineland-style social Catholicism. After the war in Afghanistan started, the murmur grew louder and more distinct, especially among the 'Hitler Youth generation'. These older Germans, who had consciously experienced National Socialism and significantly shaped post-war German political culture – on the whole both anti-communist and pro-Western – now crossed political lines to express their concerns about the United States. The growing number of opponents to the invasion of Afghanistan included a broad range of public figures such as Rudolf Augstein, founder and publisher of the weekly *Der Spiegel* and Lothar de Maizière, a moderate Christian Democrat and the last prime minister of East Germany.[19] Erhard Eppler, an old-style Social Democrat, suggested that Europe might offer the United States lessons in how to deal with conflicts in a peaceful way.[20] Leftwing historian Hans-Ulrich Wehler, during a roundtable on Afghanistan in Berlin, started talking about Palestine as a bloody wound kept open by Israel, a thesis that he then tied into a suggestion that Air Force generals were once again in charge of setting the course of world history. For this allegation, he supplied a litany of disasters: Dresden, Vietnam and Serbia, in addition to Afghanistan.[21] Klaus Zwickel, then chairman of IG Metall, Germany's largest and most influential labour union, called on the United States to 'stop the bombardment of Afghanistan immediately', and Günter Gaus, a former member of the late Willy Brandt's government, made remarks about the 'unscrupulousness of carpet bombing and the use of cluster bombs' at a time when an average of fifteen fighter planes were operating over a territory larger than France. The vice-president of the German Parliament, Antje Vollmer of the Greens, worried whether the United States was prepared to 'convert the war against the Taliban into a world-wide campaign against an unlimited number of potential fallback territories' such as Somalia or Pakistan.[22] Meanwhile the controversial author Martin Walser said Europe was obliged to 'tell the friend that historical failures and aberrations cannot be corrected through war but solely through peace'.[23]

A few months later, when it became clear that the campaign in Iraq was looming, the rhetoric escalated. Ulrich Wickert, a prominent German television news anchor, suggested in a magazine article that George W. Bush and Osama bin Laden shared similar 'patterns of thinking',[24] while the German fashion designer Wolfgang Joop accused the United States of committing atrocities in Afghanistan. In the run-up to the Iraq War, legitimate criticism became increasingly difficult to distinguish from basic resentments towards America, with political arguments often being prefaced by conspiracy theories. The confusion culminated during the tightly contested 2002 German election campaign, when Chancellor Schröder sought domestic political advantage by categorically rejecting German participation in any future American 'adventure'[25] in Iraq. This may have emboldened a leading parliamentarian of the governing Social Democratic Party to declare that George W. Bush behaved 'as if he were Princeps Caesar Augustus'.[26] As if this were not enough, the justice minister then drew a comparison between President Bush and Hitler, a remark that cost the minister her job.[27]

It was not only the opposition to the war that prompted people to make extreme remarks about the United States. The spectrum for interpretations of social reality in which the codeword 'America' played a crucial role has been stretched from the cultural sphere to debates about social and economic transformation. Theatre director Peter Zadek, for instance, told *Der Spiegel* in an interview that America was 'repugnant' to him because of its 'lack of culture' only to let the reader know in the next sentence that he had never been to the country. He also said the United States was ultimately 'more dangerous than the Nazis', for it did not want to conquer only Europe but the whole world.[28] Similar comparisons of National Socialism with US politics are sometimes found among intellectuals as well as young people at anti-war rallies waving banners that depict Bush with a Hitler-style moustache and comparing the bombing of Baghdad with that of Dresden.

Less aggressive but no less intriguing in this context is a variety of comments that portray the United States as the root cause for the downsizing of the German welfare system. Employing his populist instinct, Schröder vindicated his reform policies by calling them a struggle against 'American conditions', referring to the socio-economic system in the United States. During a state election campaign in 2005, the chairman of the Social Democratic Party went even further by directly attributing the repercussions of a global economy to 'American capitalists'. 'Financial investors' who try to stay 'anonymous' and 'have no face', he said, would dig into German corporations like 'swarms of locusts'. His insect metaphor quickly became a popular image of unscrupulous economic behaviour considered by many in Germany as typically American. The May 2005 issue *Metall*, IG Metall's monthly magazine, featured a cover story on US investors called: 'The Plunderers are Here.' A caricature illustrating the article showed mosquitoes attacking German factories. The caption read: 'Like mosquitoes, American financial investors suck the German economy dry'.[29]

Similar rhetoric is to be found in German debates on European Union (EU) integration, which is rarely discussed as a political and economic transformation process, but usually in pre-political terms as an issue of supposed or desired European 'identity'. These deliberations often explicitly or implicitly refer to the United States as the counter-example. Ironically, the most intense debate over European self-perception was triggered by a US politician's derisive remark about 'old Europe'. Politicians and intellectuals countered by seizing on the image of the 'old' and infusing the debate on the future of the EU's shape with traditional anti-American imagery. Being old and endowed with a long history and high culture suddenly became coalescing point for European self-awareness. Lacking positive democratic traditions and common political visions, European was conveniently conceived as non-American.

Similarly, anxieties about power and weakness on the world stage are also addressed with anti-American vocabulary. The war in Iraq brought to light the imbalance of economic vis-á-vis political and military power in United States–European relations. A well-known German commentator, criticising the political state of the EU, especially the attitude of some eastern European countries towards the Iraq War lamented, 'the EU, following Eastern enlargement, has become more American rather than more European'.[30]

Such statements and discussions have to be seen against the backdrop of the political changes that German society has undergone since the end of the Cold War. The challenges to the old, inward orientation of German foreign policy became unmistakably clear on 9/11, an event that highlighted the dramatic changes that had taken place silently and had only been partly and belatedly addressed by the interventions in Bosnia and Kosovo. 9/11 showed that a Cold War style of foreign policy abstinence was untimely and that the need to act differently in a world of new threats was palpable. In Germany, this implied a tremendous change of political and public conventions; balancing between the needs posed by new challenges and the requirements of national interest, Germany for the first time had to democratically shape its own foreign policy paradigms.

Two important challenges to these outmoded attitudes occurred within the expanse of three short years. Firstly, the 1998 general election produced a long overdue generational change, bringing the Americanised 1960s generation to power and putting an end to the prolonged existence of the Federal Republic. Secondly, with the deployment of German troops to the Balkans in 1999 and the September 11 attacks in 2001, it became obvious that Germany's role in future world politics had to be redefined. But that was not an easy task. Old political and social traditions simply vanished before new ones had emerged to replace them. The vacuum could not be filled by drawing on democratic national traditions in German foreign policy because close to none existed. In this situation, a mixture of various forms of anti-Americanism helped to establish new political and foreign policy traditions in united Germany. It could be done only negatively, the old-fashioned Federal Republic way.

Therefore, the American-armed interventions in Afghanistan and Iraq were bound to affect Germany's difficult transformation from the non-national, post-war period of the 'Bonn Republic' to the post-unification era of full sovereignty. The friction that is bound to arise in this process of re-invention is in turn compensated by disparaging America's purported lack of culture and its short history, and by pointing to alleged German pre-eminence in this field. A particular ambivalence towards power in general can be found here. It finds expression, for example, by denouncing American policies based on national interests and contrasting them with German policies supposedly based on values and ideals.[31] In 2004, during a heated debate at Yale University, Constanze Stelzenmüller, a journalist from *Die Zeit*, coined an expression for this German mindset: She called it the attitude of a 'moral superpower'.

Even if some of the aforementioned manifestations of anti-Americanism in Germany were perhaps driven to extremes by the desire to provide a European response to the current US administration's frequent rhetorical drubbings of Europe, they are on the whole full of resentment and beyond rational criticism. Such emotional outbursts do not necessarily reveal a German predisposition towards hatred of the United States, nor do they represent an all-embracing national attitude. Examining such phenomena at the level of forms of collective consciousness remains nonetheless instructive.

Modern societies are complex and consist of many different layers. As has been argued with regard to France, heterogeneous European countries are made up of countless different groups, every one of which has its 'own' image of America, which frequently changes in the light of circumstances or political events. However, it sometimes happens that this multitude of contradictory perceptions coalesces into a major trend of opinion and for a while the attitudes of the country as a whole become lopsided, standing excessively positive or negative in the face of American realities.[32]

Modes of collective consciousness are a strange phenomenon; they easily take on a life of their own when cut loose from the checks and balances of reality, particularly in times of transformation. After the Cold War, when convictions thought to be unshakable were shattered within a few months, individuals felt not only 'the right to have ... his 'opinion' ... without subjecting it to any criteria of objective truth',[33] as Theodor Adorno put it in a discussion from another time, they felt compelled to develop new opinions about the world's order, which was proving extremely resistant to being brought under one umbrella. The sole standard, to which one could relate, positively or negatively, was the one society seemingly untouched by the upheavals of the late twentieth century: the United States.

When people in Germany and other parts of the globe define their understanding of the world by distancing themselves from America, this does not necessarily indicate alienation and detachment, but rather suggests the very opposite. To define a society as strange and different, it has to be 'beyond far and near', to use Georg Simmel's words during the last *fin-de-siècle*. What is believed to be the essence of America is so much a part of daily life in Europe, or anywhere else in the world for that matter, that anybody who has seen a Hollywood movie or visited a Starbucks coffee shop feels entitled to have an opinion about the United States, its policies and its cultural standing. People feel they know what America is. This feeling proves the illusion of closeness and transparency. Yet, this is more than an illusion: this feeling merges with firsthand experiences, because the United States 'is indeed an open society. News and information circulate freely, American media organisations dot the globe, European journalists encounter no special obstacles when they work in the United States, and the number of Europeans travelling to America rises from year to year. However, behind this apparent transparency the real workings of American society are far from obvious. We believe we know a great deal about America, but in fact we know very little.'[34]

This unique context provides for the intensity with which people around the world refer to the United States, observe and misconstrue its internal workings and desperately try to derive from it a frame of reference for understanding the world. Emphasising differences is thus a function of closeness among modern societies that share a great deal with each other. 'Strangeness is not due to different and incomprehensible matters', as Simmel observed, 'it is rather caused by the fact that similarity, harmony and nearness are accompanied by the feeling that they are not really the unique property of this particular relationship'.[35] Simmel's insights were fuelled by his experiences in Berlin at the turn of the century. At that time, when the city was growing, modernising and becoming more cosmopolitan, he understood that expressions of strangeness were an integral part of an urban environment that was growing more complex and diverse as well as more simplified and uniform. Today, this dynamic is occurring around the world.

In a global public sphere marked by such a breathtaking dynamic, expressions of opinion have to be interpreted, not taken at face value. The charge that America lacks history should not be reflexively labelled a Heideggerian and Germanic attack or taken as proof that German cultural pessimism and anti-Americanism are carrying on the tradition of their nineteenth- and twentieth-century counterparts. The revival of this image is growing in importance in the post-Cold War world. Against the backdrop of a process of growing economic and political differences as well as competition between the EU and its former closest ally, the topos of an America allegedly lacking in history and culture should instead be seen as ideological compensation for a real or imagined global dominance of the United States not as a repetition of similar themes that played a role in Germany 100 years ago.

There are of course good reasons why people *imagine* the United States as having a disproportionate effect on world history. And when the forty-year era of unprecedented stability, peace and economic growth ended in 1990, ideologies became even less dependent on reality.[36] When one takes a step back, it is clear that four years after the initial outburst of German anti-war sentiment and the increasing complications in Iraq, anecdotal observations and a number of opinion polls agree not only that anti-American feelings are on the rise in Europe, but also that European societies are themselves only part of a global trend towards a resentful estrangement from the United States. However, neither common sense nor poll results (with their seductive aura of precision) provide a complete picture. The complexity of both modern anti-Americanism and current transformations in German society goes beyond empirical processing and statistical tabulations.

Although German ambivalence towards the United States certainly indulges in much of the same resentment and many of the same distorted representations that feed more uncompromising and violent forms of anti-Americanism, the two varieties are only partly comparable. The variations range from relatively mild antipathy to 'Yankee go home – and take me with you' to the absurdly radical and violent postures of certain parts of the intelligentsia in the Arab world. In a world lacking real empires in the classical sense, anti-Americanism performs several functions for those who (understandably or not) wish to see themselves in national or subjective opposition to a global force. As a universal symbol that pre-packages the world and makes it readily understandable, anti-Americanism offers a platform for communicative bonding and serves the lowest common denominator, uniting those who might otherwise have little means to associate. There is of course a desperate need for some kind of understanding of the world after the Cold War confrontation between superpowers and military blocs. The levelling power of anti-Americanism helps to simplify reality by ridding it of non-compatible, refractory dissonance. Since it helps interpret modern society, it is mostly a middle-class phenomenon, a convenient ideology for people with a certain amount of education, ambition and self-confidence to construe the world in bold terms. For its constituency, the discourse of anti-Americanism condenses overarching and sometimes overwhelming economic and cultural developments into a simplistic worldview.

Such false abstractions are found in everyday practices in many societies. Although America serves as the prism through which the world is interpreted, it is nevertheless important to recognise that these ideas and opinions, although wrong-headed and full of resentment, do not easily translate into action. Only a very specific set of circumstances is capable of transforming felt ambivalence into violent rebellion – a rule that applies to attitudes towards the United States as much as towards any other perceived power.

History does not repeat itself, nor do forms of consciousness. Genuine ambivalence towards the United States does not 'promote or confirm the pre-existing concepts of America constructed by Heidegger and others'.[37] Some have gone so far as to assume a revival of a long-standing German obsession with American power, which flourished at different occasions, at the dawn of the twentieth century, during the interwar period, throughout the 1950s and during the 1980s debates over nuclear missiles. Alas, the notion that the 'anti-American discourse has not changed much' is equally flawed.[38]

The German middle classes have undergone an Atlantic transition during the 1950s and 1960s and experienced a profound modernisation process. Newly educated communities have replaced the older German bourgeoisie and are separated from previous anti-American ideologies by half a century and two global wars. The difference is partly reflected in the fact that today nobody wants to be seen as truly anti-modern or anti-American. Ambivalence towards the United States persists because opinion leaders and other members of the educated middle classes have yet to find their place in a society where modernisation is still perceived as Americanisation. At the same time, they have failed to pursue a more independent path towards inventing new political traditions. Pacifism and neutrality were not only an important part of the post-Nazi legacy, but also central to the establishment of a domestic democratic tradition; now, however, one might well ask whether this is now inadequate and prevents

German society from establishing a democratic foreign policy tradition capable of overturning its considerable deficit in the field. German foreign policy, once the plaything of Bismarck and Prussian aristocrats, was an undemocratic feature of Germany's constitutional monarchy, and in many ways, the dream of a restored empire, the quintessence of an anti-democratic foreign policy, was crucial to the rise of National Socialism. Indeed, such knowledge plays a role in shaping the taboo against having a foreign policy, a taboo that continues to hobble, even as it moderates and informs, German attempts to engage positively with the one country that dominates international politics, the United States.

The current blend of military responsibility, new democratic policies and stubborn resentment that characterises German society and politics are indicators of an increasing desire to overcome past practices and the rhetoric of neutral exceptionalism. This is why the present form of anti-Americanism cannot be equated with either its predecessors of the 1920s or militant Islam. Today's anti-Americanism is a different phenomenon, more ambivalent than *anti*. German society underwent dramatic changes in the second half of the Cold War and was part of the Atlantic revolution. This transformation also codifies the new anti-American resentment of not wanting to be seen as either anti-modern or anti-American. If this dialectic is appreciated, instead of being misused for short-sighted political gain, the reconstruction of the West could finally begin.

About the Series Editor and Contributors

Series Editor

Brendon O'Connor is a senior lecturer in the Department of Politics and Public Policy at Griffith University, Australia. In 2006 he was a Fulbright Fellow at Georgetown University. He is the author of *A Political History of the American Welfare System: When Ideas Have Consequences* (2004) and co-editor with Martin Griffiths of *The Rise of Anti-Americanism* (2006).

Contributors

Shahram Akbarzadeh is the director of the Centre for Muslim Minorities and Islam Policy Studies, School of Political and Social Inquiry, Monash University, Australia.

Kylie Baxter is a research assistant in the Centre for Muslim Minorities and Islam Policy Studies, and a PhD candidate in the School of Political and Social Inquiry, Monash University, Australia.

D. Jason Berggren is a PhD candidate in the Department of Political Science, Florida International University.

Konstantina E. Botsiou is a lecturer in modern and contemporary history, University of Athens.

Richard Boyd is an assistant professor in the Department of Political Science, University of Wisconsin-Madison.

Mary Buckley is a fellow and Director of Studies in Social and Political Sciences at Hughes Hall, University of Cambridge.

John Callaghan is a professor of politics at the University of Wolverhampton, United Kingdom.

Paola Cesarini is an assistant professor in the Department of Political Science, Providence College.

John Chiddick is a lecturer in politics at La Trobe University, Australia.

Richard Crockatt is a professor of American studies at the University of East Anglia, United Kingdom.

Sergio Fabbrini is a professor of political science at the University of Trento.

Barbara Fried is a PhD candidate in the Sociology Department at Hannover University, Germany, and is currently a visiting scholar at the Center of European Studies at the University of California Berkeley.

Navraj Singh Ghaleigh is a lecturer in public law, Edinburgh Law School, University of Edinburgh.

Martin Griffiths is an associate professor in the Department of International Business and Asian Studies at Griffith University.

Marianne Hanson is a reader in international relations in the School of Political Science and International Studies, and director of the Rotary Center for International Studies in Peace and Conflict Resolution at the University of Queensland.

Kenneth J. Heineman is a professor of history at Ohio University.

Cheryl Hudson is the assistant director of Academic Programme at the Rothermere American Institute, University of Oxford, and a PhD candidate in American history at Vanderbilt University, Nashville, TN.

Pierangelo Isernia is a professor in the Center for the Study of Political Change, University of Siena.

Iyanatul Islam is a professor in the Department of International Business and Asian Studies at Griffith University.

John Kane is a professor in the Department of Politics and Public Policy, Griffith University, Australia.

Ashley Lavelle is a lecturer in the Department of Politics and Public Policy at Griffith University.

Alan McPherson is an associate professor in the Department of History, Howard University, United States.

Andrei S. Markovits is the Karl W. Deutsch Collegiate Professor of Comparative Politics and German Studies at the University of Michigan.

Iwan Morgan is a professor Institute in the for the Study of the Americas, University of London.

John E. Moser is an associate professor of history, Ashland University, United States.

Colin Nettelbeck is a professorial fellow in the School of Languages and Linquistics, University of Melbourne, Australia.

Kim Richard Nossal is a professor in the Department of Political Studies, Queen's University, Canada.

Terry O'Callaghan is a senior lecturer in the School of International Studies at the University of South Australia.

Brendon O'Connor is a senior lecturer in the Department of Politics and Public Policy, Griffith University, Australia.

Jacinta O'Hagan is a fellow in the Department of International Relations at the Australian National University.

Michael O'Keefe is a lecturer in politics at La Trobe University.

Graeme Orr is an associate professor in the Law School, University of Queensland, Australia.

Inderjeet Parmar is the director of the Center for International Politics and senior lecturer in the Department of Politics at the University of Manchester.

Haig Patapan is an associate professor in the Department of Politics and Public Policy, Griffith University, Australia.

Nicol C. Rae is a professor in the Department of Political Science, Florida International University.

Lars Rensmann is the DAAD Assistant Professor of Political Science, University of Michigan.

Michael Schiavone is a lecturer in the School of Political and International Studies, Flinders University, Australia.

Robert Singh is a professor of politics at Birkbeck College, University of London.

Alan Tidwell is the director of the Center for Australian and New Zealand Studies, Edmund A. Walsh School of Foreign Service, Georgetown University.

Brandon Turner is a PhD candidate in the Department of Political Science, University of Wisconsin-Madison.

Ian Tyrrell is a professor in the School of History at the University of New South Wales, Australia.

Irwin M. Wall is an emeritus professor of history at the University of California, Riverside.

Guanhua Wang is an associate professor in the Department of History, University of Connecticut.

Deborah E. Ward is an assistant professor of political science, Seton Hall University, United States.

Michael Werz serves as the director of the Hessen Universities Consortium in New York and is a Transatlantic Fellow at the German Marshall Fund of the United States in Washington, DC.

Michael Wesley is a professor of Asian studies and director of the Griffith Asia Institute at Griffith University.

Notes

Series Preface
1. Geoff Elliot, 'Osama bin Saving all His Love for Whitney,' *Australian* (August 23, 2006),8.
2. Seymour Martin Lipset, *American Exceptionalism* (New York: Norton, 1996).

Introduction: Causes and Sources of Anti-Americanism
1. Tony Judt makes this link with sport-utility vehicles (SUVs) in 'Anti-Americanism Abroad,' in *The Rise of Anti-Americanism*. Edited by Brendon O'Connor and Martin Griffiths (London: Routledge, 2007).
2. Amnesty International, 'Guantánamo Bay – A Human Rights Scandal,' http://www.web.amnesty.org/pages/guantanamobay-index-eng.
3. John Micklethwait and Adrian Wooldridge, *The Right Nation: Conservative Power in America* (New York: Penguin, 2004).
4. Pew Research Center for the People and the Press, 'American Character Gets Mixed Reviews,' June 23, 2005.
5. Ibid.
6. See Tony Judt, *Past Imperfect* (Berkeley: University of California Press, 1992).
7. Collected by Pierangelo Isernia, cited in Philip Everts, 'Images of the US – Three Theories of Anti-Americanism,' Workshop on Anti-Americanism in Comparative Historical Perspective, European Consortium for Political Research, Nicosia, Cyprus, April 25–30, 2006. Explanatory note from Philip Everts: 'Combined Net Scores ("favorable" minus "unfavorable") are given for France, Germany, Italy and United Kingdom. Averages have been calculated for years for which more polls were available. Data for missing years have been interpolated. Polls were not always held in all countries and the average figure presented in the graph sometimes may hide important differences among the four countries. Given the generally fairly positive results in terms of sympathy, trust with respect to the United States that these surveys tend to produce it is somewhat awkward and biased to (continue to) use the term "anti- Americanism" for this indicator.'

Chapter 1: What is Anti-Americanism?
1. Throughout this chapter I use a variety of abbreviated ways of talking about the United States of America, i.e., the US, the United States and America. I know some people find the use of the term 'America' inappropriate, but the abbreviation 'America' to me seems quite different from the words 'the Americas' or 'North America'. Most people seem to accept that the people of the United States of America are to be called Americans; from this it would seem reasonable to suggest that these Americans come from America.
2. Oscar Wilde, 'The American Invasion,' *Virtual Library*, http://www.farid-hajji.net/books/en/Wilde_Oscar/spp-chap07.html.
3. Theodore Zeldin, 'The Pathology of Anti-Americanism,' in *The Rise and Fall of Anti-Americanism: A Century of French Perception*. Edited by Denis Lacorne, Jacques Rupnik and Marie-France Toinet (London: Macmillan, 1990), 41.
4. Similarly Richard Crockatt argues: 'Even these polarities scarcely meet the case; they are the beginning of analysis, not the end of it. The point should be clear. Simplified images are dangerous tools of analysis and are certainly dangerous politically.' Crockatt, *America Embattled: September 11, Anti-Americanism and the Global Order* (London: Routledge, 2003), xii–xiii.
5. James Russell Lowell, 'On a Certain Condescension in Foreigners,' *Atlantic Monthly*, XXIII (1869), 89.

6. Marcus Cunliffe makes this point stating America 'has supplied an extraordinary drama (or melodrama) peopled with scouts and trappers, Yankees and Cavaliers, cowboys and Indians, sheriffs and badmen, Huck Finns and Nigger Jims, Abe Lincolns and Huey Longs, preachers and robber barons, do-gooders and con-men, Al Capones and J. Edgar Hoovers, hobos and work-bosses, loners and Babbitts. No other nation has produced so rich a cast of symbolic characters for modern times.' Quoted in Henry Fairlie, 'Anti-Americanism at Home and Abroad,' *Commentary* (December 1975), 31.

7. Henry Pelling, *America and the British Left* (New York: New York University Press, 1957), 161.

8. Moisés Naím writes: 'In France, the editor of *Le Monde Diplomatique* summarized his view of the world's reaction: "What's happening to [Americans] is too bad, but they had it coming."' Naím, 'Anti-Americanisms,' *Foreign Policy* (January–February 2002), 104–105. This view conflates people with governments in a manner I find highly questionable. However, the flip side of this response is the claim of American innocence. A classic example of this claim was made by Donald Rumsfeld in 2004 when he said: 'I think that people who think that terrorists pick and choose discriminately don't understand how it works. The United States had done nothing on September 11th when 3,000 people were killed.' Rumsfeld, 'Transcript of the Prime Minister The Hon John Howard MP Joint Press Conference with Secretary of Defense Donald Rumsfeld' (press conference held at the Pentagon, Washington, DC), http://www.pm.gov.au/news/interviews/Interview1469.html (cited July 18, 2005). The terrorist attacks of 9/11 were inexcusable, but America has certainly done a lot more than 'nothing' on the world stage.

9. Todd Gitlin, 'Anti-Anti-Americanism,' *Dissent* (Winter 2003), 103–106.

10. This point follows the advice of James Madison in the *Federalist Papers* (#63), where he declared that 'in doubtful cases, particularly where the national councils may be warped by some strong passion or momentary interest, the presumed or known opinion of the impartial world may be the best guide to be followed.' Of course the outside world is seldom, if ever, impartial, but the principle is still a good one. Alexander Hamilton et al., *The Federalist Papers* (New York: New American Library, 1961).

11. Pelling made a similar point about a different time period in his *America and the British Left* (1957, 6): 'The historical perspective provided by these studies inevitably suggests that dangerous distortion of the facts is likely to take place among those who commit themselves most fully to an *a priori* view of politics. Socialists of the mid-twentieth century seem to be often as blind to the merits of American society as Radicals of the mid-nineteenth century were blind to its faults.'

12. Grunberg writes: 'Even though the 9/11 attacks clearly marked the United States as a target and victim, a majority of Europeans considered that American foreign policy had been a contributing factor (GMF survey). Sixty-three percent of the French were of this opinion, but 57 percent of the British as well.' Gérard Grunberg, 'Anti-Americanism in French and European Public Opinion,' in *With Us or Against Us: Studies in Global Anti-Americanism.* Edited by Tony Judt and Denis Lacorne (New York: Palgrave Macmillan, 2005), 63.

13. Paul Hollander, 'Introduction: The New Virulence and Popularity,' in *Understanding Anti-Americanism.* Edited by Paul Hollander (Chicago: Ivan R. Dee, 2004), 16.

14. Pew Research Center for the People & the Press, 'A Year After Iraq War,' March 16, 2004.

15. See BBC, 'What the World Thinks of America.' (2003) http://www.news.bbc.co.uk/2/hi/americas/2994924.stm. Similar results were seen in the Euorobarometer survey of October 2003. See Marta Lagos, 'Threat to World Peace and the Role of the USA,' *International Journal of Public Opinion Research,* 16, 1 (Spring 2004), 91–95.

16. Pew Research Center for the People & the Press, 'A Year after Iraq War,' March 16, 2004.

17. Max Rodenbeck, 'The Truth about Jihad,' *New York Review of Books* (August 11, 2005).

18. Friedman writes 'It is the rare author who, like Rolf Winter and Alfred Mechtersheimer, openly acknowledges his own Anti-Americanism.' Max Paul Friedman, 'Cold War Critiques from Abroad: Beyond a Taxonomy of Anti-Americanism,' *GHI Bulletin*, 34 (Spring 2004).

19. The abuse of the term 'liberal' in post-1960s US politics is a classic example. See Brendon O'Connor, *A Political History of the American Welfare System* (Lanham: Rowman & Littlefield, 2004).

20. Kenneth Minogue, 'Anti-Americanism: A View from London,' *The National Interest* (Spring 1986), 43. On this issue, also see Hubert Vedrine, 'On Anti-Americanism,' *Brown Journal of World Affairs*, X, 2 (Winter/Spring 2004), 117–122. The popular internet encyclopedia *Wikipedia* similarly notes this usage of the term 'Anti-Americanism': '[T]he term is rarely employed as a self-identifier (i.e., "I am anti-American …") as this inherently implies bias. Instead, it is used most often as a pejorative by those who feel the United States is unfairly disparaged. The term may be employed, for instance, as a slur against groups or arguments critical of American policy.' http://www.en.wikipedia.org/wiki/Anti-Americanism (cited september 12, 2005).

21. For examples of the misuse of the term 'Anti-Americanism' in Australian politics see: Steve Lewis, 'PM Forced into Another Sugar Rescue,' *Australian* (February 11, 2004); Michelle Grattan, 'US Aware of Latham's "Dislike",' *Age* (April 13, 2004); Greg Sheridan, 'Labor's Anti-Americanism Won't Wash,' *Australian* (June 17, 2004), 11; 'Labor Shows Knee-Jerk Anti-Americanism over FTA – Howard,' *AAP* (August 21, 2004); Janet Albrechtsen, 'On Uncle Sam, Latham's Spots Aren't Changing,' *Australian* (August 4, 2004).

22. This work offers a laundry list of reasons why people dislike America, and at times, they rightly point out the contradictions within American society. However, their analysis is often too glib and logic at times deserts them, such as in the following paragraph: 'The rest of the world is more alert to the contradictions within America and its history than Americans themselves; more intrigued and interested to explore these contradictions than Americans are prepared to participate in such debate. As President Clinton noted in a speech at the University of California in 1997: "We were born with a declaration of independence which asserted that we were all created equal and a constitution that enshrined slavery. We fought a bloody civil war to abolish slavery but we remained unequal by law for another century. We advanced across the continent in the name of freedom, yet in doing so we pushed Native Americans off their land. We welcome immigrants, but each new wave has felt the sting of discrimination."' Ziauddin Sardar and Merryl Wyn Davies, *Why Do People Hate America?* (Cambridge: Icon Books, 2002), 59. Are they forgetting that Bill Clinton is an American, and a rather prominent one at that? We should expect much more from these best-selling authors.

23. 'The *New York Review of Books* marketed itself in Europe in 2003 with a cartoon of George W. Bush in the garb of a Roman emperor, next to the slogan "There is another America – and we need to hear from it."' John Micklethwait and Adrian Wooldridge, *The Right Nation: Conservative Power in America* (New York: Penguin, 2004), 292.

24. Andrei Markovits, *Uncouth Nation* (Princeton, Princeton University Press, 2007).

25. Naím, 'Anti-Americanisms,' *Foreign Policy* (January–February 2002), 104–105.

26. Alvin Rubinstein and Donald Smith, 'Anti-Americanism in the Third World,' *Annals of the American Academy of Political Science*, 497 (1998).

27. Robert Singh, 'Are We All Americans Now? Explaining Anti-Americanisms,' in *The Rise of Anti-Americanism*. Edited by Brendon O'Connor and Martin Griffiths (London: Routledge, 2005).

28. Peter Katzenstein and Robert Keohane, 'Varieties of Anti-Americanisms' (Paper presented at the annual meeting of the American Political Science Association, Washington, DC, US, August 31–September 1, 2005).

29. Moisés Naím, 'The Perils of Anti-Americanism lite,' *Foreign Policy* (May/June 2003).

30. Denis Lacorne and Tony Judt, 'The Banality of Anti-Americanism,' in *With Us or Against Us*. Edited by Judt and Lacorne, 1.

31. Potter Stewart was struggling to precisely define pornography [see Justice Potter Stewart, concurring in *Jacobellis v. Ohio* (378 US 134, 1964)].

32. 'States Go under Microscope,' *Courier Mail* (April 20, 2005).

33. Pew Research Center for the People & the Press, 'American Character Gets Mixed Reviews,' June 23, 2005, 59–60.

34. Pew Research Center for the People & the Press, 'America's Image Slips, but Allies Share US Concerns over Iran, Hamas,' June 13, 2006, 30–31.

35. Pew Research Center for the People & the Press, 'American Character Gets Mixed Reviews,' 45–46.

36. Pew Research Center for the People & the Press, 'American Character Gets Mixed Reviews,' 1.

37. Zeldin, 'The Pathology of Anti-Americanism,' in *The Rise and Fall of Anti-Americanism*. Edited by Lacorne, Rupnik and Toinet.

38. Marie-France Toinet, 'Does Anti-Americanism Exist?' Ibid, 220.

39. Kimball takes this outlook when he writes 'Anti-Americanism has almost nothing to do with *criticism*. It is more a pathology than a position, operating not by evidence but emotion.' Roger Kimball, 'Anti-Americanism Then and Now,' in *Understanding Anti-Americanism*. Edited by Hollander, 240. More hysterical on this issue is Medved, who describes Anti-Americanism as 'the world's most dangerous, powerful and pathological hatred', which 'needs to be punished and rooted out, not respectfully analyzed'. Michael Medved, 'World's Most Dangerous Hatred,' http://www.worldnetdaily.com/news/article.asp?ARTICLE_ID=25296.

40. Toinet, 'Does Anti-Americanism Exist?' 225–226.

41. Singh, 'Are We All Americans Now?'

42. Arundhati Roy, 'Anti-Americanism: Hallowed Be Thy Name,' *Arts and Opinion*, 2, 1 (2003).

43. Not one of the books I have come across on prejudice has a listing for Anti-Americanism in the index.

44. Nick Cohen, 'Why It Is Right to Be Anti-American,' *New Statesman* (January 14, 2002).

45. Gitlin, 'Anti-Anti-Americanism,' 103–106.

46. In the same article, Cohen writes: 'However worthy individual thinkers and protesters may be, there are now no convincing radical movements in America, and haven't been for years,' Cohen, 'Why It Is Right to Be Anti-American'.

47. Paul Hollander, *Anti-Americanism: Irrational and Rational* (New York: Transaction, 1995), 334.

48. Ivan Krastev, 'The Anti-Americanism Century,' *Journal of Democracy*, 15, 2 (2004), 5.

49. James Ceaser, 'The Philosophical Origins of Anti-Americanism in Europe,' in *Understanding Anti-Americanism*. Edited by Paul Hollander (Chicago: Ivan R. Dee, 2004), 45.

50. Michael Freeden, *Ideology: A Very Short Introduction* (Oxford: Oxford University Press, 2003); Michael Freeden, *Ideologies and Political Theory* (Oxford: Clarendon Press, 1996).

51. The idea that ideology was a tool of the powerful and thus that the study of ideology is crucially the study of power relations has also long been central to Marxist thinking. See Terry Eagleton, *Ideology: An Introduction* (London: Verso, 1991), 5–7.

52. Tony Judt, *Past Imperfect* (Berkeley: University of California Press, 1992), 190–191.

53. Minogue, 'Anti-Americanism,' 44.

54. Michael Freeden, 'Editorial: Fundamentals and Foundations of Ideologies,' *Journal of Political Ideologies,* 10, 1 (2005), 3.

55. Michael Freeden, 'Editorial: Ideological Boundaries and Ideological Systems,' *Journal of Political Ideologies,* 8, 1 (2003); Freeden, *Ideology: A Very Short Introduction;* Freeden, *Ideologies and Political Theory.*

56. Mark Falcoff, 'Cuban Anti-Americanism: Historical, Popular, and Official,' in *Understanding Anti-Americanism.* Edited by Paul Hollander (Chicago: Ivan R. Dee, 2004), 197.

57. Ceaser, 'The Philosophical Origins of Anti-Americanism in Europe,' in *Understanding Anti-Americanism.* Edited by Paul Hollander (Chicago: Ivan R. Dee, 2004), 45.

58. Andrei Markovits, *Uncouth Nation* (Princeton: Princeton University Press, 2007); Andrei Markovits, 'European Anti-Americanism (and Anti-Semitism): Ever Present though Always Denied,' Center for European Studies Working Paper Series #108 (Harvard University, 2004).

59. Michael Freeden, 'Is Nationalism a Distinct Ideology?' *Political Studies,* XLVI (1998), 748–750.

60. Quoted in Michael Kazin, 'The Party of Fear,' *The Nation* (February 20, 1989). Hofstadter's words echo G. K. Chesterton's much quoted 'America is the only nation in the world that is founded on a creed. That creed is set forth with dogmatic and even theological lucidity in the Declaration of Independence.'

61. Ian Tyrrell, 'American Exceptionalism in an Age of International History,' *American Historical Review,* 96, 4 (1991).

62. Theodore Roosevelt quoted in Toinet, 'Does Anti-Americanism Exist?' 219.

63. Seymour Martin Lipset, *American Exceptionalism* (New York: Norton, 1996), 19.

64. Books that go along way to rebuffing Hartz and providing a more balanced understanding of the role of conservatism in America include: Theodore Lowi, *The End of the Republican Era* (Norman: University of Oklahoma Press, 1995); Anatol Lieven, *America Right or Wrong* (New York: Oxford University Press, 2004); Micklethwait and Wooldridge, *The Right Nation: Conservative Power in America* (New York: Penguin, 2004), 292.

65. Although I am less confident than Crockatt about what exactly Americanism might be, he is dead right in suggesting that Anti-Americanism is simply not a rejection of the American creed or the American example; it is commonly tinged with feelings of disappointment that America has not lived up to its ideals and rhetoric. Crockatt, *America Embattled,* 38.

66. Denis Lacorne, 'Anti-Americanism and Americanophobia' in *With Us or Against Us.* Edited by Judt and Lacorne, 47–52.

Chapter 2: The Anti-Americanism Mindset

1. By using the term 'America' and 'American' throughout this study to denote the political entity of 'The United States of America', I beg the indulgence of all readers who reside north or south of the respective borders of the United States and are thus, of course, 'American', though not citizens of the United States. I am using the concepts 'America' and 'American' not in their wider and more accurate geographic meaning but in their much more commonly used manner as representing one country, the United States of America. But particularly in a work on 'Anti-Americanism', I feel justified in doing so, since the term itself has always applied 'exclusively to the United States, and not to Canada or Mexico or any other nation of the New World. Many who complain bitterly that the United States has unjustifiably appropriated the label of America have nonetheless gladly allowed that Anti-Americanism should refer only to the United States.' James Ceaser,

'A Genealogy of Anti-Americanism,' *Public Interest* (Summer 2003). As to the surveys, the best known is the BBC's study of eleven countries for the television programme, 'What the World Thinks of America' (BBC News, 'Poll Suggests World Hostile to US'). The show was aired on Tuesday, June 17, 2003. In addition, there are the following seven studies by the Pew Foundation Survey Reports – Global Attitudes/International: 'Views of a Changing World 2003,' June 3, 2003; 'America's Image Further Erodes: Europeans Want Weaker Ties,' March 18, 2003; 'Among Wealthy Nations … ,' December 19, 2002; 'What the World Thinks in 2002,' December 4, 2002; 'Americans and Europeans Differ Widely on Foreign Policy Issues,' April 17, 2002; 'America Admired, Yet Its New Vulnerability Seen as a Good Thing, Say Opinion Leaders,' December 19, 2001; and 'Bush Unpopular in Europe, Seen as Unilateralist,' August 15, 2001. Some of these titles reflect the afore-mentioned malaise with and antipathy towards America on the part of much of the world, including Europe. Finally, there was a detailed survey conducted in August 2003 by the German Marshall Fund of the United States and Compagnia di San Paolo of Turin in seven European countries (German, France, Britain, Italy, the Netherlands, Poland and Portugal) and the United States, where the growing and deepening European aversion to America is amply documented.

2. Pierantelo Isernia, 'The Nature of the Beast: Anti-Americanism in Western Europe,' (Unpublished paper, January 2005).

3. Floyd Norris, 'Showdown Looms in Europe over Proposals on Accounting,' *New York Times* (July 11, 2003).

4. The very best article in recent times on Anti-Americanism is Fouad Ajami's 'The Falseness of Anti-Americanism,' *Foreign Policy* (September 2003).

5. Jon Elster, *Alchemies of the Mind: Rationality and the Emotions* (Cambridge: Cambridge University Press, 1999), 65. Elster himself attributes the distinction between anger and hatred to Aristotle's *Nicomachean Ethics*.

6. For an excellent article demonstrating how American intellectuals have cultivated Anti-American views, see Ian Buruma, 'Wielding the Moral Class,' *Financial Times Weekend Magazine* (September 13, 2003).

7. For a fine article showing how Michael Moore's work has a completely different meaning in the United States and in Europe, see Andrian Kreye, 'Zugpferd des Antiamerikanismus: Schlecht recherchiert, ohne Kontext: Warum ist Michael Moore in Europa so erfolgreich?' *Süddeutsche Zeitung* (October 11, 2003). The author makes it clear that whereas in the United States Moore's popularity bespeaks his humorous and biting depiction of a conservative administration and establishment, in Europe Moore embodies little more than a foil behind which one can safely voice one's Anti-Americanism without being accused of holding such a prejudice since – after all – Michael Moore, a *bona fide* American, says the same things.

8. For a detailed discussion of Michael Moore, see Andrei Markovits, *Amerika, Dich hasst sich's besser. Antiamerikanismus und Antisemitismus in Europa* (Hamburg: Konkret-Literatur Verlag, 2004).

9. Meredith Woo-Cummings, 'Unilateralism and Its Discontents: The Passing of the Cold-War Alliance and Changing Public Opinion in the Republic of Korea,' (Unpublished paper, University of Michigan, 2003.)

10. Berndt Ostendorf, 'The Final Idiocy of the Reversed Baseball Cap: Transatlantische Widersprüche in der Amerikaniserungsdebatte,' *Amerikastudien/American Studies,* 44, 1 (1999); Berndt Ostendorf, 'Why Is American Popular Culture So Popular? A View from Europe,' *Amerikastudien/American Studies,* 46, 3 (2001). I will only look at the European side of this *folie à deux* in this study, not the American.

11. Paul Hollander, *Anti-Americanism: Critiques at Home and Abroad, 1965–1990* (New York: Oxford University Press, 1992), 339 (emphasis in original). In addition to Hollander's key book on this topic, I would like to mention three others that, in my view,

offer the most comprehensive analysis on this topic. For Germany, it is clearly Dan Diner's *Feindbild Amerika: Über die Beständigkeit eines Ressentiments* (Munich: Propylaen Verlag, 2002). For France it is Philippe Roger's *L'Ennemi Américain: Généalogie de l'antiaméricanisme français* (Paris: Editions du Seuil, 2002); and for Canada, Mario Roy's *Pour en finir avec l'antiaméricanisme* (Québec: Boréal, 1993). I have yet to find comparable books for Anti-Americanism in Britain and Italy.

12. A British economist writing in the *Atlantic Monthly* in 1901 used the phrase Anti-Americanism explicitly, and made clear what it was about. To a 'despairing (European) envy of her prosperity and success' was coupled with a disagreeable new sense of impotence: commercial, diplomatic and moral. 'Cultured Europeans intensely resent the bearing of Americans; they hate the American form of swagger, which is not personal like the British, but national.' Here was a country 'crudely and completely immersed in materialism'. Little wonder that 'Anti-Americanism (sic) was on the march'. From David W. Ellwood, 'A Brief History of European Anti-Americanism'. (Unpublished paper, delivered at the 2003 convention of the Organization of American Historians, Memphis, Tennessee, April 6, 2003.)

13. Justice Potter Stewart, concurring in *Jacobellis v. Ohio* (378 US 134, 1964).

14. I am purposely using the French word 'ressentiment' instead of the English 'resentment' because – as Max Scheler in his brilliant treatment of this topic demonstrates – the French term includes dimensions of envy, jealousy and above all lingering hate arising from a certain degree of impotence that the English does not. See Max Scheler, *Ressentiment*. Edited, with an introduction, by Lewis Coser, and translated by William Holdheim (Glencoe: The Free Press, 1961). Of course the concept of *ressentiment* plays a central role in Friedrich Nietzsche's work as well, in which it connotes impotence, hatred, envy, and repressed feelings of revenge.

15. Ira Strauss, 'Is It Anti-Americanism or Anti-Westernism?' (Unpublished paper, 2003).

16. Georges de Buffon, 'Of the Varieties in the Human Species,' in *Barr's Buffon: Buffon's Natural History Containing a theory of the Earth, a General History of Man, of the Brute Creation, and of Vegetables, Minerals, Etc.* (London: T. Gillet, 1807), volume 4 (of 10), 306–352.

17. Cornelius de Pauw, 'Recherches philosophiques sur les américains' in idem, *Oeuvres philosophiques* (1974), Volume I, II.

18. Diner discusses de Pauw, de Buffon and other authors and thinkers of the time in his superb *Feindbild Amerika: Über die Bestätigung eines Ressentiments* (Munich: Propylaen Verlag, 2002).

19. Herbert J. Spiro, 'Anti-Americanism in Western Europe' in 'Anti-Americanism: Origins and Context,' ed. Thomas Perry Thornton. A special edition of *The Annals of the American Academy of Political and Social Science* (Beverly Hills: Sage Publications, 1988), 124.

20. The ideas regarding Tocqueville hail from an unpublished research proposal that John Torpey wrote in an application to Vienna's IFK.

21. Josef Joffe, 'Who's Afraid of Mr. Big?' *National Interest* (Summer 2001).

22. Heinrich Heine (trans. Frederic Ewen and Robert Holub) 'Ludwig Boerne: A Memorial (Second book),' in *The Romantic School and Other Essays*. Edited by Jost Hermand and Robert Holub (New York: Continuum 1985), 263.

23. Hartmut Wasser, 'Die Deutschen und Amerika,' *Politik und Zeitgeschichte* (Beilage zur Wochenzeitung *Das Parlament*) June 26, 1976.

24. Three articles have proven particularly useful for my research on these Anti-American attitudes by these giants of German culture, politics, literature and philosophy: Manfred Henningsen, 'Das Amerika von Hegel, Marx und Engels,' *Zeitschrift für Politik* (München), 20, 3 (1973); Wasser, 'Die Deutschen und Amerika,' *Politik und Zeitgeschichte* (Beilage zur Wochenzeitung *Das Parlament*) (June 26, 1976); and Günter Moltmann,

'Anti-Americanism in Germany: Historical Perspectives,' *Australian Journal of Politics and History*, 21, 2 (August 1975).

25. Ceaser, 'A Genealogy of Anti-Americanism,' *Public Interest* (Summer 2003).

26. Ibid.

27. All these quotations are from Peter Gay, *Freud: A Life for Our Time* (New York: W. W. Norton, 1988), 563, 570.

28. When Secretary of Defense Donald Rumsfeld made his provocative remark about 'Old Europe', with which he meant to dismiss the alliance of France and Germany against the Bush administration's Iraq policy, one of Germany's newspapers of record, the *Frankfurter Allgemeine Zeitung*, responded by publishing a long article which featured the voices of many leading French and German intellectuals. Sure enough, one German intellectual, the artist Jochen Gerz, centered his entire response on America's marginalisation of its native population, thus implying that the United States is not a democracy. See Jochen Gerz, 'Not in Our Name,' as part of the larger article entitled 'Das alte Europa antwortet Herrn Rumsfeld,' *Frankfurter Allgemeine Zeitung* (January 24, 2003).

29. Gernot Erler, Michael Mueller and Angelica Schwall-Dueren, 'Die Geburt einer Nation II,' *Frankfurter Rundschau* (March 11, 2003). As we will see below, this is a pattern pursued by many European intellectuals in the current cross-Atlantic debate with the United States whereby these intellectuals attempt to enhance the validity of their criticism of America and American policy by ostensibly following in the footsteps of 'good', i.e. internationalist and enlightened Americans such as Abraham Lincoln and Woodrow Wilson.

30. Roger, *L'Ennemi Américain: Généalogie de l'antiaméricanisme français*, 156. According to Roger, the South became a sentimental favorite in the right Parisian circles in the era of Napoleon III.

31. For Charles Dickens, see *American Notes* and *Martin Chuzzlewit*. For Frances Trollope, see *Domestic Manners of the Americans*. For Evelyn Waugh see *Decline and Fall*, *Vile Bodies* and *The Loved One*. Knut Hamsun's pro-peasant and later pro-Nazi views featured a vehement antipathy towards all things American. He had visited the United States twice: the first time he worked as a streetcar conductor in Chicago; the second time as a farmhand in North Dakota. Joseph de Maistre's work extols pre-revolutionary authoritarianism that spurns liberal democracy and can be construed as one of the precursors to the views of Charles Maurras, the fascist editor of *L'Action Française*. For Stendhal, freedom in the United States did not protect against social pressure and did not permit the creation of genius in art and politics.

32. Günter Bischof, 'Is There a Specific Austrian Anti-Americanism after World War II?' (Unpublished paper presented at the 2003 conference of the Organization of American Historians, Memphis, Tennessee, April 6, 2003, 34.) Bischof writes: 'Reading immediate "gut-feeling" internet responses by Austrians on any given day in *Der Standard* or *Die Presse* indicates raw public opinion among Austrians who read quality newspapers. The letter-to-the-editor pages in the *Neue Kronenzeitung* reveal the worst in Austrian Anti-Americanism. While Anti-Americanism may be on the rise in Austria and more lurid in some instances, the old stock images of European and Austrian resentment are still the same.' Ibid.

33. I am grateful to David Buch for this important point.

34. Andrei Markovits, 'Anti-Americanism and the Struggle for a West Germany Identity,' in *The Federal Republic of Germany at Forty*. Edited by Peter Merkl (New York: New York University Press, 1989), 42, 43.

35. There are many books dedicated solely to expressing antipathy towards Manchester United. Among the better known are *Manchester United Ruined My Life*, *Red Devils: A History of Man United's Rogues and Villains*, and *Yessss!!!: United in Defeat*, the latter being an especially evocative expression of *Schadenfreude* at its purest. As for parallels

concerning the New York Yankees, one only need think of the immensely popular musical 'Damn Yankees', in which the Yankees are equated with the devil. And pertaining to Harvard, I have never heard colleagues refer to any other university as the 'evil empire'.

36. Jochen Bittner, 'Umfrage: Blackbox Weisses Haus – Je komplizierter die Weltlage, desto fester glauben die Deutschen an Verschwörungstheorien,' *Die Zeit* (July 31, 2003).

Chapter 3: Americanisation and Anti-Americanism

1. That there exists a clear discrepancy – but also a certain underlying congruence – between how the European elite media view and interpret the United States and how the 'regular' European 'man in the street' does, is best described by a French baseball fan's statement: 'It's the media that make this distaste for the United States, but the people aren't in favor of it.' As quoted in John Vinocur, 'Continental Divide: Despite Some Promising Signs, Europe Is Still a Baseball Backwater,' *New York Times* (July 19, 2003).

2. Andrei S. Markovits, *Amerika, dich hasst sich's besser. Antiamerikanismus und Antisemitismus in Europa* (Hamburg: Konkret-Literatur Verlag, 2004).

3. For more details: ibid, Chapter 3.

4. Andrei S. Markovits and Steven Hellerman, *Offside: Soccer and American Exceptionalism* (Princeton: Princeton University Press, 2001); Andrei S. Markovits and Steven Hellerman, 'The "Olympianization" of Soccer in the United States,' *American Behavioral Scientist,* 46, 11, (July 2003), 1553–1549.

5. See particularly Chapter 6 and Appendix B in Markovits and Hellerman, *Offside*.

6. As quoted in Andrei S. Markovits, 'Reflections on the World Cup'98,' *French Politics and Society,* 16, 3 (Summer 1998), 1.

7. See the segment on this controversy on ESPN, 'Outside the Lines' of May 31, 2005.

8. See 'US-Firmen in Deutschland. Die Aussauger,' *metall; Das Monatsmagazin*, May 2005, cover story.

9. 'Die Pluenderer sind da,' ibid.

10. Hubert Vedrine, *Les Cartes de la France a L'heure de la Mondialisation* (Paris: Fayard, 2000), 9.

11. For a succinct summary of this argument, see Dmitry Shlapentokh, 'The New Anti-Americanism: America as an Orwellian Society,' *Partisan Review,* LXIX, 2 (2002).

12. Andrei S. Markovits, 'Deutscher Hochmut statt internationaler Solidarität – ein trauriger Vorfall,' *Gewerkschaftliche Monatshefte,* 52, 3 (March 2001), 186–188.

13. See, for example, 'Trauer, Entsetzen und Suche nach Konsequenzen,' http://www.Polizei.bayern.de/schutz/sich_kontr/sicherheit.htm.

14. 'Wie in Amerika', Kronen-Zeitung (August 14, 2003).

15. As cited in Joseph Joffe, 'Who's Afraid of Mr. Big?' *National Interest* (Summer 2001).

16. Far and away, the most prominent interpretation of this increasing clash between Europe and the United States – that Europeans are from Venus and Americans from Mars – is, of course, Robert Kagan's superb book *Of Paradise and Power: America and Europe in the New World Order* (New York: Alfred A. Knopf, 2003).

17. Joffe, 'Who's Afraid of Mr. Big?'

18. Vedrine in his book *La Cartes de la France à L'heure de la Mondialisation*, as cited in Joffe, 'Who's Afraid of Mr. Big?'

19. Peter Zadek, 'Kulturkampf? Ich bin dabei. Mir ist Amerika zutiefst zuwider,' *Der Spiegel* (July 14, 2003). As is so typical of many of the most rabid anti-Americans, Zadek proudly exclaims that he has never been to the United States nor does he ever intend to visit it.

20. As quoted in Richard Bernstein, 'Europe Awaits, with Bated Breath,' *New York Times* (May 31, 2003).

21. Max Scheler, *Ressentiment* (New York: Free Press of Glencoe, 1961), 24.

22. Dominique Strauss-Kahn, 'Die Geburt einer Nation,' *Frankfurter Rundschau* (March 11, 2003). This is a verbatim German translation of the French original.

23. Jürgen Kaube, 'Sind wir denn vernünftig?' *Frankfurter Allgemeine Zeitung* (June 2, 2003).

24. Jan Ross, 'Die Geister des Pralinengipfels,' *Die Zeit* (June 5, 2003).

25. Habermas – Rede, 'Teilz: Ueber die Zukunft Europas,' *Der standard*, March, 10, 2006.

26. Lars Rensmann, 'Europeanism and Americanism in the Age of Globalization: Hannah Arendt on the Europe and America and Implications for a post - National Identity of the EU Polity,' *European Journal of Political Theory,* 5, 2 (2006), 139 – 170.

27. Hannah Arendt, *Essays in Understanding,* 1930 –1954. Edited by Jerome Kohn (New York: Harcourt, Brace and Co., 1994), 416 passim.

28. Ibid., 412.

29. Ibid., 415.

30. Ibid., 427.

Chapter 4: Guns, Capital Punishment and Anti-Americanism

1. Walter R. Mead, 'The Case Against Europe,' *Atlantic Monthly* (April 2002), 26.

2. Hugh Brogan, 'A Tale of Two Republics,' *Times Higher Education Supplement* (August 5, 2005), 16–17.

3. Quoted in Barry Rubin and Judith C. Rubin, *Hating America: A History* (Oxford: Oxford University Press, 2004), 202.

4. John Mickelthwait and Adrian Wooldridge, *The Right Nation: Conservative Power in America* (London: Allen Lane, 2004), 368.

5. Christopher Meyer, *DC Confidential: The Controversial Memoirs of Britain's Ambassador to the US at the Time of 9/11 and the Iraq War* (London: Weidenfeld and Nicolson, 2005), 184–185.

6. Mickelthwait and Wooldridge, *The Right Nation,* 367.

7. Stuart Banner, *The Death Penalty: An American History* (Cambridge, MA: Harvard University Press, 2002), 301.

8. Ibid., 275–276.

9. Jonathan Freedland, *Bring Home the Revolution* (London: Fourth Estate, 1998), 31–33.

10. Richard Posner, *Law, Pragmatism and Democracy* (Cambridge, MA: Harvard University Press, 2003), 159.

11. James Jacobs, *Can Gun Control Work?* (New York: Oxford University Press, 2002).

12. Jan Dizard, *Guns in America: A Reader.* Edited by Robert Merrill Muth and Stephen Andrews, Jr. (New York: New York University Press, 1999), 13.

13. Jean-Francois Revel, *Anti-Americanism* (San Francisco: Encounter Books, 2003), 87.

14. 'After Tookie,' *Economist* (December 17, 2005), 10–11.

15. See Hugo A. Bedau, Editor, *The Death Penalty in America: Current Controversies,* 3rd ed. (Oxford: Oxford University Press, 1997).

16. Robert Spitzer, *The Politics of Gun Control* (Chatham, NJ: Chatham House, 1995).

17. See, for example, the intense debates and highly polarised reactions to both the relatively 'pro-control' arguments of Michael Bellesiles, *Arming America: The Origins of a National Gun Culture* (New York: Alfred Knopf, 2000) and the relatively 'pro-gun' John Lott, *More Guns, Less Crime* (Chicago: The University of Chicago Press, 1998).

18. Revel, *Anti-Americanism,* 78.

19. Mickelthwait and Wooldridge, *The Right Nation,* 369.

20. *Times* (December 14, 2005), 18.

21. 'After Tookie,' *Economist* (December 17, 2005), 48.

22. Cited in Margaret Talbot, 'Supreme Confidence: The Jurisprudence of Antonin Scalia,' *New Yorker* (March 28, 2005), 54.

23. Ibid., 42.

24. Antonin Scalia, *A Matter of Interpretation: Federal Courts and the Law* (Princeton, NJ: Princeton University Press, 1997), 137, n. 13.

25. Laurent Cohen-Tanugi, *An Alliance At Risk: The United States and Europe Since September 11* (Baltimore: Johns Hopkins Press, 2003), 123–124.

26. Mickelthwait and Wooldridge, *The Right Nation*, 280.

27. John Peterson and Mark A. Pollack, Editors, *Europe, America, Bush: Transatlantic Relations in the Twenty-First Century* (London: Routledge, 2003), 140.

28. Cohen-Tanugi, *An Alliance At Risk*, 124.

29. Robert Singh, 'Are We All Americans Now? Explaining Anti-Americanisms?' in *The Rise of Anti-Americanism*. Edited by Brendon O'Connor and Martin Griffiths (London: Routledge, 2005), 25–47.

Chapter 5: George W. Bush, Religion and European Anti-Americanism

1. Michael Corbett and Julia M. Corbett, *Politics and Religion in the United States* (New York: Garland Publishing, 1999), 55–62.

2. Robert B. Fowler, Allen D. Hertzke, and Laura R. Olson, *Religion and Politics in America: Faith, Culture, and Strategic Choices*, 2nd ed. (Boulder: Westview Press, 1999), 5.

3. Louis Hartz, *The Liberal Tradition in America: An Interpretation of American Political Thought Since the Revolution* (New York: Harcourt Brace and Company, 1955); James Chace, 'Imperial America and the Common Interest,' *World Policy Journal* (Spring 2002), 1–9; Michael Elliott, 'The Trouble with Saving the World,' *Time* (December 30, 2002–January 6, 2003), 108–112.

4. David Chidester, *Patterns of Power: Religion and Politics in American Culture* (Englewood Cliffs, NJ: Prentice Hall, 1988), 101.

5. Please note that the Gallup Organization, the Pew Research Center for the People & the Press, and the Pew Global Attitudes Project bear no responsibility for the analyses or interpretations presented here.

6. Quoted in Joshua Muravchik, 'The European Disease,' *The American Enterprise*, http://www.theamericanenterprise.org/issues (cited December 2002).

7. Jessica Mathews, 'Estranged Partners,' *Foreign Policy* (November/December 2001), 48–53.

8. 'Bush Unpopular in Europe, Seen as Unilateralist,' *Pew Research Center Survey Report*, August 15, 2001.

9. Andrew Kohut, 'Anti-Americanism: Causes and Characteristics,' *Pew Global Attitudes Project*, http://www.people-press.org/commentary (cited December 10, 2003).

10. 'America's Image Slips, But Allies Share US Concerns Over Iran, Hamas,' *Pew Global Attitudes Project: 15-Nation Survey*, http://www.pewglobal.org/reports/display.php?ReportID=252 (cited June 13, 2006), 1.

11. Ibid., 13.

12. Peter Finn, 'Anti-War Theme Strains US–German Ties,' *Miami Herald* (September 24, 2002), 3A.

13. Jere Warren, 'World Peace Survey,' *Miami Herald* (January 1, 2004), 28A.

14. 'America's Image Slips, but Allies Share US Concerns over Iran, Hamas,' 3.

15. Ibid., 11–12.

16. Jean-Francois Revel, 'Europe's Anti-American Obsession,' *The American Enterprise*, http://www.theamericanenterprise.org/ (cited December 2003).

17. Jacques Chirac, 'Interview with James Graff and Bruce Crumley,' *Time* (February 24, 2003), 32–33.

18. See Mark Patinkin, 'US Almost Alone, But Right,' *Miami Herald* (April 2, 2003), 11B; Michael Elliott, 'Can This Marriage Be Saved?' *Time* (February 24, 2003), 30–31.

19. Max J. Castro, 'Europe Not Thrilled with Bush,' *Miami Herald* (August 21, 2001), 7B.

20. Paul Geitner, '"America First" Environmental Stand Angers Europeans,' *Associated Press* (March 30, 2001); Ron Hutcheson, 'Europeans Give Bush a Heated Welcome,' *Miami Herald* (June 13, 2001), 1A; Ron Hutcheson, 'In Europe, President is Defiant on Missile Defenses,' *Miami Herald* (July 20, 2001), 1A.

21. Quoted in Hutcheson, 'Europeans Give Bush a Heated Welcome.'

22. Jerome Socolovsky, 'On Road, President Will Find Disdain over Death Penalty,' *Miami Herald* (June 10, 2001), 9A.

23. Ron Hutcheson and Warren P. Strobel, 'Bush Will Face Tough Crowd in Europe,' *Miami Herald* (June 10, 2001), 1A.

24. Muravchik, 'The European Disease'; Andres Oppenheimer, 'Relations between US, Canada Are the Latest Casualty of Iraq War,' *Miami Herald* (April 17, 2003), 22A.

25. Brian Anderson, 'Secular Europe, Religious America,' *Public Interest* (Spring 2004).

26. Peter Berger, 'Secularism in Retreat,' *National Interest* (Winter 1996).

27. Andrew Kohut and Bruce Stokes, *America Against the World: How We Are Different and Why We Are Disliked* (New York: Times Books, 2006), 91–119.

28. Jeffery L. Sheler, 'The Ways of Worship,' *US News and World Report: Mysteries of Faith* (2004) 7.

29. Steven Muller, 'Time to Kill – Employment in Europe,' *National Interest* (Summer 1997); Peter Berger, 'Religion and the West,' *National Interest* (Summer 2005); Grace Davie, 'Believing Without Belonging: Just How Secular is Europe?' The Pew Forum on Religion and Public Life, Key West, Florida, Event Transcript, http://www.pewforum.org/events (cited December 5, 2005), 10, 18, 30; Karsten D. Voigt, 'Religion is the Wild Card in Transatlantic Relations,' *EU Observer*, http://www.euobserver.com/7/21839 (cited June 16, 2006).

30. Jacques Delors quoted in Peter Ford, 'What Place for God in Europe?' *Christian Science Monitor*, http://www.csmonitor.com/2005/0222/p01s04-woeu.html (cited February 22, 2005).

31. Voigt, 'Religion Is the Wild Card.' Europeans are not alone in holding such views. Because of the important electoral role of religious conservatives in President Bush's reelection, American historian Garry Wills described the 2004 election as 'the day the Enlightenment went out' in the United States. *New York Times* (November 4, 2004).

32. Francois Heisbourg quoted by E. J. Dionne, Jr., 'God and Foreign Policy: The Religious Divide Between the US and Europe,' The Pew Forum on Religion and Public Life, Washington, DC, Event Transcript, http://www.pewforum.org/events (cited July 10, 2003), 1.

33. David Frum, *The Right Man: An Inside Account of the Bush White House* (New York: Random House, 2003), 17.

34. George W. Bush, 'State of the Union Address,' White House News Releases, http://www.whitehouse.gov/news/releases/2004/01/ (cited January 20, 2004); 'Remarks via Satellite to the National Association of Evangelicals Convention,' White House News Releases, http://www.whitehouse.gov/news/releases/2004/03/20040311-1.html (cited March 11, 2004).

35. George W. Bush, 'Remarks During Visit of Japanese Prime Minister Junichiro Koizumi,' White House Press Releases, http://www.whitehouse.gov/news/releases/2001/09/20010925-1.html (cited September 25, 2001); George W. Bush, 'Remarks at Welcoming Ceremony for Aid Workers Rescued from Afghanistan,' White House News Releases, http://www.whitehouse.gov/news/releases/2001/11/20011126-1.html (cited November 26, 2001); 'Remarks on the South Lawn of the White House Upon Arrival,' http://www.whitehouse.gov/news/releases/2001/09/20010916-2.html (cited September 16, 2001).

36. George W. Bush, 'Address to the Nation on Iraq,' White House News Releases, http://www.whitehouse.gov/news/releases/2003/03/20030317-7.html (cited March 17, 2003); 'Radio Address to the Nation,' White House News Releases, http://www.whitehouse.gov/news/releases/2003/03/20030301.html (cited March 1, 2003).

37. Toby Harnden, 'Bin Laden is Wanted: Dead or Alive, Says Bush,' *Daily Telegraph*, http://www.telegraph.co.uk/news/main.jhtml?xml=/news/2001/09/18/wbush18.xml (cited September 18, 2001).

38. George W. Bush, 'National Day of Prayer and Remembrance Proclamation for the Victims of the Terrorist Attacks on September 11,' White House Press Releases, http://www.whitehouse.gov/news/releases/2001/09/20010913-7.html (cited September 13, 2001).

39. George W. Bush, 'Address Before a Joint Session of Congress,' White House Press Releases, http://www.whitehouse.gov/news/releases/2001/09/20010920-8.html (cited September 20, 2001).

40. Ibid.

41. George W. Bush and Laura Bush, 'Interview with Diane Salvatore in Crawford, Texas,' *Ladies' Home Journal* (August 2004), 110.

42. 'Bush: "Bring on" Attackers of US Troops,' *Associated Press* (July 2, 2003).

43. George W. Bush, 'Remarks at Joint Press Conference with British Prime Minister Tony Blair, Spanish Prime Minister Jose Maria Aznar, and Portuguese Prime Minister Jose Manuel Barroso in the Azores,' White House News Releases, http://www.whitehouse.gov/news/releases/2003/03/20030316-3.html (cited March 16, 2003).

44. George W. Bush, 'State of the Union Address,' White House News Releases, http://www.whitehouse.gov/news/releases/2002/01/20020129-11.html (cited January 29, 2002).

45. Ibid., January 20, 2004.

46. George W. Bush, 'Remarks at the Religious Broadcasters Convention in Nashville, Tennessee,' White House News Releases, http://www.whitehouse.gov/news/releases/2003/02/20030210-5.html (cited February 10, 2003).

47. Quoted in Michael Duffy, 'Trapped by His Own Instincts,' *Time* (May 6, 2002), 27.

48. George W. Bush, 'Interview with Evan Thomas and Tamara Lipper,' *Newsweek* (September 6, 2004), 39.

49. Bush, 'Remarks at the National Day of Prayer and Remembrance at the Washington National Cathedral,' White House News Releases, http://www.whitehouse.gov/news/releases/2001/09/20010914-2.html (cited September 14, 2001).

50. Bush, 'State of the Union Address,' January 29, 2002.

51. Bush, 'Address to the Nation,' White House Press Releases, http://www.whitehouse.gov/news/releases/2001/09/20010911-16.html (cited September 11, 2001).

52. 'Among Wealthy Nations, US Stands Alone in Its Embrace of Religion,' *Pew Global Attitudes Project Commentary* (December 19, 2002); 'Americans and Europeans Differ Widely on Foreign Policy Issues,' *Pew Global Attitudes Project Report* (April 17, 2002).

53. Voigt, 'Religion Is the Wild Card.' Gregory A. Smith and Peyton M. Craighill, 'Do the Democrats Have a "God Problem"?: How Public Perceptions May Spell Trouble for the Party,' Pew Research Center, http://www.pewresearch.org/obdeck/?ObDeckID=35 (cited July 6, 2006).

54. Joe Klein, 'Why Not Kill Dictators with Kindness?' *Time* (March 10, 2003), 21.

55. Joe Klein, 'The Blinding Glare of His Certainty,' *Time* (February 24, 2003), 19.

56. Peter Rodman, quoted in Joseph S. Nye, Jr., *The Paradox of American Power: Why the World's Only Superpower Can't Go It Alone* (New York: Oxford University Press, 2002), 147.

57. Klein, 'The Blinding Glare of His Certainty'; See also Martin E. Marty, 'The Sin of Pride,' *Newsweek* (March 10, 2003), 32–33.

58. D. Jason Berggren and Nicol C. Rae, 'Jimmy Carter and George W. Bush: Faith, Foreign Policy, and an Evangelical Presidential Style,' *Presidential Studies Quarterly*, 36 (December 2006), 606–632.

59. Grace Davie, *Europe: The Exceptional Case* (London: Darton, Longman, and Todd Ltd, 2002), xi, 19; Davie, 'Believing Without Belonging,' 3.

60. Andrew M. Greeley, *Religion in Europe at the End of the Second Millennium: A Sociological Profile* (New Brunswick, NJ: Transaction Publishers, 2003), 19.

61. Grace Davie, *Religion in Britain Since 1945: Believing Without Belonging* (Oxford: Blackwell, 1994).

62. Grace Davie, *Religion in Modern Europe: A Memory Mutates* (Oxford: Oxford University Press, 2000), 38–81.

63. Grace Davie, 'Religion and Laicite,' in *Modern France: Society in Transition*. Edited by Malcolm Cook and Grace Davie (London: Routledge, 1999), 201; Davie, 'Believing Without Belonging' 21; Ford, 'What Place for God in Europe?'. According to the 2003 Pew Religion and Public Life Survey, 72% of Americans said they would be 'comfortable' with a political leader saying, 'The Constitution promises freedom of religion, not freedom from religion.' Only 23% said they would be uncomfortable with such an utterance.

64. Berger, 'Religion and the West.'

65. 'Americans and Canadians: The North American Not-So-Odd Couple,' *Pew Global Attitudes Project Commentary* (January 14, 2004).

66. Mark Silk, 'Preface' to the *Religion by Region Series, Religion and Public Life in the South: In the Evangelical Mode* (Walnut Creek, CA: AltaMira Press, 2005), 5.

67. See Gary C. Jacobson, *A Divider, Not a Uniter: George W. Bush and the American People* (New York: Longman, 2006); Jeffrey M. Jones, 'Views of Bush Reach New Heights of Polarization,' *Gallup Poll News Service* (October 21, 2004); Jeffrey M. Jones, 'Bush Ratings Show Historic Levels of Polarization,' *Gallup Poll News Service* (June 4, 2004).

68. Reportedly, according to a journalist for *The Economist*, on one occasion when British Prime Minister Tony Blair and President George W. Bush met, they 'got down on their knees and prayed' together. Evidently in disgust, Blair spokesman Alistair Campbell said, 'We don't do God' and left the room. Adrian Wooldridge, 'Believing Without Belonging,' 19.

69. To Dean's remark, North Carolina Senator and a rival of Dean's for the nomination, John Edwards quipped, 'Coming to the South during the church hour on a Sunday morning to tell southerners what they should believe is not the way to reach out to southern Democratic voters.' Jim VandeHei, 'Dean Crafts Own "Southern Strategy,"' *Washington Post* (December 8, 2003), A6.

70. Garry Wills, *Under God: Religion and American Politics* (New York: Simon and Schuster, 1990), 60–61.

71. E. J. Dionne, 'Believing Without Belonging,' 28.

72. Kevin Phillips, *American Theocracy: The Peril and Politics of Radical Religion, Oil, and Borrowed Money in the 21st Century* (New York: Viking, 2006); Christine Todd Whitman, *It's My Party Too: The Battle for the Heart of the GOP and the Future of America* (New York: Penguin Press, 2005).

73. Phillips, *American Theocracy*, 133. For Phillip's full comments regarding the South's role in American politics and the Republican Party, see Chapters 5–6, 132–217.

74. See Chapters 3–4 in Whitman, *It's My Party Too*, 71–141.

75. Peter Applebome, *Dixie Rising: How the South is Shaping American Values, Politics, and Culture* (San Diego, CA: Harcourt Brace and Company, 1996), 120. Applebome noted, too, that Mississippi's Trent Lott, future Republican Senate Majority Leader, once said that 'the spirit of Jefferson Davis lives' again in the Republican Party. In a 1984 interview with a neo-Confederate publication, Lott explained, 'I think that a lot of the fundamental principles that Jefferson Davis believed in are very important today to people

all across the country, and they apply to the Republican Party. It is the more conservative party. It is the party more concerned about not having government dominance. It is the party that believes that the least government is the best government. ... The platform we had in Dallas, the 1984 Republican platform, all the ideas we supported there – from tax policy to foreign policy, from individual rights to neighborhood security – are things that Jefferson Davis and his people believed in.' Applebome, *Dixie Rising*, 121. One columnist has even asserted that George W. Bush is 'the most dangerous president' since 'the Confederacy's Jefferson Davis', who also 'had a relentlessly regional perspective', 'a clear sense of estrangement from that part of America that did not support him', whose 'values were militaristic', and who 'had dreams of building an empire at gunpoint'. Consequently, this writer advocated, 'as with Davis, obtaining Bush's defeat is an urgent matter of national security – and national honor'. Harold Meyerson, 'The Most Dangerous President Ever,' *The American Prospect*, http://www.prospect.org/web/page.ww?section=root& name=ViewPrint&articleId=6770 (cited May 1, 2003).

76. 'Among Wealthy Nations, US Stands Alone in its Embrace of Religion,' *Pew Global Attitudes Project Commentary*.

77. Jimmy Carter, *The Hornet's Nest: A Novel of the Revolutionary War* (New York: Simon & Schuster, 2003), ix.

78. Linda Lyons, 'Religiosity Compass Points South,' *Gallup Poll News Service* (January 14, 2003); Jeffrey Jones, 'Tracking Religious Affiliation, State by State,' *Gallup Poll News Service* (June 22, 2004).

79. John Green, Lyman A. Kellstedt, Corwin Smidt, and James Guth, 'The Soul of the South: Religion and the New Electoral Order,' in *The New Politics of the Old South: An Introduction to Southern Politics*. Edited by Charles Bullock III and Mark Rozell (Lanham, MD: Rowman and Littlefield Publishers, 1998), 261; Flannery O'Connor quoted in Edwin M. Yoder, Jr., 'Foreword' to John Shelton Reed, *The Enduring South: Subcultural Persistence in Mass Society* (Chapel Hill, NC: University of North Carolina Press, 1974), xvi.

80. Albert L. Winseman, 'Americans Have Little Doubt God Exists,' *Gallup Poll News Service* (December 13, 2005).

81. Here are the sources for each of the countries reported in Table 4: for the American states and the United States, Frank Newport, 'Church Attendance Lowest in New England, Highest in South,' *Gallup Poll News Service* (April 27, 2006); for the four American regions, D. Jason Berggren and Nicol C. Rae, 'The American South: The "Bible Belt" of America (and the Western World?),' Paper presented at the 2006 annual meeting of the Southern Political Science Association in Atlanta, Georgia; for Malta, Slovakia, Cyprus and Lithuania, Robert Manchin, 'Religion in Europe: Trust Not Filling the Pews,' *Gallup Poll News Service* (September 21, 2004); average scores for Poland, Slovenia, Austria, Hungary and the Czech Republic from Manchin, 'Religion in Europe: Trust Not Filling the Pews,' and Ford, 'What Place for God in Europe?'; average scores for Ireland, Italy, Portugal, Greece and Denmark, Davie, *Europe: The Exceptional Case*, 6, Manchin, 'Religion in Europe: Trust Not Filling the Pews,' and Ford, 'What Place for God in Europe?'; average scores for Northern Ireland and Iceland, Davie, *Europe: The Exceptional Case*, 6, and 'How Many People Go Regularly to Weekly Religious Service?' Ontario Consultants on Religious Tolerance, http://www.religioustolerance.org/rel_rate.htm; for Canada, Julie Ray, 'Worlds Apart: Religion in Canada, Britain, US,' *Gallup Poll News Service* (August 12, 2003); for Mexico, Turkey, Croatia, Romania, Australia, Bulgaria, Georgia Republic, Moldova, Ukraine, Armenia, Montenegro, Serbia, Belarus and Russia, 'How Many People Go Regularly to Weekly Religious Service?'; average scores for Spain and Sweden, Davie, *Europe: The Exceptional Case*, 6, Manchin, 'Religion in Europe: Trust Not Filling the Pews,' Ford, 'What Place for God in Europe?' and 'How Many People Go Regularly to Weekly Religious Service?'; average score for Great Britain, Davie, *Europe: The*

Exceptional Case, 6, Ray, 'Worlds Apart: Religion in Canada, Britain, US,' and Ford, 'What Place for God in Europe?'; for Luxembourg, Ford, 'What Place for God in Europe?'; average scores for Belgium, the Netherlands and Germany, Davie, *Europe: The Exceptional Case*, 6, Ford, 'What Place for God in Europe?', 'How Many People Go Regularly to Weekly Religious Service?'; for France, Davie, *Europe: The Exceptional Case*, 6, and Ford, 'What Place for God in Europe?'; average scores for Switzerland and Norway, Ford, 'What Place for God in Europe?', 'How Many People Go Regularly to Weekly Religious Service?'; average scores for Latvia and Estonia, Manchin, 'Religion in Europe: Trust Not Filling the Pews,' and 'How Many People Go Regularly to Weekly Religious Service?'; average score for Finland, Davie, *Europe: The Exceptional Case*, 6, Manchin, 'Religion in Europe: Trust Not Filling the Pews,' and 'How Many People Go Regularly to Weekly Religious Service?'.

82. Davie, 'Religion and Laicite'; Davie, *Religion in Modern Europe: A Memory Mutates*, 9.

83. Davie, *Europe: The Exceptional Case*, 6.

84. Davie, *Europe: The Exceptional Case*, 29; Pippa Norris and Ronald Inglehart, *Sacred and Secular: Religion and Politics Worldwide* (New York: Cambridge University Press, 2004), 94; Augustus B. Cochran, III, *Democracy Heading South: National Politics in the Shadow of Dixie* (Lawrence, KS: University Press of Kansas, 2001), 235–236 n40.

85. Albert L. Winseman, 'Who Has Been Born Again?' *Gallup Poll News Service* (January 18, 2005).

86. Frank Newport and Joseph Carroll, 'Another Look at Evangelicals in America Today,' *Gallup Poll News Service* (December 2, 2005); Joseph Carroll, 'Republicans, Democrats Differ on What Is Morally Acceptable,' *Gallup Poll News Service* (May 24, 2006).

87. Albert L. Winseman, 'Eternal Destinations: Americans Believe in Heaven, Hell,' *Gallup Poll News Service* (May 25, 2004); Jennifer Robison, 'The Devil and the Demographic Details,' *Gallup Poll News Service* (February 25, 2003).

88. Lydia Saad, 'Religion is Very Important to Majority of Americans,' *Gallup Poll News Service* (December 5, 2003); Frank Newport, 'Twenty-Eight Percent Believe Bible is Actual Word of God,' *Gallup Poll News Service* (May 22, 2006); Frank Newport, 'Six in 10 Americans Agree that Gay Sex Should Be Legal,' *Gallup Poll News Service* (June 27, 2003); Frank Newport, 'Americans Turn More Negative Toward Same-Sex Marriage,' *Gallup Poll News Service* (April 19, 2005); Lydia Saad, 'NRA Viewed Favorably by Most Americans,' *Gallup Poll News Service* (April 15, 2005).

89. Josephine Mazzuca, 'American and Canadian Views on Abortion,' *Gallup Poll News Service* (September 24, 2002); Lydia Saad, 'Abortion Views Hold Steady Over Past Year,' *Gallup Poll News Service* (June 2, 2003); Frank Newport, 'Third of Americans Say Evidence Has Supported Darwin's Evolution Theory,' *Gallup Poll News Service* (November 19, 2004).

90. Josephine Mazzuca, 'Should Democrats Head North?' *Gallup Poll News Service* (December 14, 2004).

91. Frank Newport and Joseph Carroll, 'Support for Bush Significantly Higher Among More Religious Americans,' *Gallup Poll News Service* (March 6, 2003); Frank Newport, 'Support for War Modestly Higher Among More Religious Americans,' *Gallup Poll News Service* (February 27, 2003).

92. Frank Newport, 'Protestants and Frequent Churchgoers Most Supportive of Iraq War,' *Gallup Poll News Service* (March 16, 2006).

93. Tom Strode, 'US Launches Iraq Campaign; "Last Resort," SBC Leaders Say,' *Baptist Press News*, http://www.baptistpress.org/bpnews.asp?ID=15488 (cited March 20, 2003).

94. 'Resolution No. 2 on the Liberation of Iraq,' 2003 SBC Annual Meeting, Phoenix, Arizona, http://www.sbcannualmeeting.net/sbc03/resolutions/sbcresolution.asp?ID=2 (cited June 17–18, 2003).

95. George W. Bush, 'Video Remarks to the Southern Baptist Convention Annual Meeting,' White House News Releases, http://www.whitehouse.gov/news/releases/2005/06/20050621-3.html (cited June 21, 2005).

96. Clyde Wilcox, *Onward Christian Soldiers? The Religious Right in American Politics* (Boulder, CO: Westview Press, 2000), 77.

97. James W. Lamare, Jerry L. Polinard and Robert D. Wrinkle, 'Texas: Religion and Politics in God's Country,' in *The Christian Right in American Politics: Marching to the Millennium.* Edited by John C. Green, Mark J. Rozell and Clyde Wilcox (Washington, DC: Georgetown University Press, 2003), 59–78; James W. Lamare, Jerry L. Polinard and Robert D. Wrinkle, 'The Christian Right in God's Country: Texas Politics,' in *Prayers in the Precincts: The Christian Right in the 1998 Elections.* Edited by John C. Green, Mark J. Rozell and Clyde Wilcox (Washington, DC: Georgetown University Press, 2000), 41–58; Michael Lind, *Made in Texas: George W. Bush and the Southern Takeover of American Politics* (New York: Basic Books, 2003).

98. George W. Bush, *A Charge to Keep* (New York: William Morrow and Company, 1999), 14–22; David Aikman, *A Man of Faith: The Spiritual Journey of George W. Bush* (Nashville, TN: W Publishing Group, 2004), 85–110.

99. Howard Fineman, 'Apocalyptic Politics,' *Newsweek* (May 24, 2004), 55.

100. John Podhoretz, *Bush Country* (New York: St. Martin's Griffin, 2005), 36; see also John Micklethwait and Adrian Wooldridge, *The Right Nation: Conservative Power in America* (New York: Penguin Books, 2005), 27–39; Fred Barnes, *Rebel-in-Chief* (New York: Crown Forum, 2006), 46–50.

101. Kenneth T. Walsh, *From Mount Vernon to Crawford: A History of the Presidents and Their Retreats* (New York: Hyperion Books, 2005), 236.

102. Ibid., 271.

103. Ibid., 258.

104. Michael Lind, 'Mapquest.Dem,' *Prospect* (January 2005), 18–22.

105. Bill Clinton, 'Remarks at the Funeral of Coretta Scott King in Lithonia, Georgia,' transcript available at the Clinton Foundation website, http://www.clintonfoundation.org/mediacenter-speeches.htm (cited February 7, 2006).

106. George H.W. Bush, *George Bush: Man of Integrity* (Eugene, OR: Harvest House Publishers, 1988), 33.

107. George H.W. Bush, *All the Best, George Bush: My Life in Letters and Other Writings* (New York: Lisa Drew Book/Scribner, 1999), 319.

108. See George H.W. Bush, *Looking Forward: An Autobiography* (New York: Doubleday, 1987), 27, 69.

109. Bush, *A Charge to Keep*, x.

110. Ibid., 44–45.

111. Ibid., 45.

112. Ibid., 8–13.

113. Ibid., 9.

114. Ibid., 13.

115. Ibid., 136.

116. Phillips, *American Dynasty*, 214–215; Podhoretz, *Bush Country*, 41.

117. Phillips, *American Dynasty*, 215.

118. Ibid., 223–228.

119. Ibid., 216.

120. Ibid., 140.

121. George W. Bush, 'Interview with J. Lee Grady and Carol Chapman Stertzer,' *Charisma*, http://www.beliefnet.com/story/47/story_4705.html (cited August 29, 2000).

122. Seymour Martin Lipset, *American Exceptionalism: A Double-Edged Sword* (New York: W.W. Norton and Company, 1996), 65; Lipset, *Continental Divide: The*

Values and Institutions of the United States and Canada (New York: Routledge, 1990), 76–79.

123. Hartz, *The Liberal Tradition in America*, 37.

124. Ron Hutcheson, 'War Decision a Leap of Faith That Could Change the World,' *Miami Herald* (March 9, 2003), 20A; Susan Page, 'War May Realign World and Define a Presidency,' *USA Today* (March 17, 2003), 1A; Michael Kinsley, 'The Power of One,' *Time* (April 21, 2003), 86; Steven E. Schier, '"Typing" the George W. Bush Presidency,' *The Forum*, 3, 4 (2006), Article 3.

125. Quoted in Fawn Vrazo and Daniel Rubin, 'As war looms, Europe's harsh view of Bush worsens,' *Miami Herald* (February 25, 2003), 24A.

126. Earl Black and Merle Black, *The Vital South: How Presidents are Elected* (Cambridge, MA: Harvard University Press, 1992).

127. Davie, *Europe: The Exceptional Case*, ix; see also Davie, 'Believing Without Belonging: Just How Secular is Europe?' 2–3, 20, 31.

Chapter 6: Anti-Americanism and the American Personality

1. Seymour M. Lipset, *The First New Nation: The United States in Historical and Comparative Perspective* (New York: Basic Books, 1963).

2. John Winthrop, 'A Model of Christian Charity,' in *Pragmatism and Religion*. Edited by Stuart Rosenbaum (Urbana, IL: University of Illinois Press, 2003), 21–23.

3. Thomas Paine, *Common Sense*. Edited by Isaac Kramnick (London: Penguin, 1986), 84–94.

4. Thomas Jefferson, 'Declaration of Independence,' in *Selected Writings of Thomas Jefferson*. Edited by Harvey Mansfield (Wheeling, IL: Crofts Classics, 1979), 7–8.

5. Andrei Markovits, 'European Anti-Americanism (and Anti-Semitism): Ever Present though Always Denied,' Center for European Studies Working Paper Series #108, Minda De Gunzburg Center for European Studies, Harvard University, 3.

6. As cited in James Ceaser, 'A Genealogy of Anti-Americanism,' *Public Interest*, 152 (Summer, 2003), 12.

7. Alexis de Tocqueville, *Democracy in America*. Edited by J. P. Mayer (New York: Harper, 1988), 'Author's Introduction,' 11–13.

8. Ibid., Vol. 1, Pt. 1, Ch. 3, 54.

9. Ibid., Vol. 2, Ch. 10, 460.

10. Ibid., Vol. 2, Pt. 2, Ch. 13, 536.

11. Ibid., Vol. 2, Pt. 2, Ch. 13, 536–538.

12. Ibid., Vol. 2, Pt. 1, Ch. 10, 460.

13. Ibid., Vol. 2, Pt. 3, Ch. 5, 579.

14. Ibid., Vol. 2, Pt. 2, Ch. 18, 550–551.

15. Ibid., Vol. 2, Pt. 2, Ch. 2, 507.

16. Ibid., Vol. 1, Pt. 1, Ch. 3, 55.

17. Ibid., Vol. 1, Pt. 1, Ch. 3, 56.

18. Ibid., Vol. 2, Pt.1, Ch. 9–19.

19. Ibid., Vol. 1, Pt. 2, Ch. 7, p. 247; Vol. 2, Pt. 1, Ch. 2, 434–436.

20. Ibid., Vol. 1, Pt. 1, Ch. 2, 46–47.

21. Ibid., Vol. 2, Pt. 2, Ch. 12, 534–535.

22. Ibid., Vol. 1, Pt. 1, Ch. 2, 42–43.

23. Ibid., Vol. 1, Pt. 2, Ch. 7, 254–255.

24. Ibid., Vol. 1, Pt. 2, Ch. 6, 242–243.

25. Ibid., Vol. 2, Pt. 3, Chs. 9–12, 590–603.

26. This Tocquevillean vision of nineteenth-century America as the golden age of local associations and civic engagement has been popularized and widely disseminated by the

work of Robert Putnam, *Bowling Alone: The Collapse and Revival of American Community* (New York: Simon & Schuster, 2000).

27. Tocqueville, *Democracy in America*, Vol. 1, Pt. 2, Ch. 4, 192–193.

28. Ibid., Vol. 1, Pt. 2, Ch. 7, 248.

29. See especially, Arthur M. Schlesinger, Jr., *The Vital Center: The Politics of Freedom* (Boston: Houghton Mifflin, 1949).

30. Tocqueville, *Democracy in America*, Vol. 2, Pt. 2, Ch. 2, 506–507.

31. Ibid., Vol. 2, Pt. 2, Ch. 2, 508.

32. See for example, Theodor Adorno et al., *The Authoritarian Personality* (New York: Harper, 1950); cf. *Democracy in America*, Vol. 2, Pt. 4, Ch. 6, 690–702.

33. David Riesman, *The Lonely Crowd: A Study of the Changing American Character* (New Haven: Yale University Press, 1950); Robert Bellah et al., *Habits of the Heart: Individualism and Commitment in American Life* (Berkeley: University of California Press, 1985).

34. Tocqueville, *Democracy in America*, Vol. 1, Pt. 2, Ch. 6, 237.

35. Dickens's character Martin Chuzzlewit has scarcely left the boat upon his arrival in New York harbor before being accosted by Colonel Diver, an American newspaper publisher who demands that Martin sing the nation's praises and repudiate the old world for its misery, ignorance, poverty, and crime. Charles Dickens, *The Life and Adventures of Martin Chuzzlewit* (London: Penguin, 1999), Chapter 16.

36. Tocqueville, *Democracy in America*, Vol. 2, Pt. 3, Ch. 3, 567–571.

37. Ibid., Vol. 2, Pt. 3, Ch. 3, 569.

38. Ibid., Vol. 2, Pt. 3, Ch. 14, 606.

39. It is possible that Tocqueville has Mrs. Trollope's pretensions in mind when he writes the following about manners in *Democracy in America*, Vol. 2, Pt. 3, Ch. 14, 607: 'The English make game of American manners, but it is odd that most of those responsible for those comic descriptions belong themselves to the English middle classes, and the cap fits them very well too. So these ruthless critics generally themselves illustrate just what they criticize in America; they do not notice that they are abusing themselves, to the great delight of their own aristocracy.'

40. All references are to Donald Smalley's excellent critical edition of Frances Trollope's *Domestic Manners of the Americans* (New York: Knopf, 1949), 45.

41. Trollope, *Domestic Manners of the Americans*, 46.

42. Ibid., 37.

43. Ibid., 18–19.

44. Ibid., 37.

45. Ibid., 142.

46. Ibid., 100.

47. Ibid., 99–100.

48. Ibid., 100.

49. Ibid., 100.

50. Ibid., 425.

51. Ibid., 425.

52. Ibid., 71.

53. Henry James, *The American Scene* (New York: St. Martin's, 1987), 233–234.

54. Trollope, *Domestic Manners of the Americans*, 305.

55. Ibid., 309.

56. Ibid., 248.

57. Ibid., 186.

58. Ibid., 186n.

59. Ibid., 121.

60. Ibid., 116.

61. Ibid., 119–120.

62. Ibid., 119.

63. Ibid., 123–124.

64. Ibid., 121.

65. Ibid., 154–155.

66. James, *The American Scene*, 233.

67. Tocqueville, *Democracy in America*, Vol. 1, Pt. 1, Ch. 2, 49.

68. For a polemical and often inaccurate critique of Tocqueville's limitations in this regard, see August Nimtz, *Marx, Tocqueville, and Race in America* (Lanham, MD: Lexington Publishers, 2003). For a more balanced assessment see Rogers Smith, 'Beyond Tocqueville, Myrdal, and Hartz: The Multiple Traditions in America,' *American Political Science Review,* 87 (September, 1993), 549–566.

69. For some like Richard Hunt, Marx's treatment of America is marginal to his central political concerns, amounting to a doctrine of '[American] political exceptionalism'. Cf. Hunt, *The Political Ideas of Marx and Engels* (Pittsburgh: University of Pittsburgh Press, 1984), 85. For others like August Nimtz, democratic institutions in the US 'played a crucial role in the conclusions [Marx and Engels] reached on the road to becoming communists'. Nimtz, *Marx, Tocqueville, and Race in America*, ix.

70. Saul K. Padover, Editor, *The Karl Marx Library*, Vol. 2: *On America and the Civil War* (New York: McGraw-Hill, 1972–1977), 'Editor's Introduction,' xi.

71. Marx, 'On the Jewish Question,' in *The Marx-Engels Reader*. Edited by Robert Tucker (New York: Norton, 1972), 31.

72. The articles attributed to Marx during the first year of this engagement with the Tribune were actually written by Frederick Engels. Until 1852, Marx was unable to write at a high level in English. See Padover, 'Editor's Introduction', *On America and the Civil War*, xvi.

73. More broadly, for Marx, the very notion of a people having something like an essential 'character' independent of its material conditions is something to be resisted, and whatever particular or distinctive national cultures or consciousness of nationality might exist will be swept away by the globalizing effects of civil society. See especially, Marx, 'Communist Manifesto,' in *The Marx-Engels Reader*, 475–477, 489.

74. Marx, 'The Grundrisse,' in *The Marx-Engels Reader*, 241.

75. Marx, 'Debates on Freedom of the Press and Publication,' in *The Karl Marx Library*, Vol. 4, *On Freedom of the Press and Censorship*. Edited by Padover (New York: McGraw-Hill, 1972–1977), 34; 'Critique of the Gotha Program,' in *The Marx-Engels Reader*, 539–540.

76. Marx, 'On the Jewish Question,' 33; Marx, 'The London Times on the Orleans Princes in America,' in *On America and the Civil War*, 85.

77. Marx, 'The American Budget and the Christian-German One,' in *On America and the Civil War*, 9.

78. Marx, 'On the Jewish Question,' 40–46, esp. 43.

79. Marx, '18th Brumaire of Louis Napoleon' in *The Marx-Engels Reader*, 602.

80. Despite America's rapid economic development, Marx continued to classify the Americas as European colonies well into the second half of the nineteenth century. See especially Marx, *Capital*, Vol. 1. (London: Penguin, 1976), 580, 931.

81. Marx, '18th Brumaire of Louis Napoleon,' 602.

82. Marx, 'On the Jewish Question,' 49.

83. Marx, '18th Brumaire of Louis Napoleon,' 602.

84. Marx, 'On the Jewish Question,' 31.

85. Ibid.

86. Ibid., 35.

87. Ibid., 31.

88. Ibid., 49.

89. Marx, 'The North American Civil War,' in *On America and the Civil War*, 78; Marx, 'The Civil War in the United States,' in *On America and the Civil War*, 93.

90. Marx, 'The North American Civil War,' in *On America and the Civil War*, 78.

91. Marx, 'Letter to Engels (in Manchester) [London, October 29, 1862]' in *On America and the Civil War*, 263; 'Letter to Engels (in Manchester) [London, September 10, 1862]' in *On American and the Civil War*, 261.

92. Marx, 'American Affairs,' in *On America and the Civil War*, 171; Marx, 'Letter to Engels (in Manchester) [London, October 29, 1862]' in *On America and the Civil War*, 263; Marx, as cited in Padover, 'Editor's Introduction' in *On America and the Civil War*, xxvi.

93. Engels, 'Engels to Marx,' in Karl Marx and Frederick Engels, *The Marxist Library*, Vol. XXX: *The Civil War in the United States*. Edited by Richard Enmale (New York: International Publishers, 1937), 265.

94. Marx, *Capital*, 1014.

95. Marx, 'The Civil War in France' in *The Marx-Engels Reader*, 627–628.

96. Antonio Gramsci, 'Americanism and Fordism,' in *An Antonio Gramsci Reader*. Edited by David Forgacs (New York: Schocken Books, 1988), 275–299.

97. Ibid., 290.

Chapter 7: The Environment and Anti-Americanism

1. Thanks to Majid Rizvi for excellent research assistance and to Rachel Cohen for occasional mopping of brow.

2. Brendon O'Connor, 'The Last Respectable Prejudice?' *Australian Book Review* (October 2003); 'What Is Anti-Americanism?' in *Anti-Americanism* (Vol. 1). Edited by Brendon O'Connor (Westport: Greenwood Press, 2007).

3. *Oxford English Dictionary*, 2nd ed., s.v. 'prejudice'.

4. Alvin Rubinstein and Donald Smith, 'Anti-Americanism in the Third World,' *The Annals of the American Academy of Political and Social Science*, 497 (1988), 35–45.

5. Theodore Zeldin, 'The Pathology of Anti-Americanism' in *The Rise and Fall of Anti-Americanism*. Edited by Denis Lacorne, Jacques Rupnik, and Marie-France Toinet (Basingstoke: Macmillan, 1990), 35.

6. Marie-France Toinet, 'Does Anti-Americanism Exist?' in *The Rise and Fall of Anti-Americanism*, 219.

7. Aristotle famously linked the quality of air and climate to the 'exhalations' of a polity in *The Politics* (New York: Viking Penguin, 1981); Hippocrates made a similar but distinct connection between climate and health and national character in *Corpus Hippocraticum* (Amsterdam: A.M. Hakkert, 1961).

8. *Réflexions critiques sur la poésie et sur la peinture* (Paris: n.p., 1719).

9. *Dictionnaire de Biographie Francaise*, s.v. 'Du Bos,' quoted in James Fleming, *Historical Perspectives on Climate Change* (New York: Oxford University Press, 1998), 12.

10. Fleming, *Historical Perspectives on Climate Change*, 13.

11. Du Bos' work came to North America via David Hume and his *Of the Populousness of Ancient Nations*, which noted that the climate of Europe had changed gradually over two millennia as forests were cut down, swamps drained, agriculture organized on a large scale, etc., whilst America had undergone a similar change in merely two centuries. David Hume, 'Of the Populousness of Ancient Nations,' in *Essays, Moral, Political, and Literary* (Oxford: Oxford University Press, 1963), 381.

12. Georges-Louis Leclerc, *Histoire Naturelle* (Paris: n.p., 1802), quoted in Fleming, *Historical Perspectives on Climate Change*, 24.

13. *Notes of the State of Virginia* (Gloucester, MA: Peter Smith, 1976).

14. Fleming, *Historical Perspectives on Climate Change*, Chapter 2.

15. With James Madison, Jefferson is credited with making the first simultaneous meteorological measurements in 1778.

16. Fleming, *Historical Perspectives on Climate Change*, 40–41.

17. Ibid.

18. In 1864, Congress donated the Yosemite Valley to the state of California for preservation as the world's first state park.

19. Undertaken in 1916, at the instigation of President Woodrow Wilson.

20. See Philippe Sands, *Lawless World: America and the Making and Breaking of Global Rules* (London: Allen Lane, 2005), 74.

21. See David Blackbourn, *The Conquest of Nature: Water, Landscape and the Making of Modern Germany* (London: Jonathan Cape, 2006).

22. Richard Nixon, *The Memoirs of Richard Nixon* (New York: Grosset and Dunlap, 1978), 1, 4; Stephen Ambrose, *Nixon: The Education of a Politician, 1913–1962* (New York: Simon and Schuster, 1987), 27.

23. Richard Lazarus, 'A Different Kind of "Republican Moment" in Environmental Law,' *Minnesota Law Review,* 87, 4 (2003), 999.

24. *New York Times*, January 2, 1970, 1, 20. The NEPA has been described as 'the world's first comprehensive environmental protection regime', see Sands, *Lawless World*. Among other things, the Act provided federal assistance in the development and operation of state coastal zones plans, mandated exhaustive studies prior to the approval of large federal projects and established a powerful Council on Environmental Quality.

25. See J. Brooks Flippen, *Nixon and the Environment* (Albuquerque: University of New Mexico Press, 2000), 53–55.

26. Ibid., Chapters 1 and 2.

27. See Sands, *Lawless World*. In 1972, Nixon proposed a new legal instrument, 'for the nations of the world to agree to the principle that there are certain areas of such unique worldwide value that they should be treated as part of the heritage of all mankind and accorded special recognition as part of a World Heritage Trust'. The World Heritage Convention was adopted in 1972, with the USA the first country to ratify.

28. Quoted in Richard Lazarus, *The Making of Environmental Law* (Chicago: University of Chicago Press, 2004).

29. Ibid.

30. Ibid.

31. The average votes in favour of major environmental legislation during the 1970s were as follows: Senate: 70 versus 5; House: 331 versus 30. See Lazarus, 2004.

32. From the 'environmental balance sheet' cannot be excluded the use of defoliants in the Vietnam War. Variously named Agents Pink, Green, Purple, Blue, White and Orange according to their strength, from 1961 to 1971 these chemicals were used to devastating human and environmental effect. See Christopher Hitchens, 'The Vietnam Syndrome,' *Vanity Fair* (August 2006). Crediting Nixon for overseeing the non-use of this policy is difficult to stomach, although he evidently did not devise or initiate it. In any event, it is unlikely that strictly *environmental* considerations ever entered into the calculus for their use or cessation.

33. M. J. Molina and F. S. Rowland, 'Stratospheric Sink for Chlorofluromethanes: Chlorine Atom-Catalysed Destruction of Ozone,' *Nature*, 249 (1974), 810–812.

34. Jim Hansen, 'The Threat to the Planet,' *New York Review of Books*, 53, 12 (July 13, 2006).

35. United States Environmental Protection Agency, 'Protection of Stratospheric Ozone; Final Rule,' *Federal Register*, 53 (1988), 30566–30602.

36. Richard Benedict, *Ozone Diplomacy: New Directions in Safeguarding the Planet* (Cambridge, MA: Harvard University Press, 1998).

37. Sands, *Lawless World*, 75.

38. In May 1985, the British Atlantic Survey reported that between 1977 and 1985, the ozone layer over the Antarctic had been reduced by 40 percent.

39. See Hansen, 'The Threat to the Planet.'

40. See generally, Andrew Jordan, Editor, *Environmental Policy in the European Union*, 2nd Editor. (London: Earthscan, 2005) and Ludwig Krämer, 'The Single European Act and Environmental Protection: Reflections on Several New Provisions,' *Common Market Law Review* (1987), 659. Prior to the Single European Act, several discrete environmental measures were passed by the European legislature, including the Council Directive 76/464/EEC on the pollution caused by certain dangerous substances discharged into the aquatic environment, the Community and Council Directive 75/439/EEC on the disposal of waste oils. Both were justified on the basis of fundamental economic freedoms, not environmental protection.

41. Sands, *Lawless World*.

42. Ibid.

43. The IPCC was created in 1988 by the United Nation's Environment Program and the World Meteorological Organisation. It was set up 'anticipating the critical role that scientific consensus would play in building the political will to respond to climate change'. David Hunter et al., *International Environmental Law and Policy* (New York: Foundation Press, 2002), 590.

44. Intergovernmental Panel on Climate Change, *Climate Change: The IPCC Scientific Assessment* (IPCC: 1990).

45. For a full listing of the policies adopted by various nations, see the International Energy Agency's report, *Climate Change Policy Initiatives* (Paris: OECD, 1992).

46. *Economic Report of the President* (Washington, DC: US Government Printing Office, 1990).

47. Ibid., 223.

48. See Donald Goldberg, 'As the World Burns: Negotiating the Framework Convention on Climate Change,' *Georgetown International Environmental Law Review*, 5, 2 (1993), 39.

49. Ibid., 251.

50. See Ozone Action, *The Ties that Bind* (Ozone Action: 1996).

51. For a general account of these issues that argues for the environmental credentials of the Clinton administrations, see Sheila Cavanagh et al., 'National Environmental Policy During the Clinton Years,' Faculty Research Working Paper Series, Paper RWP01-027, John F Kennedy School of Government, Harvard University (June, 2001).

52. Ibid., 29.

53. This resolution is known as the Byrd–Hagel Resolution. As a matter of US constitutional law, international agreements are ratified only when signed by the President *and* approved by a two-thirds majority of the Senate. Accordingly, even if a US President is willing to sign an international treaty, it will have force of domestic law only if the Senate is like-minded.

54. For a detailed, official history of the Kyoto negotiations, see Joanna Depledge, 'Tracing the Origins of the Kyoto Protocol: An Article-by-Article Textual History,' United Nations Framework Convention on Climate Change, FCCC/TP/2000/2 (2002).

55. See Robert Stavin, 'What Can We Learn from the Grand Policy Experiment? Lessons from SO_2 Allowance Trading,' *Journal of Economic Perspectives*, 12, 3 (1998), 69–88.

56. See Cavanagh, 'National Environmental Policy,' 30.

57. For full details, see Chad Damro and Pilar Luaces Mendez, 'Emissions Trading at Kyoto: From EU Resistance to Union Innovation,' in *Environmental Policy in the European Union*. Edited by Jordan.

58. Scott Barrett, *Environment and Statecraft* (Oxford: OUP, 2003).

59. White House Press Release, Statement by the President, *Federal Document Clearing House Transcripts*, December 10, 1997.

60. Ron Suskind, *The Price of Loyalty* (New York: Simon and Schuster, 2004), 60.

61. Ibid., 105.

62. Ibid., 104–106.

63. Ibid., 98–99.

64. Ibid., 98–99.

65. *The Financial Times*, March 6, 2001.

66. Ibid., 113.

67. Ibid., 118–119.

68. Ibid., 119.

69. Ibid., 119.

70. Ibid., 121–122.

71. See the EPA's list of state action plans on global warming http://www.yosemite.epa.gov/globalwarming/ghg.nsf/actions/StateActionPlans?Open.

72. Marc Gunther, 'The Green Machine,' *Fortune* (August 28, 2006), 34.

73. Jeffrey Garten, 'A Foreign Policy Harmful to Business,' *Business Week* (October 14, 2002), 72.

74. Toinet, 'Does Anti-Americanism Exist?' 219.

75. See Sands, *Lawless World*.

76. Suskind's ghosted memoirs of Paul O'Neill, *The Price of Loyalty*.

77. See the Joint Science Academies' Statement: Global Response to Climate Change, http://www.royalsoc.ac.uk/document.asp?latest=1&id=3222 (cited June 7, 2005).

Chapter 8: American Democracy and Anti-Americanism Since 2000

1. My thanks to Brendon O'Connor, Andrew Geddis and Rick Hasen for helpful comments, and to Chad Gear for research assistance.

2. For an illustration, see the exchange between an American journalist and passer-by in Germany on November 12, 2000, relayed in Mark Hertsgaard, *The Eagle's Shadow: Why America Fascinates and Infuriates the World* (Sydney: Allen & Unwin, 2002), 147–148.

3. Vicent Jorge Silva, 'American Fiction,' *Diário de Notícias* (Lisbon), November 17, 2000.

4. Scott Atran, 'The Emir: An Interview with Abu Bakar Ba'asyir, Alleged Leader of the Southeast Asian Jemaah Islamiyah Organization,' *Spotlight on Terror,* 3, 9 (2005), http://www.jamestown.org/terrorism/news/article.php?articleid=2369782.

5. John Lennon/Plastic Ono Band, 'Give Peace a Chance' (1969).

6. I give that definition, aware that 'Americanism' has an older, homegrown, political provenance, attributed to Teddy Roosevelt, in William Safire's definition: 'Patriotic political philosophy, sometimes abused by chauvinists.' See Marie-France Toinet, 'Does Anti-Americanism Exist?' in *The Rise and Fall of Anti-Americanism: A Century of French Perception.* Edited by Denis Lacorne, Jacques Rupnik, and Marie-France Toinet (trans. Gerald Turner) (Basingstoke: Macmillan, 1990), 219. The words 'Americanism' and 'Americanize' are in truth somewhat older than Roosevelt. James Murray described them as necessary inclusions in the first fascicle or part of what became the *Oxford English Dictionary*, despite the Dictionary's rule against proper names derived from geography. See Simon Winchester, *The Meaning of Everything: The Story of the Oxford English Dictionary* (Oxford: Oxford University Press, 2002), 144.

7. Canadians seem acutely aware of US values and ideologies, and like to believe they do not share them, yet find them threatening to their sovereignty. See Sherry Devereaux Ferguson et al., 'As Others See the United States: A View from Canada,' in *Images of the United States Around the World.* Edited by Yahya R. Kamalipour (Albany: State University of New York Press, 1999), 157.

8. Compare the account of Anti-Americanism as informed by the sense that the United States has failed to live up to its Romantic idealism, e.g. Paul Hollander, 'Introduction: the New Virulence and Popularity,' in *Understanding Anti-Americanism: Its Origins and Impact at Home and Abroad*. Edited by Paul Hollander (Chicago: Ivan R Dee, 2004), 10–11, drawing on Bruce S. Thornton.

9. Innumerable reams were written about the breakdown of the electoral process in 2000; the neatest account, for non-Americans or non-electoral junkies, is Daniel Lowenstein, 'Lessons from the Florida Controversy,' in *Realising Democracy*. Edited by Graeme Orr et al. (Sydney: The Federation Press, 2003), 7–25.

10. Filipe Perez Roque, Press Conference, New York, November 9, 2000.

11. Richard Beeston, 'US Foes Gleeful at Voting "Fraud,"' *The Times* (London) (November 10, 2000), 5, quoting *Babel* (Iraqi newspaper).

12. Richard Hasen, 'Beyond the Margin of Litigation: Reforming US Election Administration to Avoid Election Meltdown,' *Washington & Lee Law Review*, 62 (2005), 937.

13. See http://www.cbsnews.com/stories/2000/11/10/politics/main248544.shtml.

14. Frank Devine, 'US Democracy Buried Beneath a Lather of Lawyers,' *The Australian* (December 7, 2000), 11. Devine, an Australian, is a former editor of the *New York Post*.

15. Gay Alcorn, 'Nobody Won; America Lost,' *The Sydney Morning Herald* (December 14, 2000), 1, 8.

16. Anneliese Rohrer, 'The World of George Jr,' *Die Presse* (Vienna) (December 15, 2000), 2.

17. Editorial, 'Electoral Archaism,' *Le Monde* (November 4, 2000).

18. Editorial, 'Judges Govern America,' *Le Monde* (December 14, 2000).

19. Editorial, 'Judgement Day Makes Losers of Everyone', *The Australian* (December 14, 2000), 10. *The Australian* is the national flagship of the News Limited empire, having been personally founded by Rupert Murdoch.

20. See the selection printed in *The Times* (London), December 9, 2000, 5.

21. Frederick Kempe, 'Whatever Happened to America's Golden Rules,' *The Wall Street Journal Europe* (November 15, 2000), 7.

22. Richard Dawkins, 'Bin Laden's Victory: A Political System That Delivers This Disastrous Mistake Needs Reform,' *The Guardian*, www.guardian.co.uk/comment/ story/0,3604,919538,00 (cited March 22, 2003). The related critique is that Bush is a puppet of more Machiavellian masters. See, for example, James Moore and Wayne Slater, *Bush's Brain: How Karl Rove made George W. Bush Presidential* (New York: Wiley, 2003). For an argument that Americans, in electing and re-electing Bush, Strom Thurmond, Sonny Bono, Clint Eastwood and assorted widows of politicians, are using elections as a form of patronage to reward 'good' people or minor celebrities, see James A. Gardner, 'Giving the Gift of Public Office,' *Buffalo Law Review*, 53 (2005), 859.

23. Aka 'BRCA', the *Bipartisan Campaign Finance Reform Act 2002* (US).

24. For a summary of the legal thicket, see Trevor Potter and Paul S. Ryan, 'United States,' in *Lobbying, Government Relations and Campaign Finance Worldwide*. Edited by T. D. Grant (New York: Oceania Publications, 2005).

25. There is an enormous critical literature. See, for example, Kevin Phillips, *American Dynasty* (New York: Viking, 2004), John Judis, *The Paradox of American Democracy* (New York: Routledge, 2001) and William Greider, 'The Grand Bazaar,' in *Who will Tell the People* (New York: Simon & Schuster, 1993).

26. Daniel Lowenstein, 'On Campaign Finance Reform: the Root of All Evil Is Deeply Rooted,' *Hofstra Law Review*, 18 (1989), 301.

27. In truth, with the exception of the racist 'white primaries' of the South (see the later heading of 'Race' in this chapter), primaries were not intended to weaken US parties, but to

ameliorate problems with the caucus and convention systems of nominating candidates. See Alan Ware, *The American Direct Primary* (Cambridge: Cambridge University Press, 2002).

28. Compare Norway, for example, which until recently had no campaign finance law, in large part as its (two) television networks were state run and only faced a commercial, terrestrial competitor in 1992.

29. The governing Supreme Court precedent is *Buckley v Valeo* 424 US 1 (1976). For discussion on the role of money (its lure and aversion) in comparative electoral cultures, see Graeme Orr, 'The Ritual and Aesthetic in Electoral Law,' *Federal Law Review,* 32 (2004), 441–449.

30. Peter Singer, *The President of Good and Evil: The Ethics of George W. Bush* (Melbourne: Text, 2004).

31. 'Robertson: US should assassinate Venezuela's Chavez,' *CNN.com*, http://www.edition.cnn.com/2005/US/08/23/robertson.chavez.1534/ (cited August 23, 2005).

32. See http://www.whitehouse.gov/news/releases/2005/09/20050905-10.html.

33. The reports, from the Palestinian leadership, were not denied by the White House: 'Bush: God made me do it,' http://www.news.com.au/story/0,10117,16843124-401,00.html (cited October 7, 2005).

34. A larger number favors teaching evolution, even though a majority of Americans cling to creationist over evolutionary accounts in their private beliefs: Gallup poll data http://www.gallup.com/poll/content/default.aspx?ci=1690.

35. Gallup poll data http://www.gallup.com/poll/content/default.aspx?ci=17176. The margins preferring less to more religious influence were: US, +7 percent, Canada, +19 percent, Britain, +16 percent. Given the more pronounced level of religious influence in the United States, one might expect the margin of aversion to be higher; but it may also be that perceptions of excessive religiosity in US politics has fed a higher intolerance of boundary blurring in the other countries surveyed. In each country, a plurality was content with the current level of religious influence.

36. A turnaround of 15 percent: see Gallup poll data http://www.gallup.com/poll/content/default.aspx?ci=1690&pg=4.

37. Gallup poll data http://www.gallup.com/poll/content/default.aspx?ci=1690.

38. Gore sought recounts in only selected counties, and then only of 'undervotes' (ballots that machines had mistakenly read as identifying no vote), and not 'overvotes' (ballots that had been rejected as including two votes, when, for example, an overly cautious elector had punched the card for 'Gore,' then written in his name as well.) See Lowenstein, 'Lessons from the Florida Controversy,' 22–23; and Dan Keating, 'Democracy Counts: the Media Consortium Florida Ballot Project', Paper presented at the annual meeting of the American Political Science Association, Boston, US, August–September, 2002, http://www.aei.org/docLib/20040526_KeatingPaper.pdf.

39. Daniel Henninger, '10000 Lawyers Mass to Attack 2004 Election,' *wsj.com*, http://www.opinionjournal.com/columnists/dhenninger/?id=110005821 (cited October 29, 2004).

40. Alexis de Tocqueville, *Democracy in America*, vol. 1 (1835), chapter XVI. See further H. Kwasi Prempeh, 'Lawyers and Liberal Democracy,' *Journal of Democracy,* 11 (2000), 71.

41. *Baker v Carr* 369 US 186 (1962), *Gray v Sanders* 372 US 368 (1963), *Wesberry v Sanders* 376 US 1 (1964), *Reynold v Sims* 377 US 533 (1964).

42. Lani Guinier, *The Tyranny of the Majority: Fundamental Fairness in Representative Democracy* (New York: The Free Press, 1995).

43. Republican officials in Florida were accused of heavily purging black felons, but not Latino or white felons. Such claims are firmly part of international folklore about Florida 2000. See, for example, the comments, five years on, at the Australian politics website *crikey.com.au*, http://www.crikey.com.au/articles/2005/10/12-1611-6935.html.

Democrat officials in Florida were counter-accused of too lightly enforcing the felony-disenfranchisement rules: see Guy Stuart, 'Databases, Felons, and Voting: Bias and Partisanship of the Florida Felons List in the 2000 Elections,' *Political Science Quarterly,* 119 (2004), 435.

44. *Hirst v United Kingdom* (No 2), European Court of Human Rights, October 6, 2005.

45. To compare Australia, see Graeme Orr, 'Ballotless and Behind Bars: the Denial of the Franchise to Prisoners,' *Federal Law Review,* 26 (1998), 72–74.

46. Daniel Lowenstein, *Election Law: Cases and Materials* (Durham: Carolina Academic Press, 1995), 319–324.

47. George Will, 'VRA, All of It, Forever?' *Newsweek* (October 10, 2005).

48. Dan Froomkin, 'A Polling Free-Fall among Blacks,' *washingtonpost.com,* http://www.washingtonpost.com/wp-dyn/content/blog/2005/10/13/BL2005101300885.html (cited October 13, 2005).

49. Post WWII alone, Australia has had five national elections at which the party that won government did not achieve 50 percent of the 'two-party preferred' vote.

50. I am indebted to Andrew Geddis for pointing this out.

51. The Federal Elections Commission only regulates campaign finance, and then only in relation to federal elections.

52. Alec Ewald, 'American Voting: the Local Character of Suffrage in the United States,' (Ph.D. diss., University of Massachusetts, 2005).

53. Hasen, 'Beyond the Margin of Litigation.'

54. Daniel P. Tokaji, 'Early Returns on Election Reform: Discretion, Disenfranchisement, and the Help America Vote Act,' *The George Washington Law Review,* 73 (2005), 1701, arguing that post-2000 reform contributed to problems in the 2004 election, especially in vesting too much discretion in local officials.

55. Kevin Rudd, quoted in 'Labor Backs Four-Year Term Plan,' *theage.com.au,* www.theage.com.au/news/national/labor-backs-four-year-term-plan/2005/09/30/1127804637279.html (cited September 30, 2005).

56. Rafael Pintor et al., *Voter Turnout Since 1945: A Global Report* (Stockholm: International IDEA, 2002), 78–79, lists the US as 120 in 169 nations in terms of post-war turnout. Yet at an average of 66.5 percent it is only 3 percent behind Japan, and between 6 and 8 percent behind Korea, France and the UK.

57. John Fund, 'Gerhard on the Fall: Anti-Americanism Reaches Its Limit in Germany,' *wsj.com Opinion Journal,* http://www.opinionjournal.com/diary/?id=110006726 (cited May 23, 2005).

58. Daniel W. Drezner, 'Friendly Fire,' *The New Republic Online,* http://www.danieldrezner.com/policy/friendlyfire.htm (cited April 9, 2003).

59. Garry Wills, *A Necessary Evil: A History of American Distrust of Government* (New York: Simon & Schuster, 1999).

60. Political legend has it that British Opposition Leader Neil Kinnock's 'triumphalism' at his Labour party's launch in the 1992 general election cost him dearly. Kinnock's riding of the crest of the crowd's energy, punching the air and declaring 'Alright, alright, alright' may have seemed unseemly to many British electors; it would have seemed tame to most Americans.

61. BBC World Service/Gallup International, 'Voice of the People – 2005,' reproduced at Rick Hasen's *Election Law* web log, http://www.electionlawblog.org/archives/BBC%20Democracy%20tables.pdf. Yet, perhaps reflecting a less hierarchical society, Americans were more sanguine than Western Europeans about whether their country was 'governed by the will of the people,' with a response of – 23%, compared with – 34% for Europeans. Scandinavians aside, the question drew a heavily negative response worldwide.

62. Lowenstein, 'Lessons from the Florida Controversy,' 23–25. For the counter-argument that the Republicans stole the election, see Hertsgaard, *The Eagle's Shadow,* 147–167.

63. Marc Young, 'Opinion: Germany's Electoral Circus,' *Deutsche Welle*, http://www.dw-world.de/dw/article/0,2144,1714524,00.html (cited September 20, 2005).

64. Richard Crockatt, *America Embattled: September 11, Anti-Americanism and the Global Order* (London: Routledge, 2003), 24–33. Anxiety over terrorism may be driving America to embrace the methods of empire more than ever: Benjamin Barber, *Fear's Empire: War, Terrorism and Democracy* (New York, WW Norton & Co, 2003). If so, the cycle reproduces itself: Chalmers Johnson, *Blowback: The Costs and Consequences of American Empire* (New York: Henry Holt and Co, 2000).

65. Geraldine Doogue's interview with Premier Bob Carr, 'Bob Carr on the US,' *ABC Radio National*, http://www.abc.net.au/sundayprofile/stories/s1138579.htm (cited June 27, 2004). The quote finishes with a dose of liberalism and Realpolitik: 'The capacity to project that power right around the globe is by any historical sense, an empire. But it's an empire that acts not infrequently on humanitarian impulses, and second, it's an empire that offers real benefits to a country like Australia, which is [sic] a comfortable relationship with it.'

66. Henry David Thoreau, *Walden, or, Life in the Woods; On the Duty of Civil Disobedience* (New York: Collier, 1962).

67. Walter Russell Mead, *Special Providence: American Foreign Policy and How It Changed the World* (New York: Alfred A Knopf, 2001).

Chapter 9: Bush, the Iraq War and Anti-Americanism

1. David W. Ellwood, *Anti-Americanism in Western Europe: A Comparative Perspective* (Bologna: The Johns Hopkins University, Occasional Paper, n. 3, 1999).

2. Brendon O'Connor and Martin Griffiths, Editors. *The Rise of Anti-Americanism* (London: Routledge, 2005).

3. David W. Ellwood, 'Comparative Anti-Americanism in Western Europe,' in *Transactions, Transgressions, Transformations: American Culture in Western Europe and Japan*. Edited by Heide Fehrenbach and Uta G. Poiger (New York: Berghahn, 2000); Edited by Sergio Fabbrini, *The United States Contested: American Unilateralism and European Discontent* (London: Routledge, 2006).

4. William Drzdick, 'Even Allies Resent US Dominance,' *Washington Post* (November 4, 1997), 1.

5. William Wallace, 'Living with the Hegemon: European Dilemmas,' in *Critical Views of September 11: Analysis From Around the World*. Edited by E. Hershberg and K. W. Moore (New York: New Press, 2002).

6. Volker A. Berghahn, *America and the Intellectual Cold Wars in Europe* (Princeton: Princeton University Press, 2001).

7. Sergio Fabbrini, 'The Domestic Sources of European Anti-Americanism,' *Government and Opposition*, 37, 1 (2002), 3–14.

8. The communist left became the largest political force after World War II in countries such as Italy and France and was also very influential in democratic Greece, Spain and Portugal.

9. Seymour M. Lipset and Gary Marks, *It Didn't Happen Here: Why Socialism Failed in the United States* (New York: W.W. Norton, 2000).

10. Barry Rubin and Judith C. Rubin, *Hating America: A History* (Oxford: Oxford University Press, 2004), Chapter 3.

11. Anthony Giddens and Will Hutton, 'In Conversation,' in *Global Capitalism*. Edited by Anthony Giddens and Will Hutton (New York: The New Press, 2000), 15.

12. Rubin and Rubin, *Hating America*, Chapter 4.

13. James W. Ceaser, *Reconstructing America. The Symbol of America in Modern Thought* (New Haven: Yale University Press, 1997).

14. Gordon Wood, *The Radicalism of the American Revolution* (New York: Alfred A. Knopf, 1992).

15. Robert H. Wiebe, *Self Rule: A Cultural History of American Democracy* (Chicago: The University of Chicago Press, 1995).

16. Michela Nacci, *L'anti-americanismo in Italia negli anni Trenta* (Turin: Bollati Boringhieri, 1989).

17. Seymour M. Lipset, *American Exceptionalism: A Double-Edge Sword* (New York: Norton, 1996); Michael Kazin, *The Populist Persuasion: An American History* (New York: Basic Books, 1995).

18. Gary Wills, *Papal Sin: Structure of Deceit* (New York: Random House, 2001).

19. Michael Walzer, *What It Means to Be an American: Essays on the American Experience* (New York: Marsilio, 1996), 108.

20. Carol S. Steiker, 'Capital Punishment and American Exceptionalism' in *American Exceptionalism and Human Rights*. Edited by Michael Ignatieff (Princeton: Princeton University Press, 2005).

21. Lipset, *American Exceptionalism*, 19.

22. Jacob Neusner, Editor, *World Religions in America: An Introduction* (Louisville: Westminster John Knox Press, 2003).

23. Michael Walzer, *On Toleration* (New Haven: Yale University Press, 1999), 67.

24. Norberto Bobbio, *Sinistra e destra* (Rome: Donzelli, 1994); Stephen Holmes, *The Anatomy of Antiliberalism* (Cambridge: Harvard University Press, 1993).

25. Sergio Fabbrini, 'Layers of Anti-Americanism: Americanization, American Unilateralism and Anti-Americanism in a European Perspective,' *European Journal of American Culture*, 23, 2 (2004), 79–94.

26. James Petras and Henry Veltmeyer, *Globalization Unmasked: Imperialism in the 21st Century* (London: Zed Books, 2001); Chalmers Johnson, *Blowback: The Costs and Consequences of American Empire* (New York: Metropolitan Books, 2000); Malcom Waters, *Globalization* (London: Routledge, 1996).

27. Will Hutton, 'America's Global Hand,' *The American Prospect*, 11 (December 6, 1999), 54.

28. Chalmers Johnson, *The Sorrows of Empire: How the American People Lost* (New York: Metropolitan Books, 2004).

29. Francis Fukuyama, *Trust: The Social Virtues and the Creation of Prosperity* (London: Hamish Hamilton, 1995), 353.

30. Lynda L. Kaid and Christine Holtz-Bacha, Editors, *Comparative Perspective on Political Advertising* (Thousand Oaks: Sage, 1994).

31. See, for a recent overview of this issue, Jeff Manza, Fay Lomax Cook, and Benjamin I. Page, Editors, *Navigating Public Opinion. Polls, Policy, and the Future of American Democracy* (Oxford: Oxford University Press, 2002).

32. Ziauddin Sardar and Merryl Wyn Davies, *Why Do People Hate America?* (Cambridge: Icon Books, 2002).

33. See, for example, Fareed Zakaria, 'The Politics of Rage: Why Do They Hate Us?' *Newsweek* (October 15, 2001); but see *contra* Timothy Mitchell, 'American Power and Anti-Americanism in the Middle East,' in *Anti-Americanism*. Edited by Andrew Ross and Kristin Ross (New York: New York University Press, 2004).

34. See Walter Russell Mead, 'Why Do They Hate Us? Two Books Take Aim at French Anti-Americanism,' *Foreign Affairs* (March–April, 2003).

35. Tod Lindberg, 'Why Others Have Mixed Feelings About Us,' *Washington Times* (January 15, 2002).

36. Washington Post/Kaiser Family Foundation/Harvard University, June 13–23, 2002, N=1,402.

37. The data discussed here have been collected from the set of Pew surveys, the Transatlantic Trends Surveys, Eurobarometer and the Gallup international surveys, carried out between 2001 and 2006 in several European countries and elsewhere in the world.

38. This figure updates the information in Pierangelo Isernia's 'Anti-Americanism and European Public Opinion during the Iraq War,' in *The United States Contested*. Edited by Fabbrini and also in Isernia's 'Anti-Americanism in Europe During the Cold War,' in *Anti-Americanisms in World Politics*. Edited by Robert O. Keohane and Peter J. Katzenstein (Ithaca: Cornell University Press, 2006).

39. Using the raw data in Figure 2, we first normalized the four series and then converted them into an index computed as 100 plus the percentage of those in favor of the United States minus the percentage of those opposed to the United States. We then standardized each score, using the mean average and standard deviation across the four series. These calculations were done for all four series.

40. James A. Stimson, *Public Opinion in America: Moods, Cycles, and Swings* (Boulder: Westview, 1991), 36–39.

41. In fact, the four series move quite in parallel, with an average correlation between pairs of 0.617, with only the British–France pair less than 0.5 (at 0.377) and only one pair higher than 0.8 (Italy–Germany, at 0.865).

42. In Figure 2, the 2003 data overlook this recovery being a yearly average of different surveys, but this fact can be seen from the raw data in Figure 1. Positive feelings go from a net average feeling of 47 down to –7 in February 2003, to the all time lowest –31 in March 2003 (the start of the Iraq War) but feelings entered positive territory again by April 2003.

43. Richard Crockatt, *America Embattled. September 11, Anti-Americanism and the Global Order* (London: Routledge, 2003).

44. For a discussion of how anti-Americanism has been measured in survey research, see Isernia, 'Anti-Americanism in Europe During the Cold War'.

45. Richard J. Davidson, 'On Emotion, Mood, and Related Affective Constructs,' in *The Nature of Emotion: Fundamental Questions*. Edited by Paul Ekman and R. J. Davidson (New York: Oxford, University Press, 2004), 52.

46. See, for example, Timothy Garton Ash, *Free World: Why a Crisis of the West Reveals the Opportunity of Our Time* (Allen Lane: Penguin Books, 2004).

47. Princeton Survey Research Associates International for *Newsweek*, March 13–14, 2003, N=1,004 adult population.

48. Ibid., July 29–30, 2004, N=1,190 only registered voters.

49. Ibid., September 30–October 2, 2004, N=1,144.

50. The data comes from different surveys carried out by the German Marshall Fund of the United States and the Compagnia di San Paolo (*Transatlantic Trend Survey*), the Pew Research Center for People and the Press, the Chicago Council of Foreign Relations, and the USIA.

51. Philip H. Gordon and Jeremy Shapiro, *Allies at War: America, Europe and the Crisis over Iraq* (New York: McGraw-Hill, 2004), 47.

52. The relatively lower level of disapproval for the death penalty, where *only* 64% disapproved, is mostly due to the strong plurality of Britons approving Bush's support for the death penalty. In the other three countries, disapproval is in the order of 70% for the death penalty also.

53. The correlation between Bush's job approval and EU/US interests getting closer, staying the same or going further apart is very weak (Pearson's r –0.095 and Kendall's tau-b –0.077, both significant at the level 0.001, with two tails). This is a clear indication that in August 2002, Bush's personal image was only marginally related to the assessment of the EU/US relationship.

54. SOFRES for the French–American Foundation, May 16–18, 2000.

55. SOFRES for *Le Nouvel Observateur*, November 1–2, 2001.

56. EMNID for the Ministry of Defence, November 12–15, 2001.

57. *Global Express Monitor*, November 19–December 17, 2001.

58. Comparing this question with the previous one, asked by Gallup in the same period, shows that an explicit reference to Al Qaeda and its leader Osama Bin Laden did not apparently move public opinion in either direction.

59. Bob Woodward, *Plan of Attack* (New York: Simon & Schuster, 2004).

60. Philip Everts and Pierangelo Isernia, 'The Polls – Trends: The War in Iraq,' *Public Opinion Quarterly*, 69, 2 (2005), 264–323.

61. For the data on the Transatlantic Trend Survey 2006, see http://www.transatlantic trends.org/, and for the European Elite Survey 2006, see http://www.gips.unisi.it/circap/ees_overview.

Chapter 10: The Washington Consensus and Anti-Americanism

1. John Williamson, 'Did the Washington Consensus Fail?' Address at Center for Strategic and International Studies, Washington, DC, US, http://www.iie.com/publications/papers/paper.cfm?researchid=488 (cited November 6, 2002).

2. For insightful analysis, see Robert Singh, 'Are We All Americans Now? Explaining Anti-Americanisms,' in *The Rise of Anti-Americanism*. Edited by Brendon O'Connor and Martin Griffiths (London: Routledge, 2006), 25–47.

3. Brendon O'Connor, 'What Is Anti-Americanism: Tendency, Prejudice or Ideology?' Keynote Address, Anti-Americanism: A Symposium, Institute for the Study of the Americas, London, UK, October 21, 2005.

4. John Williamson, 'What Washington Means by Policy Reform,' in *Latin American Adjustment: How Much Has Happened*. Edited by John Williamson (Washington, DC: Institute for International Economics, 1990), 5–20.

5. Moises Naim, 'Fads and Fashions in Economic Reforms: Washington Consensus or Washington Confusion?' *Third World Quarterly*, 21 (June, 2000), 505–528.

6. David Harvey, *A Brief History of Neoliberalism* (New York: Oxford University Press, 2005), 13.

7. Ibid., 64–86; S. Bessis, *Western Supremacy: The Triumph of an Idea* (London: Zed Books, 2003), 99–130.

8. Quoted in John Williamson, 'What Should the Bank Think About the Washington Consensus?' Paper prepared as background for the World Bank's Development Report 2000, www.iie.com/publications/papers/paper/cfm?ResearchID=351 (cited July 1999).

9. Ibid.

10. Robin Broad and John Cavanagh, 'The Death of the Washington Consensus?' *World Policy Journal*, 16 (Fall, 1999), 79–88.

11. M. Destler, *American Trade Politics* (Washington, DC: Institute for International Economics, 1995); Robert Baldwin and Christopher S. Magee, *Congressional Votes: From NAFTA Approval to Fast-Track Defeat* (Washington, DC: Institute of Economics, 2000).

12. Quoted in Will Hutton, *The World We're In* (London: Little Brown, 2002), 199. See, also, Stiglitz's oeuvres, *Globalization and Its Discontents* (London: Allen Lane, 2002); *The Roaring Nineties: Seeds of Destruction* (London: Allen Lane, 2003).

13. James Wolfensohn, 'People First,' *Paul Hoffman Lecture*, http://www.worldbank.org/html/extdr/extme/jwsp0529.htm (cited May 29, 1997); R. W. Stevenson, 'A chief banker for nations at the bottom of the heap,' *New York Times* (September 14, 1997). Wolfensohn typically pronounced the Washington Consensus no longer relevant. Speaking in Shanghai on May 25, 2004, he declared that it had been 'dead for years' and had been 'replaced by all sorts of other consensuses.' Quoted in Simon Maxwell, 'The Washington Consensus is dead! Long live the meta-narrative,' Overseas Development Institute, Working Paper 243, January 2005.

14. Daniel Yergin and Joseph Stanislaw, *The Commanding Heights: The Battle for the World Economy* (New York: Touchstone, 2002), 237; Williamson, 'What Should the Bank think about the Washington Consensus?'

15. Frances Stewart, Comments on John Williamson, 'The Washington Consensus Revisited,' in *Economic and Social Development into the XXI Century*. Edited by Louis Emmerij (Washington, DC: Inter-American Development Bank, 1997), 69.

16. Richard Crockatt, 'Anti-Americanism and the Clash of Civilizations,' in *The Rise of Anti-Americanism*. Edited by O'Connor and Griffiths, 126. For a classic study of this credo, see Seymour Martin Lipset, *American Exceptionalism* (New York: Norton, 1996).

17. Max Lerner, *America as a Civilization: Life and Thought in the United States Today* (New York: Simon & Schuster, 1957), 61–62.

18. Thomas Friedman, *The Lexus and the Olive Tree* (New York: Farrar, Strauss, & Giroux, 1999), 28. According to Friedman, what was at stake in global politics was acceptance of the benefits of globalization (represented by the ultimate consumer product, the Lexus luxury car) or outworn dedication to territory or ideology (represented by the olive tree).

19. In a National Security Strategy of Engagement and Enlargement (February 1996), the Clinton administration saw its three main foreign policy goals – to enhance US security, to bolster economic prosperity and to promote democracy – as intertwined. It declared, 'These goals are supported by ensuring America remains engaged in the world and by enlarging the community of secure, free markets and democratic nations.' The Bush administration's national security strategy statements of 2002 and 2006 expressed similar goals. In its introduction, the latter declared that one of the two pillars of US foreign policy was to promote freedom, justice and human dignity by working against tyranny, promoting democracy and extending prosperity through 'free and fair trade'.

20. George Bush, 'Securing Freedom's Triumph,' *New York Times* (September 11, 2002).

21. George W. Bush, State of the Union Address, www.whitehouse.gov (cited January 20, 2004).

22. Charles Kupchan, *The End of the American Era: US Foreign Policy and the Geopolitics of the Twenty-first Century* (New York: Alfred A. Knopf, 2002), 60.

23. Hutton, *The World We're In*, 199–207 [quotation, 199]. Significantly, Hutton sought to distinguish between traditional American liberalism of the New Deal variety, of which he approved, and the new economic neoliberalism, which he associated with 'rampant inequality and an increasingly feral capitalism,' 3–4.

24. Friedman, 273, 285.

25. Mark T. Berger and Mark Beeson, 'Lineages of Liberalism and Miracles of Modernization,' *Third World Quarterly*, 19 (November 3, 1998), especially 494–500. The World Bank hesitantly recognized the capability of the state in its report, *The East Asian Miracle: Economic Growth and Public Policy* (Oxford: Oxford University Press, 1993) and more directly in its *World Development Report: The State in a Changing World* (Oxford: Oxford University Press, 1997).

26. Chalmers Johnson, *Blowback: The Costs and Consequences of American Empire* (London: Little Brown, 2000), 193–215. For a less critical assessment, see Yergin and Stanislaw, *The Commanding Heights*, 139–184.

27. Charles Krauthammer, 'What Caused Our Economic Boom?' *Washington Post* (January 5, 1998).

28. Takashi Kawachi, 'A New Backlash against American Influence,' *Japan Echo* (April 1998), 44–47; Philip Courtenay, 'Versions of Capitalism Vie for Ascendancy in Asia,' *Free China Journal* (March 19, 1999), 7. Significantly, when blaming 'villainous acts of sabotage' by international speculators for precipitating the crisis, Prime Minister Mahathir Mohamad of Malaysia singled out New York–based George Soros as the main culprit rather than hedge fund managers working from London. See Yergin and Stanislaw, *The Commanding Heights*, 180.

29. Mark Landler, 'Gore, in Malaysia, Says Its Leaders Suppress Freedom,' *New York Times* (November 17, 1998); Tom Plate, 'Gore's Inept Criticism of the Malaysian President Has Hurt the US All Over Asia,' *Los Angeles Times* (November 24, 1998).

30. Kupchan, *The End of the American Era*, 59; Johnson, *Blowback*, 211.

31. Marshall Auerback and Patrick Smith, 'Japan, for One, is Finally Learning to Say "No",' *International Herald Tribune* (February 1, 1999). Sakakibara was known as 'Mr. Yen' for his role in currency management and had previously published a defence of his country's industrial policy. See Eisuke Sakakibara, *Beyond Capitalism: The Japanese Model of Market Economics* (Lanham, MD: University Press of America, 1993) and 'Globalization and Diversity,' in *Economic and Global Development*. Edited by Emmerij, 62–69.

32. See, for example, Angel Ubide, 'Europe Needs Its Own Koizumi,' *Newsweek* (April 3, 2006), 43. In 2000, a think tank convened by the Tokyo government to set a national agenda for the new century recommended that Japan should look to foster greater individualism, less conformity and more risk-taking in the place of economic decision-making by consensus. As one analyst noted, this called for 'the absorption of the idiosyncrasy of the US as the essence of the new mentality.' See Alfredo Toro-Hardy, *The Age of Villages: The Small Village vs. the Global Village* (Bogota: Villegas Editores, 2002), 100.

33. Joshua Cooper Ramo, 'The Beijing Consensus: Notes on the New Physics of Chinese Power' (London: Foreign Policy Center, 2004), 39 http://www.fpc.org.uk/fsblog/244.pdf. See, also, Eric Teo Chu Cheow, 'US–China Ideological Rivalry Heats Up,' *The Japan Times* (January 6, 2006).

34. Timothy Garton Ash, 'Old Britain, New Britain,' *The Guardian* (June 12, 2003).

35. Ross McKibbin, 'How to Put the Politics Back into Labour,' *London Review of Books* (August 7, 2003).

36. For a similar view, see John Kay, 'The Real Economy,' *Prospect* (May 2003), 26–30. This deems Bill Clinton's address to the G-7 meeting at Denver in June 1997 a particularly hubristic celebration of the American model as the way forward for global prosperity because it ignored the social problems of the free market in the United States, notably income inequality, high crime and social dislocation. Kay quotes an unnamed British official attending the event who noted the discrepancy between the economic boastfulness of his American counterparts and their warnings to 'us not to stray too far from our hotel at night'. Kay, 'The Real Economy,' *Prospect* (May 2003), 28.

37. Hutton, *The World We're In*, 2–3, [4 quotation], 11–19, 208–256, 352–370.

38. Margaret Blunden, '"Anglo-Saxon Model" Wears French Clothes,' *International Herald Tribune* (June 8, 2005).

39. See, for example, comments by Labour MP and former Europe Minister Denis MacShane in his article 'The Politics of Protest,' *Newsweek* (April 3, 2006), 22–23. Commenting on street demonstrations in France against a reform replacing existing protections against lay-offs with a two-year probationary period for workers hired under age 26, MacShane declared that the demonstrations were in denial of 'the modern narrative' that would rescue the national economy from entrenched immobility. With some smugness, he avowed that France (and Italy) needed to copy the examples of America and Britain, which they had once derided as 'the sick man of Europe'.

40. Stephen Castle, 'Chirac Wins Battle to Defend his EU Vision Against Britain's Free-Market Liberalism,' *The Independent* (March 23, 2005). Chirac is also reported to have told his own ministers that liberalism 'is an ideology quite as harmful as Communism, and like Communism, it will go to the wall'. See Blunden, '"Anglo-Saxon Model" Wears French Clothes.'

41. Luke Harding, 'Schroder Bows Out with Swipe at Blair,' *The Guardian* (October 13, 2005).

42. David Hojman, 'The Political Economy of Recent Market Conversions in Latin America,' *Journal of Latin American Studies*, 26 (1994); Philip Oxhorn and Graciela Ducatenzeiler, eds., *What Kind of Democracy? What Kind of Market? Latin America in the Age of Neoliberalism* (University Park: Pennsylvania State University Press, 1998); Laura Carlsen and Tom Barry, *US Hegemony or Global Good Neighbor Policy?* International Relations Center Americas Program Special Report (2004).

43. Ronaldo Munck, '"Neoliberalism," Necessitarianism, and Alternatives in Latin America: There Is No Alternative (TINA)?' *Third World Quarterly*, 24 (June 2003), 495–512; Kurt Weyland, 'Neopopulism and Neoliberalism in Latin America: How Much Affinity?' *Third World Quarterly*, 24 (December 2003), 1095–1116.

44. 'Redrawing the Political Map,' *The Economist* (November 26, 2005), 65–66. See, also, Marcela Sanchez, 'A New Latin Consensus,' *Washington Post* (July 16, 2005).

45. For a sympathetic study, see Richard Gott, *Hugo Chavez and the Bolivarian Revolution* (London: Verso, 2005), and for a contrary view, see Javier Corrales, 'Hugo Boss,' *Foreign Policy* (January/February 2006), 32–40. In an attempt to counter what he saw as American anti-Latin Americanism, Chavez also challenged the 'cultural dictatorship' of the United States, particularly the tendency of Hollywood to portray the continent as a haven of drug barons, violent street gangs and kidnappers. To this end, he provided $11 million to set up a Venezuelan film studio in addition to the 70 percent funding that his government provided for Telesur, the Caracas-based news channel that opponents have dubbed 'Telechavez'. See Martin Hodgson, 'Chavez launches homegrown Hollywood,' *The Guardian* (June 5, 2006).

46. Monte Reel and Michael Fletcher, 'As Bush Meets with Allies in Argentina, Rally Led by Chavez Turns Violent,' *Washington Post* (November 5, 2005).

47. Michael Shifter and Vinay Jawahar, 'The Divided States of the Americas,' *Current History* (February 2006), 52–53.

48. Those Latin American officials who had pursued the Washington Consensus were broadly condemned in popular opinion as toadies of the United States and betrayers of the national interest. According to one such criticism, 'When someone keeps companies with the chief supporters of a certain kind of economic policy it is clear where his interests lie.' See Xavier Cano Tamayo, 'Burying the "Washington Consensus",' Global Policy Forum, http://www.globalpolicy.org/socecon/bwi-wto/imf/2003/0226bury.html (cited February 26, 2003).

49. Peter Hakim, 'Is Washington Losing Latin America?' *Foreign Affairs* (January/February, 2006), 47–50.

50. Joseph Stiglitz, 'Argentina Shortchanged: Why the Nation that Followed the Rules Fell to Pieces,' *Washington Post* (May 12, 2002).

51. For differing assessments of the crisis, see: Alan Cibils, Mark Weisbrot, and Debayanyi Kar, *Argentina Since Default: The IMF and the Depression*, Center for Economic and Policy Research, http://www.cepr.net/publication/argentina_2002_09_03htm, which holds the IMF to blame; and Paul Bluestein, *And the Money Kept Rolling In (And Out): Wall Street, the IMF, and the Bankrupting of Argentina* (Washington, DC: Public Affairs, 2005), which blames Argentine government ineptitude and Wall Street greed.

52. Anthony Faiola, 'Economic Crisis Spurs Anger: Latin America's Resentment Feeds Anti-US Sentiments,' *Washington Post* (May 19, 2002); Roger Burbank, 'Argentina's President Faces Off With IMF,' http://www.zmag.org/content/showarticle.cfm?ItemID=5014 (cited February 20, 2004).

53. Omar Encarnacion, 'Lula's Big Win,' *World Policy Journal* (Winter 2002–2003), 76; Kenneth Rapoza, 'Learning to Samba; Brazil and the Bretton Woods Institutions,' http://www.worldpress.org/print_article.cfm?article_id=934(cited November 27, 2002); Stiglitz, 'Argentina Shortchanged'.

54. Faiola, 'Economic Crisis Spurs Anger'; Encarnacion, 'Lula's Big Win,' 73.

55. Hakim, 'Is Washington Losing Latin America?' 42–43. Chile and Mexico, Latin America's representatives on the United Nations Security Council in 2003 and two of Washington's closest allies in the region, opposed a resolution endorsing the invasion of Iraq. In total, of 34 Latin American and Caribbean countries, only seven supported the war. The latter comprised the five Central American republics and the Dominican Republic, which were in trade negotiations with the United States at the time, and the seventh was Columbia, which received over $600 million annually in US military aid.

56. Dan Glaister, 'US on Sidelines as Latin American Voters Prepare to Redraw Continent,' *The Guardian* (November 14, 2005).

57. Larry Rohter and Elizabeth Bumiller, 'Hemispheric Summit Marred by Violent Anti-Bush Protests,' *New York Times* (November 5, 2005); Reel and Fletcher, 'As Bush Meets with Allies.'

58. Lula interview by editors *of O Estado de Sao Paulo,* translated as 'Brazil Wants Autonomy,' *New Perspectives Quarterly,* 20 (Winter 2003); Encarnacion, 'Lula's Big Win,' 73–77.

59. Larry Elliot, 'Who Needs the Hand of God?' *The Guardian* (March 7, 2005).

60. Given Maradona's popularity throughout the continent, Chavez's propaganda makes much of their connection. See, for example, Mike Whitney, 'Panicky Bush Slinks Away from Chavez,' http://www.venezuelaanalysis.com/articles.php?artno=1596 (cited November 7, 2005).

61. Uki Goni, 'Argentina's Unorthodox Rehab,' *The Guardian* (January 10, 2006).

62. David Erikson, 'Castro and Latin America: A Second Wind,' *World Policy Journal,* XXI (Spring 2004). See, also, Cuban dissident Paul Rivero, 'False Friends,' *Newsweek* (March 20, 2006), 42.

63. Joseph Contreras, 'Castro's Comeback,' *Newsweek* (March 20, 2006), 40–42.

64. Hakim, 'Is Washington Losing Latin America?' 49.

65. Lula, 'Brazil Wants Autonomy.' See too, Encarnacion, 'Lula's Big Win,' 73–77; and Hakim, 'The Reluctant Partner,' *Foreign Affairs* (January/February 2004), 114–123.

66. David Harvey, *The New Imperialism* (New York: Oxford University Press, 2005), 130.

67. James Dunkerley, 'The United States and Latin America in the Long Run (1800–1945),' in *The United States and Latin America: The New Agenda.* Edited by Victor Bulmer-Thomas and James Dunkerley (London: Institute of Latin American Studies, 1999), 24. For a more polemical assessment, see Peter Smith, *Talons of the Eagle: Dynamics of US-Latin American Relations* (New York: Oxford University Press, 1996).

68. Carlos Albert Montaner, 'Anti-Americanism Has Become Ideology,' http://www.firmaspress.com/577.htm (cited November 8, 2005).

69. 'ALBA: Bolivarian Alternative for Latin America and the Caribbean,'http://www.venezuelaanalysis.com/docs.php?dno=1010 (cited January 30, 2004).

70. Niall Ferguson, 'Meanwhile ... Have You Seen What's Been Happening in Bush's backyard?' *www.opinion.telegraph.com* (cited February 12, 2006); Richard Gott, 'The Challenge in the South,' *The Guardian* (December 20, 2005).

71. Dan Glaister, 'Triumph for Bolivia's Candidate of the Poor,' *The Guardian* (December 20, 2005); Steve Bogan, 'Coca Is a Way of Life,' *The Guardian* (February 9, 2006); Vinay Jawahar, 'LA: Looking Left,' *The Internationalist* 3 www.thedialogue.org/publications/oped/feb06/jawahar_0227.asp#top (cited Spring, 2006).

72. Coca leaf, used for tea and herbal remedies in Bolivia, is the only cash crop that indigenous and impoverished cocaleros can grow as a cash crop. However, the United States calculated that only 5,000 hectares of the 27,700 hectares taken up in its cultivation in Bolivia went on traditional usage and the rest was taken up by cocaine production. Bolivian growers feel they are being penalized to solve the cocaine habits of Americans, which should be dealt with through action within the United States' own borders. As one

cocalero put it, 'If it was left up to the Americans, all the crops would be eradicated and we would starve. We would have no way to make an income.' See Bogan, 'Coca is a Way of Life.'

73. Jorge Castaneda, 'Why Chile Really Matters,' *Newsweek* (March 27, 2006).

Chapter 11: American Popular Culture and Anti-Americanism

1. Rob Kroes, *If You've Seen One, You've Seen the Mall: Europeans and American Mass Culture* (Urbana: University of Illinois Press, 1996), 155.

2. Ibid., 156.

3. John Rockwell, 'The New Colossus: American Culture as Power Export,' *The New York Times* (January 30, 1994), Section 2, A1, A30.

4. Ibid., Section 2, A1.

5. Six Feet Under's creator Alan Ball explained that the show was ultimately life-affirming: 'Everybody dies. Until you face the truth of your own mortality, you can't really start to live.' See 'Life and Loss' video, downloadable from http://www.tv.com /six-feetunder/show/3223/videos.html?tag=tabs;videos.

6. This point is well made by Christopher Lasch in *The Culture of Narcissism* (New York: W.W. Norton & Co., 1979). Lasch argues that a distorted fear and denial of death emerges with the narcissistic personality since narcissists are unwilling to give up their wealth, power and fame to future generations and they therefore seek to prolong their own youth and ultimately biological life indefinitely.

7. Todd Gitlin, 'Anti-Anti-Americanism,' *Dissent* (February 1, 2003).

8. James Ceaser, 'A Genealogy of Anti-Americanism,' *The Public Interest* (Summer 2003).

9. Theodor Adorno and Max Horkheimer, *Dialectic of Enlightenment* (London: Verso Press, 1979), 132. It is worth noting that the book was written during the Frankfurt School thinker's time of wartime exile in the United States.

10. Ibid., 120.

11. Heidegger quoted in Ceaser, 'A Genealogy of Anti-Americanism.'

12. Herbert Schiller, *Communication and Cultural Domination* (New York: International Arts and Sciences Press, 1976). See also Livingston A. White, 'Reconsidering Cultural Imperialism Theory,' *Transnational Broadcasting Studies* No. 6 (Spring/Summer, 2001) and Rese Anne Sims, 'The United States vs. The World: A Theoretical Look at Cultural Imperialism,' (undated), http://www.utexas.edu/ftp/pub/eems/cultimp. 38._.html.

13. See Hugh Wilford, 'Winning Hearts and Minds: American Cultural Strategies in the Cold War,' *Borderlines: Studies in American Culture*, 1, 4 (1994), 315–326; Richard Pells, *Not Like Us: How Europeans Have Loved, Hated, and Transformed American Culture Since World War II* (New York: Basic Books, 1997).

14. Margaret Wertheim quoted in Ziauddin Sardar and Merryl Wyn Davies, *Why Do People Hate America?* (Cambridge: Icon Books, 2002), 117.

15. Ibid., 118, 131.

16. Ibid., 121.

17. Ibid., 124.

18. Ziauddin Sardar and Merryl Wyn Davies, *American Dream, Global Nightmare* (Cambridge: Icon Books, 2004).

19. Benjamin R. Barber, 'Jihad vs. McWorld,' *Atlantic Monthly* (March 1992), 4.

20. Barber lists Kurds, Basques, Puerto Ricans, Ossetians, East Timoreans, Quebecois, the Catholics of Northern Ireland, Abkhasians, Kurile Islander Japanese, the Zulus of Inkatha, Catalonians, Tamils and Palestinians as examples of the forces of Jihad. Barber, 'Jihad vs. McWorld,' *Atlantic Monthly* (March 1992), 4.

21. Heinz Ickstadt, 'Uniting a Divided Nation: Americanism and Anti-Americanism in Post-War Germany,' *European Journal of American Culture*, 23, 2 (2004), 160.

22. Nina Bernstein, 'Young Germans Ask: Thanks for What?' *New York Times* (March 9, 2003).

23. Ickstadt, 'Uniting a Divided Nation,' 165.

24. Jean Baudrillard, *America* (trans. Chris Turner) (London: Verso Press, 1988), 76.

25. Frank Viviano, 'Bitter Debate in Europe on US Role: Washington's Dominance of Nato Creates Waves of Anti-Americanism,' *San Francisco Chronicle*, 5 April, 1999, 1, 7. See also the discussion comparing various national Anti-Americanisms in Europe in Sergio Fabbrini, 'Layers of Anti-Americanism: Americanization, American Unilateralism and Anti-Americanism in a European Perspective,' *European Journal of American Culture*, 23, 2 (2004), 79–94.

26. Richard Kuisel, *Seducing the French: The Dilemma of Americanization* (Berkeley and Los Angeles: University of California Press, 1993).

27. See Seong Cheol Kim, 'Cultural Imperialism on the Internet,' *The Edge: The E-Journal of Intercultural Relations*, 1, 4 (Fall 1998) and Chris Yeomans, 'The Coca-Colonisation of European Culture,' *Café Babel*. Current Internet usage figures for EU countries are available at http://www.internetworldstats.com/stats9.htm (cited October 25, 2004). Sweden has the highest usage rate in the EU at 74.9% penetration.

28. See George McKay, 'Downsizing America,' in *Yankee Go Home & Take Me with U.* Edited by George McKay (Wiltshire: Sheffield Academic Press, 1997).

29. George McKay, 'Anti-Americanism, Youth and Popular Music, and the Campaign for Nuclear Disarmament in Britain,' in *Anti-Americanism at Home and Abroad*. Edited by Sylvie Mathe (Aix-en Provence: University of Provence Press, 2000).

30. See Joseph Nye, 'Globalization Is Not Americanization,' *The Taipei Times* (October 22, 2004); Terry Eagleton, *The Idea of Culture* (Oxford: Blackwell Publishers, 2000), 12.

31. Richard Pells, 'From Modernism to the Movies: The Globalization of American Culture in the Twentieth Century,' *European Journal of American Culture*, 23, 2 (2004), 152. We might even go further than Pells and argue that the United States not only draws together disparate cultures but also reinvigorates them and creates then anew.

32. Fabbrini, 'Layers of Anti-Americanism,' 83; Pells, 'From Modernism to the Movies,' 148–151; Neal Gabler, *An Empire of Their Own: How Jews Invented Hollywood* (New York: Anchor Books, 1998).

33. Fabbrini, 'Layers of Anti-Americanism,' 83; Ron Robin quoted in Sims, 'The United States vs. The World,' 1.

34. Radley Balko, 'Globalization and Culture: Americanization or Cultural Diversity?' *A World Connected*, http://www.aworldconnected.org/article.php/486.html (cited 21 January 2004); Nye, 'Globalization Is Not Americanization.'

35. Balko, 'Globalization and Culture'; Livingston A. White, 'Reconsidering Cultural Imperialism Theory'; Pells, 'From Modernism to the Movies'; Emine Saner, 'King of Bollywood,' *The Guardian*, 4 (August, 2006), 6–9.

36. Pells, 'From Modernism to the Movies,' 152.

37. Anthony D. Smith, 'Towards a Global Culture?' *Theory, Culture & Society*, 7 (1990), 171–191.

38. Balko, 'Globalization and Culture'; Livingston A. White, 'Reconsidering Cultural Imperialism Theory'; Sims, 'The United States vs. The World.'

39. For a discussion of the redundancy of the traditional political labels of left and right, see Anthony Giddens, *Beyond Left and Right: The Future of Radical Politics* (Cambridge: Polity Press, 1994) For an analysis of the decline of solidarities, see Robert D. Putnam, *Bowling Alone* (New York: Simon & Schuster, 2000).

40. Eagleton, *The Idea of Culture*, 95.

41. Meera Nanda quoted in ibid., 76.

42. Ibid., 123.

Chapter 12: Modernity, Resentment and Anti-Americanism

1. For examples of recent discussions of Anti-Americanism, see Barry Rubin and Judy C. Rubin, *Hating America: A History* (Oxford: Oxford University Press, 2004); Andrei Markovits, *Amerika dich haßt sich's besser* (Hamburg: Konkret Verlag, 2004); Dan Diner, *Feindbild Amerika* (Munich: Propyläen, 2002).

2. See Georg Kamphausen, *Die Erfindung Amerikas in der Kulturkritik der Generation von 1890* (Weilerswist: Velbrück Wissenschaft, 2002).

3. Quoted in James Ceaser, 'A Genealogy of Anti-Americanism,' *Public Interest,* 152 (2003), 14.

4. Anton Kaes, 'Massenkultur und Modernität. Notizen zu einer Sozialgeschichte des frühen amerikanischen und deutschen Films', in *Amerika und die Deutschen. Bestandsaufnahme einer 300-jährigen Geschichte.* Edited by Frank Tommer (Opladen: Westdeutscher Verlag, 1986), 651–665.

5. Donald Young, *American Minority Peoples* (New York: Harper & Brothers, 1932), 55. See also Richard Pells, *From Modernism to the Movies* (New Haven: Yale University Press, forthcoming).

6. Diner, *Feindbild Amerika,* 178ff.

7. Detlev Claussen, 'Die amerikanische Erfahrung der Kritischen Theoretiker,' in *Keine Kritische Theorie ohne Amerika.* Edited by Detlev Claussen et al. (Frankfurt am Main: Neue Kritik, 2000), 29.

8. Emmanuel Todd, *After the Empire* (New York: Columbia University Press, 2003).

9. Eric Hobsbawm and Terence Ranger, Editors, *The Invention of Tradition* (Cambridge: Cambridge University Press, 1983).

10. Theodor W. Adorno et al., *The Authoritarian Personality* (New York: Harper, 1950), 727.

11. Gilles Kepel, *Jihad: The Trail of Political Islam* (London: I.B. Tauris, 2001); Gilles Kepel, *The War for Muslim Minds: Islam and the West* (Cambridge: Harvard University Press, 2004).

12. Diner, *Feindbild Amerika,* 180.

13. Kanan Makiya, *Republic of Fear* (Berkeley: University of California Press, 1998); here, Part Two, 'The Legitimation of Ba'athism.'

14. Detlev Claussen, *Aspekte der Alltagsreligion* (Frankfurt am Main: Neue Kritik, 2000).

15. Norbert Muhlen, 'German "Anti-Americanism": East and West Zones,' *Commentary,* 15, 2 (1953).

16. Diner, *Feindbild Amerika,* 19.

17. Hannah Arendt, 'The Aftermath of Nazi Rule. A Report from Germany,' *Commentary,* 10, 4 (1950), 343.

18. Gerrit-Jan Berendse, 'German Anti-Americanism in Context,' *Journal of European Studies,* 33, 3/4 (2003), 335, 344.

19. See, for example, Rudolf Augstein, 'Wie man Terroristen fördert,' *Der Spiegel* (November 5, 2001).

20. Remarks made at a panel discussion under the title 'Lässt sich so die Welt befrieden? Lehren aus dem 11. September' at the Akademie der Künste in Berlin on November 11, 2001.

21. Remarks made at a roundtable discussion on September 11 at the Wissenschaftszentrum Berlin, November 2001.

22. Antje Vollmer, 'Es geht um nicht weniger als Krieg und Frieden,' *Frankfurter Rundschau* (November 9, 2001).

23. Martin Walser, 'Stoppt diesen Krieg,' *Stern* (November 15, 2001), 54.

24. Ulrich Wickert, 'Was haben George W. Bush und Osama bin Laden gemeinsam?' *Max* (October 2001).

25. Quoted in Ralf Beste et al., 'Du musst das hochziehen,' *Der Spiegel* (March 24, 2003), 52.

26. Quoted in 'Irak lobt Bundesregierung, SPD verschärft Kritik an USA,' *Welt am Sonntag* (September 8, 2002), 1.

27. Quoted in 'Däubler unter Druck,' *Die Tageszeitung* (August 20, 2002), 2.

28. Interview with Peter Zadek, 'Kulturkampf? Ich bin dabei!' *Der Spiegel* (July 14, 2003), 140.

29. Peter Rügemer, 'Die Plünderer sind da,' *Metall, Das Monatsmagazin der IG Metall* (May 2005), 14–17.

30. Heribert Prantl, '"Ich verstehe Sie nicht"; Gaullisten gegen Atlantiker: Der Urkonflikt Europas und der Krieg,' *Süddeutsche Zeitung* (January 31, 2003), 13.

31. For example, Gret Haller, *Politik der Götter. Europa und der neue Fundamentalismus* (Berlin: Aufbau Verlag, 2005).

32. Denis Lacorne and Jacques Rupnik, 'France Bewitched by America,' in *The Rise and Fall of Anti-Americanism. A Century of French Perception.* Edited by Denis Lacorne et al. (Basingstoke: Macmillan, 1990), 2.

33. Adorno et al., *The Authoritarian Personality*, 722 footnote.

34. Denis Lacorne, 'Anti-Americanism and Americanophobia: A French Perspective,' unpublished manuscript.

35. Kurt H. Wolff, trans. and ed., *The Sociology of Georg Simmel* (New York: Free Press, 1950), 402 and 408.

36. See Berendse, 'German Anti-Americanism in Context,' 334.

37. Ceaser, 'A Genealogy of Anti-Americanism,' 16.

38. Ivan Krastev, 'The Anti-American Century?' *Journal of Democracy,* 15, 2 (2004), 6.

Index

11/9 *see* Berlin Wall, fall of
15 February, 2003 *see* 'united Europe'
2000 Election, international response to
  165–8
9/11 tragedy 38–40, 267–8
  contemporary European anti-
    Americanism 86–9
  and New Intellectual World Order
    267–9
  sympathy for America 201, 206, 259
  versus 11/9 263
  world opinion for and against America 4
  see also Bush administration

Abramovich, Roman 45–6
Adorno, Theodor 246, 247, 258, 283
'age of ideologies' 16
Al Qaeda 5, 205, 211
Allen, Woody 243
Alltagsreligion ('everyday religion') 273
Altman, Robert 243
America
  anti-communist mission 223
  'anti-Paradise' 34
  aspirations of global mission 222
  'Bible belt of the Western World' 96
  civic associations 120–1
  communist view of 189
  condemnation on political
    immaturity 33
  corrosiveness of ideals and
    ideologies 250
  difference between Europe and 191
  domestic manners of Americans 122–9
  Europe's condescension, ridicule,
    irritation and *ressentiment* on 41–9
  and European Catholic world 191
  and European conservative right 191
  European image of 54–8
  and European neo-fascist parties 191
  and European rightist parties 190–1
  fanatical haters of 13, 193–4
  global attitudes towards 4, 10
  global icons 1, 294–6
  gun-regulatory regime 73, 74–5
  immature patriotism 122
  misguided spirit of individualism 121
  'moral superpower' 282
  as most advanced economic force
    267–9

national security strategies 222
Nazi's hatred of 36–7
'othering' 49–54
personification of values of democracy
  and equality 116–17
political lineage and popularity 169–70
post–Cold War foreign policy 222
promotion of a free-market agenda 217
promotion of market democracy 222
public prayer 175
race in US politics 177–9
rapid social mobility 118–19
religion and evangelisation in politics
  172–7
religious divide between Europe and
  92–6
religious pluralism 192
as replica of the world 256
as representative of evil aspects of
  modernisation 55
respect for other cultures 249–50
role of money in politics 170–1
rootlessness 33
self-examination and self-understanding
  250–1
slavery in 127
symbol of modernity 54–5
symbol of radical modernisation 55
threat to world peace 87, 189
views on 1, 289
view on modern mass culture 265–6
after World War II 55
America and the British Left 294–11
American Bar Association 179
American Beauty 242
American competitiveness 168
American cultural imperialism 248–9
American culture 37–8
American culture industry, theory of
  246–7, 258–9
American democracy and anti-
  Americanism (since 2000)
  criticisms 168
  dynasty and celebrity 168–70
  international response to 2000 election
    165–8
  low voter turnout, disinterest and
    disengagement 181–2
  promotion 193
  race 177–9

religion and Evangelisation 172–6
role of money in politics 170–2
systemic flaws 179–81
American Dream 249
American Dream, dark side of 59–60
American electoral college system
179–80
The American Enemy 15
American environmental activism 149–50
American environmentalism
accidental environmentalism 144–8
decline and fall 157–61
definition in the environmental
dimension 139–41
development of international
environmental agreements 148–51
in early America 141–4
global warming and climate change
151–4
Kyoto Protocol and Clinton
administration 154–7
American Exceptionalism 17
American exceptionalism 67, 116, 222
American feminism 47
American individualism 47, 116, 121, 192
American materialism 118–19
American movies 241–4
American music 244–5
and other music 257
American nationalism 7, 18, 230
American personality
democratic equality 118–22
economic dimensions 116
manners 122–9
capitalism and American spirit 129–34
political dimensions 116
religious dimensions 116
views on 115–16
American pluralism 2, 192, 256
American popular culture 239, 240–1
analysis by Heidegger 247
clothing (denim jeans) and 244–5
criticism on 241, 259–62
'cowboy pants' 245
domination in international markets
257
experiences by the rest of the world
241–2
fall of politics and rise of culture
259–62
forms of cultural anti-Americanism
245–55

impact of American movies 243–4
music 244
television and 242–3
American puritanism 47
American religious exceptionalism 92–6
American social dislocation 69
American social mobility 118–20
American South 96–7
attitudes towards atheists 99–103
belief in God and personal importance
of religion 97–9
Bible belt of the Western World 96–7
and Europe 95
party values 103–5
American unilateralism 231
American violence 68–71
American–European *folie à deux* 27–9
American–European relations 23
Americanisation 7, 21, 42, 245, 252, 253,
254–5, 266, 267, 268, 286
anti-Americanism 41–54
British responses to 254
France and 253
French responses to 253
of German youth 48
globalisation and 193, 255–9
of 'McWorld' 251–2
perceptions on the process 253
sensitivity to 254–5
Americanism 17–19, 56, 164–5, 217,
297n65
core values of 218
versus anti-Americanism 59
Amerikanertum 34
'Amerikanische Verhältnisse' (American
conditions) 42, 48
Ang, Ien 258
Anglo-American liberalism 224
Anglo-Saxon model *see* Washington
Consensus
anti-American ideology 16–18
anti-American mood 6, 189, 195, 199
anti-American prejudice
markers 13
views on 14–15
anti-Americanism
in American mass media 199
and anti-Bushism 187–8
in Argentina 230–4
in Britain 254
causes and sources xiii–xiv
characteristics 25–6

conceptualising 7–18
contemporary 24, 27, 134–7
in contemporary Western Europe 23
core markers 2
criticism of American system and
American policies 189
debates on 6–7
definition in the environmental
dimension 139–41
definition (Hollander) 29–30
as a distorted perception of real 264
and ethno-religious ideologies 271–4
European antipathy 24, 27–9, 30–8
evolution in Western Europe 194–8
example from soccer 43–5
Germany's stance in 32–8
in historical transformation (Germany)
274–8
as an ideology 9, 15–18, 218
impact of American movies and
television 242–4
as an 'ism' 164–5
Korean versus European 27
Kyoto Protocol and 156–7
lack of definitions 6–7
levelling power of 285
markers of prejudice 13
in the Middle East 194
misinterpretation of 11
as one side of dichotomy 8, 9
pathological definition 12–13
as a pathology 8, 12–13, 218
political function in Europe's state-
building process 49–54
as a politicised term 5
as a prejudice 8, 13–15, 218
reasons for further analysis 21
religion – contributing factor to 85
as a tendency 8, 9–11, 217–18
term usage 5
usage of the term (Wikipedia) 295n20
varieties of 217–18
versus Americanism 59
Western critics and protestors 255–6
see also 9/11; capital punishment; gun
ownership in America; Iraq War
Anti-Ballistic Missile Treaty 88, 203
'anti-Bushism' 11, 161–2, 187–8, 214–15
anti-globalisation movement 223–4
anti-modern ideologies 272–3
'Anti-Terrorism and Effective Death
Penalty Act' 63

Arendt, Hannah 54–6, 277
Ash, Timothy Garton 6
Asia-Pacific Economic Cooperation
(APEC) forum 224
atheists, attitudes towards 99–103
Atlantic alliance, Euro-American relations
since 187
Augstein, Rudolf 279
Austrian anti-Americanism 35–6
'Axis of Evil' rhetoric 89–92

Ball, Alan 242
Banner, Stuart 64
Barber, Benjamin 251
'battle of Seattle' 223
Baudrillard, Jean 39, 253
The Beatles 256
Beijing Consensus 226
Bellah, Robert 121
Berger, Peter 93
Berlin Wall, fall of 53, 56, 263
Bernstein, Nina 252
Big Brother 261
Bill Haley and His Comets 254
Bill of Rights 66
bin Laden, Osama 4, 12–13, 39, 89,
205, 279
bio-terrorism see cultural imperialism
Bischof, Günter 35–6, 300–32
Blair, Tony 226
Blüm, Norbert 278
Bolivarian vision 229–30
Bowling for Columbine (documentary film)
xiv, 26, 62
Brando, Marlon 244
Breyer, Stephen (Justice) 81
Broder, Henryk 113
Broecker, Mathias 39
Brokeback Mountain 69
Brown, Gordon 226
Buffy the Vampire Slayer 242
de Buffon, Count 31, 143
Burkhardt, Jacob 33
Bush administration 3, 9, 11, 14, 21, 24,
29, 38, 50, 51, 188, 227–8
compare Clinton, Bill
Bush v Gore 176
Bush, George H. W. 106, 109–10
accusations on moneyed interests 171
attitude towards global warming, Kyoto
Protocol and international law
157–61, 203

autobiography of 110–12
'Axis of Evil' rhetoric 89–92, 210
A Charge to Keep 110–12
compared to Caesar Augustus and
  Adolph Hitler 87
'compassionate conservatism' 175–6
contemporary anti-Americanism in
  Western Europe 24
difference between George H. W. Bush
  and 112
election in 2000 163–4
European anti-Americanism and
  199–205
European feelings towards 88
Europeans disturbed by religious
  characteristics 96–7
extradition of terror suspects 63
as governor of Texas 63
increase in negative global attitudes
  towards America 10
messianic mission 112–13
national security strategies 222–3
prejudice against 18
rejection of liberal elitism 106
religion in the presidency of 94–5
religious characteristics 96–7
Southern religious exceptionalism 95
speech on Hurricane Katrina 173–4
summoning religious language 173–4
support for gun rights and judicial
  killings 62–3
support from religious Americans
  104–5
testimonies of faith 111–12
'them versus us' politics 21
'typical American' 18
as unilateralist 206
versus Osama bin Laden 4, 39
views on Bush as president 63
views on foreign affairs 201
see also 'anti-Bushism'; Bush
  administration

Caeser, James 15, 17, 246
Calvinistic Protestantism 85
capital punishment
  Christians and 81
  constitutional protection 66, 67–8
  Europe versus America 64
  political dimensions 75–8
  public opinion surveys 65
  rationality and public policy 72–5

reasons for criticism 59–60
support from Al Gore, John McCain
  and Bill Bradley 63
Cardoso, Fernando Henrique 233
Carrio, Elisa 230
Carte Blanche 278–86
Carter, Jimmy 92, 96
Castaneda, Jorge 236
Castro, Fidel 9, 17, 166, 233,
  235, 236
A Charge to Keep 110–12
Chavez, Hugo 229–30, 235
  *Alternativa Bolivariana para las
  Americas* (ALBA) 235
Chicago School and devotees of public
  choice theory 221
Chidester, David 85
Chirac, Jacques 87, 227, 254
Cimino, Michael 251
The Civil War in France 133
Civilisation and Its Discontents 34
Claussen, Detlev 273
Clean Air Act 146, 155
Clean Water Act 147
Clinton, Bill 46, 50
  'Anti-Terrorism and Effective Death
  Penalty Act' 63
  approval of Clinton administration
  86–7
  extradition of terror suspects 63
  and judicial killings 63
  Kyoto Protocol and Clinton
  administration 155
  national security strategies 222–3
  remarks on George H. W. Bush 109
  United States' popularity among
  Europeans 86
Coats, Daniel 278
Cohen, Nick 14, 296n46
Cohen-Tanugi, Laurent 82, 83–4
Cold War 24, 69, 190, 193, 253, 284,
  285, 286
  anti-American moods in Europe
  after 189
  transatlantic alliance post 86, 187–8,
  192, 197–8
Colombani, Jean-Marie 39
Common Sense 115
Congress for Cultural Freedom 248
Coppola, Francis Ford 243
Critical Reflections on Poetry and Painting
  141–2

Crockatt, Richard 18, 293–4
cultural Americanisation 7, 246, 252, 259, 267
cultural anti-Americanism
    contemporary 241, 246, 247–8, 252, 254–5
    forms of 245–55
    growth of 259
cultural imperialism 248
    see also American cultural imperialism
cultural relativism 260
culture
    anthropological definition 239
    mass 240
    popular versus high 240
    see also popular culture
Cunliffe, Marcus 294–6

The Daily Mirror 63
Davie, Grace 93, 100–1
Davies, Merryl Wyn 249–51
Davis, Miles 244
Dawkins, Richard 169
Dean, James 244
death penalty in America see judicial killings
Death Row see death penalty in America
The Deer Hunter 251
degeneration thesis 31
Democracy in America 118
Der Spiegel 113, 280
Derrida, Jacques 52
Dialectic of Enlightenment 246
Die Presse 129
Die Zeit 282
Dionne, E. J. 95
diplomatic ostracism 92
Domestic Manners of the Americans 123
Drezner, Daniel 183
Du Bos, Abbé Jean-Baptiste 141, 142
Dukakis, Michael 94–5

Eagleton, Terry 255, 260
Earth Day 145, 147
'East Asian economic miracle' 224
Eco, Umberto 52
The Economist 72–3, 229
L'Effroyable Imposture 39
Egyptian Muslim Brotherhood 272
El Pais 52
Elliott, Michael 50
Engels. Friedrich 15, 132, 133

Environics survey 206
environmental law and policy, contemporary 150–1
Environmental Protection Agency 146, 158
Environmental Species Act 147
Eppler, Erhard 279
Eurobarometer survey 87
Europe
    anti-Americanism in historical perspective 188–93
    attitude towards Bush and American foreign policy 202
    contemporary anti-Americanism in 86–9
    difference between America and 191
    elite versus mass opinion on America 36–8, 49–50
    evolution of anti-Americanism 194–8
    Michael Moore's popularity 26
    modernisation in 265
    opinion on America 4
    positive attitude towards United States 188
    post–Cold War transatlantic alliance 86, 187–8, 192, 197–8
    power over America post–World War II and Cold War 69
    religious divide between America and 93–6
    ressentiment to rebellion 49–54
    ressentiment towards America 30–8, 299n14
    support for Iraq War 210
    trend in support for United States and Bush 199–205
    weapons of mass destruction 211
European anti-Americanism 24, 27–9, 37–8, 47–9
    in Bush era 199–205
    between 9/11 and Iraq War 205–9
    comparative perspective 193–8
    contemporary 86–9
    in historical perspective 188–93
    and the Iraq War 209–13
European churches 93
European Elite Surveys 215
European secular exceptionalism 94
European social model 218
European–American folie à deux 27–9
evangelical Protestantism 85, 89, 175

Evangelicalism 85
Ewald, Alec 180–1

Fahrenheit 9/11 (documentary film) 26, 62
Feinberg, Richard 231
Ferguson, Niall 235
Financial Times 159
firearms *see* guns
Fordschritt 275
Fox, Vincente 233
France
    anti-Americanism and 23
    anti-Americanism and Iraq War
    209–14
    anti-Americanism between 9/11 and
    Iraq War 205–9
    anti-Americanism during Bush era
    199–205
    approval of foreign policy during
    Clinton presidency 86
    attitude towards America 4, 11
    contemporary anti-Americanism 86–9
    evolution of anti-Americanism 188
    firearms in 75
    religion and liberty in 120
    ressentiment to rebellion 49–54
    view on 9/11 39
Frankfurter Allgemeine Zeitung 52
Free Trade Area of the Americas (FTAA)
    229–30
Freeden, Michael 15, 16
Freedland, Jonathan 65
French anti-Americanism 15–16
Freud, Sigmund 34
Freund, Charles Paul 257
Friedman, Thomas 222, 223
Fukuyama, Francis 193
Furman v Georgia (1972) 77

Gallup International Survey 65, 103, 104,
    106, 174, 175, 194, 205, 206, 207, 208
Gaus, Günter 279
Gay, Peter 34
Gaye, Marvin 244
Germany
    'Amerikanische Verhältnisse' 42–3
    American films in 241
    American music in 252
    anti-Americanism and Iraq War
    209–14
    anti-Americanism between 9/11 and
    Iraq War 205–9

anti-Americanism during
    Bush era 199–205
anti-Americanism in historical
    transformation 274–8
anti-Americanism in 17, 23, 32–8, 196
anti-Semitism in 29, 40
approval of foreign policy during
    Clinton presidency 86
attitudes towards America 4, 10
contemporary anti-Americanism 86–9
evolution of anti-Americanism
    188, 194
impact of American modern mass
    culture 265–6
'locust' affair 46
'New Germany' 278–86
religion in 97–9
ressentiment to rebellion 49–54
Giddens, Anthony 190
Gitlin, Todd 2, 14, 245
Glazer, Malcom 45–6
Global Issues Monitor Survey 206
Global Nightmare 249
global warming 151–4
globalisation 38, 134, 188, 192–3, 217,
    218, 219, 220, 223, 225, 227, 233,
    255–9, 268
Gore, Al 18, 63, 88, 166, 225
Gott, Richard 235
Graham, Billy 89, 111
Gramsci, Antonio 134
Greeley, Andrew 93
Grunberg, Gérard 294n12
The Guardian 6
Guinier, Lani 177
gun clubs 82–3
gun ownership in America
    civilisation and morality 78–83
    constitutional protection 66, 67–8
    criticism from European elites 62
    political dimensions 75–8
    rationality and public policy 72–5
    reasons for criticism 59–60
    support by George W. Bush 62–3
gun ownership and violence in Europe
    64, 75
gun-related deaths 70
Gutierrez, Lucio 229

Habermas, Jürgen 52
    criticisms on 53–4
Haldeman, Bob 147

Hartz, Louis 18
Harvey, David 220
Hasen, Rick 181
Hegel, Georg Wilhelm Friedrich 33
Heidegger, Martin 34, 247, 258, 265, 285
Heine, Heinrich 33
Hofstatder, Richard 17
Hollander, Paul 29
Hollywood 250, 256, 257, 266–7
Horkheimer, Max 246, 247, 258
Hussein, Saddam 105, 204, 209, 210–11,
   212, 213, 214
Hutton, Will 190, 192, 223, 227
hyperpuissnace 46, 198

Ickstadt, Heinz 252
ideology
   Antoine Destutt de Tracy 15
   Marx and Engels 15, 132, 312–69
   pejorative understanding 15
Inacio, Luiz 'Lula' da Silva 229, 232–4
indirect election 179
Intergovernmental Negotiating Committee
   on Climate 151
Intergovernmental Panel on Climate
   Change (IPCC) 151–2
*International Covenant on Civil and
   Political Rights* 182
IPOS/REID 205
Iraq War 2, 3–4
   and anti-Americanism 187–8, 196,
      197, 200
   articles on 52
   European anti-Americanism and
      209–14, 215, 281
   European anti-Americanism between
      9/11 and 205–9
   European opposition to 88
   global attitudes towards America
      10–11
   religious Americans and 104
   transatlantic crisis around 187–8
Isernia, Pierangelo 23, 187

Jackson, Michael 244
Jacobs, James 71, 73
James, Henry 126
Jefferson, Thomas 115, 141, 143
Johnson, Chalmers 224
Johnson, Robert 244
Jones, Ernest 34
Joop, Wolfgang 279

judicial killings 60, 63, 66–9, 72
Judt, Tony 6, 7

Katzenstein, Peter 7
Kaube, Jürgen 53
Keohane, Robert 7
Kimball, Roger 296n39
Kirchner, Nestor 229, 233
Klein, Joe 92
Klein, Naomi 249
Kohut, Andrew 86
Koizumi, Junichiro 226
Kolodko, Grzegorz 220
Kraus, Karl 275
Krauthammer, Charles 225
Kuisel, Richard 253
'Kulturkampf' 51
Kyoto Protocol on global warming 88,
   139, 154–7

Latin America and Washington Consensus
   218, 219, 228–34
Leclerq, Georges Louis *see* de Buffon,
   Count
Lenau, Nikolaus 38
liberal democracy 61, 66
liberal egalitarianism 227
Libération 52
Liebes, Tamar 258
Lipset, Seymour Martin 17
Look Back in Anger 254
The (London) Times 78
Lost in Translation 244
Lowell, James Russell 1
Lula *see* Inacio, Luiz 'Lula' da Silva

McCain-Feingold Act 171
Mckay, George 255
'McWorld' 251
Madison, James 144, 294n10
de Maizière, Lothar 279
Manchester United 40, 45, 46, 300n35
Maradona, Diego 232–3
market fundamentalism 217
Markovits, Andrei 6, 17, 116
Marshall Plan 248, 275
Marx, Karl 116, 117
   capitalism and American spirit 129–34
mass cultural production 239–40
mass culture 36, 240
   criticisms on 266–7
'mass society' 121

May, Karl 34–5
Merkl, Angela 227
Metall 46, 280
Meyssan, Thierry 39
Miami Herald 88
Michaels, Eric 258
Mickelthwait, John 77
Minogue, Kenneth 5, 16
modern anti-Americanism 273, 284
modern ideologies 268, 270, 272
modern social organisation 270
modern societies 282
modernity 265
Molina, Mario 148, 149, 150
Le Monde 39, 52, 86
Montaner, Carlos Alberto 235
de Montesquieu 142
Montreal Protocol on Substances the
    Deplete the Ozone Layer 149–54
Moore, Michael 26, 62, 251
    Bowling for Columbine (documentary
    film) xiv, 26, 62
Morales, Evo 235–6

Naím, Moisés 6, 7, 294–8
National Environmental Policy Act 146
national identity crisis, French and British
    254
National Park Service 144
National Socialism 276, 278, 280, 286
neoliberal globalisation 217, 218,
    219–24
neoliberalism 221–2, 224, 227, 228, 233
New Deal liberalism 227
New-York Daily Tribune 129
The New York Review of Books 6,
    295n23
New York Times 198, 222, 231, 252
New Yorker 6
new world order 219, 267–9
News and World Report 88
Newsweek International 50
Nietzsche, Friedrich 34, 116
    notion of cultural struggle 274
Nixon, Richard 144–5
    focus on environmentalism 145–6
No Logo 249
'no regrets policy' 152–3
non-Americans
    criticisms on firearms and death penalty
    59–60
    respect for American domestic order 72

North Atlantic Treaty Organisation
    (NATO) 197
Noticias 230

O'Neill, Paul 157–8, 160, 231
Oil & Gas Journal 158
Ortega, Daniel 236
Osborne, John 254
'othering' United States 49–54
ozone depletion 148

Paine, Thomas 115
pan-European nationalism 54, 55
de Pauw, Cornelius 31
Pelling, Henry 1–2, 294n11
Pells, Richard 256, 257
Pentagon *see* 9/11
Peterson, John 83
Pew Global Attitudes Project survey 6
Pew Global Attitudes Project 96
Pew Research Center 4, 86, 201
Pew surveys 4, 6, 10, 11, 87, 194, 203,
    206, 208, 211
Phillips, Kevin 95
    difference between the two Bush
    presidents 112
Pollack, Mark 83
Pop Idol 261
popular culture
    fall of politics and rise of 259–62
    role of media technologies 239
    versus high culture 240
    versus mass culture 240
    see also American popular culture
Posner, Richard 65, 76
Powell, Colin 231
'precautionary principle' 150
The President of Good and Evil 173
Presley, Elvis 244
Princeton Survey Research Associates
    201, 210
prisoner disenfranchisement 178
pro-Americanism 9, 10
public opinion surveys 3, 9, 23,
    29, 65

Quiroga, Jorge 235

Rau, Johannes 278
religion
    American South 96–7
    Bible belt of Western world 96–7

church attendance gap between Europe and America 103
and personal importance 97–9
Southern and Republican Party values 104
Texas – Protestant and church-going state 105–9
transatlantic belief in God 97–9
Religion by Region 94
religious fundamentalism 50, 272, 273
Republica 52
Revel, Jean-François 15, 72, 75, 76, 183
comments on Europe's anti-American obsession 87–8
Riesman, David 121
The Rise and Fall of Anti-Americanism 12
Robins, Ron 256
Roger, Philippe 15
Rolling Stones 256
Rorty, Richard 52
Roosevelt, Theodore 17, 171
Ross, Jan 53
Rowland, Sherwood 148, 149, 150
Roy, Arundhati 13
Rubinstein, Alvin 6–7
Rumsfeld, Donald 294–8

Sakakibara, Eisuke 225
Sardar, Ziauddin 249–51
satellite television 256–7
Savater, Fernando 52
Scalia, Antonin (Justice) 80, 81–2
Schadenfreude 39, 40
Schama, Simon 6, 33
Scheler, Max 51
Schiller, Herbert 248
Schröder, Gerhard 42, 48, 227, 278, 279, 280
Schumpeter, Joseph 264
Schwarzenegger, Governor Arnold 78–9
Scorsese, Martin 243
Sectarian Protestantism 191
security, privatisation of 70
September 11 *see* 9/11
Shaw, George Bernard 1
Sheler, Jeffery 88
Silk, Mark 94
Simmel, Georg 283
Singh, Robert 7, 12
Six Feet Under 242–3
Smith, Anthony 258
Smith, Donald 6–7

Sombart, Werner 190
The Sopranos 242
Southern Baptist Convention (SBC) 105
Southern religious exceptionalism 92–6
Soviet Union, fall of 24
Spiro, Herbert J. 32
Spitzer, Robert 73
Springsteen, Bruce 251
La Stampa 52
state socialism 268
Stelzenmüller, Constanze 282
Stewart, Potter (Justice) 7, 30
Stiglitz, Joseph 221
Strauss, Ira 3
Strauss, Levi 244
Strauss-Kahn, Dominique 52
Süddeutsche Zeitung 52
Sumner, William Graham 264
The Supremes 244
SWG survey 207, 208

Taliban regime 86, 89, 205, 214, 279
The Temptations 244
Tocqueville, Alexis de 116, 117
democratic equality in America 117, 118–22
Tocqueville, Alexis de 12, 32, 55
prediction on rise of superpowers 32
Todd, Emmanuel 269
Toinet, Marie-France 12, 140
Tokyo Foreign Correspondents' Club 225
Tönnies, Ferdinand 264
Transatlantic Trend Surveys 188, 210, 213, 214, 215
Trollope, Frances 116, 117
Republican rudeness 122–9

'un-American' 188–91
UN Conference on Environment and Development (UNCED) 152
'united Europe' 51
United Kingdom
anti-Americanism between 9/11 and Iraq War 205–9
anti-Americanism during Bush era 199–205
capital punishment in 65, 76
evolution of anti-Americanism 188, 194
gun regulations 76
gun violence 75
Washington Consensus and 226

United Nations Framework Convention on
Climate Change (UNFCCC) 153–4
United States National Academy of
Sciences 149
United States *see* America
US politics
lineage and popularity 168–70
race in 177–9
religion and Evangelisation 172–7
role of money 170–2
systemic flaws 179–81
US war on terrorism 206–7
see also 9/11

Vasquez, Tabare 233
Vattimo, Gianni 52
Vedrine, Hubert 50–1, 53
Veintitres 230
Velez, Alvaro Uribe 233
Vienna Convention for the Protection of
Ozone Layer 149–54
violence, America versus Europe
68–71
Vollmer, Antje 279
Voting Rights Act 178
'vulgarisation' 239–40

Wall Street Journal Europe 168
Wall Street Journal 183
Walser, Martin 279
Walzer, Michael 191–2
Washington Consensus, and anti-
Americanism
acceptance in Latin America 228–34
Asian animus versus 224–6
criticism from Japan 225
European antipathy to 'Anglo-Saxon
model' 226–8
ideological variety of anti-Americanism
218
and neoliberal globalisation 219–24
to rescue Latin America from economic
stagnation 219

role of World Bank 224
symbol of neoliberal globalisation 220
universalisation of 219–20
Washington Post 95, 198
Weber, Max 264
Wehler, Hans-Ulrich 279
Western media 258, 283
Whitman, Christine Todd 95, 158–9
Why Do People Hate America? 6, 249,
295n22
Wickert, Ulrich 279
Wilde, Oscar 1
Williams, Stanley 'Tookie' (convicted
murderer) 78–9
Williamson, John 217, 219, 220, 221
Wills, Gary 94–5
Wilson, Woodrow 92, 190
Winthrop, John 115
Wirth, Timothy 155
With us or against us 7, 9
Wolfensohn, James 221
Wonder, Stevie 244
Woo-Cummings, Meredith 27
Wooldridge, Adrian 77
Work Foundation 227
world opinion
on America 4, 10
on American public policy
rationales 72
shifting tendencies 10–11
World Trade Center *see* 9/11
World Values Survey 103

Yorna, Jorge 230
YOUGOV poll 207

Zadek, Peter 280
Zeldin, Theodore 12, 140
Zoellick, Robert 234
Zwickel, Klaus 279